Herbs, Spices, and Medicinal Plants:
Recent Advances in Botany, Horticulture, and Pharmacology
Volume 1

LYLE E. CRAKER, *Editor-in-Chief*
Department of Plant and Soil Sciences
University of Massachusetts
Amherst, MA 01003 U.S.A.

JAMES E. SIMON, *Editor-in-Chief*
Department of Horticulture
Purdue University
West Lafayette, IN 47907 U.S.A.

Board of Editors

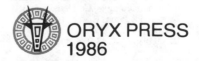

ORYX PRESS
1986

The rare Arabian Oryx is believed to have inspired the myth of the unicorn. This desert antelope became virtually extinct in the early 1960s. At that time several groups of international conservationists arranged to have 9 animals sent to the Phoenix Zoo to be the nucleus of a captive breeding herd. Today the Oryx population is over 400 and herds have been returned to reserves in Israel, Jordan, and Oman.

Warning: The medicinal and other uses of herbs described in this volume have been included for informational and study purposes only. The authors and publishers neither advocate nor prescribe the use of any herb for medicinal or other purposes. Please note that some herbs mentioned in this book could be poisonous. The authors and publisher assume no liability for omissions or for use or misuse of information contained herein.

Library of Congress Cataloging in Publication Data
Main entry under title:

Herbs, spices, and medicinal plants.

  Includes bibliographies.
  1. Herbs—Collected works.   2. Spices—Collected works.   3. Medicinal plants—Collected works.
4. Pharmacology—Collected works.   I. Craker, Lyle E.
II. Simon, James E.
SB107.H47   1985   635.7   85-11551
ISBN 0-89774-143-9 (v. 1)

Contents

Preface

With this publication, we initiate a new series devoted to the study of herbs, spices, and medicinal plants. Although utilized for thousands of years as condiments, medicines, fragrances, dyes, and ornaments, scientific information on the botany, horticulture, and pharmacology associated with the growing and using of this group of plants has been limited. Each of the sequential volumes of this series will review and summarize the most recent available information within selected subject areas, providing the reader with an introduction to the herbs, spices, and medicinal plants and a ready, authoritative reference for detailed study on the botany, horticulture, and pharmacology of these plants.

The more than one billion dollars per year worldwide trade in herbs, spices, and medicinal plants testifies to their market value. Yet, the importance of these plants is more than economic as the scientific study of herbs, spices, and medicinal plants has made significant contributions to the understanding of physiological processes in the biosynthesis of natural plant products and in the ecological relationships of plants within their environment. Herbs, spices, and medicinal plants continue to serve important traditional and ritualistic functions for many groups of people throughout the world.

Scientific investigations have been initiated in many countries as the potential food and health contributions of these plants are recognized. The continual search for and interest in natural plant products to use in the flavor and medicinal industries has acted as a catalyst for exploring the methodologies involved in obtaining the required plant material and probing the botanical, chemical, ecological, and pharmacological relationships among plants. With this increased interest in herbs, spices, and medicinal plants, professionals and field specialists associated with trade, horticulture, and chemistry have made an ever-increasing demand for recent and accurate information on plant culture and pharmacology. However, few scientific references that can provide an in-depth review of current research developments on herbs, spices, and medicinal plants are available.

The editors-in-chief, being plant physiologists interested in the growth and biochemistry of herbs, spices, and medicinal plants and keenly aware of the long and laborious process involved in gathering scientific information, felt a special contribution to the study of these plants could be made by producing a forum for presentation and review of research work. After a careful and considerable exploration of ideas, an annual collection of invited papers summarizing the recent advances in herbs, spices, and medicinal plants appeared to best serve the needs of all.

We have been joined in this endeavor by the board of editors, an international group of scientists committed to the advancement of this discipline. A special acknowledgment must also be made to the contributors of this volume who, upon invitation, undertook the rigorous work and research necessary to prepare a thorough review in their specialty area.

To this beginning, Volume 1 of *Herbs, Spices, and Medicinal Plants: Recent Advances in Botany, Horticulture, and Pharmacology*, is launched.

Lyle E. Craker
James E. Simon

Acknowledgments

The editors-in-chief wish to express special thanks to their patient families during the dreaming, writing, and compiling involved in the publication of this first volume of *Herbs, Spices, and Medicinal Plants: Recent Advances in Botany, Horticulture, and Pharmacology, Volume 1*. We very much appreciate the initial financial support of the University of Massachusetts Graduate School and College of Food and Natural Resources. The preparation of this volume was greatly aided by the library work of Mr. John Gancarski and Ms. Alena Chadwick, the typing of Ms. Debbie Clark, and the proofreading of Ms. Marie Iken.

Contributors to Volume 1

T. Adzet   Department of Pharmacognosy and Pharmacodynamics, University of Barcelona, Barcelona, Spain

J. Bernáth   Research Institute for Medicinal Plants, Budakalasz, Hungary

R. Croteau   Institute of Biological Chemistry, Washington State University, Pullman, Washington, USA

A. Dafni   Institute of Evolution, Haifa University, Haifa, Israel

J. Friedman   Department of Botany, the G.S. Wise Faculty of Life Sciences, Tel-Aviv University, Ramat Aviv, Israel

C. Mann   Department of Medicinal Chemistry and Pharmacognosy, College of Pharmacy, University of Minnesota, Minneapolis, Minnesota, USA

D. Palevitch   Department of Medicinal and Spice Crops, Agricultural Research Organization, The Volcani Center, Bet Dagan, Israel

T. Robinson   Department of Biochemistry, University of Massachusetts, Amherst, Massachusetts, USA

E.J. Staba   Department of Medicinal Chemistry and Pharmacognosy, College of Pharmacy, University of Minnesota, Minneapolis, Minnesota, USA

P. Tétényi   Research Institute for Medicinal Plants, Budakalasz, Hungary

A.O. Tucker   Department of Agriculture and Natural Resources, Delaware State College, Dover, Delaware, USA

Z. Yaniv   Department of Medicinal and Spice Crops, Agricultural Research Organization, The Volcani Center, Bet Dagan, Israel

An Introduction to the Scientific Literature on Herbs, Spices, and Medicinal Plants

L.E. Craker
Department of Plant and Soil Sciences, University of Massachusetts, Amherst, MA 01003

A.F. Chadwick
Science Libraries, University of Massachusetts, Amherst, MA 01003

J.E. Simon
Department of Horticulture, Purdue University, West Lafayette, IN 47907

The beginnings of scientific literature on herbs, spices, and medicinal plants can be linked to the very earliest of writings. Instructions for making and using plant-based medicinal preparations are recorded on Egyptian papyri dating from 2000 B.C., with this material appearing to be copied from other sources written several centuries earlier (2, 3, 12). The legendary Chinese Emperor Shen Nung is credited with composing an herbal of over 100 items in c. 2700 B.C., forming the basis for China's purportedly oldest medical text, *Shen Nung Pen Tsao* (2, 12). Other early texts, scriptures, and tablets from throughout the world indicate the use of plants as pharmaceuticals, spices, and dyes, suggesting the development and recording of recipes and methodologies for selection and application of plant material (4, 5, 8, 11, 13).

The systematic separation and categorization of herbs and other plants according to morphological traits appear to have begun with the publication of *Historia Plantarum* and *De Causis Plantarum,* both written by Theophrastus of Eresus (c. 372–286 B.C.), a colleague of Aristotle in Plato's academy and considered the father of modern botany (6, 7). Dioscorides, a Greek physician in the first century A.D., expanded on the work of Theophrastus by assembling *De Materia Medica,* a listing of approximately 600 plants that included names, botanical and habitat descriptions, preparations, and medicinal and aromatic uses (7).

De Materia Medica remained the classical authority in Europe for the next 1,500 years, frequently reproduced, but seldom augmented, leaving the science of botany to be described as degenerating "into a drug list" after 200 A.D. (7). A Chinese herbal, *Tzu-I Pên Tshao Ching,* appeared in c. 500 B.C. and incorporated several earlier works (7, 12). Although the dates of writing are uncertain, ranging between 800 B.C. and 400 A.D., the Indian medical manuscripts *Charaka Samhita* and *Susruta Samhita* list approximately 500 herbal drugs (2, 12).

During the Middle Ages, Avicenna (Ibn Sina) and others from the Middle East, North Africa, and Moslem Spain made significant additions to the number of plants that could be used for medicinal purposes (2, 7). In Medieval Europe, herbals became the major form of codified plant knowledge but provided little enlightenment as essentially unrecognizable illustrations for describing plants and unverified directions for medicinal preparations (derived from writings of Theophrastus and Dioscorides) were utilized. The *Herbarum Vivae Eicones,* produced by Otto Brunfels in 1530, relied on Greek and Roman sources for information but did contain accurate illustrations of the plants (1).

TABLE 1. Research Reports on Dill and Parsley for 1920 through 1980[a].

Number of Reports						
Dill	0	0	0	1	1	5	12
Parsley	0	0	3	3	7	10	42
Lettuce[b]	5	5	14	13	32	49	149
Tomato[b]	13	34	70	93	146	300	507
Year of Publication	1920	1930	1940	1950	1960	1970	1980

[a]From citations in *Chemical Abstracts,* Chemical Abstracts Service, The American Chemical Society, Columbus, Ohio.
[b]The number of research reports on lettuce and tomato have been included for comparison.

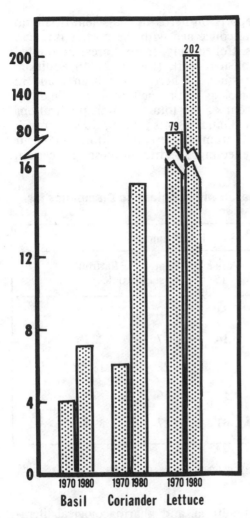

Figure 1. The Scientific Literature on Basil and Coriander. Numbers of research articles are from a count of 1970 and 1980 citations listed for each plant in the U.S. National Agricultural Library database, AGRICOLA. The number of research reports on lettuce has been included for comparison.

The *Herball* of Nicholas Culpeper, published in 1652, and the *Herball* of John Gerard, published in 1597 and expanded by Thomas Johnson in 1633, gained wide recognition and use. The Johnson revision of Gerard's *Herball* contained accurate descriptions of plants and was used by physicians and apothecaries. However, Culpeper's *Herball,* while extremely popular, did not contribute to scientific knowledge and erroneously connected plants with astrological events and the "Doctrine of Signatures" (13). The distillation of essential oils did become widespread in the 1500s and, during this time, physic gardens were established by medical schools and societies of apothecaries (9, 14).

"Modern" research on herbs, spices, and medicinal plants has expanded to study a wide variety of topical areas connected to the botany, horticulture, and pharmacology of these plants. A recent bibliographic review of the scientific literature on herbs of the temperate zone associated over 10,000 authors with published research articles related to this group of plants covering the period from 1971 through 1980 (10). As evidenced by dill and parsley (Table 1), the number of published scientific reports has increased throughout the last 50 years. A comparison of the amount of basil and coriander research literature listed by the United States National Agricultural Library database (AGRICOLA) in 1970 and 1980 indicates a similar increase in publications (Figure 1).

The majority of research reports on herbs in the scientific literature during this time period were concerned with the horticulture and production ecology of the plants. Collectively, these 2 areas accounted for over 38 percent of the published work (Figure 2). In addition, significant contributions to the study of herbs have been made in botany, chemistry, and pharmacology with each of these fields of study contributing over 10 percent of the total research publications on herbs and aromatic and medicinal plants during 1971 through 1980. Differences in the distribution of research effort do occur among the plants, however, reflecting specific interests in certain species (Table 2).

TABLE 2. Distribution of Research within Scientific Disciplines for Selected Herbs[a].

Research Area	Plant Material		
	Anise	Poppy	Saffron
	(% of published articles)		
Chemistry	31	12	14
Botany	14	17	22
Horticulture	12	28	18
Pharmacology	12	16	7
Other[b]	31	27	39

[a]Data from Simon *et al.* (10).
[b]Including bionomics, production ecology, culinary studies, perfumery, natural dyes and ornamental applications, and commerce.

Dividing the botanical, horticultural, and pharmacological literature on herbs into subcategories demonstrates specific areas of scientific interest in the herb plants (Figure 3). Within botany, most research publications focus on growth and development of the plants; within horticulture, most research publications report on plant breeding and crop production; within pharmacology, most research publications concern pharmacognosy of the plants or plant extracts. An area where increased numbers of scientific articles have been published in recent years is in tissue culture, which has gone from the publication of 9 reports in 1971 to 25 in 1980.

Mint was the most frequently reported herb, spice, or medicinal plant in the scientific literature during 1971 through 1980 with over 500 published research articles containing information associated with

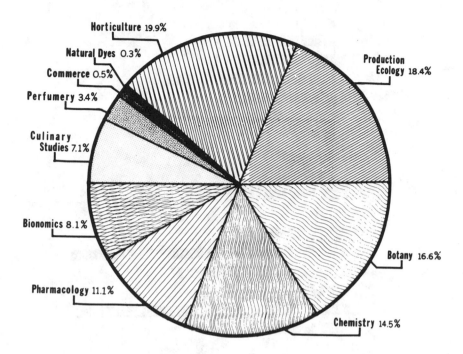

Figure 2. Distribution of Scientific Literature among Various Disciplines. Data on 64 herbs and aromatic and medicinal plants of the temperate zone. From Simon *et al.* (10).

mint plants. Articles in botany and horticulture accounted for over 50 percent of the research literature on mint (Table 3). In the pharmacological area, research on licorice, foxglove, and ginseng was the most frequently published.

Studies on herbs, spices, and medicinal plants are being conducted on a global basis with scientists in many countries contributing to the scientific literature on these plants. Reports on the horticulture of mint (the crop with the largest number of scientific reports) can be identified with authors from 26 countries. Most of the scientific literature contributions on horticulture of mint are published in the U.S.S.R. (Table 4).

Yet, a close examination of the literature indicates the amount of research on most herbs, spices, and medicinal plants remains quite limited; the number of reported research articles for 1971 through 1980 averaged approximately 750 per year for 64 plant categories or only about 12 articles for each plant each year. This relatively low average number of published research papers must be viewed with caution, of course, as great variation in economic value and commercial use exists among the 64 plant types examined, influencing the

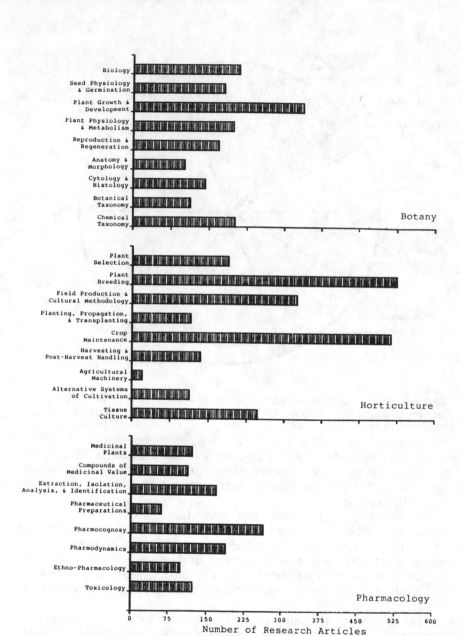

Figure 3. Scientific Literature on Herbs, Spices, and Medicinal Plants within Botany, Horticulture, and Pharmacology. Data from Simon *et al.* (10).

demand and need for scientific studies. An indication of the small number of research reports on the botany, horticulture, and phar-

TABLE 3. Distribution of Botany, Horticulture, and Pharmacology Literature among Plants[a].

Botany		Horticulture		Pharmacology	
		Most Publications			
Plant	No.[b]	Plant	No.	Plant	No.
Mint	146	Mint	255	Licorice	95
Mustard	103	Capsicum Pepper	181	Foxglove	69
Onion	73	Poppy	103	Ginseng	69
Poppy	68	Onion	96	Poppy	65
Capsicum Pepper	66	Sesame	88	Angelica	61
		Least Publications			
Dittany of Crete	1	Goldenrod	2	Caper	2
Southernwood	1	Wintergreen	2	Dittany of Crete	2
Chervil	0	Caper	1	Lemon Verbena	2
Henna	0	Dittany of Crete	1	Lavender	1
Lobelia	0	Goldenseal	0	Southernwood	1
				Horehound	0
				Horseradish	0

[a]Data from Simon *et al.* (10).
[b]Number of publications, 1971 through 1980.

macology of some herbs, spices, and medicinal plants is presented in Table 3. For one plant—Dittany of Crete—less than one research report per year (a total of 7 identified articles) was published over the 10-year period from 1971 through 1980. For caper, goldenseal, and southernwood, less than 2 research reports per year were published.

Unfortunately, the large number of countries doing research on herbs, spices, and medicinal plants has resulted in a wide variety of research reports scattered in numerous journals and reports, making a comprehensive bibliographic review and an accurate count of scientific publications on specific herbs difficult. For example, with basil, 73 percent of the research papers were reported in separate journals for 1971 through 1980 (Table 5). Only 13 percent of the research papers on parsley during this same time period could be associated with scientific journals having 3 or more articles on parsley.

Scientific literature is the collection of research information and, as such, serves as the reservoir of knowledge about a subject. The literature codifies the subject material, maintains a historical record on experimental trials, and aids in problem solving through education and communication about facts and ideas. As the scientific literature

TABLE 4. Origin of Published Research Studies on Mint[a].

Country	Contribution (%)
France	9
Germany	6
India	17
USSR	19
United States	10
Other[b]	31
Unidentified[c]	8

[a]Data from Simon *et al.* (10). Authors were affiliated with specific countries by language and origin of publication.
[b]A total of 26 countries could be associated with publications on mint.
[c]Author(s) could not be identified with any specific country.

TABLE 5. The Distribution of Research Reports among Literature Sources[a].

Number of Sources with:	Basil	Parsley
1 article	120	180
2 articles	25	40
3 articles	7	10
4 articles	8	10
5 articles	1	5
6 articles	2	5
7 articles	1	2

[a]Identified literature, 1971 through 1983.

on herbs, spices, and medicinal plants develops, more exchange of information should occur, helping to advance the science of these plants.

REFERENCES

1. Arber, Agnes. 1953. From medieval herbalism to the birth of modern botany. *In* E.A. Underwood, ed. *Science Medicine and History.* Vol. 1. Oxford University Press, London. pp. 317–336.

2. Castiglioni, Arturo. 1958. *A History of Medicine,* 2d ed. Alfred A. Knopf, New York. 1192 p.

3. Dawson, W.R. 1953. Egypt's place in medical history. *In* E.A. Underwood, ed. *Science Medicine and History.* Vol. 1. Oxford University Press, London. pp. 47–60.

4. Forbes, R.J. 1964. Dyes and dyeing. *In* R.J. Forbes. *Studies in Ancient Technology.* Vol 4. E.J. Brill, Leiden. pp. 99–150.

5. Forbes, R.J. 1965. Cosmetics and perfumes in antiquity. *In* R.J. Forbes. *Studies in Ancient Technology.* Vol. 3. E.J. Brill, Leiden. pp. 1–50.

6. Greene, E.L. 1983. *Landmarks of Botanical History.* Part I. F.N. Egerton, ed. Stanford University Press, Stanford, CA. 505 p.

7. Morton, A.G. 1981. *History of Botanical Science.* Academic Press, New York. 474 p.

8. Partington, J.R. 1953. Chemistry in the ancient world. *In* E.A. Underwood, ed. *Science Medicine and History.* Vol. 1. Oxford University Press, London. pp. 35–46.

9. Rea, C.B. and J. Rea. 1973. *Circa Instans.* [Rea], Bryan, TX. 426 p.

10. Simon, J.E., A.F. Chadwick, and L.E. Craker. 1984. *Herbs: An Indexed Bibliography, 1971–1980—The scientific literature on selected herbs, and aromatic and medicinal plants of the temperate zone.* Archon Books, Hamden, CT. 770 p.

11. Thompson, R. Campbell. 1924. *The Assyrian Herbal.* Luzac, London. 294 p.

12. Thorwald, Juergen. 1962 *Science and Secrets of Early Medicine: Egypt, Mesopotamia, India, China, Mexico, Peru.* Thames and Hudson, London. 331 p.

13. Trease, George Edward. 1964. *Pharmacy in History.* Baillière, Tindall and Cox, London. 265 p.

14. Urdang, George. 1948. The origin and development of the essential oil industry. *In* Ernest Guenther, ed. *The Essential Oils.* Vol. 1. Van Nostrand, New York. pp. 3–13.

Chemotaxonomic Aspects of Essential Oils*

Peter Tétényi
**Research Institute of Medicinal Plants, Budakalasz,
Hungary**

CONTENTS

I. INTRODUCTION

Although data on infraspecific differences in volatile oils may be
traced back to an earlier period, chemotaxonomy arose and was first
proposed as a special term at the Wageningen Symposium in 1957
(56), where several papers were read on special essential oils con-
stituting "chemical races" (30,46,48,50). Hegnauer (31) added em-
phasis and support to the concept of chemotaxonomy in 1958.

Since this introduction, the major disagreement in
chemotaxonomic classification has been with the 2 different meanings
associated with volatile oils. One meaning, as indicated by Hegnauer
(32), considers the artificial nature of essential or volatile oils as
related to their technical origin. In extraction processes, like steam
distillation, differential solubilities may produce different quantities

---

*Based on a plenary lecture given at the XII Essential Oil workshop in
Weihenstephan (FRG) 1983.

and ratios of ingredients than are actually present within the tissue. However, since it is evident that essential oils are present *in vivo,* the terms essential oils and volatile oils. do not refer only to technical products. Plants produce and/or store (in special secretory organs) essential oils. These natural oils are comparable with and also determinant of the subsequent yield and composition of steam-distilled oil. Therefore, it is possible to draw correct conclusions on the nature of the accumulating plant if chemotaxonomic evaluation of volatile oils is carried out on the extracted products that represent physiological active compounds (47).

The second difficulty in defining an essential oil relates to the natural substances per se. Formed and accumulated substances cannot solely characterize the production of a special taxon (57,59), as substances result from a course of biosynthesis. Identical substances in different species may be developed through entirely different biosynthetic routes and thus, the formation, but never the substance, has chemotaxonomic value. Comparative physiology data (8) have demonstrated that different plants can synthesize the same substance through 2 specific and characteristic, yet different, biochemical routes (Figure 1) and clearly indicate that one should not separate the substance production from the plant.

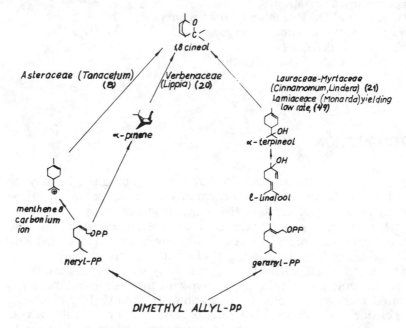

Figure 1. Biosynthesis Pathways for 1,8 Cineol by Different Plant Families. Numbers in parentheses indicate references.

Hegnauer (32) has speculated that, for chemotaxonomic evaluation, only essential oil constituents that attain at least one percent should be considered. However, the requirement that plants have this level of oil before using the constituent in chemotaxonomic evaluation is unacceptable as essential oils are naturally complicated products made of many compounds and cannot be entirely described by the major chemical constituents alone. Over 400 constituents have been determined in "Mousse de Chene's" oil (22) and illustrate the difficulty of using only those oil components of a high percentage.

A more reasonable approach is to characterize the complex of the oil through all of the constituents, since these reflect the genetic background of the enzyme systems and thus demonstrate biogenetic relations. As the enzymes have been coded by DNA and RNA, constituents in an essential oil are, as a consequence, "fingerprints" to the genetic makeup of the plant. This understanding agrees with the concept of Culberson's chemosyndrome (13), today's generally accepted term.

Complex biosynthesis reflects on the nature of the plant and not on the thesis provided by Stahl (51) that substances are stored as packages in plants. Production of plant products depends on plant structure as well as the plant's genetic and phylogenetic background in building an entity of life. The term allelochemicals has no declarative power but demonstrates how plant production of substances, as a phylogenetic accommodation to the environment, is furthered and developed as a complex in reality (24).

II. HISTORICAL PERSPECTIVE

Remarkably, very few studies deal with essential oils from the point of chemotaxonomy. After the Wageningen Symposium in 1957, no chemotaxonomic evaluation was published until 1965 (39). As pointed out by McKern (39), there was no assigned section on essential oils in the monographs of either Alston and Turner (3) or of Swain (54) that were published in 1963.

A historical survey presented by McKern (39) mentions that Baker and Smith (6) observed the characteristic presence of phyllocladenes and isophyllocladenes as early as 1910 in *Gymnosperms*. Data from the monograph on *Eucalyptus* oils by Baker and Smith (7), the publication series on *Orthodon* by Fujita (19), the studies on *Pinus* by Erdtman (16) and by Mirov (42), and observations since 1950 on ethereal oils of the genera *Backhousia*, *Melaleuca*, and *Leptosperum*, made the so-called "frequency rule" (the rarer a molecule occurs, the greater its value in taxonomy) (26) theoretically unacceptable to McKern (39). The difficulty of essential oil chemotaxonomy rests in the fact that not all products become volatile under steam pressure and, therefore, the selection of products of plants whose boiling points are between 150°C and 350°C as keys to identification is very arbitrary (39). In view of this, one must take into consideration whether certain essential oil components may serve as genuine "taxonomic tracers" (39).

In 1973, Flake and Turner (18) evaluated the utility and potential value of various volatile constituents as taxonomic characters and concluded that terpenes were ideal characters for systematic purposes, especially at and below the generic level. By using terpenes, considerable insight can be obtained about speciation and adaptational processes occurring within a given taxon.

Concern with the various hypotheses on the biological significance of formation and storage of essential oils, as related to qualitative and quantitative differentiation within species, has been raised (60). The infraspecific chemical differences of volatile oil accumulation may be frequently attributed to ecologic, geographic, and local factors rather than to introgressive hybridization. A tabular account concerning polychemistry in essential oil-containing taxa of the *Cormophytes* has been presented (60).

In a comprehensive report, Hegnauer (33) dealt with the term of essential oils (glycosidic-bonded olfactory substances, mustard oils, and flower scents), describing the range of essential oils in the plant kingdom and the different causes of their qualitative variation. A chemotaxonomic evaluation based on volatile oils in various plant taxa and on the range of various oil constituents suggested making use of both studies for understanding the variation and formation of taxa in nature as well as in the natural classification of plants (31).

III. ESSENTIAL OIL PLANTS AND CONSTITUENTS

The experimental line detailing the range of essential oils and their constituents in the plant kingdom occurs phylogenetically first in brown and red algae and in fungi (33). A systematic value may be given to bryophytes among which Marchantiales and Jungermanniales of the liverworts class have corpuscles of essential oil containing sesquiterpenoid molecules as taxon characteristics (5). Researchers in Japan (43) have analyzed aromatic ether as the main component of the *Leptolejeunea* oil. One can draw chemotaxonomic conclusions from most internal and/or external glandular hairs in *Filices*.

Among the gymnosperms, it is the Coniferopsida and the Taxopsida which store essential oils and balms in schizogenous exocretory organs and canals. In addition, one may find resins in Cycadopsida and Chlamydospermae. As main characteristics, diterpene hydrocarbons for coniferous oils and tropolone derivatives from plants in the family of Cupressaceae should also be mentioned (17).

Essential oil-containing taxa are widespread, not only on different levels of angiosperms but also conforming to its whole range of 111 families (23). Among the angiosperm taxa, one may attribute as main characteristics, various chemotaxonomic values to essential oils of Magnoliiflorae, Araliiflorae (superorders), Rutales and Zingiberales (orders), Myrtaceae and Piperaceae (families), Saturejoideae and Asteroideae (subfamilies), *Cannabis* and *Cymbopogon* (genera), and some *Polygonum* and *Cyperus* (species).

However, there are, of course, differences in frequency, as illustrated in Figure 2. Additional examples of the hierarchical categories

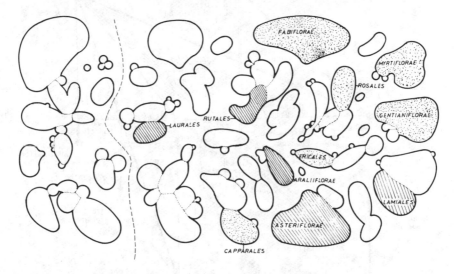

Figure 2. Characterization of Essential Oil Containing Taxa of Flowering Plants. Striking frequency: ▨ = high, ▒ = low, ☐ = absent.

that are definitely *not* essential oil-synthesizing taxa are known, which means that this property is induced phylogenetically and is a consequence of differentiation belonging to various levels. In the essential oil-accumulating taxa, one may always find special glandular hairs or other excreting organs as well as special components.

The second type of chemotaxonomic research is the investigation within larger, limited, systematic units of the occurrence of certain essential oil constituents or special oils. With the most practical objectives in mind, these kinds of studies can lead to very interesting theoretical results. Baker and Smith (7), closely examining the large genus of *Eucalyptus* for cineol and for pinene, were able to define a very good system of taxonomic classification that was phylogenetically valid. In the juvenile stage and in the adult period, the archaic species produce essential oils rich in pinene while seedlings of more recent species transform this metabolite in their second and third year of life into an essential oil spectrum true to the species, producing a considerable quantity of cineol (40). In later studies, Fujita (20) examined the components of coniferous oils and surveyed various taxa of *Lippia* (Verbenaceae), *Satureja* (Lamiaceae), and *Asarum* for several components, that led to his famous cubic system based on biochemical aspects (Figure 3).

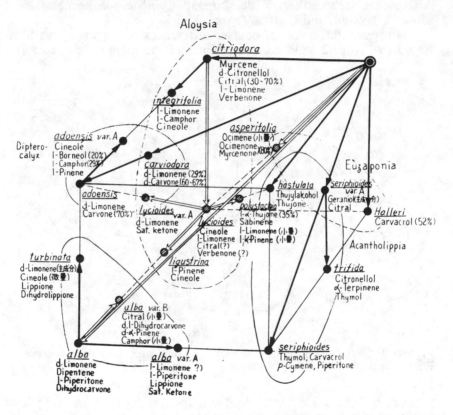

Figure 3. Cubic System for the Genus *Lippia*. Data developed by Fujita (20).

Research on chemical constituents is continuing. Kolesnikova *et al.* (35) report 35 chemical combinations of essential oils in the leaves of species of Juglandaceae found in the Soviet Union. Komae *et al.* (36) have surveyed 22 species of 8 genus of the family Lauraceae for mono- and sesquiterpene components of essential oils. After a study lasting several years, Zhou (66) has discovered, among other *Cinnamomum* taxa in China, a new safrole-producing species (the *Cinnamomum petrophilum* N. Chao that contains 3 to 4 percent essential oil [97 to 98 percent safrole] in the leaves).

IV. CHEMOTAXONOMIC EVALUATIONS

An aspect in chemotaxonomic evaluation is studies that draw new conclusions on a taxa's systematic position by elaborating data of previous trends. Baker and Smith (7) demonstrated that essential oils of the genus *Angophora* bear a close resemblance in their spectra to the genus *Eucalyptus* but only in the so-called pinene group of species. The veins of the leaves are also similar in the 2 genera, but this change conforms to the phellandrene increase in other species of *Eucalyptus.* Thus, the evolution of *Eucalyptus* from *Angophora* is documented, and this leads to new taxonomic and phylogenetic conclusions.

Hegnauer (33) gives 2 excellent examples for this kind of chemotaxonomic conclusion. In the past, the family Pittosporaceae was classified in the superorder of Rosanae. However, a large number of species of this family contain essential oils in their schizogenic vessels and reservoirs. This is not the case in other taxa belonging to Rosanae but occurs in the superorder of Aralianae, especially in species of the family Araliaceae and Apiaceae. Takhtajan (55) has classified 12 other families into the latter superorder that have nothing to do with essential oil production. For this reason, Hegnauer (33) states that, in this case, essential oils represent a feature that encourages the division and new classification of Aralianae. By accepting this concept, Dahlgren (15) was able to build up from Pittosporales and Araliiales the superorder of Araliiflorae. The families not accumulating essential oil are placed in the superorder of Corniflorae.

A second example is the separation within the Lamiaceae family by Hegnauer (33). Only one of its subfamilies, that of Saturejoideae, is rich in essential oils, with the other 4 (Prostantheroideae, Ajugoideae, Scutellarioideae, and Stachyoideae) being mostly poor in oil and having elaborate iridoid glycosides that are never found in the oil-containing subfamily. Thus, the confirmation of a distinct process of differentiated terpenoid chemism within the family is possible. As taxonomists introduce this reality, the 2 taxa will be separately described, discriminated, and classified in the systematic hierarchy.

The next aspect of chemotaxonomic evaluation is that of phylogeny. The descension of *Eucalyptus,* described above, was found on a purely theoretical basis. Nevertheless, in this aspect of research, there is a range of concrete palaeontologic studies such as the findings of phytane and pristane radicals of chlorophyll in fossilization (11). So far, however, no information on residues of essential oil in petrifaction, except for that of amber, is available. Therefore, one can do nothing more than consider some theoretical consequences. The genus *Satureja* (Lamiaceae), where Fujita (21) presents differentiated production of essential oil constituents, is a precedent. Isolation is also reflected in chemical features of different species of the genus and gives evidence of the last stage in the Tertiary period with respect to the separation of continents.

The theory of continental drift is reflected in the mode of appearance of essential oil constituents in plants now growing both in Africa and South America (20). While *Satureja calamintha* Scheele (a species in Turkey) has 20 percent d-pulegone in its essential oil, *Satureja abyssinica* Briq. (a species in Tanzania) contains d-pulegone (48 percent) and also d-isomenthone (42 percent). *Satureja odora* Epling (a species in Argentina) contains d-pulegone (70 percent), d-isomenthone (10 percent), and the constituent lippione (10 percent). The importance of lippione can be deduced from the essential oil of *Satureja parvifolia* Epling, which contains this constituent and its derivative through reduction of dehydrolippione. Thus, the continental drift has caused, in this detectable way, an established variation (Figure 4).

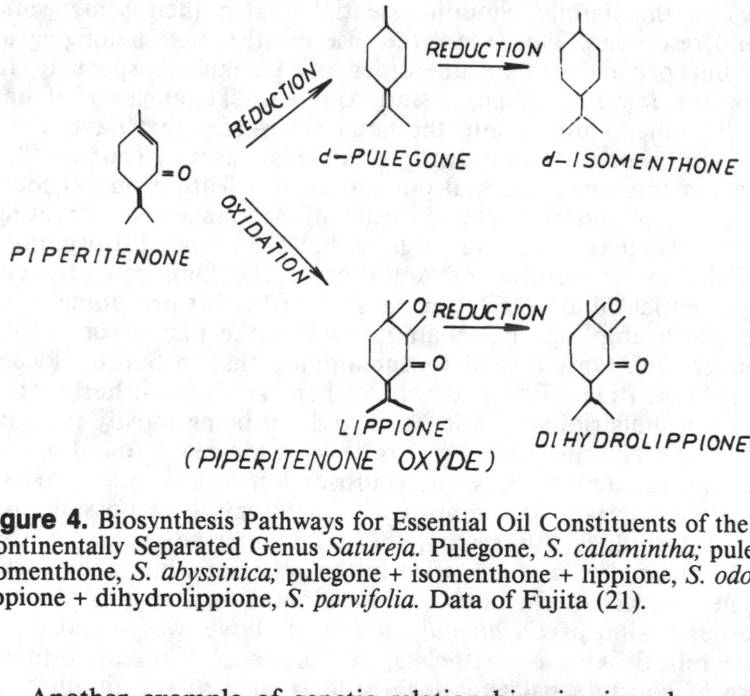

Figure 4. Biosynthesis Pathways for Essential Oil Constituents of the Continentally Separated Genus *Satureja.* Pulegone, *S. calamintha;* pulegone + isomenthone, *S. abyssinica;* pulegone + isomenthone + lippione, *S. odora;* lippione + dihydrolippione, *S. parvifolia.* Data of Fujita (21).

Another example of genetic relationships is given by evaluation of the oil constituent baeckol. First found in eastern Australia in the leaf oil of 2 Myrtaceae species, *Baeckea imbricata* Gaerth. Druce and *Darwinia procera* Briggs (45), this constituent was later reported in the non-Australian *Baeckea frutescens* L. and in the essential oil of the West Australian *Calythrix angulata* Lindl. The synthesis of baeckol thus shows, in an impressive manner, the migration of the family Myrtaceae from Southeast Asia to western and to eastern Australia (39).

V. ECOLOGICAL ASPECTS

The ecological aspect of chemotaxonomy is a most interesting field of research. As an example, much circumstantial work has been conducted for many years to clarify the causes of difference in the genus *Thymus*. Beginning with Granger *et al.* (25) and with definitive results from Adzet *et al.* (2), numerous experiments conducted with a number of species and infraspecific taxa of spontaneous occurrence indicate this genus originates from the Tertiary period in the western Mediterranean region. In the western part of the study area, only taxa of arborescent habit were found, but progressively northeastward, more herbaceous, creeping taxa were encountered. This mode of accommodation has allowed *Thymus* to push far into the European continent. The adaptability is reflected in the essential oil constituents and composition (Figure 5). As a principal component, the

Chemotypes	*longiflorus membranaceus autoninae*	*mastichina*	*aestivus*	*hiemalis*	*piperella*	*zygis*	*vulgaris*	*nitens*	*herba-barona*
Cineole	●		●	○			●··	○	
Borneol (camphor)			○	●					
Thymol, carvacrol			?*		●	●	●	●	●
(γ-Terpinene)									
trans-Thuyanol-4	●						●		
Terpineol-4						●	●		
linalool							●		
α-Terpineol							●···	●	
Geraniol							●		
Carvone									●

● chemotypes, certain
○ chemotypes, doubtful
* chemotype, detected, but seems to be *T. aestivus* x *T. vulgaris*
** chemotype, present in Spain, absent in France
*** chemotype, present in France, but seem to be absent in Spain

Figure 5. Differentiation of *Thymus* taxa According to Their Essential Oil Constituents. Data of Adzet *et al.* (2).

western taxa produce 1, 8-cineol while the eastern, dry regions produce thymol and carvacrole.

The influence of winter can also be observed. Where the temperatures of winter drop below freezing with much snow, the taxa with geraniol are found; where temperatures are more mild with little snow, species containing 1-terpineol dominate. For plants growing in places with a humid climate all year (like the near-Atlantic region), the taxa show linalool as the principal component.

The studies of Stahl (52) on the variability of the Icelandic *Thymus praecox* Opiz. ssp. *arcticus* (E. Durand) Jalas demonstrated that essential oils of this taxon differ from other species of *Thymus* primarily by the lack of phenols. The oil type of *Thymus arcticus* is characterized by the monoterpene ester linalyl acetate, which shows a remarkable similarity with *Thymus serpyllum* L. ssp. *tanaensis* (Hyl.) Jalas. Of the examined individual plants, 92 percent belong to the linalyl acetate taxon while the others contain little linalyl acetate and are differentiated according to the pattern of sesquiterpene. In the humid environment of the Gulf Stream on the Atlantic coast of Europe, linalool is present as a direct derivative.

A second example of ecologic chemotaxonomy comes from Hayashi *et al.* (27) in their study of the subgenus *Heterotropa* of *Asarum,* represented in Japan with 23 species of the existing 40. Examination of 5 section members verified that, according to groupings of essential oils, a differentiation between western and eastern regions of Japan is observed. Species with an essential oil composition of safrole, elemicin, and terpene-rich series (chemical groups A, B, and C) (Figure 6) have been noted in the West and species containing essential oil with elemicin trimethoxytoluene or elemicin tetramethoxybenzene (chemical groups D and E) have been noted in the East. In another specialization, *Asarum* species living outside Japan have no asatone in their volatile oil, but this component is always found in the oils of plants originating from Japan.

These ecologic-chemotaxonomic data clearly show the physiologic accommodation of plants to climatic conditions. Thus, an important part of the theory of Vavilov (63) on gene centers, such as that of homologous lines which was later extended by Nilov (44) to the biochemical characters of related species on the basis of their similarity in chemism, can be explained. Certain parallelisms in essential oil production, as in the case of various *Thymus* species, demonstrate that identical reaction norms are effective. For this reason, one may find, for example, the same borneol-accumulating infraspecific taxa in different species, indicating in this way a chemically homologous line.

VI. INFRASPECIFIC SYSTEMATIZATION

The most interesting aspect of chemotaxonomy would appear to be the infraspecific systematization. Stapf (53), who as early as 1906 observed such infraspecific chemical essential oil differences without any morphological ones in *Cymbopogon nardus* L. Rendle, was the first to describe plants producing the phenomenon known as "physiological races." However, intrinsic differences only represent a proper base if this sign of polychemism is tested and established through genetic verification. Thus, in the study of hereditary processes of infraspecific chemical characters, Hefendehl and Romero-Fonseca (29) are correct in describing chemogenetics as production of special constituents of essential oils under fairly strict genetic control. Many genetic analyses (29, 65) confirm the heredity of biosynthetic routes leading to the determined essential oil composition of plants.

Infraspecific polychemism of this kind is known in both essential oil-containing families of Hepaticae and in 4 of the 5 families of Gymnospermae. More than one-third of all essential oil-accumulating

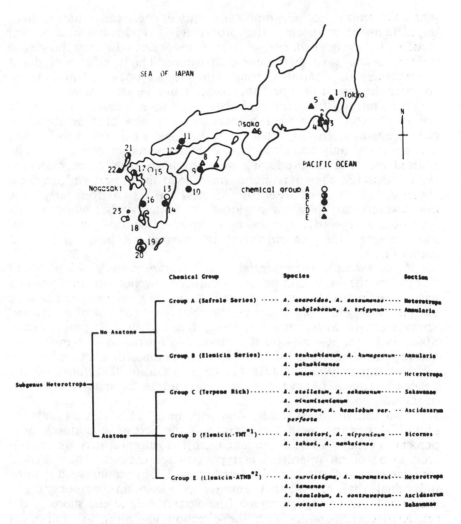

Figure 6. Chemodifferentiation and Distribution of *Asarum* Subgenus *Heterotropa* in Japan. Numbers indicate different species. Data of Hayashi *et al.* (27).

families of Angiospermae have species that are infraspecifically differentiated in their chemical characters. These supporting data indicate that polychemism is a general feature in the plant kingdom. Hereditary heterogeneity in metabolism always becomes manifested in a certain phase of plant ontogenesis (58, 61).

Hegnauer (33) calls infraspecific populations or groups of populations different in a biochemical sense chemodemes. These chemodemes are closely linked with cytologic, ecologic, or topographic phenomena. Chemotype is a term designed for individual plant differences. For geographically limited, chemically characterized populations of a species, the proper term is chemodeme. Recent studies of Biering *et al.* (9) on *Asarum europaeum* L. show how such differentiations take their course in nature. This species includes 4 chemodemes in Central Europe with the asarone-containing taxon covering the largest area and the isoelemicine the smallest area.

If chemical differentiation is conceived to be a result of breeding, the new taxon is regarded botanically as a new chemocultivar. A chemocultivar's self-support is restricted since a cultivar is multiplied and preserved only under the care of humans. As many economically utilized essential oil-producing varieties have such chemocultivars, the infraspecific chemotaxonomy has a great theoretical and practical significance in the breeding of new taxa. Theoretically, the microevolutionary basis of phylogenesis, imitating that which in nature occurs regularly, creates new varieties identical in form, but more adapted for our objectives in essential oil productivity and composition.

As an example, the essential oil of *Ocimum suave* Willd. plants in Kenya has the main component as methyl eugenol and in Tanzania has the main component as eugenol. In a study on variation among samples of origins from Rwanda, the volatile oil content of individual samples proved to be rather variable, from 0.04 to 1.88 percent (62). Statistically, the Rwanda plant material has proved to be significantly heterogeneous. Studies of the chemical composition of individual *Ocimum sauve* Willd. plants (Table 1) indicate that most of the collected samples (90 percent) have eugenol as the main constituent of the oil.

Two individual samples, one containing 51.3 percent eugenol plus 13.4 percent methyl eugenol and the second containing 36.2 percent eugenol plus 12.5 percent methyl isoeugenol, may be considered to be of an intermediate type, perhaps hybrids. These hybrid samples were collected on the territory of Kibuye along with a third individual that has methyl eugenol as the main component (42 percent). From Cyangugu region (the western side at the shore of the sea Kivu corresponding with the direction to Zaire), an individual sample with 42.5 percent methyl eugenol and 28.2 percent eugenol was discovered. One sample collected from the area of Byumba contained 37.4 percent methyl isoeugenol as the main component and only 9.2 percent eugenol, the lowest amount of eugenol of all samples. Samples originating from Ruhengeri (H) contain α-bergamotene instead of β-bisabolene.

According to the data, the real cause of previously reported differences in plant types may have been dependent upon the different locations from which plant material was collected. Conforming to its area and geographical distribution, the chemism of the species *Ocimum suave* Willd. is differentiated. In Rwanda, 3 subspecies can be found: chssp. *eugenol,* chssp. *methyl eugenol,* and chssp. *methyl isoeugenol.* The transition among these chemosubspecies seems to be

TABLE 1. Chemical Composition of the Essential Oil from Some Individual Ocimum suave Willd.

Sample	Constituent[a]								
	1	2	3	4	5	6	7	8	9
	(percent of total oil)[b]								
47 C	26.0	3.4		8.0				54.9	
55 C	21.0	3.7		6.8				65.0	
52 C	17.0	2.0		13.4				57.9	
74 C	14.2	10.0		21.8				38.9	
09 C	10.0	1.9		9.2				72.9	
76 C	4.0	1.3		4.8				80.9	2.0
58 G	5.0	6.0		12.0	14.2			43.7	
66 I	18.2			12.1	12.0		3.8	9.2	37.4
34 B	18.2			10.0	11.4			51.7	
61 F	9.1	8.2		14.0	10.8			36.2	12.5
28 G	5.9	5.0		11.0	10.3			56.4	
65 F	9.0	9.9		9.4	9.0		42.0	12.7	
33 B	13.8	13.0		11.0	8.2			46.6	
27 G	6.0	5.7		4.4	4.0		3.4	68.5	
29 H	5.8	6.0		8.6		10.0		59.1	
30 H	6.0	10.0		7.2		6.0		65.8	
03 C	25.0	6.4		10.2		2.9		45.1	
10 C	15.0	3.4		9.4			5.1	59.0	
20 F	5.8	5.0		17.7			13.4	51.3	
14 E	4.0	2.7	2.0	16.1			42.5	28.2	

[a]1. β-ocimene, 2. unknown, 3. estragol, 4. β-cubebene; 5. β-bisobolene, 6. α-bergamotene, 7. methyl-eugenol, 8. eugenol, 9. methyliso-eugenol.
[b]Calculated from data at TLC chromatogram on 3 percent NPS and 3 percent OV-17 columns.

continuous so that this can be viewed as a variation of cline type (Figure 7).

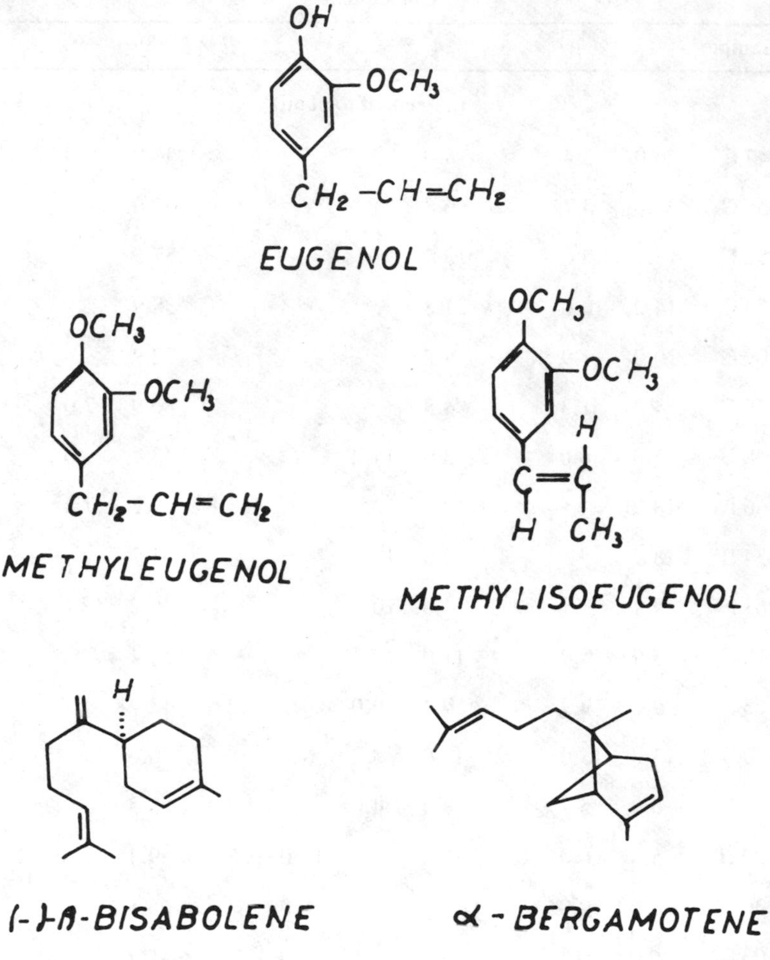

EUGENOL

METHYLEUGENOL

METHYLISOEUGENOL

(-)-ß-BISABOLENE   ∝-BERGAMOTENE

Figure 7. Main Constituents of Differentiated Infraspecific Chemotaxa of *Ocimum suave* Willd. in Rwanda.

The difference between α-bergamotene and β-bisabolene is, however, at a lower level and can be evaluated as an alternative chemical variation. Only within the chemosubspecies *eugenol* taxon has the chemovariety α-*bergamotene* been separated. The chemovariety β-*bisabolene* occurs in all 3 chemosubspecies. Further studies are necessary to clarify whether an immigration of various taxa took place into Rwanda or if the primary occurrence was in Rwanda, corresponding to a gene center, with introduction in other territories through an adaptation, followed by a biochemical-physiological differentiation.

One could infinitely enumerate examples of essential oil-containing plant species, but as a summary, rough figures indicate that, from among over 130 genera of flowering plants, more than 400 species are found in which infraspecific chemical differentiation occurs. An inventory of these families is unnecessary because data on the infraspecific essential oil differences are regularly reported by Lawrence (37, 38).

From the practical point of view, the interest in systematizing according to infraspecific chemical differences appears in the study of Wagner (64) on the classification of hop varieties. Harmonious flavor and a few amaroids characterize the European varieties as compared to the American varieties that are rich in amaroids and have a strong intrusive aroma. Characteristic of American varieties are the α-acids as well as a positively correlated ratio between these and the β-fraction. A high value of the α-acids and the β-fraction provides the best quality for the dried material. Thus Wagner (64) could construct from over 40 varieties, a line from the best quality ('Srebrjanka' and 'Wurtemberger') to the strongest aroma ('Aurora' and 'Apollon').

Since the number of infraspecific chemical taxa may be very large (as in the case of *Humulus lupulus*), computers have recently been used to process the numerous chemical data. From the results obtained in this manner, a new aspect has developed: numerical chemotaxonomy. The numerical chemotaxonomy approach has been used in the past 10 years for various chemotaxonomic problems, including those with essential oil-containing plants. In the case of *Juniperus ashei* Buchh., which is native in Texas and regarded as a typical specimen for the western introgression through *Juniperus pinchotii* Sudw. and *Juniperus virginiana* L., no indication could be found for introgression or hybridization from the oil analysis of various populations. As a real cause of the variation observed in *Juniperus ashei* Buch., Adams *et al.* (1) could demonstrate that this species originated from *Juniperus saltillensis* Hall through rapid radiation and penetration into Texas (during the Tertiary period), becoming differentiated and specialized. This research continues with *Juniperus virginiana* L. (12).

As a further example of the value of computers in processing chemical data, one can examine the results of Zavarin *et al.* (65), where 6 Asiatic species of *Abies* were separated by computerizing the information of their essential oils and using "similarity indices" to discriminate among groupings.

Finally, one can explore the studies on *Tanacetum vulgare* (61) where, after the chemically differentiated taxa were clarified, the biochemical relation within the species could be demonstrated. A proper clustering was obtained through selected mathematical calculations. First, a version of the rapid McQueen method (4) of low memory requirement was utilized to provide a classification according to principal constituents, separating 11 various chemotaxa (Figure 8). This grouping was classified so that frequency of the individuals

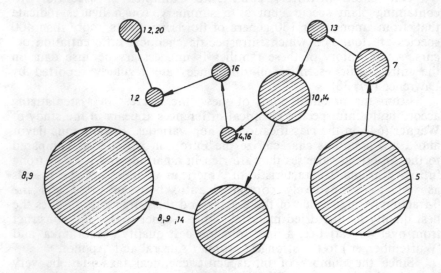

Figure 8. Clustering in *Tanacetum vulgare* as Produced by the MacQueen Method (4). Numbers represent dominant essential oil constituents; (5) artemisiaketone; (7) β-thujone; (8) trans- chrysanthenol; (9) trans-chrysanthenyl acetate; (10) borneol + bornyl acetate; (12) thujyl alcohol; (13) lyratol + lyratyl acetate; (14) trans-chrysanthenyl acetate + borneol; (16) borneol + piperitone; and (20) thujyl alcohol + umbellulone.

containing *trans*-chrysanthenol + *trans* -chrysanthenyl acetate (90 samples), artemisiaketone (84 samples), and *trans* -chrysanthenyl acetate + borneol (62 samples) predominated. Occurrence of individuals containing borneol + bornyl acetate (41 samples) was considered significant. For the other groups, a small entity number was characteristic but, by this method, the groups of α-thujone and β-thujone, thujyl alcohol, lyratol + umbellulone, and piperitone were separated.

The second technique used to demonstrate biochemical relationships was the clique method (10) where pairs of proper correlation (constituents of essential oils that are coupled) were selected. The clique method delineated the joining of *trans* -chrysanthenol and *trans* -chrysanthenyl acetate (Figure 9). The pinene + camphene, the 1,8-cineol + yomogi alcohol, the *trans* -chrysanthenol + artemisia ketone, the umbellulone + unknown, and the borneol + bornyl acetate couples were assessed as cliques also. Cliques of lower levels are formed by those containing pinene + piperitone, camphene + cineol, thujyl alcohol + piperitone, and camphene + thujone + campher.

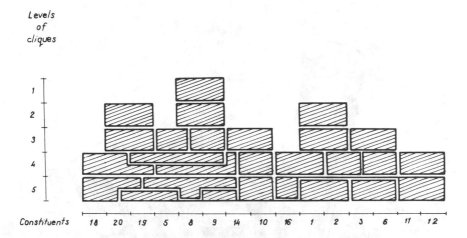

Levels
of
cliques

Figure 9. Cluster Hierarchy of Constituents in Essential Oil of *Tanacetum vulgare* as Derived by the Clique Method (10). Numbers represent essential oil constituent: (1) pinene, (2) camphene, (3) 1,8-cineol, (6) yomogi alcohol, and (18) davanone. There was no affinity for constituents 4, 7, 13, and 15. Other constituents are unidentified.

By comparatively evaluating both methods in examining constituent differentiation in the essential oil of *Tanacetum vulgare* and in the path of biosynthesis, a genealogic dendrogram conforming to Dahlgren's idea of representation (14) can be prepared. The different levels of this "tree" are due to the elongation of the carbon skeleton of constituents. Synthesis routes are differentiated in acyclic, monocyclic, biocyclic, and irregular terpenes. "Branches" conform to the terpenoid differentiation and are located as the 2 mathematical methods indicate their position (Figure 10).

Both cluster types have been determined; that is, *trans*-chrysanthenol + *trans*-chrysanthenyl acetate containing taxa, irregular compound containing taxa, or borneol + bornyl acetate (monocyclic) containing taxa (61). The McQueen cluster (4) was useful for delimiting taxa-accumulating artemisia ketone (irregular), thujone (bicyclic), or lyratol + lyratyl acetate (acyclic). Essential oil "branches" were found by the clique method (10), separating taxa with constituents *trans*-chrysanthenol + artemisia ketone (irregular), pinene + camphene (monocyclic), or thujyl alcohol + piperitone (bicyclic) and mixed, cineol + yomogi alcohol (monocyclic + irregular) and piperitone + pinene (bicyclic + monocyclic).

Although these groupings helped to construct the dendrogram, neither of the 2 methods pointed out the theoretically interesting and most practical infraspecific chemical taxon, the one determined by Hethelyi *et al.* (34) and having davanone as the main constituent.

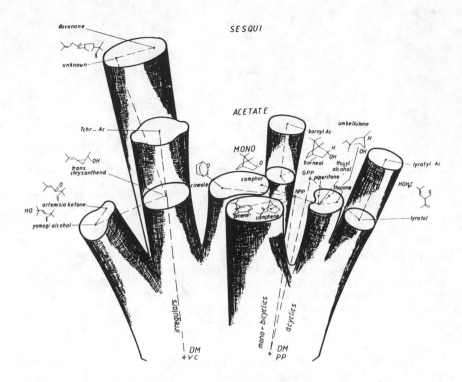

Figure 10. Dendrogram of Biosynthesis Pathways for Essential Oil Constituents Found in *Tanacetum vulgare.*

However, these conclusions are drawn only from spontaneous individuals that are clones in a Hungarian botanic garden. Such ubiquitous species like *Tanacetum vulgare,* occurring from Finland through Japan to Canada, need more study before the infraspecific chemodifferentiation can be definitely understood.

VII. CONCLUSIONS

The various but interdependent chemotaxonomic aspects characterized (with several examples) in this review are helping to form a better understanding of the plant kingdom and to find functional-biochemical connections in addition to structural-morphological ones. The earlier the more recent systematics become integrated, the earlier "this terrible mixture of Science and Art," as systematization was defined by Merxmüller (41), can be transformed into exact chemotaxonomy.

VIII. REFERENCES

1. Adams, P.R., R. Rudloff, T.A. Zavarin, and L. Hoppe. 1980. The terpenoids of an ancestral species pair of *Juniperus.* Biochem. Syst. Ecol. 8:35.

2. Adzet, T., R. Granger, J. Passet, and R. San Martin. 1977. Le polymorphisme chimique dans le genre *Thymus.* Sa signification taxonomique. Biochem. Syst. Ecol. 5:269–272.

3. Alston, R.E. and B.L. Turner. 1963. *Biochemical Systematics.* Prentice-Hall, Englewood, NJ.

4. Anderberg, M.R. 1973. *Cluster Analysis for Applications.* Academic Press, New York.

5. Andersen, N.M., Y. Ohta, C.B. Lin, M. Kramer, K. Allison, and S. Hunneck. 1977. Sesquiterpenes of thalloid liverworts of the genera *Concephalum, Lununlaria, Metzgeria* and *Riccardia.* Phytochemistry 16:1727–1729.

6. Baker, R.T. and H.G. Smith. 1910. *A research on the pines of Australia.* Government Printer, Sydney, pp. 419–426.

7. Baker, R.T. and H.G. Smith. 1920. *A research on the Eucalypts, especially in regard to their essential oils. Government Printer,* Sydney, pp. 135–412.

8. Bell, E.A. and B.V. Charlwood. 1980. Secondary plant products. *Encyclopedia of Plant Physiology,* New Series Vol. 8. Springer- Verlag, New York, pp. 23–50.

9. Biering, W.E., I. Burgert-Hansing, and H. Jork. 1976. Ist es gerechtfertigt bei *Asarum europaeum* von chemischen Rassen zu sprechen? Planta Med. 29:132–147.

10. Bron, C. and J. Kerbosch. 1975. Algorithm 457—Finding all cliques of an indirected graph. Comm. ACM, 16:575–577.

11. Chaloner, W.G. and K. Allen. 1970. Paleobotany and phytochemical phylogeny. *In* J.B. Harborne, ed. *Phytochemical Phylogeny.* Academic Press, London. pp. 21.

12. Comer, C.W., R.P. Adams, and D.F. van Haverbeke. 1982. Infra- and inter- specific variation at *Juniperus virginiana* and *J. scopulorum* seedlings based on volatile oil composition. Biochem. Syst. Ecol. 10:297–306.

13. Culberson, C.F. and W.L. Culberson. 1976. Chemosyndromic variation in lichens. Quart. J. Am. Soc. Plant Taxon. 1:331–340.

14. Dahlgren, R.M.T. 1977. A commentary on a diagrammatic presentation of the angiosperms in relation to the distribution of character states. *In* K. Kubitzki, ed. *Flowering Plants.* Springer-Verlag, New York. Plant System Evol. Suppl. 1:253–284.

15. Dahlgren, R.M.T. 1980. A revised system of classification of the angiosperms. Bot. J. Linn. Soc. 80:91–124.

16. Erdtman, H. 1956. Organic chemistry and conifer taxonomy. *In* A. Todd, ed. *Perspectives in Organic Chemistry.* Interscience Publisher Ltd., London. pp. 453–485.

17. Erdtman, H. and T. Norin. 1966. The chemistry of the order *Cupressales* Fortschr. Chemie Org. Naturst. 24:206–287.

18. Flake, R.M. and B.L. Turner. 1973. Volatile constituents, especially terpenes, and their utility and potential as taxonomic characters in populational studies. *In* G. Bendz and J. Santesson, ed. *Nobel Symposium 25.*

Chemistry in Botanical Classification. Academic Press, New York. pp. 123–128.

19. Fujita, Y. 1951. Fundamental studies of essential oils. Ogawa Koryojiho *(Ogawa Perfume Times).* No. 202:4–62.

20. Fujita, Y. 1965. Cubic system of classification of the genus *Lippia* (Verbenaceae) by the constituents of essential oils. 3. Rep. Gov., Ind. Res. Inst. Osaka. No. 306. pp. 21–25.

21. Fujita, Y. 1967. The theory of continental drift viewed from the chemical constituents of plants. J. Jpn. Bot. 42:91–95, 278–280.

22. Gavin, J., G. Nicollier, and R. Tobacchi. 1978. Composantes volatiles de la "mousse de chène" *(Evernia Prunastri* L. Arch.). Helv. Chim. Acta 61:352.

23. Gildemeister, E. and F. Hoffman. 1958–1961. *Die ätherischen Öle.* Akad. Verlag, Berlin. Vol. IV.–VII.

24. Gottlieb, O.R. 1982. *Micromolecular Evolution, Systematics and Ecology.* Springer-Verlag, New York. 170 p.

25. Granger, R., R. San Martin, T. Adzet, and R. Verdier. 1963. Variation des huiles essentielles de *Thymus vulgaris.* France Parf. 6:225–245.

26. Hänsel, R. 1956. Pflanzenchemie und Pflanzenverwandtschaft. Arch. Pharm. (Weinheim, Ger.). 289:619–630.

27. Hayashi, N., M. Sholichin, T. Sakao, Y. Yamamura, and H. Komae. 1980. An approach to chemotaxonomy of the *Asarum* Subgenus *Heterotropa.* Biochem. Syst. Ecol. 8:109–114.

28. Hefendehl, F.W. 1973. Der Einsatz genetischer Experimente zur Aufklärung der Biogenese von ätherischen Ölen. Planta Med. 23:301–307.

29. Hefendehl, F.W. and L. Romero-Fonseca. 1976. Analyse des ätherischen Öls von *Elyonurus viridulus.* Planta Med. 30:125–140.

30. Hegnauer, R. 1957. Die Bedeutung der chemischen Rassen fur die Arzneipflanzenforschung. Pharm. Weekbl. 92:860–870.

31. Hegnauer, R. 1958. Chemotaxonomische Betrachtungen. Pharm. Acta Helv. 33:287–296.

32. Hegnauer, R. 1962. *Chemotaxonomie der Pflanzen. Basel.* Birkhäuser Verlag, Stuttgart. Vol. 1. p. 114.

33. Hegnauer, R. 1978. Die systematische Bedeutung der ätherischen Öle. Dragoco Rep. 24:203–230.

34. Héthelyi, E., R. Tétényi, J.J. Kettenes-van den Bosch, C.A. Salemink, W. Heerna, C. Vershuis, J. Kloosterman, and G. Sipna. 1981. Essential oils of five *Tanacetum vulgare* genotypes. Phytochemistry 20:1847–1850.

35. Kolesnikova, R., M. Ulukina, and R. Derjuzhkin. 1983. The peculiarities of the essential oils composition of the leaves of walnuts of Juglandaceae Family. Int. Congr. Essent. Oils, 9th. 1983. Abstr. 50.

36. Komae, H., N. Hayashi, and T. Sakao. 1983. Essential oils and their constituents of *Lauraceae* in Japan, Int. Cong. Essent. Oils, 9th. 1983. Abstr. 16.

37. Lawrence, B.M. 1976. Progress in essential oils. Perfum. Flavor. 1:1–5.

38. Lawrence, B.M. 1984. Progress in essential oils. Perfum. Flavor. 9:23–31.

39. McKern, H.H.G. 1965. Volatile oils and plant taxonomy. J. Proc. R. Soc. N.S.W. 98:1–10.

40. McNair, J.B. 1945. Some comparison of chemical ontogeny with chemical phylogeny in vascular plants. Lloydia 8:145–169.

41. Merxmüller, H. 1977. Summary lecture. *In* K. Kubitzki, ed. *Flowering Plants.* Springer-Verlag, New York. Plant Syst. Evol. Suppl. 1:397–405.

42. Mirov, N.T. 1961. Composition of gum terpentines of pines. US Dep. Agric. Techn. Bull. No. 1239.

43. Nakayama, M., A. Matsuo, T. Kami, and S. Hayashi. 1979. Volatile from *Leptolejeunea elliptica.* Phytochemistry, 18:328.

44. Nilov, V.I. 1937. Chemical variation of plants. Rep. Acad. Sci. USSR. Biol Ser. 6. 1709-1732.

45. Penfold, A.R. 1922. The essential oil of *Backousia myrtifolia.* Part 1. J. Proc. R. Soc. N.S.W. 56:125–129.

46. Rovesti, P. 1957. Recherches sur les essences de quelques chemotypes de Labiees. Pharm. Weekblad 92:830–832.

47. Schilcher, H. 1977. Vorschlag zu einer biologisch orientierten Definition der ätherischen Öle. Dtsche. Apoth. Ztg. 117:89–91.

48. Schratz, E. 1957. Der Einfluss der Umwelt auf den Gehalt der Pflanzen an ätherischen Öl. Pharm. Weekbl. 92:781–792.

49. Scora, W.R. and J.D. Mann. 1967. Essential oil synthesis in *Monarda punctata.* Lloydia 30:236–241.

50. Stahl, Eg. 1957. Chemische Rassen bei Pflanzen mit terpenoiden Inhaltstoffen. Pharm. Weekbl. 92:829–842.

51. Stahl, Eg. 1971. Chemische Rassen bei Arzneipflanzen mit ätherischen Ölen. Pharm. Weekbl. 106:237–244.

52. Stahl, El. 1982. Studie zur Variabilitat des ätherischen Öls aus *Thymus praecox* Opiz. ssp. *arcticus,* E. Durand, Jalas islandische Vorkommen. Ber. Fschgst. Neori M. Hverageroi, Island, No. 38. p. 69.

53. Stapf, O. 1906. The oil grasses of India and Ceylon, *Cymbopogon, Vetiveria* and *Andropogon* spp. Kew Bull. 8:297.

54. Swain, T. 1963. *Chemical Plant Taxonomy.* Academic Press, London.

55. Takhtajan, A. 1973. The chemical approach to plant classification with special reference to the higher taxa of Magnoliophyta. *In* G. Bendz and J. Santesson, ed. Nobel Symposium 25. *Chemistry in Botanical Classification.* Academic Press, New York. pp. 17–28.

56. Tétényi, P. 1958. Proposition à propos de la nomenclature des races chimiques. Taxon VII: 40–41. Wageningen conference lecture, 1957.

57. Tétényi, P. 1965. Infraspecific chemical taxa and breeding of medicinal plants. Hung. Agric. Rev. 9:10–11.

58. Tétényi, P. 1970. *Infraspecific Chemical Taxa of Medicinal Plants.* Akad. Kiadó, Budapest. 225 p.

59. Tétényi, P. 1973. Homology of biosynthetic routes: The base in chemotaxonomy. *In* G. Bendz and J. Santesson, eds. Nobel Symposium 25. *Chemistry in Botanical Classification.* Academic Press, New York. pp. 67–78.

60. Tétényi, P. 1975. Chemical polymorphish and chemical polytypism in essential oil producing plant species. Planta Med. 28:244–256.

61. Tétényi, P., J. Fischer, A. Csiszar, E. Hethélyi, and P. Kaposi. 1979. Approach to infraspecific chemical taxonomy of *Tanacetum vulgare* L. by mathematical means. *In* Int. Congr. Essent. Oils, 7th. 1977. Kyoto. pp. 198–199.

62. Tétényi, P., E. Héthelyi, L. van Puyvelde, and F. Ayobangira. 1983. Essential oil variation of *Ocimum suave* in Rwanda. Int. Congr. Essent. Oils, 9th. 1983 Abstr. 28.

63. Vavilov, N.I. 1920. Zakoni homologitseskih rjadov. Trudi III. sjezda po szelekcii. Saratov 82.

64. Wagner, T. 1983. Kolicina in sostava grencicnih smalkemotaksonomska karakteristika hmeljnih sort. Farmacev. Restriz. 34:77–83.

65. Zavarin, E., K. Snajberk, and W.B. Critchfield. 1978. Geographic differentiation of monoterpenes from *Abies procera* and *Abies magnifica*. Biochem. Syst. Ecol. 6:267–278.

66. Zhou, R.J. 1983. A new species of safrole-containing plant yangui, *Cinnamomum Petrophilum* N. Chao Sp. Int. Congr. Essent. Oils, 9th. 1983. Abstr. 18.

Botanical Nomenclature of Culinary Herbs and Potherbs

Arthur O. Tucker
**Department of Agriculture and Natural Resources,
Delaware State College, Dover, DE 19901**

CONTENTS

I. INTRODUCTION

The need for correct identification and uniform nomenclature of herbs is well-illustrated in numerous papers on chemistry, pharmacognosy, physiology, genetics, and karyology. Furthermore, many researchers rarely see the original wild-collected plants, but instead, rely upon the purity of the dried herb or essential oil. As a result, the interpretation of this literature is often suspect.

A prime example is *Origanum*. Ietswaart (106), in his revision of the genus, stated: "None of the chemical data mentioned have been used as criteria for delimitation of *Origanum,* its sections or species. The first reason for this is that the data are too fragmentary. Secondly, many authors gave no or incomplete and inaccurate data about morphology, geography and taxonomy of the plants used." Chemists rarely file herbarium vouchers!

In particular, the identification of oregano is usually stated incorrectly. Greek or Italian oregano (*Origanum vulgare* subsp. *hirtum*) is collected from the wild, along with other species. This admixture confuses the correct identity of the commercial product. Actually, oregano is a flavor rather than one or a few species (28, 184), a fact which produces even further confusion.

Four other examples are sage, mint, lavandin, and savory. Dalmatian sage *(Salvia officinalis)*, Greek sage *(S. fruticosa)*, and their hybrids are often collected and sold in various mixtures but simply labeled as "Dalmatian sage" (187). Botanists and chemists have both been guilty of naming any pubescent, spicate *Mentha* as *M. longifolia* (horsemint), while they are often working on pubescent clones of *M. spicata* (spearmint) (82, 83, 185). While perfumers are quite familiar with the differences between lavandin *(Lavandula x intermedia)* and lavender *(L. angustifolia)*, horticulturists seem to be totally unfamiliar with lavandin and call both "lavender" (186). Summer savory *(Satureja hortensis)* has been commercially adulterated with winter savory *(S. montana)* and za'atar hommar *(Thymbra spicata)* (94, 95).

Clearly, researchers must attempt to work with materials from correctly identified plants. Local botanic gardens or herbaria allied with universities are often more than willing to help in such identification. Citation of herbarium vouchers becomes a necessity if any research is to remain valid for the future.

II. DEFINITION OF HERB AND POTHERB

Herbs and spices have little food value and are primarily used for flavoring foods and beverages. Writers have continually wrestled with the distinction between herb and spice (4, 125, 142, 182, 208). While botanists define herbs as nonwoody plants, horticulturalists generally state that herbs can be grown in temperate climates while spices must be imported from the tropics. Some definitions also attempt to define herbs and spices by the plant organ or pungency. The American Spice Trade Association (3) and writers who emphasize the trade aspect (151) avoid this dichotomy and call both spices. This is in part due to the legal definition of spices by American trade and tariff regulations as "aromatic vegetable substances (including seeds, leaves, stems, bark, roots, or other relevant plant parts) from which virtually none of the volatile oil or other flavoring principle has been removed" (80).

For the purpose of this review, a culinary herb is defined in the popular sense as a plant which can be usually grown in temperate regions and is used (or has been used) in minor quantities to flavor foods and beverages; no distinction is made as to woodiness, plant organ, or pungency. A potherb is defined here as a leafy plant (from both temperate and tropical climates) which can be used in minor quantities as an adjunct to salads.

These definitions are purposely broad in order to include certain species (*e.g., Piper auritum, Dianthus caryophyllus, Blumea balsamifera,* and *Petasites japonicus)* which might otherwise "fall through the cracks" in strict legal or scientific definitions of herbs, spices, essential oil plants, medicinal plants, fruits, or vegetables.

III. ORGANIZATION OF LIST

An initial survey of herbs, potherbs, spices, medicinal plants, essential oil crops, and sweetener plants produced a list of 401 genera, 120 of which could be considered as herbs or potherbs (in whole or part). This list does not include vegetables, fruits, strict hallucinogens, fixed oil crops, insecticide plants, dyes, and some major beverages (tea, cacao, and cola).

The following list of over 290 species and hybrids was compiled through a survey of many books on herbs and economic plants (44, 142, 169, 182, 210, 221). Guides to the correct nomenclature (90, 119, 129, 149, 206, 209) included many regional floras. The list conforms to the rules listed in the *International Code of Botanical Nomenclature* (214) and the *International Code of Nomenclature for Cultivated Plants* (24). Generic citations follow *Index nominum genericorum* (68); literature citations directly following the Latin names conform to *Taxonomic Literature* (176); other literature references refer to citations in the reference section. Common names are listed as English (Eng.), French (Fr.), German (Ger.), Italian (It.), Spanish (Sp.), Japanese (Jap.), Chinese (Chin.), Arabic (Ar.), Greek (Gk.), Vietnamese (Viet.), Indian, Malay, etc.

For guides to the "correct" pronunciation of the Latin names, the reader is directed to W.T. Stearn's *Botanical Latin* (180). Guides to English pronunciation are also listed in the "References" section of this chapter (7, 73, 173).

IV. LIST OF CULINARY HERBS AND POTHERBS SUMMARY

This list is organized phylogenetically by family (a standard taxonomic practice), but the genera and species within each family are arranged alphabetically. The following genera are included.

Cupressaceae: *Juniperus*
Liliaceae: *Allium*
Iridaceae: *Crocus*
Saururaceae: *Houttuynia*
Piperaceae: *Piper*
Moraceae: *Humulus*
Polygonaceae: *Polygonum, Rumex*
Chenopodiaceae: *Atriplex, Chenopodium*
Caryophyllaceae: *Dianthus, Stellaria*

Ranunculaceae: *Caltha, Nigella*
Lauraceae: *Laurus, Lindera, Persea, Sassafras, Umbellularia*
Papaveraceae: *Papaver*
Brassicaceae (Cruciferae): *Alliaria, Armoracia, Barbarea, Brassica, Cardamine, Cochlearia, Eruca, Lepidium, Nasturtium, Sinapis, Wasabia*
Capparaceae: *Capparis*
Rosaceae: *Filipendula, Prunus, Rosa, Sanguisorba*
Fabaceae (Leguminosae): *Aspalathus, Trigonella*
Oxalidaceae: *Oxalis*
Tropaeolaceae: *Tropaeolum*
Rutaceae: *Ruta, Zanthoxylum*
Bixaceae: *Bixa*
Violaceae: *Viola*
Apiaceae (Umbelliferae): *Anethum, Angelica, Anthriscus, Carum, Centella, Coriandrum, Crithmum, Cryptotaenia, Cuminum, Eryngium, Ferula, Foeniculum, Hydrocotyle, Levisticum, Ligusticum, Myrrhis, Oenanthe, Petroselinum, Pimpinellia, Trachyspermum*
Boraginaceae: *Borago, Symphytum*
Verbenaceae: *Aloysia, Lantana, Lippia*
Lamiaceae (Labiatae): *Acinos, Agastache, Calamintha, Coleus, Cunila, Glechoma, Hedeoma, Hyptis, Hyssopus, Lavandula, Melissa, Mentha, Monarda, Monardella, Nepeta, Ocimum, Origanum, Perilla, Phlomis, Poliomintha, Pycnanthemum, Rosmarinus, Salvia, Satureja, Sideritis, Thymbra, Thymus*
Solanaceae: *Capsicum*
Scrophulariaceae: *Limnophila*
Rubiaceae: *Galium*
Valerianaceae: *Valeriana, Valerianella*
Asteraceae (Compositae): *Artemisia, Balsamita, Blumea, Brickellia, Cacalia, Calendula, Chamaemelum, Chamomilla, Chrysanthemum, Cichorium, Cirsium, Helichrysum, Inula, Kalimeris, Petasites, Solidago, Tagetes, Tanacetum, Taraxacum*

V. LIST OF CULINARY HERBS AND POTHERBS

Cupressaceae

Juniperus L., Sp. pl. 1038. 1753.
    Literature: 56.
    Species:
    Juniperus communis L., Sp. pl. 1040. 1753: common juniper (Eng.), genévrier (Fr.), genièvre commune (Fr.), Wacholder (Ger.), ginepro (It.), enebro (Sp.).

Liliaceae

Allium L., Sp. pl. 295. 1753.
Literature: 20, 93, 115, 178, 179, 219
Species:
Allium fistulosum L., Sp. pl. 301. 1753: Welsh onion (Eng.), cibol
(Eng.), stone leek (Eng.), ciboule (Fr.), Schnittzwiebel (Ger.),
cipoletta (It.), ceboletta (Sp.), negi (Jap.).
Allium kurrat Schweinf. ex K. Krause in Notizbl. Bot. Gard.
Berlin-Dahlem 9(87):523. 1926. *(A. porrum* L. var.
aegyptiacum Schweinf.; *A. porrum* auct., non L.): kurrat
(Ar.), kurrat baladi (Ar.), kurrat nabati (Ar.).
While *Hortus Third* (129) classifies *A. kurrat* and *A. porrum*
as groups within *A. ampeloprasum* L., Bonnet (20) maintains
that *A. porrum* is a distinct species; *A. kurrat* is as distinct as
A. porrum and would seem to deserve similar recognition.
Further study is needed.
Allium sativum L., Sp. pl. 296. 1753: garlic (Eng.), ail (Fr.),
Knoblauch (Ger.), aglio (It.), ajo (Sp.).
Three varieties exist:
var. *sativum:* the cultivated garlic.
var. *ophioscorodon* (Link) Döll, Rhein. Fl. 197. 1843: serpent
garlic (Eng.), rocambole (Eng.), giant garlic (Eng.), ail
rocambole (Fr.), Rocambol (Ger.), aglio d'India (It.).
var. *pekinense* (Prokh.) Maek. apud Makino, Ill. Fl. Japan.
748. 1954: Peking garlic (Eng.), ta suan (Chin.), ninniku
(Jap.).
Allium schoenoprasum L., Sp. pl. 301. 1753: chives (Eng.), cive
(Eng.), ciboulette (Fr.), Schnittlauch (Ger.), cipollina (It.),
cebolleta (Sp.).
Two varieties may exist; further study is needed to define
their taxonomic integrity:
var. *schoenoprasum:* this is the commercially cultivated variety and diploid.
var. *alpinum* Gaudin, Fl. helv. 2:486. 1828 *(A. sibiricum* L.):
known as "large chives," this variety is tetraploid.
Allium scorodoprasum L., Sp. pl. 297. 1753: sand leek (Eng.),
Graslauch (Ger.).
Four subspecies exist, but subsp. *scorodoprasum* is the cultivated sand leek.
Allium tricoccum Solander in Aiton, Hort. kew. ed. 1, 1:428.
1789: ramps (Eng.), wild leek (Eng.).
Allium tuberosum Rottler ex Spreng., Syst. Veg. 2:38. 1825. *(A.
odorum* auct.): Chinese chives (Eng.), garlic chives (Eng.),
Oriental garlic (Eng.), gow choy (Chin.), chiu (Chin.), cuchay
(Chin.), kiu ts'ai (Chin.).

Iridaceae

Crocus L., Sp. pl. 36. 1753.
Literature: 22, 132.
Species:
Crocus sativus L., Sp. pl. 36. 1753: saffron (Eng.), safran (Fr.), Safran (Ger.), zafferano (It.), azafran (Sp.).
Mathew (132) considers this as a cultivated selection of the wild *C. cartwrightianus* Herb.

Saururaceae

Houttuynia Thunberg, Kongl. Vetensk. Acad. Nya Handl. 4:149, 151. 1783. (*"Houtuynia"*); corr. Thunberg, Fl. jap. 12. 1784.
Species:
Houttuynia cordata Thunberg, Fl. jap. 234. t. 26. 1784: ch'i (Chin.), chü-ts'ai (Chin.), dokudami (Jap.).

Piperaceae

Piper L., Sp. pl. 28. 1753.
Literature: 27, 177.
Species:
Piper auritum Humb., Bonpl. & Kunth, Nov. gen. sp. 1:54. 1815: makulan (Eng.), acoyo (Sp.).
Piper sanctum (Miq.) Schlecht. ex Miq., Linnaea 18:714. 1845: acuyo (Sp.), hierba santa (Sp.).

Moraceae

Humulus L., Sp. pl. 1028. 1753.
Literature: 172.
Species:
Humulus lupulus L., Sp. pl. 1028. 1753: hops (Eng.), common hop (Eng.), houblon (Fr.), Hopfen (Ger.), luppulo (It.), lupulo (Sp.).

Polygonaceae

Polygonum L., Sp. pl. 359. 1753.
Literature: 181, 218.
Species:
Polygonum hydropiper L., Sp. pl. 361. 1753: water-pepper (Eng.), yanagi-tade (Jap.), ma-tade (Jap.).
Polygonum odoratum Loureiro, Fl. cochinch. 243. 1790: rau râm (Viet.), chi krassang tomhom (Viet.).

Rumex L., Sp. pl. 333. 1753.
  Literature: 158.
  Species:
  Rumex acetosa L., Sp. pl. 337. 1753: garden sorrel (Eng.), oseille
    commune (Fr.), oseille de Belleville (Fr.), Grosser
    Sauerampfer (Ger.), acetosa maggiore (It.), acedera (Sp.).
  Rumex acetosella L., Sp. pl. 338. 1753: sheep sorrel (Eng.),
    common sorrel (Eng.), petite oseille (Fr.), Kleiner
    Sauerampfer (Ger.), acetosa minor (It.), acedera pequeña
    (Sp.).
  Rumex crispus L., Sp. pl. 335. 1753: curled dock (Eng.), patience
    frisée (Fr.), Krauser Ampfer (Ger.), romice crespa (It.),
    lapazio (It.), acedera crespa (Sp.).
  Rumex obtusifolius L., Sp. pl. 335. 1753: broad-leaved dock
    (Eng.).
  Rumex patientia L., Sp. pl. 333. 1753: patience dock (Eng.),
    oseille-épinard (Fr.), patience (Fr.), Englischer Spinal (Ger.),
    Gartenampfer (Ger.), romice domestico (It.), erba pazienza
    (It.), romanza (Sp.).
  Rumex scutatus L., Sp. pl. 337. 1753: French sorrel (Eng.), oseille
    ronde (Fr.), Rundblätteriger Ampfer (Ger.), acetosa romana
    (It.), acedera con hojas redondas (Sp.).

Chenopodiaceae

Atriplex L., Sp. pl. 1052. 1753.
  Literature: 131.
  Species:
  Atriplex hortensis L., Sp. pl. 1053. 1753: mountain spinach
    (Eng.), garden orach (Eng.), arroche (Fr.), Gertenmelde
    (Ger.), atreplice (It.), armuelle (Sp.).
  The cultivar 'Rubra' is commonly cultivated for its blood-red
  leaves.

Chenopodium L., Sp. pl. 218. 1753.
  Literature: 23.
  Species:
  Chenopodium album L., Sp. pl. 219. 1753: lamb's quarters (Eng.).
  Chenopodium ambrosioides L., Sp. pl. 219. 1753: wormseed
    (Eng.), epazote (Sp.).
  Chenopodium bonus-henricus L., Sp. pl. 218. 1753: allgood (Eng.),
    Good King Henry (Eng.), ansérine Bon-Henri (Fr.),
    Gemeiner Gänsefuss (Ger.), Bono Enrico (It.).

Caryophyllaceae

Dianthus L., Sp. pl. 409. 1753.
  Literature: 1, 6, 45, 76, 84, 110, 140, 192.

Species:
Dianthus caryophyllus L., Sp. pl. 410. 1753: clove pink (Eng.), carnation (Eng.), oeillet-giroflée (Fr.), Gartennelke (Ger.), garofano (It.), clavel (Sp.).
Dianthus plumarius L., Sp. pl. 411. 1753: pink (Eng.).
The cultivated forms of pink are derived from hybrids with *D. gratianopolitanus* Vill., the cheddar pink.
Stellaria L., Sp. pl. 421. 1753.
   Literature: 41, 188.
   Species:
   Stellaria media (L.) Vill., Hist. pl. dauph. 3:615. 1789: chickweed (Eng.).

Ranunculaceae

Caltha L., Sp. pl. 558. 1753.
   Literature: 121, 191.
   Species:
   Caltha palustris L., Sp. pl. 558. 1753: marsh marigold (Eng.).
Nigella L., Sp. pl. 534. 1753.
   Literature: 174, 194.
   Species:
   Nigella sativa L., Sp. pl. 534. 1753: black cumin (Eng.), black caraway (Eng.), fennel flower (Eng.), nutmeg flower (Eng.), Roman coriander (Eng.), cheveux de Vénus (Fr.), nigelle (Fr.), Schwarzkümmel (Ger.), nigella (It.), neguilla (Sp.), pasionara (Sp.).

Lauraceae

Laurus L., Sp. pl. 369. 1753.
   Literature: 175.
   Species:
   Laurus nobilis L., Sp. pl. 369. 1753: Grecian laurel (Eng.), sweet bay (Eng.), laurier (Fr.), Lorbeer (Ger.), alloro (It.), lauro (It.), laurel (Sp.).
   This species is known in 3 forms:
   f. *nobilis:* typical Grecian laurel (Eng.).
   f. *angustifolius* (Nees) Markgr. in Hegi, Ill. Fl. Mitt.-Eur. ed. 2. 4(1):15. 1958: narrow-leaved Grecian laurel (Eng.).
   f. *crispa* (Nees) Markgr. in Hegi, Ill. Fl. Mitt.-Eur. ed. 2. 4(1):15. 1958: wavy-leaved Grecian laurel (Eng.).
Lindera Thunberg, Nova Gen. Pl. 64. 1783.
   Literature: 175.
   Species:
   Lindera benzoin (L.) Blume, Mus. bot. 1:324. 1851: spice bush

(Eng.).

Persea Mill., Gard. dict. abr. ed. 4. 1754.
  Literature: 175.
  Species:
  Persea borbonia (L.) Sprengel, Syst. 2:268. 1825: red bay (Eng.),
    sweet bay (Eng.).

Sassafras Nees, Laurac. Expos. 17. 1833.
  Literature: 175.
  Species:
  Sassafras albidum (Nutt.) Nees, Syst. laur. 490. 1836: sassafras
    (Eng.), filé (Creole).

Umbellularia (Nees) Nutt., N. Amer. Sylv. 1:87. 1842.
  Literature: 175.
  Species:
  Umbellularia californica (Hook. & Arnott) Nutt., N. Amer. Sylv.
    1:87. 1842: California bay (Eng.), California laurel (Eng.).

Papaveraceae

Papaver L., Sp. pl. 506. 1753.
  Literature: 47, 122, 145.
  Species:
  Papaver somniferum L., Sp. pl. 508. 1753: opium poppy (Eng.),
    poppyseed (Eng.), pavot (Fr.), Mohn (Ger.), papavero (It.),
    adormidera (Sp.).

Brassicaceae (Cruciferae)

Alliaria Heist. ex Fabr., Enum. 161. 1759.
  Literature: 8, 33.
  Species:
  Alliaria petiolata (Bieb.), Cavara   Grande, Boll. Orto Bot. Napoli
    3:418. 1913 [*A. officinalis* Andrz. ex Bieb.; *Sisymbrium
    alliaria* (L.) Scop.]: garlic mustard (Eng.), alliaire (Fr.),
    Lauchhederich (Ger.), Lauchkraut (Ger.), alliaria (It.),
    aglliaria (It.), erísimo (Sp.).

Armoracia P. Gaertn., B. Mey. & J. Scherbius, Oekon. Fl. Wetterau
    2:426. 1800.
  Literature: 9, 74, 75, 160.
  Species:
  Armoracia rusticana P. Gaertn., B. Mey. & J. Scherbius, Oekon.
    Fl. Wetterau 2:426. 1800. (*A. lapathifolia* Gilib., *Cochlearia
    armoracia* L.): horseradish (Eng.), raifort (Fr.), Meerrettich
    (Ger.), ramolaccio (It.), rabano rusticano (Sp.).

Barbarea R. Br. in Aiton & W. T. Aiton, Hortus kew. ed. 2. 4:109.

1812.
Literature: 10.
Species:
Barbarea verna (Mill.) Aschers., Fl. Brandenburg 1:36. 1860: american cress (Eng.), scurvy grass (Eng.), winter cress (Eng.), cresson de terre (Fr.), Amerikanische Perennirende Winterkresse (Ger.).
Barbarea vulgaris R. Brown in Aiton and W. T. Aiton, Hortus kew., ed. 2. 4:109. 1812: yellow rocket (Eng.), barbarea (It.).

Brassica L., Sp. pl. 666. 1753.
Literature: 96, 156, 213.
Species:
Brassica juncea (L.) Czern., Consp. Pl. Charc. 8. 1859: Indian mustard (Eng.), brown mustard (Eng.), moutarde de Chine à feuille de chou (Fr.), Rutensenf (Ger.), Sareptasenf (Ger.), senape indiana (It.), mostaza de Indias (Sp.).
Brassica nigra (L.) W. Koch in Röhling, Deutschl. Fl. ed. 3. 4:713. 1833: black mustard (Eng.), moutarde noir (Fr.), Schwarzen Senf (Ger.), senape nera (It.), mostaza negra (Sp.).

Cardamine L., Sp. pl. 654. 1753.
Literature: 116
Species:
Cardamine amara L., Sp. pl. 656. 1753: bitter cress (Eng.), large bitter cress (Eng.).
Cardamine nasturtioides Bertero, Mercurio Chileno. 12:600. 1829.
Cardamine pensylvanica Muhl., Cat. pl. Amer. sept. 60. 1813: bitter cress (Eng.).
Cardamine pratensis L., Sp. pl. 656. 1753: cuckoo flower (Eng.), cresson des prés (Fr.), cressonnette (Fr.), Wiesenkresse (Ger.), Wiesenschaumkraut (Ger.), billeri (It.), crescione dei prati (It.), cardamine (It.), viola da pesci (It.), cardamina (Sp.), berros de prado (Sp.).
Cardamine yezoensis Maxim., Bull. Acad. Imp. Sci. Saint-Pétersbourg 18:277. 1873: wasabi (Jap.).

Cochlearia L., Sp. pl. 647. 1753.
Literature: 40.
Species:\
Cochlearia officinalis L., Sp. pl. 647. 1753: scurvy grass (Eng.), cochlearia officinal (Fr.), Löffelkraut (Ger.), coclearia (It., Sp.).

Eruca Mill., Gard. Dict. Abr. ed. 4. 1754.
Literature: 193.
Species:
Eruca vesicaria (L.) Cav., Descr. Pl. 426. 1802: rocket salad (Eng.), roquette (Fr.), Rauke (Ger.), rucola (It.), ruchetta (It.),

jaramago (Sp.), oruga (Sp.).
This species is known with the following subspecies:
subsp. *vesicaria.*
subsp. *sativa* (Mill.) Thell. in Hegi, Ill. Fl. Mitt.-Eur.
4(1):201. 1918: the cultivated rocket salad.

Lepidium L., Sp. pl. 643. 1753.
Literature: 102, 146.
Species:
Lepidium sativum L., Sp. pl. 644. 1753: garden cress (Eng.),
pepper grass (Eng.), upland cress (Eng.), cresson alénois (Fr.),
Garten-Kress (Ger.), agretto (It.), mastuerzo (Sp.), lepidio
(Sp.).

Nasturtium R. Brown in Aiton and W. T. Aiton, Hortus kew. ed. 2.
4:109. 1812.
Literature: 105, 211.
Species:
Nasturtium officinale R. Br. in Aiton and W. T. Aiton, Hortus
kew. ed. 2. 4:111. 1812 [*Rorippa nasturtium-aquaticum* (L.)
Hayek]: watercress (Eng.), cresson de fontaine (Fr.),
Brunnenkresse (Ger.), nasturzio aquatico (It.), berro (Sp.).

Sinapis L., Sp. pl. 668. 1753.
Literature: 36.
Species:
Sinapis alba L., Sp. pl. 668. 1753 [*Brassica alba* (L.) Boiss.]:
white mustard (Eng.), moutarde blanc (Fr.), Gelber Senf
(Ger.), Echter or Weisser Senf (Ger.), senapa bianca (It.),
mostaza blanca (Sp.), mostaza silvestre (Sp.).
Two subspecies are known, but subsp. *alba* is the white
mustard.
Sinapis arvensis L., Sp. pl. 668. 1753 (*S. orientalis* L.): charlock
(Eng.).

Wasabia Matsumura, Bot. Mag. (Tokyo) 13:71. 1899.
Literature: 103.
Species:
Wasabia japonica (Miq.) Matsumura, Index pl. jap. 2(2):161.
1912. [*Eutrema wasabi* (Sieb.) Maxim.; *W. tenuis* (Miq.)
Matsumura]: Japanese horseradish (Eng.), wasabi (Jap.).

Capparaceae

Capparis L., Sp. pl. 503. 1753.
Literature: 97.
Species:
Capparis spinosa L., Sp. pl. 503. 1753: capers (Eng.), câpre (Fr.),
Kapernstrauch (Ger.), Kaper (Ger.), cappero (It.), cabriola
(Sp.), alcaparna (Sp.), tápana (Sp.).

Rosaceae

Filipendula Mill., Gard. dict. abr. ed. 4. 1754.
  Literature: 11, 170.
  Species:
  Filipendula multijuga Maxim., Acta Horti Petrop. 6:247. 1879:
    meadowsweet (Eng.).
  Filipendula purpurea Maxim., Acta Horti Petrop. 6:248. 1879:
    meadowsweet (Eng.).
  Filipendula ulmaria (L.) Maxim., Acta Horti Petrop. 6(1):251.
    1879 (*Spiraea ulmaria* L.): queen-of-the-meadow (Eng.),
    meadowsweet (Eng.), reine-des-prés (Fr.), ulmaire (Fr.),
    Mädesüss (Ger.), olmaria (It.), regina dei prati (It.), barba
    (Sp.).

Prunus L., Sp. pl. 473. 1753.
  Literature: 118, 217.
  Species:
  Prunus laurocerasus L., Sp. pl. 474. 1753: cherry laurel (Eng.).
  Prunus mahaleb L., Sp. pl. 474. 1753: mahaleb cherry (Eng.), St.
    Lucie cherry (Eng.), "mahlepi" (Eng.), mahleb (Gk.).

Rosa L., Sp. pl. 491. 1753.
  Literature: 16, 55, 123, 124, 159.
  Species:
  Rosa alba L., Sp. pl. 492. 1753: white rose (Eng.).
    The type of this species is often called 'Semiplena.'
    'Suaveolens,' which is planted in Bulgaria as a windbreak
    around the damask rose fields, is similar but has more petals.
  Rosa canina L., Sp. pl. 491. 1753: dog rose (Eng.), doghip (Eng.).
  Rosa centifolia L., Sp. pl. 491. 1753: cabbage rose (Eng.), Pro-
    vence rose (Eng.), rose de Mai (Fr.).
  Rosa damascena Mill., Gard Dict. ed. 8. 1768: summer damask
    rose (Eng.).
    The status of this species is uncertain since Herrmann pub-
    lished *R. damascena* in 1762 (Herrmann's description may
    also embrace a different rose).
    'Trigintipetala' is the principal cultivar in commercial
    cultivation and known as the "Kazanlik rose"; this cultivar is
    confused in the horticultural trade with 'Prof. Emile Perrot,'
    'Alika,' and 'Bella Donna.'
    Rosa damascena Mill. var *semperflorens* (Loisel. & Michel)
    Rowley (*R. bifera* Pers.) is the autumn damask rose.
  Rosa gallica L., Sp. pl. 492. 1753: French rose (Eng.), Provins
    rose (Eng.).
    At least 2 cultivars were once commercially cultivated:
    'Conditorum': Hungarian rose (Eng.).
    'Officinalis': apothecary rose (Eng.), 'red damask' (Eng.),
      great rose of Provins (Eng.).

Rosa rubiginosa L., Mantissa pl. 564. 1771 (*R. eglanteria* L., nom. ambig.): eglantine (Eng.), sweet briar (Eng.), églantier (Fr.).

Rosa rugosa Thunberg, Fl. jap. 213. 1784: rugosa rose (Eng.), ramanas rose (Eng.), Japanese rose (Eng.).

Sanguisorba L., Sp. pl. 116. 1753.
Literature: 157.
Species:
Sanguisorba minor Scop., Fl. Carn. ed. 2. 1:110. 1772: burnet (Eng.), garden burnet (Eng.), grande pimprenelle (Fr.), pimprenelle commune des prés (Fr.), Grosser Wiesenknopf (Ger.), Pimpinelle (Ger.), pimpinella (It.), pimpinela (Sp.), salvastrella (Sp.).
The subsp. *minor* (*Poterium sanguisorba* L.) is burnet.
Sanguisorba officinalis L., Sp. pl. 116. 1753: great burnet (Eng.), burnet bloodwort (Eng.).

Fabaceae (Leguminosae)

Aspalathus L., Sp. pl. 711. 1753.
Literature: 48, 49, 78, 143.
Species:
Aspalathus linearis (N. L. Burm.) R. Dahlgren, Op. Bot. 9:283. 1963: red bush tea (Eng.), rooibus (Afrikaans).

Trigonella L., Sp. pl. 776. 1753.
Literature: 113.
Species:
Trigonella foenum-graecum L., Sp. pl. 777. 1753: fenugreek (Eng.), fenugrec (Fr.), Bockshornklee (Ger.), Griechisch Heu (Ger.), fieno greco (It.), alholva (Sp.), fenogreco (Sp.).

Oxalidaceae

Oxalis L., Sp. pl. 433. 1753.
Literature: 107, 108, 222.
Species:
Oxalis acetosella L., Sp. pl. 433. 1753: wood sorrel (Eng.), alléluia (Fr.), oxadille blanche (Fr.), petit oseille (Fr.), surette (Fr.), Sauerklee (Ger.), acetosella (It.), acederilla (Sp.), oxadile blanca (Sp.).
Oxalis corniculata L., Sp. pl. 435. 1753: yellow sorrel (Eng.), creeping wood sorrel (Eng.), creeping oxalis (Eng.).
Oxalis pes-caprae L., Sp. pl. 434. 1753: Bermuda buttercup (Eng.), soursob (Eng.).
Oxalis spiralis Ruiz & Pav. ex G. Don, Gen. hist. 1:755. 1831 (*O. pubescens* Humb., Bonpl. & Kunth): chulco (Sp.).

Oxalis stricta L., Sp. pl. 435. 1753: upright yellow wood sorrel (Eng.).

Tropaeolaceae

Tropaeolum L., Sp. pl. 345. 1753.
  Literature: 26.
  Species:
  Tropaeolum brasiliense Casar., Atti Terza Riunione Sci. Ital. 512. 1841.
  Tropaeolum majus L., Sp. pl. 345. 1753: nasturtium (Eng.), Indian cress (Eng.), capucine (Fr.), cresson d'Inde (Fr.), Kapuzinerkresse (Ger.), nasturzio (It.), capuchina (Sp.), nasturcia (Sp.).

Rutaceae

Ruta L., Sp. pl. 383. 1753.
  Literature: 183.
  Species:
  Ruta graveolens L., Sp. pl. 383. 1753: rue (Eng.), herb-of-grace (Eng.), rue odorante (Fr.), Gartenraute (Ger.), Raute (Ger.), Weinkraut (Ger.), Weinraute (Ger.), ruta (It.), ruda (Sp.).

Zanthoxylum L., Sp. pl. 270. 1753.
  Literature: 216.
  Species:
  Zanthoxylum alatum Steudel, Nom. ed. 2. 2:796. 1841: winged prickly ash (Eng.), Chinese pepper (Eng.), Szechuan pepper (Eng.), hua-chiao (Chin.).
  Zanthoxylum piperitum DC, Prodr. 1:725. 1824: prickly ash (Eng.), san-shō (Jap.).

Bixaceae

Bixa L., Sp. pl. 512. 1753.
  Literature: 5.
  Species:
  Bixa orellana L., Sp. pl. 512. 1753: annatto (Eng.), achiote (Sp.).

Violaceae

Viola L., Sp. pl. 933. 1753.
  Literature: 46, 165, 212.
  Species:
  Viola alba Besser, Prim. fl. Galiciae austriac. 1:171. 1809: Parma violet (Eng.).

This species can be divided into 3 subspecies, but subsp. *alba* is the one commonly cultivated.

Viola odorata L., Sp. pl. 934. 1753: sweet violet (Eng.).
Viola sororia Willd. is often sold as this species in the horticultural trade.

Viola suavis Bieb., Fl. Taur.-Cauc. 3:164. 1819: Russian violet (Eng.).

Apiaceae (Umbelliferae)

Anethum L., Sp. pl. 263. 1753.
Literature: 195.
Species:
Anethum graveolens L., Sp. pl. 263. 1753: dill (Eng.), aneth (Fr.), Dill (Ger.), aneto (It.), eneldo (Sp.), aneldo (Sp.).
Anethum sowa Roxb. ex Flem., As. Res. 11:156. 1810: Indian dill (Eng.), satapashpi (Indian), sowa (Indian), suwa (Indian).

Angelica L., Sp. pl. 250. 1753.
Literature: 29.
Species:
Angelica archangelica L., Sp. pl. 250. 1753: angelica (Eng., It., Sp.), angélique (Fr.), Angelika (Ger.), Engelwurz (Ger.).
This species can be divided into 2 subspecies, but subsp. *archangelica* is the cultivated angelica.
Angelica atropurpurea L., Sp. pl. 251. 1753: purple angelica (Eng.), American angelica (Eng.).
Angelica keiskei (Miq.) Koidz., Fl. symb. orient.-asiat. 45. 1930: Japanese angelica (Eng.), ashitaba (Jap.).
Angelica ursina (Rupr.) Maxim., Bull. Acad. Imp. Sci. Saint-Pétersbourg 22:258. 1876: Japanese angelica (Eng.), ezo-nyū (Jap.).

Anthriscus Pers., Syn. pl. 1:320. 1805.
Literature: 30.
Species:
Anthriscus cerefolium (L.) Hoffm., Gen. pl. umbell. 41, 1814: chervil (Eng.), cerfeuil (Fr.), Kerbel (Ger.), cerfoglio (It.), perifollo (Sp.).

Carum L., Sp. pl. 263. 1753.
Literature: 196.
Species:
Carum carvi L., Sp. pl. 263. 1753: caraway (Eng.), carvi (Fr., It.), cumin des prés (Fr.), Kümmel (Ger.), hinojo de prade (Sp.), alcaravea (Sp.).
Carum roxburghianum Benth. & J. D. Hook., Gen. pl. 1:891. 1867: ajmud (Indian).

Centella L., Sp. pl. ed. 2. 1393. 1763.

Species:
Centella asiatica (L.) Urban in Martin, Fl. Bros. 11:287. 1879
(*Hydrocotyle asiatiaca* L.): tsubo-kusa (Jap.), chi-hsüeh-ts'ao
(Chin.).
Coriandrum L., Sp. pl. 256. 1753.
Literature: 197.
Species:
Coriandrum sativum L., Sp. pl. 256. 1753: coriander (Eng.),
Chinese parsley (Eng.), coriandre (Fr.), Koriander (Ger.),
corianlolo (It.), cilantro (Sp.), yüan-sui (Chin.), hu-sai
(Chin.), hsiang-sui (Chin.).
Crithmum L., Sp. pl. 246. 1753.
Literature: 198.
Species:
Crithmum maritimum L., Sp. pl. 246. 1753: samphire (Eng.),
rock samphire (Eng.), bacile (Fr.), fenouil de mer (Fr.), perre-
pierres (Fr.), Meerfenchel (Ger.), critmo (It.), finocchio
marino (It.), hinojo marino (Sp.).
Cryptotaenia DC, Collect. Mem. Ombellif. 42. 1829.
Species:
Cryptotaenia canadensis (L.) DC, Collect. Mem. Ombellif. 42.
1829: honewort (Eng.).
Cryptotaenia japonica Hassk., Retzia 1:113. 1855 [*C. canadensis*
(L.) DC var. *japonica* (Hassk.) Makino]: Japanese wild
chervil (Eng.), mitsuba (Jap.).
Cuminum L., Sp. pl. 254. 1753.
Literature: 199.
Species:
Cuminum cyminum L., Sp. pl. 254. 1753: cumin (Eng.),
Kreuzkümmel (Ger.), Romischer Kümmel (Ger.), comino
(It., Sp.).
Eryngium L., Sp. pl. 232. 1753.
Literature: 17, 28, 37, 133.
Species:
Eryngium campestre L., Sp. pl. 233. 1753: field eryngo (Eng.),
snakeroot (Eng.).
Eryngium foetidum L., Sp. pl. 232. 1753: culantro (Eng., Sp.),
cilantro (Sp.), orégano de Cartagena (Sp.).
Ferula L., Sp. pl. 246. 1753.
Species:
Ferula assa-foetida L., Sp. pl. 248. 1753: asafetida (Eng.), devil's
dung (Eng.), giant fennel (Eng.), assa foetida (Fr.), férule
perisque (Fr.), Stinkasant (Ger.), Teufelsdreck (Ger.),
assafetida (It.), asafétida (Sp.).
Ferula foetida (Bunge) Regel, Trudy Imp. S.-Peterburgsk. Bot.

Sada 5:592. 1877: also sold as asafetida.

Foeniculum Mill., Gard. dict. abr. ed. 4. 1754.
Literature: 200.
Species:
Foeniculum vulgare Mill., Gard. Dict. ed. 8, No. 1. 1768: fennel
(Eng.), fenouil (Fr.), Fenchel (Ger.), finocchio (It.), hinojo
(Sp.).
Two subspecies exist, but subsp. *vulgare* is the cultivated
fennel. This subspecies also includes var. *azoricum*
(Mill.) Thell., or Florence fennel cultivated as a vegeta-
ble, and var. *dulce* Bett. & Trab., which is cultivated for
its essential oil. The cultivar 'Rubrum' is the bronze
fennel.

Hydrocotyle L., Sp. pl. 234. 1753.
Literature: 31.
Species:
Hydrocotyle sibthorpioides Lam., Encycl. Méth. Bot. 3:153. 1789:
salatoon (Malay), antanum beirit (Malay), andem (Malay).

Levisticum J. Hill, Brit. herb. (fasc. 42) 423. 1756.
Literature: 201.
Species:
Levisticum officinale Koch, Nova Acta Phys. Med. Acad. Oes.
Leop.-Carol. Nat. Cur. 12(1):101. 1824: lovage (Eng.), livèche
(Fr.), Liebstöckel (Ger.), Maggikraut (Ger.), levistico (It.),
apio de montana (Sp.), ligístico (Sp.).

Ligusticum L., Sp. pl. 250. 1753.
Literature: 202.
Species:
Ligusticum monnieri (L.) Calest. in Martelli, Webbia. 1:211. 1905
(*Selinum monnieri* L.): she chu'ang tsu (Chin.), giêng sàng
(Chin.), xà sàng (Chin.).
Ligusticum mutellina (L.) Crantz, Stirp. Austr. fasc. 3:81. 1767:
alpine lovage (Eng.).
Ligusticum scoticum L., Sp. pl. 250. 1753: northern lovage (Eng.),
Scotch lovage (Eng.), sea lovage (Eng.).

Myrrhis Mill, Gard. dict. abr. ed. 4. 1754.
Literature: 32.
Species:
Myrrhis odorata (L.) Scop., Fl. Carn. ed. 2. 1:207. 1772: garden
myrrh (Eng.), sweet scented myrrh (Eng.), fern-leaved chervil
(Eng.), cerfeuil d'Espagne (Fr.), cerfeuil musqué (Fr.), cerfeuil
odorant (Fr.), Englischer (Spanischer) Kerble (Ger.),
Wohlreichende Süssdolde (Ger.), mirride odorosa (It.),
perfolo (Sp.).

Oenanthe L., Sp. pl. 254. 1753.

Species:
Oenanthe javanica (Blume) DC, Prodr. 4:138: water dropwort
(Eng.), seri (Jap.), batjarongi (Malay), piopo (Malay),
bamboong (Malay), pampoong (Malay).

Petroselinum J. Hill, Brit. herb. 424. 1756.
Literature: 203.
Species:
Petroselinum crispum (Mill.) Nym. ex A. W. Hill, Hand-list Herb.
Plt. Kew ed. 3. 122. 1925 (*P. hortense* auct., *P. sativum*
Hoffm.): parsley (Eng.), persil (Fr.), petrosello (Fr.), Petersilie
(Ger.), prezzomolo (It.), perejil (Sp.).
This species can be divided into 3 varieties [curled parsley or
var. *crispum,* Italian parsley or var. *neapolitanum* Danert,
and turnip-rooted parsley or var. *tuberosum* (Bernh.) Crov.],
but their correct nomenclature needs study.

Pimpinella L., Sp. pl. 263. 1753.
Literature: 204.
Species:
Pimpinella anisum L., Sp. pl. 264. 1753: anise (Eng., Fr., Sp.),
anis vert (Fr.), Anis (Ger.), anice (It.).
Pimpinella major (L.) Huds. Fl. angl. 110. 1762: great burnet
saxifrage (Eng.).
Pimpinella saxifraga L., Sp. pl. 263. 1753: burnet saxifrage
(Eng.), black caraway (Eng.), pied de bouc (Fr.), bocage (Fr.).

Trachyspermum Link, Enum. Hort. Berol. Alt. 1:267. 1821.
Species:
Trachyspermum copticum (L.) Link, Enum. Hort. Berol. Alt.
1:267. 1821 (*Carum copticum* (L.) Bernh. & J. D. Hook.,
Ammi copticum L., *Trachyspermum ammi* (L.) Sprague)
ajuan (Indian), ajowan (Indian), omum (Indian).

Boraginaceae

Borago L., Sp. pl. 136. 1753.
Literature: 38.
Species:
Borago officinalis L., Sp. pl. 137. 1753: borage (Eng.), bourrache
(Fr.), Boretsch (Ger.), borrana (It.), borraja (Sp.).

Symphytum L., Sp. pl. 136. 1753.
Literature: 109, 152.
Species:
Symphytum asperum Lepech., Nova Acta Acad. Sci. Petrop.
14:422. 1805: prickly comfrey (Eng.) (includes Bocking #13).
Symphytum officinale L., Sp. pl. 136. 1753: common comfrey
(Eng.), healing-herb (Eng.), grande consoude (Fr.),
Schwarzmarz (Ger.), consolida maggiore (It.), consuelda

(Sp.).
Numerous cultivars ('Aureum,' 'Argenteum,' 'Coccineum,' 'Purpureum,' 'Variegatum,' etc.) exist.
Symphytum x *uplandicum* Nym., Syll. fl. Eur. 80. 1854: Russian comfrey (Eng.).
Russian comfrey is the hybrid of *S. asperum* x *S officinale.*

Verbenaceae

Aloysia Juss., Ann. Mus. Natl. Hist. Nat. 7:75. 1806.
Literature: 21.
Species:
Aloysia triphylla (L'Hér.) Britton, Bot. Porto Rico. 6:140. 1925
   [*Aloysia citriodora* Ortega ex Pers., *Lippia citriodora* (Ortega ex Pers.) Humb., Bonpl. & Kunth, *L. triphylla* (L'Hér.) Kuntze]: lemon verbena (Eng.), verbena (Eng.), vervein citronelle (Fr.), vervein odorante (Fr.), Zitronenkraut (Ger.), Punschkraut (Ger.), erba luisa (It.), limoncina (It.), cedrina (It.), cedrón (Sp.), luisa (Sp.), hierba luisa (Sp.), yerba luisa (Sp.).

Lantana L., Sp. pl. 626. 1753.
Literature: 28, 139.
Species:
Lantana achyranthifolia Desf., Tabl. ecole bot. ed. 3. 392. 1829
   [*L. purpurea* (Jacq.) Benth. & Hook.]: orégano (Sp.).
Lantana glandulosissima Hayek, Repert. Spec. Nov. Regni Veg. 2:161. 1906: orégano silvestre (Sp.), orégano xiu (Sp.).
Lantana hispida Humb., Bonpl. & Kunth, Nov. gen. sp. 2:260. 1817 (*L. hirsuta* Mart. & Gal.): oréganillo del monte. (Sp.).
Lantana involucrata L., Cent. pl. II. 22. 1756: orégano (Sp.).
Lantana microcephala A. Rich., Hist. phys. Cuba, pl. vasc. 2:141. 1841 [*L. citrosa* (Small) Moldenke]: orégano xiu (Sp.).
Lantana trifolia L., Sp. pl. 626. 1753: orégano (Sp.).
Lantana velutina Mart. & Gal., Bull. Acad. Roy. Sci. Bruxelles 11:325. 1844: orégano xiu (Sp.).

Lippia L., Sp. pl. 633. 1753.
Literature: 28, 139, 140.
Species:
Lippia abyssinica (Otto & Dietr.) Cufod. in Senckenberg Biol. 43:282. 1962 (*L. adoensis* Hochst.): Gambian tea bush (Eng.).
Lippia affinis Schauer in DC, Prodr. 11:576. 1847: orégano (Sp.).
Lippia cardiostegia Benth., Bot. voy. Sulphur 153. 1844: orégano montes (Sp.).
Lippia formosa T. S. Brandeg., Proc. Calif. Acad. II. 3:163. 1891: orégano (Sp.).
Lippia fragrans Turcz., Bull. Soc. Nat. Mosc. 26(2):203. 1863 [*L.*

geisseana (R. A. Phil.) Soler.]: orégano (Sp.).
Lippia graveolens Humb., Bonpl. & Kunth, Nov. gen. sp., ed. folio 2:215. 1817 (*L. berlandieri* Schauer): orégano (Eng., Sp.), Mexican oregano (Eng.), orégano cimarron (Sp.).
Lippia micromeria Schauer in DC, Prodr. 11:587. 1847: false thyme (Eng.), orégano (Sp.), orégano del pais (Sp.).
Lippia micromeria Schauer var. *helleri* (Britton) Moldenke is also harvested.
Lippia origanoides Humb., Bonpl. & Kunth, Nov. gen. sp. 2:267. 1815: orégano (Sp.), orégano del pais (Sp.).
Lippia palmeri S. Wats., Proc. Amer. Acad. 24:67. 1889: orégano (Sp.).
Lippia pseudo-thea (A. St.-Hil.) Schauer in DC, Prodr. 11:582. 1847: Brazilian tea (Eng.).
Lippia umbellata Cav., Icon. 2:75. 1793: orégano montes (Sp.).

Lamiaceae (Labiatae)

Acinos Mill., Gard. dict. abr. ed. 4. 1754.
Literature: 12, 59, 127.
Species:
Acinos alpinus (L.) Moench, Methodus. 407. 1794 [*Calamintha alpina* (L.) Lam., *Satureja alpina* (L.) Scheele]: alpine basil thyme (Eng.).
This species may be divided into 3 subspecies:
subsp. *alpinus*
subsp. *majoranifolius* (Mill.) P. W. Ball, Bot. J. Linn. Soc. 65:344. 1972 [*Melissa majoranifolia* Mill. *Calamintha alpina* (L.) Lam. subsp. *majoranifolia* (Mill.) Hayek]
subsp. *meridionalis* (Nym.) P. W. Ball, Bot. J. Linn. Soc. 65:344. 1972.
Acinos arvensis (Lam.) Dandy, J. Ecol. 33:326. 1946. [*A. thymoides* Moench, *Calamintha acinos* (L.) Clairv., *Satureja acinos* (L.) Scheele]: basil thyme (Eng.).
Agastache Clayton ex Gronov., Fl. virgin. 88. 1762.
Literature: 58, 130, 166.
Species:
Agastache foeniculum (Pursh) Kuntze, Rev. gen. pl. 511. 1891 [*A. anethiodora* Nutt. ex Britt., *Lophanthus anisatus* (Nutt.) Benth.]: anise hyssop (Eng.), blue giant hyssop (Eng.), fennel giant hyssop (Eng.), fragrant giant hyssop (Eng.).
Agastache mexicana (Humb., Bonpl. & Kunth) Lint & Epling, Amer. Midl. Nat. 33:227. 1945 [*Brittonastrum mexicanum* (Humb., Bonpl. & Kunth) Briq., *Cedronella mexicana* (Humb., Bonpl. & Kunth) Benth., *Gardoquia betonicoides* Lindl.]: Mexican giant hyssop (Eng.).
Agastache rugosa (Fisch. & C. A. Mey.) Kuntze, Rev. gen. pl.

2:511. 1891 (*Lophanthus rugosus* Fisch. & C. A. Mey.): Korean mint (Eng.), wrinkled giant hyssop (Eng.).

Calamintha Mill., Gard. dict. abr. ed. 4. 1754.
Literature: 13, 59, 171.
Species:
Calamintha nepeta (L.) Savi, Fl. Pis. 2:63. 1798: lesser calamint (Eng.).
This species may be divided into 2 subspecies:
subsp. *nepeta* [*C. nepetoides* Jordan, *Satureja calamintha* (L.) Scheele subsp. *nepetoides* (Jordan) Br.-Bl.]: this is the typical subsp.
subsp. *glandulosa* (Req.) P. W. Ball, Bot. J. Linn. Soc. 65:347. 1972 (*C. officinalis* Moench).
Calamintha sylvatica Bromf., Phytologist (Newman) 2:49. 1845: calamint (Eng.).
This species may be divided into 2 subspecies:
subsp. *sylvatica* [*Satureja calamintha (L.) Scheele subsp. officinalis* sensu Gams].
subsp. *ascendens* (Jordan) P. W. Ball, Bot. J. Linn. Soc. 65:346. 1972 (*C. menthifolia* auct., *C. officinalis* auct.).

Coleus Loureiro, Fl. cochinch. 358. 1790.
Literature: 28, 135, 136, 153.
Species:
Coleus amboinicus Loureiro, Fl. cochinch. 372. 1·790 [*Coleus aromaticus* (Roxb.) Benth.]; orégano (Eng., Sp.), Cuban oregano (Eng.), Indian borage (Eng.), Spanish thyme (Eng.), orégano brujo (Sp.), orégano de Cartagena (Sp.), orégano de España (Sp.), orégano Frances (Sp.), sugánda (Sp.).

Cunila Mill., Gard. Dict. Abr. ed. 4. 1754.
Species:
Cunila origanoides (L.) Britton, Mem. Torrey Bot. Club 5:278. 1894 (*C. mariana* L.): Maryland dittany (Eng.), stone mint (Eng.).

Glechoma L., Sp. pl. 578. 1753.
Literature: 69.
Species:
Glechoma hederacea L., Sp. pl. 578. 1753 [*Nepeta hederacea* (L.) Trevisan]: ground ivy (Eng.), gill-over-the-ground (Eng.), alehoof (Eng.), lierre terrestre (Fr.), Gundelrebe (Ger.), edera terrestre (It.), hiedra terrestre (Sp.).

Hedeoma Pers., Syn. pl. 2:131. 1806.
Literature: 28, 111.
Species:
Hedeoma floribundum Standl., Rep. Spec. Nov., Beihefte 115:31. 1939: orégano (Sp.), mapá (Sp.).
Hedeoma patens M. E. Jones, Contr. W. Bot. 12:70. 1908: orég-

ano (Sp.).

Hedeoma pulegioides (L.) Pers., Syn. pl. 2:131. 1806: American pennyroyal (Eng.), squaw mint (Eng.), stinking balm (Eng.), tickweed (Eng.), mosquito plant (Eng.).

Hyptis Jacq., Collectanea 1:101, 103. 1787.
Literature: 28, 63.
Species:
Hyptis albida Humb., Bonpl. & Kunth, Nov. gen. sp. 2:319. 1817: orégano (Sp.).
Hyptis americana Briq. in Engl. & Prantl, Nat. Pflanzenfam. ed. 1.4(3a):338. 1897: orégano (Sp.).
Hyptis capitata Jacq., Collectanea 1:102. 1787: orégano (Sp.).
Hyptis suaveolens (L.) Poit., Ann. Mus. Natl. Nat. 7:472. t. 29. f. 2. 1806: bush tea plant (Eng.), wild spikenard (Eng.), sangura (Sp.), orégano cimarron (Sp.).

Hyssopus L., Sp. pl. 569. 1753.
Literature: 53.
Species:
Hyssopus officinalis L., Sp. pl. 569. 1753: hyssop (Eng.), hysope (Fr.), Ysop (Ger.), issopo (It.), hisopo (Sp.).
This species may be divided into 4 subspecies, but subsp. *officinalis* is the one commonly cultivated.

Lavandula L., Sp. pl. 572. 1753.
Literature: 42, 81, 164, 186.
Species:
Lavandula angustifolia Mill., Gard. Dict. ed. 8, No. 2. 1768 (*L. spica* L., nom. ambig.; *L. officinalis* Chaix in Villars): common lavender (Eng.), lavande (Fr.), lavanda (It.), espliego (Sp.).
All the cultivars of common lavender are selections of subsp. *angustifolia*. The following cultivars are known with white flowers: 'Alba' and 'Nana Alba.' A cultivar with pink flowers is 'Rosea'; this is identical to 'Jean Davis' and 'Loddon Pink' and only slightly different from 'Hidcote Pink.' Cultivars with dark violet flowers include 'Dwarf Blue,' 'Hidcote,' 'Loddon Blue,' 'Middachten,' 'Nana Atropurpurea,' 'Mitcham Grey,' 'Munstead,' and 'Summerland Supreme.' Cultivars with lavender-blue flowers include 'Backhouse Purple,' 'Bowles Early,' 'Carroll,' 'Compacta,' 'Folgate,' 'Fragrance,' 'Graves,' 'Gray Lady,' 'Gwendolyn Anley,' 'Irene Doyle,' 'Maillette,' 'Twickel Purple,' 'Warburton Gem,' and 'Wilderness.'
Lavandula x *intermedia* Emeric ex Loisel., Fl. Gal. 2:19. 1828 (*L. hybrida* Reverchon ex Briq., *L. hortensis* Hy): lavandin (Eng., Fr.), lavandino (It.).
Lavandula x *intermedia* is the natural and artificial hybrid of *L. angustifolia* x *L. latifolia*. One white-flowered cultivar

('Alba') is known. The following are cultivars with lavender-
blue flowers: 'Abrialii,' 'Dutch,' 'Grappenhall,' 'Grey Hedge,'
'Grosso,' 'Hidcote Giant,' 'Maime Épis Tête,' 'Old English,'
'Provence,' 'Seal,' 'Silver Gray,' 'Standard,' 'Super,' and
'Waltham.'

Lavandula latifolia Medik. Bot. Beob. 1783:135. 1784 (*L. spica*
auct., non L.): spike or spike lavender (Eng.), lavande aspic
(Fr.).

Lavandula stoechas L., Sp. pl. 573. 1753: French lavender (Eng.),
lavande stéchas (Fr.).
Six subspecies are known, but subsp. *stoechas* is the most
important. The only cultivar ('Alba') differs from the species
in its white flowers.

Melissa L., Sp. pl. 592. 1753.
Literature: 70.
Species:
Melissa officinalis L., Sp. pl. 592. 1753: lemon balm (Eng.), balm
(Eng.), mélisse (Fr.), Zitronmelisse (Ger.), cedrina (It.),
melisa (Sp.), toronjil (Sp.).
Two subspecies are known, but subsp. *officinalis* is commer-
cially cultivated.

Mentha L., Sp. pl. 576. 1753.
Literature: 82, 83, 185.
Species:
Mentha aquatica L., Sp. pl. 576. 1753: water mint (Eng.), bergamot mint (Eng.), menthe aquatique (Fr.), Wasserminze
(Ger.), menta d'acqua (It.), menta acqua di colonia (It.).
While the bergamot mint (orange or lemon mint) has been
previously designated as *M.* x *piperita* L. nm. *citrata* (Ehrh.)
Boivin (*M. odorata* Sole), all clones examined so far differ
from *M. aquatica* in one gene for male sterility and the genes
for linalool/ linalyl acetate (versus menthofuran in *M.
aquatica*). Thus, bergamot mint is actually a selection of *M.
aquatica*, but the correct infraspecific taxon is unknown.

Mentha canadensis L., Sp. pl. 577. 1753 [including *M. arvensis* L.
var. *villosa* (Benth.), S. R. Stewart, *M. arvensis* L. var.
glabrata (Benth.) Fern., and *M. arvensis* L. f. *piperascens*
Malinv. ex Holmes]: corn mint (Eng.), Japanese peppermint
(Eng.), North American field mint (Eng.), hakka (Jap.).
While this species has been previously considered as an
infraspecific taxon of *M. arvensis* of Europe, *M. canadensis*
differs in chromosome number, distribution, and chemistry
and should be considered as a species. The names of the
infraspecific taxa of North America vs. Japan are still unknown.

Mentha x *gracilis* Sole, Menth. brit. 37. t. 16. 1798 (*M. gentilis*
auct., non L.): Scotch spearmint (Eng.), red mint (Eng.).

As shown in a review of the Linnaean types of *Mentha* (185), the type of *M. gentilis* L. is really *M. arvensis* L.; thus Sole's name is probably correct for this taxon.

Mentha x *piperita* L., Sp. pl. 576. 1753: peppermint (Eng.), menthe poivrée (Fr.), Pfefferminze (Ger.), menta piperita (It.), menta (Sp.).

Mentha x *piperita* is a sterile hybrid of *M. aquatica* x *M. spicata.*

Mentha pulegium L., Sp. pl. 577. 1753: English pennyroyal (Eng.), pouliot (Fr.), Polei (Ger.), puleggio (It.), poleo (Sp.).

Mentha spicata L., Sp. pl. 576. 1753 (*M. viridis* L., *M. longifolia* auct. angl. & amer., non L.): spearmint (Eng.), baume vert (Fr.), menthe verte (Fr.), Grüne Minze (Ger.), mentastro verde (It.), hierbabuena (Sp.), menta verde (Sp.).

Mentha suaveolens Ehrh., Beitr. Naturk. 7:149. 1792 (*M. rotundifolia* auct., non L.): pineapple mint (Eng.).

Ehrhart's type is the variegated clone commonly cultivated as pineapple mint; the designation of 'Variegata' is thus superfluous. The correct name of the green taxon is unknown.

Mentha x *villosa* Huds., Fl. angl. ed. 2. 250. 1778.

This nothospecies is commonly cultivated as the following taxon:

var. *alopecuroides* (Hull) Briq., Bull. Herb. Boiss. 4:679. 1896: woolly mint (Eng.), apple mint (Eng.), Egyptian mint (Eng.), Bowles' mint (Eng.).

Monarda L., Sp. pl. 22. 1753.
Literature: 28, 77, 167.
Species:
Monarda citriodora Cervantes ex Lag., Gen. sp. pl. 2. 1816.

The following varieties are important as herbs:

var. *citriodora:* lemon beebalm (Eng.), lemon bergamot (Eng.).

var. *austromontana* (Epling) Scora, Madroño 18(4):120. 1965. (*M. austromontana* Epling): orégano (Sp.).

Monarda clinopodia L., Sp. pl. 22. 1753: beebalm (Eng.), wild bergamot (Eng.).

Monarda didyma L., Sp. pl. 22. 1753: Oswego tea (Eng.), Oswego beebalm (Eng.), monarde (Fr.), Goldmelisse (Ger.), menta rosa (It.), monarda (Sp.).

Monarda fistulosa L., Sp. pl. 22. 1753: wild bergamot (Eng.), horsemint (Eng.), beebalm (Eng.).

Monarda x *media* Willd., Enum. Hort. Berol. 1:32. 1809.

This is a hybrid series involving *M. clinopodia, M. didyma,* and *M. fistulosa.* Many of the named cultivars probably belong here.

Monarda pectinata Nutt., Acad. Phil. ser. 2. 1:182. 1847: pony beebalm (Eng.).

Monardella Benth., Labiat. gen. spec. 331. 1834.
Literature: 65.
Species:
Monardella lanceolata A. Gray, Proc. Amer. Acad. 11:102. 1876: pennyroyal (Eng.), poleo (Sp.).
Monardella macrantha A. Gray, Syn. fl. N. Amer. ed. 2. 2:459. 1886.
Monardella odoratissima Benth., Labiat. gen. spec. 332. 1834: wild pennyroyal (Eng.), western balm (Eng.).
Monardella villosa Benth., Bot. voy. Sulphur. 42. t. 21. 1844: pennyroyal (Eng.), coyote mint (Eng.), horsemint (Eng.), poleo (Sp.).

Nepeta L., Sp. pl. 570. 1753.
Literature: 189.
Species:
Nepeta cataria L., Sp. pl. 570. 1753: catnip (Eng.), catmint (Eng.), cataire (Fr.), herbe à chat (Fr.), Katzenminze (Ger.), erba dei gatta (It.), gatera (Sp.), calamento (Sp.), calaminta (Sp.).

Ocimum L., Sp. pl. 597. 1753.
Literature: 18, 19, 25, 51, 52, 144.
Species:
Ocimum basilicum L., Sp. pl. 597. 1753 (*O. americanum* L.): basil (Eng.), sweet basil (Eng.), basilic (Fr.), Basilikum (Ger.), Basilienkraut (Ger.), basilico (It.), albahaca (Sp.), tulsi (Indian).
Numerous cultivars of this species have not yet been defined according to the *International Code of Botanical Nomenclature* (214) and the *International Code of Nomenclature for Cultivated Plants* (24).
Ocimum canum Sims, Bot. Mag. 51:t. 2452. 1823 (*O. americanum* auct., non L.): hoary basil (Eng.), hairy basil (Eng.).
Ocimum gratissimum L., Sp. pl. 1197. 1753 (*O. viride* Willd.): East Indian basil (Eng.), tree basil (Eng.), shrubby basil (Eng.), vriadhatulasi (Indian), ramtulsi (Indian).
Ocimum kilimandscharicum Guerke in Engl., Pflanzenw. Ost.-Afrikas 4(C):349. 1895: camphor basil (Eng.).
Ocimum sanctum L., Mant. pl. 1:85. 1767: holy basil (Eng.), sacred basil (Eng.), bai grapao (Thai).

Origanum L., Sp. pl. 588. 1753.
Literature: 28, 72, 106, 220.
Species:
Origanum x *applii* (Domin) Boros, Bot. Közlem. 35:317. 1938: orégano (Sp.), orégano comun (Sp.), orégano del pais (Sp.).
Origanum majorana L., Sp. pl. 590. 1753 (*Majorana hortensis* Moench): sweet marjoram (Eng.), marjolaine (Fr.), Majoran (Ger.), maggiorana (It.), mejorana (Sp.).

Origanum x *majoricum* Cambess., Mem. Mus. Paris. 14:296. 1827.
> *Origanum* x *majoricum* is probably a hybrid of *O. vulgare* L. subsp. *virens* x *O. majorana*. It is variously sold as marjoram or oregano.

Origanum onites L., Sp. pl. 590. 1753: oregano (Eng.), rigani (Gk.).

Origanum syriacum L., Sp. pl. 590. 1753: za'atar (Ar.).
> *Origanum syriacum* var. *syriacum* (*O. maru* L.) is the hyssop of the Bible and sometimes used as oregano (72).

Origanum vulgare L., Sp. pl. 590. 1753.
> This species may be divided into 6 subspecies:
>
> subsp. *vulgare:* wild marjoram (Eng.), although widely sold as "oregano."
>> This subspecies has at least 3 cultivars: 'Aureum,' 'Compactum Nanum,' and 'Golden Creeping.'
>
> subsp. *glandulosum* (Desf.) Ietswaart, Tax. Rev. Origanum. 110. 1980 (*O. glandulosum* Desf.): oregano (Eng.).
>
> subsp. *gracile* (Koch) Ietswaart, Tax. Rev. Origanum. 111. 1980 (*O. tytthanthum* Gontscharov, *O. kopetdaghense* Boriss.): Russian oregano (Eng.).
>
> subsp. *hirtum* (Link) Ietswaart, Tax. Rev. Origanum. 112. 1980 (*O. hirtum* Link, *O. heracleoticum* auct., non L.): Greek or "Italian" oregano (Eng.), origan (Fr.), Dost (Ger.), origano (It.), orégano (Sp.).
>
> subsp. *virens* (Hoffmanns. & Link) Ietswaart, Tax. Rev. Origanum. 115. 1980 (*O. virens* Hoffmanns. & Link): wild marjoram (Eng.).
>
> subsp. *viride* (Boiss.) Hayek, Prod. Fl. Penins. Balc. 2:334. 1931 (*O. heracleoticum* L.): wild marjoram (Eng.), orégano (Sp.).

Perilla L., Gen. pl. ed. 6. 578. 1764.
> Literature: 162.
> Species:
> *Perilla frutescens* (L.) Britton, Mem. Torrey Bot. Club 5:277. 1894 (*P. ocymoides* L.): beefsteak plant (Eng.), perilla (Eng.), shiso zoku (Jap.).
>> Numerous varieties and forms have been named, but their taxonomic status is uncertain.

Phlomis L., Sp. pl. 584. 1753.
> Literature: 54.
> Species:
> *Phlomis fruticosa* L., Sp. pl. 584. 1753: Jerusalem sage (Eng.).
>> *Phlomis fruticosa* is sometimes used as an adulterant of sage.
> *Phlomis lychnitis* L., Sp. pl. 585. 1753: lamwick plant (Eng.).
>> *Phlomis lychnitis* is sometimes used as an adulterant of sage.

Poliomintha A. Gray, Proc. Amer. Acad. Arts 8:295. 1870.

Literature: 28, 111.
Species:
Poliomintha longiflora A. Gray, Proc. Amer. Acad. Arts 8:296. 1870.
Poliomintha longiflora var. *longiflora* is sometimes used as oregano.

Pycnanthemum Michx., Fl. bor.-amer. 2:7. 1803.
Literature: 34, 35, 79
Species:
Pycnanthemum virginianum (L.) Th. Durand & B. D. Jacks. ex B. L. Robinson & Fernald, Gray's manual. ed. 7, 707. 1908: Virginia mountain mint (Eng.), wild basil (Eng.).

Rosmarinus L., Sp. pl. 23. 1753.
Literature: 2, 190.
Species:
Rosmarinus officinalis L., Sp. pl. 23. 1753: rosemary (Eng.), romarin (Fr.), Rosmarin (Ger.), rosmarino (It.), romaro (Sp.). This species is known by the following cultivated infraspecific taxa:
var. *officinalis.*
> Derived from this variety are the cultivars 'Aureus,' 'Blue Spire,' 'Logee Blue,' 'Majorca' ('Collingwood Ingram'), 'Roman Vivace,' and 'Severn Sea.'
f. *albiflorus* Béguinot in Fiori & Paoletti, Fl. Italia. 3:14. 1903 ('Albus'): white-flowered rosemary (Eng.).
var. *angustifolius* (Mill.) Guss., Fl. sicul. podr. 1:20. 1842 (*R. angustifolius* Mill., *R. tenuifolius* Jord. & Fourr., *R. officinalis* L. var. *angustissimus* Foucaud & Mand.): pine-needled rosemary (Eng.), pine-scented rosemary (Eng.).
> Similar to this variety is the cultivar 'Benenden Blue' ('Corsican Blue').
f. *erectus* Pasq. ex Béguinot in Fiori & Paoletti, Fl. Italia. 3:14. 1903: upright rosemary (Eng.).
> This form has been given popular names which are probably not distinct from f. *erectus:* 'Fastigiatus,' 'Miss Jessopp's Upright,' and 'Pyramidalis.'
var. *prostratus* Pasq. in Cat. del Real Ort. Bot. di Napoli. 91. 1867 (*R. officinalis* L. f. *humilis* Ten., f. *procumbens* Pasq., var. *rupestris* Pasq. ex Béguinot, 'Prostratus'): prostrate rosemary (Eng.).
> Derived from this variety are the cultivars 'Golden Prostrate,' 'Huntington Carpet,' 'Kenneth Prostrate,' and 'Lockwood de Forest' (var. *lockwoodii* Hort., var. *foresteri* Hort.).
var. *rigidus* (Jord. & Fourr.) Carrière & Saint-Lag., Etude des Fleurs. 657. 1889 (*R. rigidus* Jord. & Four.).

Derived from this variety is the cultivar 'Tuscan Blue.'
f. *roseus* Pamp. in Bull. Soc. Bot. It. 16. 1914 ('Roseus'):
pink-flowered rosemary (Eng.).
Similar to this form are the cultivars 'Majorca Pink' and
'Pinkie.' 'Blue Boy' was probably derived from this
form.

Salvia L., Sp. pl. 23. 1753.
Literature: 57, 62, 86, 87, 88, 89.
Species:
Salvia clevelandii (A. Gray) Greene, Pittonia 2:236. 1892: blue
sage (Eng.).
Salvia dorisiana Standley, Ceiba 1:43. 1950: peach-scented sage
(Eng.), British Honduran sage (Eng.).
Salvia elegans Vahl, Enum. pl. 1:238. 1804 (*S. rutilans* Carrière):
pineapple-scented sage (Eng.).
Salvia fruticosa Mill., Gard. Dict. ed. 8. 1768 (*S. triloba* L. f.):
Greek sage (Eng.).
Salvia lavandulifolia Vahl, Enum. pl. 1:222. 1804: Spanish sage
(Eng.).
Salvia leucophylla Greene, Pittonia 2:236. 1892: gray sage (Eng.),
purple sage (Eng.).
Salvia officinalis L., Sp. pl. 23. 1753: Dalmatian sage (Eng.),
garden sage (Eng.), common sage (Eng.), sauge (Fr.), Salbei
(Ger.), salvia (It., Sp.).
This species has many cultivars: 'Albiflora,' 'Aurea,' 'Crispa,'
'Holt's Mammoth,' 'Icterina,' 'Latifolia,' 'Milleri,'
'Purpurascens' ('Purpurea'), 'Rubriflora,' 'Salicifolia,'
'Sturnina,' 'Tenuior,' and 'Tricolor.'
Salvia pomifera L., Sp. pl. 24. 1753 (*S. calycina* Sibth. & Sm.):
apple sage (Eng.).
Salvia sclarea L., Sp. pl. 27. 1753: clary (Eng.), clary sage (Eng.),
muscatel sage (Eng.), toute-bonne (Fr.), sauge sclarée (Fr.),
Scharlei (Ger.), sclarea (It.), hierba de los ojos (Sp.).
Salvia verbenacea L., Sp. pl. 25. 1753 (*S. clandestina* L., *S.
horminoides* Pourret): vervain sage (Eng.), wild clary (Eng.).
Salvia viridis L., Sp. pl. 24. 1753 (*S. horminum* L.): Bluebeard
sage (Eng.), Joseph sage (Eng.), red-topped sage (Eng.).

Satureja L., Sp. pl. 567. 1753.
Literature: 14, 59, 64, 72.
Species:
Satureja douglasii (Benth.) Briq. in Engl. & Prantl., Nat.
Pflanzenfam. 4(3A):300. 1896 [*Micromeria chamissonis*
(Benth.) Greene, *M. douglasii* (Benth.) Benth.]: yerba buena
(Sp.).
Satureja hortensis L., Sp. pl. 568. 1753: summer savory (Eng.),
sarriette des jardins (Fr.), Bohnenkraut (Ger.), satureia (It.),
peverella (It.), ajedrea de jardin (Sp.).

Satureja montana L., Sp. pl. 568. 1753: winter savory (Eng.), sarriette des montagnes (Fr.), Winterbohnenkraut (Ger.), Guisopillo (Ger.), santoreggia invernale (It.), hisopillo (Sp.). While at least 5 subspecies exist, subsp. *montana* is the one usually harvested as winter savory.

Satureja thymbra L., Sp. pl. 567. 1753: za'atar rumi (Ar.), za'atar franji (Ar.).

Sideritis L., Sp. pl. 574. 1753.
  Literature: 98, 150.
  Species:
  Sideritis clandestina (Bory & Chaub.) Hayek, Prodr. Fl. Penins. Balcan. 2:257. 1929.
    Two subspecies exist:
    subsp. *clandestina* (*S. theezans* Boiss. & Heldr., *S. cretica* Sibth. & Sm.).
    subsp. *cyllenea* (Heldr. ex Boiss.) Papanikolaou & Kokkini in Margaris, Koedam & Vokou, Aromatic Pl. 113. 1982 (*S. peloponnesiaca* Boiss. & Heldr.).
  Sideritis raeseri Boiss. & Heldr., Diagn. Pl. Orient. ser. 2. 3:30. 1854 (*S. syriaca* Fraas, non L.).
  Sideritis syriaca L., Sp. pl. 574. 1753 (*S. cretica* Boiss.): tsai tou vounou (Gk.).

Thymbra L., Sp. Pl. 569. 1753.
  Literature: 72, 101.
  Species:
  Thymbra spicata L., Sp. Pl. 569. 1753: za'atar hommar (Ar.), za'atar midbari (Ar.).

Thymus L., Sp. pl. 590. 1753.
  Literature: 71, 72, 114.
  Species:
  Thymus caespititius Brot., Fl. lusit. 1:176. 1804 (*T. micans* Soland. ex Lowe, *T. serpyllum* auct.): tiny thyme (Eng.), tufted thyme (Eng.).
    One cultivar ('Tuffet') is recorded.
  Thymus capitatus (L.) Hoffmanns. & Link, Fl. portug. 1:123. 1809 [*Satureja capitata* L., *Thymbra capitata* (L.) Griseb., *Coridothymus capitatus* (L.) Rchb. f.]: conehead thyme (Eng.), corido thyme (Eng.), Cretan thyme (Eng.), thyme of the ancients (Eng.), Spanish origanum (Eng.), headed savory (Eng.), za'atar farsi (Ar.).
  Thymus cephalotos L., Sp. pl. 592. 1753.
  Thymus x *citriodorus* (Pers.) Schreb. in Schweigg. & Koerte, Fl. Erlang. 2:17. 1811 (*T. lanuginosus* Mill. var. *citriodorum* Pers.; *T. serpyllum* L. var. *vulgaris* Benth.; *T. comptus* Hort., non Friv.; *T. jankae* Hort., in part non Čelak; *T. serpyllum* auct., non L., var. *citriodorus* Hort.; *T.* 'Lemoneum'): lemon thyme (Eng.).

One cultivar ('Aureus,' golden lemon thyme) is known.
Thymus herba-barona Loisel., Fl. gall. 360. 1807 (*T.* 'Nutmeg,' in part): caraway thyme (Eng.).
Thymus hirtus Willd., Enum. pl. Hort. Berol. 623. 1809.
Thymus hyemalis J. Lange, Pug. pl. hispan. 3 in Vidensk. Meddel. Dansk Naturhist. Foren. Kjøbenhavn 5:7. 1863: often incorrectly cited as the source of "Spanish verbena oil."
Thymus loscosii Willk. in Willk. & Lange, Prodr. Fl. Hisp. 2:401. 1868.
Two subspecies are recorded, but subsp. *loscosii* is most common.
Thymus mastichina L., Sp. pl. ed. 2. 827. 1763: mastic thyme (Eng.), Spanish marjoram (Eng.).
Thymus praecox Opiz, Naturalientausch 6:40. 1824.
Five subspecies are recognized, but the following is most pertinent:
subsp. *arcticus* (E. Durand) Jalas, Veröff. Geobot. Inst. ETH Stiftung Rübel Zürich 43:190. 1970 (*T. drucei* Ronn.; *T. serpyllum* auct., in part, non L.; *T. serpyllum* L. 'Carneus'; *T. serpyllum* L. 'Roseus'; *T. jankae* Hort., in part, non Čelak.; *T. minus* Hort.; *T.* 'Nutmeg,' in part): creeping thyme (Eng.), mother-of-thyme (Eng.).
This subspecies includes a number of cultivars ('Albus,' 'Annie Hall,' 'Coccineus,' 'Emerald Cushion,' 'Hall's Woolly,' 'Lanuginosus,' 'Mayfair,' 'Minor,' 'Pink Chintz,' 'White Moss,' and 'Wild Garden Lavender').
Thymus pulegioides L., Sp. pl. 592. 1753 [*T. chamaedrys* Fries; *T. serpyllum* L. subsp. *montanus* Archang.; *T. serpyllum* L. subsp. *effusus* (Host) Lyka in Hegi; *T. serpyllum* L. subsp. *carniolicus* (Borb.) Lyka in Hegi; *T. serpyllum* L. subsp. *parviflorus* (Opiz ex H. Braun) Lyka in Hegi; *T. enervius* Klok.; *T. alpestris* auct., non Tausch ex A. Kern.; *T. serpyllum* auct., in part, non L.]: mother-of-thyme (Eng.), Pennsylvania Dutch tea thyme (Eng.), wild thyme (Eng.).
At least 5 cultivars are known ('Fosterflower,' 'Gold Dust,' 'Kermesius,' 'Oregano-scented,' and 'White Magic').
Thymus quinquecostatus Čelak, Oesterr. Bot. Z. 39:263. 1899: Japanese thyme (Eng.).
Two forms are known:
f. *quinquecostatus* (*T. serpyllum* L. var. *przewalskii* Kom.; *T. serpyllum* L. var. *ibukiensis* Kudo; *T. przewalskii* (Kom.) Nakai; *T. przewalskii* (Kom.) Nakai var. *laxa* Nakai; *T. quinquecostatus* Čelak. var. *japonicus* H. Hara; *T. serpyllum* auct. Japon., non L.).
f. *albiflorus* H. Hara, Bot. Mag. (Tokyo) 51:145. 1937.
Thymus serpyllum L., Sp. pl. 590. 1753.
Two subspecies exist:
subsp. *serpyllum* [*T. serpyllum* L. subsp. *angustifolius* (Pers.)

Archang., *T. serpyllum* L. subsp. *rigidus* (Wimm. & Grab.) Lyka].
subsp. *tanaensis* (Hyl.) Jalas, Acta Bot. Fenn. 39:20. 1947. (*T. subarcticus* Klok. & Shost.).
Thymus vulgaris L., Sp. pl. 591. 1753 (*T. aestivus* Reut. ex Willk., *T. ilerdensis* F. Gonzalez ex Costa, *T. webbianus* Rouy, *T. valentianus* Rouy): garden thyme (Eng.), common thyme (Eng.), thym (Fr.), Thymian (Ger.), timo (It.), tomillo (Sp.).
Thymus zygis L., Sp. pl. 591. 1753 (*T. sabulicola* Cosson, *T. sylvestris* Hoffmanns. & Link).
Thymus 'Argenteus' (*T.* x *citriodorus* Hort. 'Argenteus,' *T. vulgaris* Hort. 'Argenteus'): silver thyme (Eng.).
Thymus 'Broad-leaf English': English thyme (Eng.).
Thymus 'Clear Gold' (*T. serpyllum* auct. 'Aureus,' in part): creeping golden thyme (Eng.), yellow transparent thyme (Eng.).
Thymus 'Long-leaf Gray' (*T. glabrescens loevyanus* Hort.; *T. lanicaulis* Hort., in part, non Ronn.; *T. thracicus* Hort., non Velen.).
Thymus 'Variegated English': variegated English thyme (Eng.).
Thymus 'Wedgewood English': Wedgewood English thyme (Eng.).
Thymus 'Woolly-stemmed Sharp' (*T. lanuginosus* auct., in part, non Mill.; *T. lanicaulis* Hort. in part, non Ronn.).

Solanaceae

Capsicum L., Sp. pl. 188. 1753.
  Literature: 50, 67, 85, 91, 92, 117.
  Species:
Capsicum annuum L., Sp. pl. 188. 1753.
  Two varieties exist:
  var. annuum.
    This includes most of the cultivated peppers as vegetables and herbs/spices. At least 5 "Groups" exist, the most pertinent of which is the Longum Group; this includes the capsicum pepper (Eng.), chili pepper (Eng.), poivre rouge (Fr.), Roter Pfeffer (Ger.), pepe di caienna (It.), pimenton (Sp.), red pepper (Eng.), and paprika (Eng.) and includes the cultivars 'Anaheim,' 'Calora,' 'Caribe,' 'Fresno,' 'Goldspike,' 'Jalapeño,' 'Mulato,' 'Pasilla' (perhaps the same as 'Ancho' and 'Poblano'), 'Sante Fe Grand,' 'Serrano,' etc.
  var. *glabriusculum* (Dunal) Heiser & Pickersgill, Baileya 19:156. 1975: bird pepper (Eng.), chiltepin (Sp.).
Capsicum baccatum L., Mant. pl. 47. 1767.
  Two varieties exist:
  var. *baccatum.*
  var. *pendulum* (Willd.) Eshbaugh, Taxon 17:51-52. 1968:

Brown's pepper (Eng.), piris (Eng.).
Capsicum chinense Jacq., Hort. Bot. Vindobon. 3:38. t. 67. 1776:
    Chinese pepper (Eng.).
Capsicum frutescens L., Sp. pl. 189. 1753: Tabasco pepper (Eng.),
    malagueta (Sp.).
    This species includes the cultivars 'Tabasco' and 'Greenleaf
    Tabasco.'
Capsicum pubescens Ruiz. & Pav., Flora peruv. prodr. 2:30.
    1799: rocoto (Sp.), chile manzana (Sp.).

Scrophulariaceae

Limnophila R. Br., Prodr. 442. 1810.
Literature: 28, 155.
Species:
Limnophila stolonifera (Blanco) Merr., Sp. Blanc. 345. 1918:
    orégano (Sp.).

Rubiaceae

Galium L., Sp. pl. 105. 1753.
Literature: 61.
Species:
Galium aparine L., Sp. pl. 108. 1753: cleavers (Eng.), goosegrass
    (Eng.).
Galium odoratum (L.) Scop., Fl. Carn. ed. 2. 1:105. 1771
    (*Asperula odorata* L.): woodruff (Eng.), sweet woodruff
    (Eng.), aspérule (Fr.), Waldmeister (Ger.), stellina odorosa
    (It.), asperula (Sp.).
Galium verum L., Sp. pl. 107. 1753: cheese rennet (Eng.), yellow
    bedstraw (Eng.), our Lady's bedstraw (Eng.), caille-lait (Fr.),
    gaillet (Fr.), Echtes Labkraut (Ger.), caglio (It.), presvola (It.),
    galio (Sp.).

Valerianaceae

Valeriana L., Sp. pl. 31. 1753.
Literature: 126, 138, 148.
Species:
Valeriana officinalis L., Sp. pl. 31. 1753: garden heliotrope (Eng.),
    garden valerian (Eng.), cat's valerian (Eng.), St. George's herb
    (Eng.), valériane (Fr.), Baldrian (Ger.), valeriana (It., Sp.).
    Three subspecies are known, but subsp. *officinalis* is the
    cultivated valerian.

Valerianella Mill., Gard. Dict. Abr. ed. 4. 1754.

Literature: 60, 66, 215.
Species:
Valerianella locusta (L.) Laterr., Fl. bordel. ed. 2. 93. 1821 [*V. olitoria* (L.) Pollich]: corn salad (Eng.), lamb's lettuce (Eng.), mâche commune (Fr.), Ackersalat (Ger.), valeriana (It.), canonigos (Sp.).

Asteraceae (Compositae)

Artemisia L., Sp. pl. 845. 1753.
Literature: 154, 163, 207.
Species:
Artemisia abrotanum L., Sp. pl. 845. 1753: southernwood (Eng.), old man (Eng.), lad's love (Eng.), citronelle (Fr.), Stabwurz (Ger.), abrotano (It., Sp.).
Artemisia absinthium L., Sp. pl. 848. 1753: wormwood (Eng.), grande absinthe (Fr.), Wermut (Ger.), assenzio (It.), ajenjo (Sp.).
Artemisia dracunculus L., Sp. pl. 849. 1753: French tarragon (Eng.), Russian tarragon (Eng.), estragon (Fr., Sp.), Estragon (Ger.), targone (It.).
The clone cultivated as French tarragon is a sterile derivative of the wild species, which is normally called Russian tarragon. The clone called French tarragon should be designated as a cultivar, 'Sativa.'
Artemisia genipi Weber in Stechm., Artem. 17. 1775 [*A. spicata* Wulfen, *A. laxa* (Lam.) Fritsch., *A. mutellina* Vill., *A. glacialis* Wulfen, non L.]: genépi (Fr.), genipi (It.).
Artemisia glacialis L., Sp. pl. ed. 2. 1187. 1763: genépi des glaciers (Fr.), Gletscherreute (Ger.).
Artemisia herba-alba Asso, Syn. Stirp. Arag. 117. 1779.
Artemisia judaica L., Amoen. acad. 4:463. 1759: semen contra (Fr.), graines à vers (Fr.).
Artemisia maritima L., Sp. pl. 846. 1753.
Artemisia pontica L., Sp. pl. 847. 1753: Roman wormwood (Eng.), small absinthe (Eng.), petite absinthe (Fr.).
Artemisia princeps Pamp., Nuovo Giorn. Bot. Ital. n.s. 36:444. 1930: Japanese mugwort (Eng.), yomogi (Jap.), kazuzaki-yomogi (Jap.).
Artemisia vulgaris L., Sp. pl. 848. 1753: mugwort (Eng.), Indian wormwood (Eng.).

Balsamita Mill., Gard. dict. abr. ed. 4. 1754.
Literature: 99.
Species:
Balsamita major Desf., Actes Soc. Hist. Nat. Paris 1:13. 1792. [*Chrysanthemum balsamita* (L.) Baill., non L.; *Pyrethrum majus* (Desf.) Tzvelev]: costmary (Eng.), mint geranium

(Eng.), alecost (Eng.), sweet Mary (Eng.), Bible leaf (Eng.), balsamite (Fr.), Balsamkraut (Ger.), balsamite (It.), balsamita (Sp.).

The status of the rayed versus the rayless taxa is uncertain. The status of this genus, in view of *Carpesium* L., also needs further study.

Blumea DC, Arch. Bot. (Paris) 2:514. 1833.
Species:
Blumea balsamifera (L.) DC, Prodr. 5:466. 1836. ngai camphor (Eng.), sambong (Malay).
Blumea chinensis (L.) DC, Prodr. 5:444. 1836: tombak-tombak (Indonesian), djonge areuj (Indonesian).
Blumea lacera (N. Burman) DC in Wight, Contrib. Bot. Ind. 14:1834.
Blumea myriocephala DC, Prodr. 5:445. 1836 [*B. lanceolaria* (Roxb.) Druce].

Brickellia Elliott, Sketch bot. S. Carolina 2:290. 1823.
Literature: 28.
Species:
Brickellia veronicifolia (Humb., Bonpl. & Kunth) A. Gray, pl. wright. 1:85. 1880: brickellbush (Eng.), orégano (Sp.).
Two varieties exist, but var. *veronicifolia* is most commonly encountered.

Cacalia L., Sp. pl. 834. 1753.
Literature: 39.
Species:
Cacalia delphiniifolia Sieb. & Zucc., Abh. Math.-Phys. Cl. Königl. Bayer. Akad. Wiss. 4[3]:190. 1846 [*Senecio zuccarinii* Maxim., *C. zuccarinii* (Maxim.) Hand.-Mazz.]: tassel flower (Eng.), momijigasa (Jap.), momiji-s·o (Jap.).
Cacalia hastata L., Sp. pl. 835. 1753.
At least 7 varieties are known, but the most pertinent is:
var. *orientalis* (Kitam.) Ohwi, Fl. jap. 884. 1965 (*C. hastata* L. var. *glabra* auct. Japon., non Ledeb.; *C. hastata* auct. Japon., non L.): yobusuma-sō (Jap.).

Calendula L., Sp. pl. 921. 1753.
Literature: 134, 137.
Species:
Calendula officinalis L., Sp. pl. 921. 1753: poet's marigold (Eng.), pot marigold (Eng.), calendula (Eng.), souci (Fr.), Ringelblume (Ger.), calendula (It., Sp.), florrancio (It.).

Chamaemelum Mill., Gard dict. abr. ed. 4. 1754.
Literature: 205.
Species:
Chamaemelum nobile (L.) All., Fl. pedem. 1:185. 1785 (*Anthemis nobilis* L.): Roman chamomile (Eng.), chamomille romain

(Fr.), Gartenkamille (Ger.), camomilla romana (It.), manzanilla romana (Sp.).

Chamomilla S. F. Gray, Nat. arr. Brit. pl. 2:454. 1821.
  Literature: 120.
  Species:
  Chamomilla recutita (L.) Rauschert, Folia Geobot. Phytotax.
    (Praha) 9:255. 1754 (*Matricaria recutita* L., *M. chamomilla*
    L. pro parte): German chamomile (Eng.), Hungarian chamo-
    mile (Eng.), sweet false chamomile (Eng.), matricaire
    camomille (Fr.), Kamille (Fr.), camomilla nostrale (It.).
  Chamomilla suaveolens (Pursh) Rydb., N. Amer. Fl. 34: 232.
    1916 [*Matricaria matricarioides* (Less.) Porter pro parte]:
    pineapple weed (Eng.).

Chrysanthemum L., Sp. pl. 887. 1753.
  Species:
  Chrysanthemum coronarium L., Sp. pl. 890. 1753: garland chry-
    santhemum (Eng.), crown daisy (Eng.), cooking chrysanthe-
    mum (Eng.), chop suey greens (Eng.), p'êng-hao (Chin.).
  Chrysanthemum x *morifolium* Ramat., J. Hist. Nat. 2:240. 1792:
    florist's chrysanthemum (Eng.), mum (Eng.), shokoyu-giku
    (Jap.).
    If the genus *Chrysanthemum* is defined *sensu stricto* (*e.g.,*
    206), then it only includes about 5 annual species of the
    Mediterranean and Eurasia. A comprehensive revision of the
    Eurasian species previously included in the *sensu lato* defini-
    tion of *Chrysanthemum* is lacking. Thus, the correct name of
    C. x *morifolium,* in respect to the genus *Dendranthema,*
    remains unknown at the present.
  Chrysanthemum segetum L., Sp. pl. 889. 1753: corn chrysan-
    themum (Eng.), corn marigold (Eng.), t'ung-hao (Chin.).

Cichorium L., Sp. pl. 813. 1753.
  Literature: 168.
  Species:
  Cichorium intybus L., Sp. pl. 813. 1753: chicory (Eng.), succory
    (Eng.), chicorée (Fr.), Zichorienwurzel (Ger.), cicoria (It.),
    achichoria de raiz (Sp.).

Cirsium Mill., Gard dict. abr. ed. 4. 1754.
  Species:
  Cirsium dipsacolepis (Maxim.) Matsum., Enum. Sci. Names 82.
    1895: thistle (Eng.), mori-azami (Jap.), yabu-azami (Jap.).

Helichrysum Mill., Gard. dict. abr. ed. 4. 1754 (*"Elichrysum"*), corr.
  Pers., Syn. pl. 2:414. 1807.
  Literature: 43.
  Species:
  Helichrysum italicum (Roth) G. Don in Loudon, Hort. brit. 342.
    1830: curry plant (Eng.), white-leaved everlasting (Eng.).

Three subspecies are known, but subsp. siitalicum [*H. angustifolium* (Lam.) DC] is the cultivated curry plant.

Helichrysum orientale (L.) Gaertn., Fruct. Sem. pl. 2:404. 1791: immortelle (Eng.), everlasting (Eng.).

Helichrysum serpyllifolium Less., Syn. gen. Compos. 277. 1832: Hottentot tea (Eng.).

Inula L., Sp. pl. 881. 1753.
Literature: 15.
Species:
Inula crithmoides L., Sp. pl. 883. 1753: golden samphire (Eng.).
Inula helenium L., Sp. pl. 881. 1753: elecampane (Eng.), scabwort (Eng.), alant (Eng.), horseheal (Eng.), yellow starwort (Eng.), aunée (Fr.), Echter Alant (Ger.), enula (It.), enula campana (Sp.).

Kalimeris (Cass.) Cass., Dict. Sci. Nat. 37:464, 491. 1825.
Species:
Kalimeris yomena Kitam., Acta Phytotax. Geobot. 6:51. 1937 [*Aster yomena* (Kitam.) Honda]: yomena (Jap.).

Petasites Mill., Gard. dict. abr. ed. 4. 1754.
Species:
Petasites japonicus (Sieb. & Zucc.) Maxim., Award 34th Denidov. Prize 212. 1866.
Two varieties are known:
var. *japonicus:* sweet coltsfoot (Eng.), fuki (Jap.).
var. *giganteus* (F. Schmidt) Kitamura, Compos. jap. 3:164. 1942: sweet giant coltsfoot (Eng.), akitabuki (Jap.).

Solidago L., Sp. pl. 878. 1753.
Species:
Solidago odora Aiton., Hort. kew. 3:214. 1789: sweet goldenrod (Eng.), fragrant goldenrod (Eng.).
Two subspecies are known, but subsp. *odora* is most often encountered.

Tagetes L., Sp. pl. 887. 1753.
Literature: 147.
Species:
Tagetes lucida Cav., Icon. 3. 1794: sweet marigold (Eng.), sweet mace (Eng.), Mexican tarragon (Eng.), anisillo (Sp.).

Tanacetum L., Sp. pl. 843. 1753.
Literature: 100.
Species:
Tanacetum vulgare L., Sp. pl. 844. 1753 [*Chrysanthemum vulgare* (L.) Bernh., non (Lam.) Gaterau; *C. tanacetum* Karsch, non Vis.]: tansy (Eng.), button bitters (Eng.), tanaisie (Fr.), Wurmkraut (Ger.), Drusenkraut (Ger.), Rainfarn (Ger.), tanaceto (It.), ariceto (It.), erba amara (It.), argentina (Sp.),

balsimita menor (Sp.), tanaceto (Sp.).
The nomenclatural status of the taxon with finely dissected leaves needs more study but would probably be best designated as 'Crispum.'

Taraxacum G. H. Weber in Wiggers, Prim. Fl. Hols. 56. 1780.
Literature: 161.
Species:
Taraxacum officinale G. H. Weber in Wiggers, Prim. Fl. Hols. 56. 1780: dandelion (Eng.), pissenlit (Fr.), dent de lion (Fr.), Löwenzahn (Ger.), Kuhblume (Ger.), dente di leone (It.), soffione (It.), diênte de leon (Sp.).
The name is used *sensu latu,* but it has never been typified, so the correct application of the name is uncertain.

VI. REFERENCES

1. Allwood, M.C. 1954. *Carnations, Pinks and All Dianthus.* Allwood Brothers, Hayward's Heath, England. 354 p.

2. Amaral Franco, J. do and M.L. da Rocha Afonso. 1972. *Rosmarinus.In* T.G. Tutin, V.H. Heywood, N.A. Burges, D.M. Moore, D.H. Valentine, S.M. Walters, and D.A. Webb, eds. *Flora Europaea.* Vol. 3. University Press, Cambridge. p. 187.

3. American Spice Trade Association. 1972. *A History of Spices.* Amer. Spice Trade Association, New York. 13 p.

4. Arctander, S. 1960. *Perfume and Flavor Materials of Natural Origin.* S. Arctander, Elizabeth, NJ. 736 p.

5. Baer, D.F. 1976. Systematics of the genus *Bixa* and geography of the cultivated annatto tree, Ph.D. thesis. University of California, Los Angeles. 239 p.

6. Bailey, L.H. 1938. *The Garden of Pinks, with Decorations.* Macmillan, New York. 142 p.

7. Bailey, R. 1948. *The Home Garden Self-pronouncing Dictionary of Plant Names.* American Garden Guild, New York. 72 p.

8. Ball, P.W. 1964. *Alliaria. In* T.G. Tutin, V.H. Heywood, N.A. Burges, D.H. Valentine, S.M. Walters, and D.A. Webb, eds. *Flora Europaea* Vol. 1. University Press, Cambridge. p. 267.

9. Ball, P.W. 1964. *Armoracia. In* T.G. Tutin, V.H. Heywood, N.A. Burges, D.H. Valentine, S.M. Walters, and D.A. Webb, eds. *Flora Europaea.* Vol. 1. University Press, Cambridge. p. 234.

10. Ball, P.W. 1964. *Barbarea. In* T.G. Tutin, V.H. Heywood, N.A. Burges, D.H. Valentine, S.M. Walters, and D.A. Webb, eds. *Flora Europaea.* Vol. 1. University Press, Cambridge. pp. 231–282.

11. Ball, P.W. 1968. *Filipendula. In* T.G. Tutin, V.H. Heywood, N.A. Burges, D.M. Moore, D.H. Valentine, S.M. Walters, and D.A. Webb, eds. *Flora Europaea.* Vol. 2. University Press, Cambridge. pp. 6–7.

12. Ball, P.W. and F.M. Getliffe, 1972 *Acinos. In* T.G. Tutin, V.H. Heywood, N.A. Burges, D.M. Moore, D.H. Valentine, S.M. Walters, and D.A.

Webb, eds. *Flora Europaea*, Vol. 3. University Press, Cambridge. pp. 165–166.

13. Ball, P.W. and F. Getliffe. 1972. *Calamintha. In* T.G. Tutin, V.H. Heywood, N.A. Burges, D.M. Moore, D.H. Valentine, S.M. Walters, and D.A. Webb, eds. *Flora Europaea*, Vol. 3. University Press, Cambridge. pp. 166–167.

14. Ball, P.W. and F.M. Getliffe. 1972. *Satureja. In* T.G. Tutin, V.H. Heywood, N.A. Burgess, D.M. Moore, D.H. Valentine, S.M. Walters, and D.A. Webb, ed. *Flora Europaea*, Vol. 3. University Press, Cambridge. pp. 163–165.

15. Ball, P.W. and T.G. Tutin. 1976. *Inula, In* T.G. Tutin, V.H. Heywood, N.A. Burges, D.M. Moore, D.H. Valentine, S.M. Walters, and D.A. Webb, eds. *Flora Europaea*, Vol. 4. University Press, Cambridge. pp. 133–136.

16. Bean, W.J. 1980. *Rosa. In* W.J. Bean, *Trees and Shrubs Hardy in the British Isles,* 8th ed. (rev.) D.L. Clarke and G. Taylor, eds. Vol. 4. John Murray, London. pp. 35–102.

17. Bell, C.R. 1963. The genus *Eryngium* in the southeastern United States. Castanea 28:73–79.

18. Bentham, G. 1832. *Ocymum. In* G. Bentham, *Labiatarum Genera Et Species.* James Ridgway & Sons, London. pp. 1–19.

19. Bentham, G. 1848. *Ocimum. In* A. deCandolle, *Prodromus Systematis Naturalis Regni Vegetabilis,* Vol. 12. Victoris Masson, Paris. pp. 31–44.

20. Bonnet, B. 1976. Le poireau (*Allium porrum* L.): Aspects botaniques et agronomiques. Revue bibliographique. Saussurea 7:121–155.

21. Botta, S.M. 1979. Las especies argentinas del género *Aloysia* (Verbenaceae). Darwiniana 22:67–108.

22. Bowles, E.A. 1952. *A Handbook of Crocus and Colchicum for Gardeners.* Bodley Head, London. 222 p.

23. Brenan, J.P.M. 1964. *Chenopodium. In* T.G. Tutin, V.H. Heywood, N.A. Burges, D.H. Valentine, S.M. Walters, and D.A. Webb, eds. *Flora Europaea,* Vol. 1. University Press, Cambridge. pp. 92–95.

24. Brickell, C.D., ed. 1980. International code of nomenclature for cultivated plants–1980. Bohn, Scheltema & Holkema, Utrecht. 32 p.

25. Briquet, J. 1897. *Ocimum. In* A. Engler and K. Prantl, *Die natürlichen Pflanzenfamilien,* Vol. 4, part 3A. Wilhelm Engelmann, Leipzig. pp. 369–372.

26. Buchenau, F. 1892. Beiträge zur Kenntnis der Gattung *Tropaeolum.* Bot. Jahrb. Syst. 15:180–259.

27. Burger, W.C. 1972. Flora Costaricensis. Family 40, Casuarinaceae. Family 41, Piperaceae. Fieldiana, Bot., Vol. 35. 227 p.

28. Calpouzos, L. 1954. Botanical aspects of oregano. Econ. Bot. 8:222–233.

29. Cannon, J.F.M. 1968. *Angelica. In* T.G. Tutin, V.H. Heywood, N.A. Burges, D.M. Moore, D.H. Valentine, S.M. Walters, and D.A. Webb, eds. *Flora Europaea,* Vol. 2. University Press, Cambridge. pp. 357–358.

30. Cannon, J.F.M. 1968. *Anthriscus. In* T.G. Tutin, V.H. Heywood, N.A. Burges, D.M. Moore, D.H. Valentine, S.M. Walters, and D.A. Webb, eds. *Flora Europaea,* .Vol. 2. University Press, Cambridge. p. 326.

31. Cannon, J.F.M. 1968. *Hydrocotyle. In* T.G. Tutin, V.H. Heywood, N.A. Burges, D.M. Moore, D.H. Valentine, S.M. Walters, and D.A. Webb, eds. *Flora Europaea,* Vol. 2. University Press, Cambridge. p. 319.

32. Cannon, J.F.M. 1968. *Myrrhis. In* T.G. Tutin, V.H. Heywood, N.A. Burges, D.M. Moore, D.H. Valentine, S.M. Walters, and D.A. Webb, ed. *Flora Europaea,* Vol. 2. University Press, Cambridge. p. 327.

33. Cavers, P.B., M.I. Heagy, and R.K. Kokron. 1979. The biology of Canadian weeds. 35. *Alliaria petiolata* (M. Bieb.) Cavara and Grande. Can. J. Pl. Sci. 59:217–229.

34. Chambers, H.L. 1961. Chromosome numbers and breeding systems in *Pycnanthemum* (Labiatae). Brittonia 13:116–128.

35. Chambers, H.L. and K.L. Chambers. 1971. Artificial and natural hybrids in *Pycnanthemum* (Labiatae). Brittonia 23:71–88.

36. Chater, A.O. 1964. *Sinapis. In* T.G. Tutin, V.H. Heywood, N.A. Burges, D.H. Valentine, S.M. Walters, and D.A. Webb, eds. *Flora Europaea,* Vol. 1. University Press, Cambridge. p. 339.

37. Chater, A.O. 1968. *Eryngium. In* T.G. Tutin, V.H. Heywood, N.A. Burges, D.M. Moore, D.H. Valentine, S.M. Walters, and D.A. Webb, eds. *Flora Europaea,* Vol. 2. University Press, Cambridge. pp. 320–324.

38. Chater, A.O. 1972. *Borago. In* T.G. Tutin, V.H. Heywood, N.A. Burges, D.M. Moore, D.H. Valentine, S.M. Walters, and D.A. Webb, eds. *Flora Europaea,* Vol. 3. University Press, Cambridge. p. 109.

39. Chater, A.O. 1976. *Cacalia. In* T.G. Tutin, V.H. Heywood, N.A. Burges, D.M. Moore, D.H. Valentine, S.M. Walters, and D.A. Webb, eds. *Flora Europaea,* Vol. 4. University Press, Cambridge. p. 206.

40. Chater, A.O. and V.H. Heywood, 1964. *Cochlearia. In* T.G. Tutin, V.H. Heywood, N.A. Burges, D.H. Valentine, S.M. Walters, and D.A. Webb, eds. *Flora Europaea,* Vol. 1. University Press, Cambridge. pp. 313–314.

41. Chater, A.O. and V.II. Ileywood. 1964. *Stellaria. In* T.G. Tutin, V.H. Heywood, N.A. Burges, D.H. Valentine, S.M. Walters, and D.A. Webb, eds. *Flora Europaea,* Vol. 1. University Press, Cambridge. pp. 133–136.

42. Chaytor, D.A. 1937. A taxonomic study of the genus *Lavandula.* J. Linn. Soc., Bot. 51:153–204.

43. Clapham, A.R. 1976. *Helichrysum. In* T.G. Tutin, V.H. Heywood, N.A. Burges, D.M. Moore, D.H. Valentine, S.M. Walters, and D.A. Webb, eds. *Flora Europaea,* Vol. 4. University Press, Cambridge. pp. 128–131.

44. Cook, A.D., ed. 1983. Oriental plants and vegetables. Pl. & Gard. Vol. 39, No. 2. 75 p.

45. Cook, J.H. 1911. Carnations and Pinks. Frederick A. Stokes, New York. 116 p.

46. Coombs, R.E. 1981. Violets: The History and Cultivation of Scented Violet. Croom Helm, London. 142 p.

47. Cullen, J. 1968. The genus *Papaver* in cultivation. 1. The wild species. Baileya 16.73–91.

48. Dahlgren, R. 1964. The correct name of the "rooibus" tea plant. Bot. Not. 117:188–196.

49. Dahlgren, R. 1968. Revision of the genus *Aspalathus.* II. The species with ericoid and pinoid leaflets. 7. Subgenus *Nortieria.* With remarks on Rooibos Tea cultivation. Bot. Not. 121:165–208.

50. D'Arcy, W.G. and W.H. Eshbaugh. 1974. New World peppers [*Capsicum*-Solanaceae] north of Colombia: A resumé. Baileya 19:93–105.

51. Darrah, H.H. 1974. Investigations of the cultivars of the basils (*Ocimum*). Econ. Bot. 28:63–67.

52. Darrah, H.H. 1980. *The Cultivated Basils.* Buckeye Printing Co., Independence, MO. 40 p.

53. DeFilipps, R.A. 1972. *Hyssopus. In* T.G. Tutin, V.H. Heywood, N.A. Burges, D.M. Moore, D.H. Valentine, S.M. Walters, and D.A. Webb, eds. *Flora Europaea,* Vol. 3. University Press, Cambridge. pp. 170–171.

54. DeFilipps, R.A. 1972. *Phlomis. In* T.G. Tutin, V.H. Heywood, N.A. Burges, D.M. Moore, D.H. Valentine, S.M. Walters, and D.A. Webb, eds. *Flora Europaea,* Vol. 3. University Press, Cambridge. pp. 144–145.

55. de la Roche, G., G.D. Rowley, A. Lawalrée, and W.T. Stearn. 1978. *Commentaries to Les Roses by P.J. Redouté, a Contribution to the History of the Genus Rosa.* De Schutter S.A., Antwerp. 387 p.

56. Den Ouden, P. and B.K. Boom. 1978. *Manual of Cultivated Conifers Hardy in the Cold- and Warm-temperate Zone,* Martinus Nijhoff, The Hague. 526 p.

57. Devetak, Z. 1963. Prilog poznavanju kadulje u Jogoslaviji. Radova Polj. Fak. 12:241–261.

58. DeWolf, G.P. 1953. Notes on cultivated Labiates. 1. *Agastache.* Baileya 1:115–117.

59. DeWolf, G.P. 1954. Notes on cultivated Labiates. 4. *Satureja* and some related genera. Baileya 2:142–150.

60. Dyal, S.C. 1938. *Valerianella* in North America. Rhodora 40:185–212.

61. Ehrendorfer, F. 1976. *Galium. In* T.G. Tutin, V.H. Heywood, N.A. Burges, D.M. Moore, D.H. Valentine, S.M. Walters, and D.A. Webb, eds. *Flora Europaea,* Vol. 4. University Press, Cambridge, pp. 14–36.

62. Epling, C. 1938. The California Salvias: A review of *Salvia* section Audibertia. Ann. Missouri Bot. Gard. 25:95–188.

63. Epling, C. 1949. Revisión del género *Hyptis* (Labiatae). Revista Mus. La Plata, Secc. Bot. 7:153–497.

64. Epling, C. and C. Jàtiva. 1966. A descriptive key to the species of *Satureja* indigenous to North America. Brittonia 18:244–248.

65. Epling, C.C. 1925. Monograph of the genus *Monardella.* Ann. Missouri Bot. Gard. Vol. 12. 106 p.

66. Ernet, D. and I.B.K. Richardson. 1976. *Valerianella. In* T.G. Tutin, V.H. Heywood, N.A. Burges, D.M. Moore, D.H. Valentine, S.M. Walters, and D.A. Webb, eds. *Flora Europaea,* Vol. 4. University Press, Cambridge. pp. 48–52.

67. Eshbaugh, W.H. 1980. The taxonomy of the genus *Capsicum* (Solanaceae)–1980. Phytologia 47:153–166.

68. Farr, E.R., J.A. Leussink, and F.A. Stafleu. 1979. *Index nominum genericorum.* Bohn, Scheltema & Holkema, Utrecht. 3 vols.

69. Fernandes, R. 1972. *Glechoma. In* T.G. Tutin, V.H. Heywood, N.A. Burges, D.M. Moore, D.H. Valentine, S.M. Walters, and D.A. Webb, eds. *Flora Europaea,* Vol. 3. University Press, Cambridge. p. 161.

70. Fernandes, R. 1972. *Melissa. In* T.G. Tutin, V.H. Heywood, N.A. Burges, D.M. Moore, D.H. Valentine, S.M. Walters, and D.A. Webb, eds. *Flora Europaea,* Vol. 3. University Press, Cambridge. pp. 162–163.

71. Flannery, H.B. 1982. A study of the taxa of *Thymus* L. (Labiatae) cultivated in the United States, Ph.D. thesis. Cornell University, Ithaca, NY. 369 p.

72. Fleischer, A., Z. Fleischer, N. Sneer, and A. Joffe. 1982. Chemical and botanical aspects of the biblical hyssop. *In* VIII International Congress of Essential Oils, October 12–17, 1982, Cannes-Grasse, France. Paper no. 212.

73. Florists' Publishing Company. 1980. *New Pronouncing Dictionary of Plant Names.* Florists' Publishing Co., Chicago. 63 p.

74. Fosberg, F.R. 1965. Nomenclature of the horseradish (Cruciferae). Baileya 13:1–3.

75. Fosberg, F.R. 1966. The correct name of the horseradish (Cruciferae). Baileya 14:60.

76. Genders, R. 1962. *Garden Pinks.* John Gifford Ltd., London. 160 p.

77. Gill, L.S. 1977. A cytosystematic study of the genus *Monarda* L. (Labiatae) in Canada. Caryologia 30:381–394.

78. Ginsberg, B. 1977. Rooibosch tea. Herbal Rev. 2(2):7–12.

79. Grant, E. and C. Epling. 1943. A study of *Pycnanthemum* (Labiatae). Univ. Calif. Publ. Bot. 20:195–240.

80. Gray, F.D. 1972. Spice trends in the United States. U.S.D.A. Econ. Res. Serv. NSF-142. 43 p.

81. Guinea, E. 1972. *Lavandula. In* T.G. Tutin, V.H. Heywood, N.A. Burges, D.M. Moore, D.H. Valentine, S.M. Walters, and D.A. Webb, eds. *Flora Europaea,* Vol. 3. University Press, Cambridge. pp. 187–188.

82. Harley, R.M. 1972. *Mentha. In* T.G. Tutin, V.H. Heywood, N.A. Burges, D.M. Moore, D.H. Valentine, S.M. Walters, and D.A. Webb, eds. *Flora Europaea,* Vol. 3. University Press, Cambridge. pp. 183–186.

83. Harley, R.M. and C.A. Brighton. 1977. Chromosome numbers in the genus *Mentha* L.J. Linn. Soc., Bot. 74:71–96.

84. Harvey, J.H. 1978. Gilliflower and carnation. Gard. Hist. 6(1):46–57.

85. Hawkes, J.G. 1972. *Capsicum. In* T.G. Tutin, V.H. Heywood, N.A. Burges, D.M. Moore, D. H. Valentine, S.M. Walters, and D.A. Webb, eds. *Flora Europaea,* Vol. 3. University Press, Cambridge. pp. 196–197.

86. Hedge, I.C. 1959. Studies in east Mediterranean species of *Salvia:* II. Notes Roy. Bot. Gard. Edinburgh 23:47–69.

87. Hedge, I.C. 1969. *Salvia. In* P.M. Synge, ed. *The Royal Horticultural Society Supplement to the Dictionary of Gardening: A Practical and Scientific Encyclopedia of Horticulture,* 2d ed. Clarendon Press, Oxford. pp. 497–504.

88. Hedge, I.C. 1972. *Salvia. In* T.G. Tutin, V.H. Heywood, N.A. Burges, D.M. Moore, D.H. Valentine, S.M. Walters, and D.A. Webb, eds. *Flora Europaea,* Vol. 3. University Press, Cambridge. pp. 188–192.

89. Hedge, I.C. 1974. A revision of *Salvia* in Africa including Madagascar and the Canary Islands. Notes Roy. Bot. Gard. Edinburgh 33:1–121.

90. Hegi, G., ed. 1963-1984. *Illustrierte FLora von Mittel-Europa,* 2d ed. Verlag Paul Parey, Berlin. 7 vols.

91. Heiser, C.B. and B. Pickersgill. 1969. Names for the cultivated *Capsicum* species (Solanaceae). Taxon 18:277–283.

92. Heiser, C.B. and B. Pickersgill. 1975. Names for the bird peppers (*Capsicum*-Solanaceae). Baileya 19:151–156.

93. Helm, J. 1956. Die zu Würz- und Speisezwecken kultivierten Arten der Gattung *Allium* L. Kulturpflanzen 4:130–180.

94. Hérisset, A., J. Jolivet, A. Zoll, and J.-P. Chaumont. 1973. A propos des falsifications de la sarriette des jardins (*Satureia hortensis* L.) Pl. Med Phytother. 7:121–134.

95. Hérisset, A., J. Jolivet, A. Zoll, and J.-P. Chaumont. 1974. Nouvelles observations concernant les falsifications de la sarriette des jardins (*Satureia hortensis* L.) Pl. Med. Phytother. 8:287–294.

96. Heywood, V.H. 1964. *Brassica. In* T.G. Tutin, V.H. Heywood, N.A. Burges, D.H. Valentine, S.M. Walters, and D.A. Webb, eds. *Flora Europaea,* Vol. 1. University Press, Cambridge. pp. 335–339.

97. Heywood, V.H. 1964. *Capparis. In* T.G. Tutin, V.H. Heywood, N.A. Burges, D.H. Valentine, S.M. Walters, and D.A. Webb, eds. *Flora Europaea,* Vol. 1. University Press, Cambridge. p. 259.

98. Heywood, V.H. 1972. *Sideritis. In* T.G. Tutin, V.H. Heywood, N.A. Burges, D.M. Moore, D.H. Valentine, S.M. Walters, and D.A. Webb, eds. *Flora Europaea,* Vol. 3. University Press, Cambridge. pp. 138–143.

99. Heywood, V.H. 1976. *Balsamita. In* T.G. Tutin, V.H. Heywood, N.A. Burges, D.M. Moore, D.H. Valentine, S.M. Walters, and D.A. Webb, eds. *Flora Europaea,* Vol. 4. University Press, Cambridge. pp. 171–172.

100. Heywood, V.H. 1976. *Tanacetum. In* T.G. Tutin, V.H. Heywood, N.A. Burges, D.M. Moore, D.H. Valentine, S.M. Walters, and D. A. Webb, eds. *Flora Europaea,* Vol. 4. University Press, Cambridge. pp. 169–171.

101. Heywood, V.H., and R.A. DeFilipps. 1972. *Thymbra. In* T.G. Tutin, V.H. Heywood, N.A. Burges, D.M. Moore, D.H. Valentine, S.M. Walters, and D.A. Webb, eds. *Flora Europaea,* Vol. 3. University Press, Cambridge. p. 170.

102. Hitchcock, C.L. 1936. The genus *Lepidium* in the United States. Madroño 3:265–320.

103. Hodge, W.H. 1974. Wasabi--Native condiment plant of Japan. Econ. Bot. 23:118–129.

104. Hottes, A.C. 1937. *The Home Gardener's Pronouncing Dictionary.* Meredith Co., Des Moines, IA. 117 p.

105. Howard, W.H. 1976. Watercress: *Rorippa nasturtium-aquaticum* (Cruciferae). *In* N.W. Simmonds, ed. *Evolution of Crop Plants.* Longman, London, pp. 62–64.

106. Ietswaart, J.H. 1980. *A Taxonomic Revision of the Genus* Origanum *(Labiatae. Leiden University Press, The Hague. 153 p.*

107. Ingram, J. 1958. The cultivated species of *Oxalis.* 1. The caulescent species. Baileya 5:22–32.

108. Ingram, J. 1959. The cultivated species of *Oxalis.* 2. The acaulescent species. Baileya 8:11–22.

109. Ingram, J. 1961. Studies in the cultivated Boraginaceae. 5. *Symphytum.* Baileya 9:92–99.

110. Ingwersen, W. 1949. *The Dianthus: A Flower Monograph.* Collins, London. 128 p.

111. Irving, R.S. 1972. A revision of the genus *Poliomintha* (Labiatae). Sida 5:8–22.

112. Irving, R.S. 1980. The systematics of *Hedeoma* (Labiatae). Sida 8:218–295.

113. Ivimey-Cook, R.B. 1968. *Trigonella In* T.G. Tutin, V.H. Heywood, N.A. Burges, D.M. Moore, D.H. Valentine, S.M. Walters, and D.A. Webb, eds. *Flora Europaea,* Vol. 2. University Press, Cambridge. pp. 150–152.

114. Jalas, J. 1972. *Thymus. In* T.G. Tutin, V.H. Heywood, N.A. Burges, D.M. Moore, D.H. Valentine, S.M. Walters, and D.A. Webb, eds. *Flora Europaea,* Vol. 3 University Press, Cambridge. pp. 172–182.

115. Jones, A.G. 1979. A study of wild leek, and the recognition of *Allium burdickii* (Liliaceae). Syst. Bot. 4:29–43.

116. Jones, B.M.G. 1964. *Cardamine. In* T.G. Tutin, V.H. Heywood, N.A. Burges, D.H. Valentine, S.M. Walters, and D.A. Webb, eds. *Flora Europaea,* Vol. 1. University Press, Cambridge. pp. 285–289.

117. Jurenitsch, J., W. Kubelka, and K. Jentzsch. 1979. Identifizierung kultivierter *Capsicum*-Sippen. Pl. Med. 35:174–183.

118. Kalkman, C. 1965. The Old World species of *Prunus* subg. *Laurocerasus* including those formerly referred to *Pygeum.* Doct. thesis. Rijksuniversiteit, Leiden, Nl. 115 p.

119. Kartesz, J.T. and R. Kartesz. 1980. *A Synonymized Checklist of the Vascular Flora of the United States, Canada, and Greenland,* Vol. II. The biota of North America. University of North Carolina Press, Chapel Hill. 500 p.

120. Kay, Q.O.N. 1976. *Chamomilla. In* T.G. Tutin, V.H. Heywood, N.A. Burges, D.M. Moore, D.H. Valentine, S.M. Walters, and D.A. Webb, eds. *Flora Europaea,* Vol. 4. University Press, Cambridge. p. 167.

121. Keener, C.S. 1977. Studies in the Ranunculaceae of the southeastern United States, VI. Miscellaneous genera. Side 7:1–12.

122. Kiger, R.W. 1975. *Papaver* in North America north of Mexico. Rhodora 77:410–422.

123. Klášterský, I. 1968. *Rosa. In* T.G. Tutin, V.H. Heywood, N.A. Burges, D.M. Moore, D.H. Valentine, S.M. Walters, and D.A. Webb, eds. *Flora Europaea,* Vol. 2. University Press, Cambridge. pp. 25–32.

124. Krüssman, G. 1981. *The Complete Book of Roses.* Transl. G. Krüssman and N. Raban. Timber Press, Portland, OR. 436 p.

125. Lamberts, M. 1984. Classifications of herbs: Popular and scientific. HortScience 19:495.

126. Lawalrée, A. 1952. Le groupe de *Valeriana officinalis* L. en Belgique. Bull. Jard. Bot. Etat 22:193–200.

127. Lawrence. G.H.M. 1961. The name of the basil thyme, *Acinos arvensis.* Baileya 9:125.

128. Lawrence, G.H.M., A.F.G. Buchheim, G.S. Daniels, and H. Dolezal, eds. 1968. *B-P-H. Botanico-Periodicum-Huntianum.* Hunt Bot. Libr., Pittsburgh, PA 1063 p.

129. Liberty Hyde Bailey Hortorium, Staff of the. 1976. *Hortus Third.* Macmillan, New York, 1290 p.

130. Lint, H. and C. Epling. 1945. A revision of *Agastache.* Ameri. Midl. Naturalist 33:207–230.

131. McNeill, J., I.J. Bassett, C.W. Crompton, and P.M. Taschereau. 1983. Taxonomic and nomenclatural notes on *Atriplex* L. (Chenopodiaceae). Taxon 32:549–556.

132. Mathew, B. 1982. *The Crocus: A Revision of the Genus* Crocus *(Iridaceae. Timber Press, Portland, OR. 127 p.*

133. Mathias, M.E. and L. Constance. 1941. A synopsis of the North American species of *Eryngium.* Amer. Midl. Naturalist 25:361–387.

134. Meikle, R.D. 1976. *Calendula. In* T.G. Tutin, V.H. Heywood, N.A. Burges, D.M. Moore, D.H. Valentine, S.M. Walters, and D.A. Webb, eds. *Flora Europaea,* Vol. 4. University Press, Cambridge. pp. 206–207.

135. Merrill, E.D. 1937. *Coleus amboinicus.* Addisonia 20:11–12, pl. 646.

136. Merrill, E.D. 1938. Sugánda: An interesting aromatic herb. Herbarist 4:5–9.

137. Meusel, H. and H. Ohle. 1966. Zur Taxonomie and Cytologie der Gattung *Calendula* Oesterr. Bot. Z. 113:191–210.

138. Meyer, F.G. 1951. *Valeriana* in North America and the West Indies. (Valerianaceae). Ann. Missouri Bot. Gard. 38:377–503.

139. Moldenke, H.N. 1971. *A Fifth Summary of the Verbenaceae, Avicenniaceae, Stilbaceae, Dicrastylidaceae, Symphoremaceae, Nyctanthaceae, and Eriocaulaceae of the World as to Valid Taxa, Geographical Distribution, and Synonymy.* H.N. Moldenke, Wayne, NJ. 2 vols.

140. Moldenke, H.N. 1978. Additional notes on the genus *Lippia.* VII. Phytologia 39:78–106.

141. Moreton, C.O. 1955. *Old Carnations and Pinks.* George Rainbird, London. 51 p.

142. Morton, J.F. 1976. *Herbs and Spices.* Golden Press, New York. 160 p.

143. Morton, J.F. 1983. Rooibos tea, *Aspalathus linearis,* a caffeineless, low-tannin beverage. Econ. Bot. 37:164–173.

144. Morton, J.K. 1962. Cytotaxonomic studies on the West African Labiatae. J. Linn. Soc. Bot. 58:231–283.

145. Mowat, A.B. and S.M. Walters. 1964. *Papaver. In* T.G. Tutin, V.H. Heywood, N.A. Burges, D.H. Valentine, S.M. Walters, and D.A. Webb, eds. *Flora Europaea,* Vol. 1. University Press, Cambridge. pp. 247–251.

146. Mulligan, G.A. 1961. The genus *Lepidium* in Canada. Madroño 16:77–90.

147. Neher, R.T. 1966. Monograph of the genus *Tagetes* (Compositae). Ph.D. thesis. Indiana University, Bloomington, 306 p.

148. Ockendon, D.J. 1976. *Valeriana. In* T.G. Tutin, V.H. Heywood, N.A. Burges, D.M. Moore, D.H. Valentine, S.M. Walters, and D.A. Webb, eds. *Flora Europaea,* Vol. 4. University Press, Cambridge. pp. 52–55.

149. Ohwi, J. 1965. *Flora of Japan.* Smithsonian Institution, Washington, DC. 1067 p.

150. Papanikolaou, K. and S. Kokkini. 1982. A taxonomic revision of *Sideritis* L. section Empedoclia (Rafin.) Bentham (Labiatae) in Greece. *In* N. Margaris, A. Koedam, and D. Vokou, eds. *Aromatic Plants: Basic and Applied Aspects.* Martinus Nijhoff, The Hague. pp. 101–128.

151. Parry, J.W. 1969. *Spices.* Chemical Publishing Co., New York. 2 vols.

152. Pawlowski, B. 1972. *Symphytum. In* T.G. Tutin, V.H. Heywood, N.A. Burges, D.M. Moore, D.H. Valentine, S.M. Walters, and D.A. Webb, eds. *Flora Europaea.* Vol. 3. University Press, Cambridge. pp. 103–105.

153. Pedley, R. and K. Pedley. 1974. *Coleus: A Guide to Cultivation and Identification.* John Bartholomew and Son, Edinburgh. 116 p.

154. Persson, K. 1974. Biosystematic studies in the *Artemisia maritima* complex in Europe. Op. Bot. Vol. 35. 188 p.

155. Philcox, D. 1970. A taxonomic revision of the genus *Limnophila* R. Br. (Scrophulariaceae). Kew Bull. 24:101–170.

156. Prakash, S. and K. Hinata. 1980. Taxonomy, cytogenetics and origin of crop Brassicas, a review, Op. Bot. Vol. 55. 57 p.

157. Proctor, M.C.F. and G. Nordborg. 1968. *Sanguisorba. In* T.G. Tutin, V.H. Heywood, N.A. Burges, D.M. Moore, D.H. Valentine, S.M. Walters, and D.A. Webb, eds. *Flora Europaea,* Vol. 2 University Press, Cambridge. pp. 33–34.

158. Rechinger, K.H. 1964. *Rumex. In* T.G. Tutin, V.H. Heywood, N.A. Burges, D.H. Valentine, S.M. Walters, and D.A. Webb, eds. *Flora Europaea,* Vol. 1. University Press, Cambridge. pp. 82–89.

159. Rehder, A. 1949. *Bibliography of Cultivated Trees and Shrubs Hardy in the Cooler Temperate Regions of the Northern Hemisphere.* Arnold Arboretum, Jamaica Plan, MA. 825 p.

160. Rhodes, A.M., J.W. Courter, and M.C. Shurtleff. 1965. Identification of horseradish types. Trans. Illinois State Acad. Sci. 58:115–122.

161. Richards, A.J. and P.D. Sell. 1976. *Taraxacum. In* T.G. Tutin, V.H. Heywood, N.A. Burges, D.M. Moore, D.H. Valentine, S.M. Walters, and D.A. Webb, eds. *Flora Europaea,* Vol. 4. University Press, Cambridge, pp. 332–343.

162. Richardson, I.B.K. 1972. *Perilla. In* T.G. Tutin, V.H. Heywood, N.A. Burges, D.M. Moore, D.H. Valentine, S.M. Walters, and D.A. Webb, eds. *Flora Europaea,* Vol. 3. Unviersity Press, Cambridge. pp. 186–187.

163. Rousi, A. 1969. Cytogenetic comparison between two kinds of cultivated tarragon (*Artemisia dracunculus*) Hereditas 62:193–213.

164. Rozeira, A. 1949. A seccão *Stoechas* Gingens, do genero *Lavandula* Linn. Broteria 19:5–84.

165. Russell, N.H. 1965. Violets (*Viola*) of central and eastern United States: An introductory survey. Sida 2:1–113.

166. Sanders, R.W. 1979. A systematic study of *Agastache* section Brittonastrum (Lamiaceae, Nepeteae). Ph.D. thesis University of Texas, Austin. 281 p.

167. Scora, R.W. 1967. Interspecific relationships in the genus *Monarda* (Labiatae). University of California Publ. Bot. Vol. 41. 59 p.

168. Sell, P.D. 1976. *Cichorium. In* T.G. Tutin, V.H. Heywood, N.A. Burges, D.M. Moore, D.H. Valentine, S.M. Walters, and D.A. Webb, eds. *Flora Europaea.* Vol. 4. University Press, Cambridge. pp. 304–305.

169. Shih-Chen, L. 1973. *Chinese Medicinal Herbs.* Transl. F.P. Smith and G.A. Stuart. Georgetown Press, San Francisco, CA 508 p.

170. Shimizu, T. 1961. Taxonomical notes on the genus *Filipendula* Adans. (Rosaceae). J. Fac. Textile Sci & Technol. Shinshu Univ. 26A(10):1–31.

171. Shinners, L.H. 1962. *Calamintha* (Labiatae) in the southern United States. Sida 1:69–75.

172. Small, E. 1981. A numerical analysis of morpho-geographic groups of cultivars of *Humulus lupulus* based on samples of cones. Can. J. Bot. 59:311–324.

173. Smith, A.W. 1972. *A Gardener's Dictionary of Plant Names: A Handbook on the Origin and Meaning of Some Plant Names.* Rev. W.T. Stearn. St. Martin's Press, New York. 391 p.

174. Sorvig, K. 1983. The genus *Nigella.* Plantsman 4:229–235.

175. Spongberg, S.A. 1975. Lauraceae hardy in temperate North America. J. Arnold Arbor. 56:1–19.

176. Stafleu, F.A. and R.S. Cowan. 1976-1983. *Taxonomic Literature.* Bohn, Scheltema & Holkema, Utrecht. 4 vols.

177. Standley, P.C. 1924. *Piper. In* P.C. Standley, *Trees and Shrubs of Mexico.* Contr. U.S. Natl. Herb. Vol. 23. pp. 145–156, 1647.

178. Stearn, W.T. 1946. Notes on the genus *Allium* in the Old World: Its distribution names, literature, classification and garden-worthy species. Herbertia 11:11–34.

179. Stearn, W.T. 1980. *Allium. In* T.G. Tutin, V.H. Heywood, N.A. Burges, D.M. Moore, D.H. Valentine, S.M. Walters, and D.A. Webb, eds. *Flora Europaea,* Vol. 5. University Press, Cambridge. pp. 49–70.

180. Stearn, W.T. 1983. *Botanical Latin: History, Grammar, Syntax, Terminology and Vocabulary.* David & Charles, London, 566 p.

181. Steward, A.R. 1930. The Polygonaceae of eastern Asia. Contr. Gray Herb. Vol. 88. 129 p.

182. Stobart, T. 1970. *Herbs, Spices and Flavourings.* Penguin Books, Middlesex, England. 320 p.

183. Townsend, C.C. 1968. *Ruta. In* T.G. Tutin, V.H. Heywood, N.A. Burges, D.M. Moore, D.H. Valentine, S.M. Walters, and D.A. Webb, eds. *Flora Europaea,* Vol. 2. University Press, Cambridge. p. 227.

184. Tucker, A.O. 1981. Which is the true oregano? Horticulture 59(7):57–59.

185. Tucker, A.O., R.M. Harley, and D.E. Fairbrothers. 1980. The Linnaean types of *Mentha* (Lamiaceae). Taxon 29:233–255.

186. Tucker, A.O. and K.J.W. Hensen. 1985. The cultivars of lavander and lavandin (Labiatae). Baileya 22:168–177.

187. Tucker, A.O., M.J. Maciarello, and J.T. Howell. 1980. Botanical aspects of commercial sage. Econ. Bot. 34:16–19.

188. Turkington, R., N.C. Kenkel, and G.D. Franko. 1980. The biology of Canadian weeds. 42. *Stellaria media* (L.) Vill. Can. J. Pl. Sci. 60:981–992.

189. Turner, C. 1972. *Nepeta. In* T.G. Tutin, V.H. Heywood, N.A. Burges, D.M. Moore, D.H. Valentine, S.M. Walters, and D.A. Webb, eds. *Flora Europaea,* Vol. 3. University Press, Cambridge. pp. 158–160.

190. Turrill, E.B. 1920. The genus *Rosmarinus.* Bull. Misc. Inform. 1920:105–108.

191. Tutin, T.G. 1964. *Caltha. In* T.G. Tutin, V.H. Heywood, N.A. Burges, D.H. Valentine, S.M. Walters, and D.A. Webb, eds. *Flora Europaea,* Vol. 1. University Press, Cambridge. p. 211.

192. Tutin, T.G. 1964. *Dianthus. In* T.G. Tutin, V.H. Heywood, N.A. Burges, D.H. Valentine, S.M. Walters, and D.A. Webb, eds. *Flora Europaea,* Vol. 1. University Press, Cambridge, pp. 188–204.

193. Tutin, T.G. 1964. *Eruca. In* T.G. Tutin, V.H. Heywood, N.A. Burges, D.H. Valentine, S.M. Walters, and D.A. Webb, eds. *Flora Europaea,* Vol. 1. University Press, Cambridge. p. 340.

194. Tutin, T.G. 1964. *Nigella. In* T.G. Tutin, V.H. Heywood, N.A. Burges, D.H. Valentine, S.M. Walters, and D.A. Webb, eds. *Flora Europaea,* Vol. 1. University Press, Cambridge. pp. 209–210.

195. Tutin, T.G. 1968. *Anethum. In* T.G. Tutin, V.H. Heywood, N.A. Burges, D.M. Moore, D.H. Valentine, S.M. Walters, and D.A. Webb, eds. *Flora Europaea,* Vol. 2. University Press, Cambridge. pp. 341–342.

196. Tutin, T.G. 1968. *Carum. In* T.G. Tutin, V.H. Heywood, N.A. Burges, D.M. Moore, D.H. Valentine, S.M. Walters, and D.A. Webb, eds. *Flora Europaea,* Vol. 2. University Press, Cambridge. p. 354.

197. Tutin, T.G. 1968. *Coriandrum. In* T.G. Tutin, V.H. Heywood, N.A. Burges, D.M. Moore, D.H. Valentine, S.M. Walters, and D.A. Webb, eds. *Flora Europaea,* Vol. 2. University Press, Cambridge. p. 328.

198. Tutin, T.G. 1968. *Crithmum. In* T.G. Tutin, V.H. Heywood, N.A. Burges, D.M. Moore, D.H. Valentine, S.M. Walters, and D.A. Webb, eds. *Flora Europaea,* Vol. 2. University Press, Cambridge. p. 333.

199. Tutin, T.G. 1968. *Cuminum. In* T.G. Tutin, V.H. Heywood, N.A. Burges, D.M. Moore, D.H. Valentine, S.M. Walters, and D.A. Webb, eds. *Flora Europaea,* Vol. 2. University Press, Cambridge. p. 351.

200. Tutin, T.G. 1968. *Foeniculum. In* T.G. Tutin, V.H. Heywood, N.A. Burges, D.M. Moore, D.H. Valentine, S.M. Walters, and D.A. Webb, eds. *Flora Europaea,* Vol. 2. University Press, Cambridge. p. 341.

201. Tutin, T.G. 1968. *Levisticum. In* T.G. Tutin, V.H. Heywood, N.A. Burges, D.M. Moore, D.H. Valentine, S.M. Walters, and D.A. Webb, eds. *Flora Europaea,* Vol. 2. University Press, Cambridge. p. 358.

202. Tutin, T.G. 1968. *Ligusticum. In* T.G. Tutin, V.H. Heywood, N.A. Burges, D.M. Moore, D.H. Valentine, S.M. Walters, and D.A. Webb, eds. *Flora Europaea,* Vol. 2. University Press, Cambridge. p. 356.

203. Tutin, T.G. 1968. *Petroselinum. In* T.G. Tutin, V.H. Heywood, N.A. Burges, D.M. Moore, D.H. Valentine, S.M. Walters, and D.A. Webb, eds. *Flora Europaea,* Vol. 2. University Press, Cambridge. p. 352.

204. Tutin, T.G. 1968. *Pimpinella. In* T.G. Tutin, V.H. Heywood, N.A. Burges, D.M. Moore, D.H. Valentine, S.M. Walters, and D.A. Webb, eds. *Flora Europaea,* Vol. 2. University Press, Cambridge. pp. 331–333.

205. Tutin, T.G. 1976. *Chamaemelum. In* T.G. Tutin, V.H. Heywood, N.A. Burges, D.M. Moore, D.H. Valentine, S.M. Walters, and D.A. Webb, eds. *Flora Europaea,* Vol. 4, University Press, Cambridge. p. 165.

206. Tutin, T.G., V.H. Heywood, N.A. Burges, D.M. Moore, D.H. Valentine, S.M. Walters, and D.A. Webb, eds. 1964–1980. *Flora Europaea,* University Press, Cambridge. 5 vols.

207. Tutin, T.G., K. Persson, and W. Gutermann. 1976. *Artemsia. In* T.G. Tutin, V.H. Heywood, N.A. Burges, D.M. Moore, D.H. Valentine, S.M. Walters, and D.A. Webb, eds. *Flora Europaea,* Vol. 4. University Press, Cambridge, pp. 178–186.

208. Tyner, G.E. 1974. The dispersal of culinary herbs in relation to the contemporary California herb industry. Ph.D. thesis. University of California, Los Angeles. 164 p.

209. United States Department of Agriculture. 1982. National List of Scientific Plant Names. Soil Conservation Service SCS-TP-159. 2 vols.

210. Uphof, J.C.T. 1968. *Dictionary of Economic Plants.* 2d ed. J. Cramer. 591 p.

211. Valentine, D.H. 1964. *Nasturtium. In* T.G. Tutin, V.H. Heywood, N.A. Burges, D.H. Valentine, S.M. Walters, and D.A. Webb, eds. *Flora Europaea,* Vol. 1. University Press, Cambridge. pp. 284–285.

212. Valentine, D.H., H. Merxmüller, and A. Schmidt. 1968. *Viola. In* T.G. Tutin, V.H. Heywood, N.A. Burges, D.M. Moore, D.H. Valentine, S.M. Walters, and D.A. Webb, eds. *Flora Europaea,* Vol. 2. University Press, Cambridge. pp. 270–282.

213. Vaughan, J.G. 1977. A multidisciplinary study of the taxonomy and origin of *Brassica* crops. BioScience 27:35–40.

214. Voss, E.G., ed. 1983. *International Code of Botanical Nomenclature.* Bohn, Scheltema & Holkema, Utrecht. 472 p.

215. Ware, D.M.W. 1983. Genetic fruit polymorphism in North American *Valerianella* (Valerianaceae) and its taxonomic implications. Syst. Bot. 8:33–44.

216. Waterman, P.G. 1975. New combinations in *Zanthoxylum* L. (1753). Taxon 24:361–366.

217. Webb, D.A. 1968. *Prunus. In* T.G. Tutin, V.H. Heywood, N.A. Burges, D.M. Moore, D.H. Valentine, S.M. Walters, and D.A. Webb, eds. *Flora Europaea,* Vol. 2. University Press, Cambridge. pp. 77–80.

218. Webb, D.A. and A.O. Chater. 1964. *Polygonum. IN* T.G. Tutin, V.H. Heywood, N.A. Burges, D.H. Valentine, S.M. Walters, and D.A. Webb, eds. *Flora Europaea,* Vol. 1. University Press, Cambridge. pp. 76–80.

219. Wilde-Dufjes, B.E.E. de. 1973. Typification of 23 *Allium* species described by Linnaeus and possibly occurring in Africa. Taxon 22:57–91.

220. Xifreda, C.C. 1983. Sobre oreganos cultivados en Argentina. Kurtziana 16:133–148.

221. Yashiroda, K. 1968. Japanese herbs and their uses. Pl. & Gard. Vol. 24, No. 2. 72 p.

222. Young, D.P. 1968. *Oxalis. In* T.G. Tutin, V.H. Heywood, N.A. Burges, D.M. Moore, D.H. Valentine, S.M. Walters, and D.A. Webb, eds. *Flora Europaea,* Vol. 2. University Press, Cambridge. pp. 192–193.

Biochemistry of Monoterpenes and Sesquiterpenes of the Essential Oils

Rodney Croteau
Institute of Biological Chemistry, Washington State University, Pullman, WA 99164

CONTENTS

I. INTRODUCTION

The most frequently used method for isolating fragrant plant principles is steam distillation, which yields the essential oils or essences. Various extractive techniques are employed to isolate odorous plant substances in the form of tinctures, infusions, concretes, and related resinoids, the volatile fractions of which are similar to essential oils in containing, as major constituents, low molecular weight aliphatics, benzenoids, and terpenoids. The most characteristic, diverse, and perhaps the most economically significant (106, 193) group of compounds present in these products is the C_{10} (mono-) and C_{15} (sesqui-) terpenoids, whose origin and fate are the subject of this review.

The monoterpenes, of which several hundred individual compounds in this group are known, comprise some 30 basic carbon skeletons, while the sesquiterpenes, of which many thousand individuals have been described, are divided into approximately 200 skeletal types (99, 100, 120, 137). Although production of monoterpenoid and sesquiterpenoid substances is not restricted to higher plants, most of the common structural representatives are produced by them (126). The latter observation is not so surprising when one considers that these 2 groups of natural products are synthesized and accumulated by over 50 plant families, from the Pinaceae to the Orchidaceae and from the Ranunculaceae to the Asteraceae and Lamiaceae (119, 129). Perhaps more surprising, considering the formidable synthetic talents of higher plants and the evolutionary time scale for development, is that all of the biogenetically feasible skeletal arrangements have not yet been encountered (201).

Comprehensive treatment of monoterpene and sesquiterpene biochemistry is well beyond the scope of this article's focus (essential oils, i.e., the classical steam-volatile terpenoids). Thus, neither the cyclopentanoid monoterpene glycosides nor the sesquiterpene lactones and other more complex oxygenated derivatives are covered here, in spite of the fact that our present concepts of sesquiterpene biochemistry are based largely on studies of these latter metabolites (42). Rather, a general overview of key features of the metabolism of monoterpene and sesquiterpene olefins and their simple oxygenated relatives is provided, with a focus on comparative aspects using selected examples for illustration. More comprehensive treatment of the subject is available in recent reviews (42, 55, 60, 66, 67), and the field is surveyed periodically (187).

II. SITES OF SYNTHESIS

The accumulation or secretion of monoterpenes and sesquiterpenes has been observed in every plant organ and is virtually always associated with the presence of well-defined secretory structures such as oil cells, glandular trichomes (Figure 1), oil or resin ducts, or glandular epidermis (157). Although varying enormously in gross morphology and fine structure (108, 194), a common feature of these secretory structures is an extracytoplasmic (often extracellular) cavity in which the relatively toxic terpenoid oils and resins appear to be sequestered. This anatomic feature distinguishes the "essential oil plants" (118, 196) from others in which terpenes are produced as trace constituents that either volatilize inconspicuously or are rapidly metabolized.

Numerous studies employing microanalytical techniques (3, 133, 135, 195, 215) have confirmed earlier microscopic evidence (1, 2,

Figure 1. Scanning electron micrograph of the dorsal surface of a sage (*Salvia officinalis*) leaf. The ontogenic sequence from capitate sessile glands with one (A), 2 (B), and 4 (C) secretory cells to the peltate gland with 8 secretory cells and greatly enlarged oil-filled cavity (D) is illustrated. The diameter of the mature peltate gland is about 0.06 mm. Also visible in the field is a stalked capitate gland with a single terminal secretory cell (E).

125, 217) that the secretory structures do, in fact, contain the monoterpenes and sesquiterpenes characteristic of the plant, and there is little doubt that such structures represent the major sites of terpene accumulation. Several lines of evidence indicate that the secretory structures are also the primary site of mono- and sesquiterpene biosynthesis. Thus, isolated leaf epidermis from *Marjorana hortensis* Moench (containing intact glandular trichomes) possesses the same ability to convert [U-^{14}C] sucrose to constituent monoterpenes as the intact leaf, while the isolated mesophyll layer is inactive in synthesizing monoterpenes from the same precursor (64). Glandular trichomes are capable of incorporating basic precursors such as labeled acetate and mevalonate into their constituent terpenoids (98, 158, 163, 217), demonstrating that the requisite biosynthetic capability is present in such structures. A similar argument (121) has been made regarding the biosynthetic capability of the epithelial cells (a specialized type of parenchyma) lining conifer resin ducts or cavities into which the terpenes are eventually deposited. The levels of incorporation of exogenous precursors into the monoterpenes and sesquiterpenes of most tissues are rather low, relative to other terpenoid classes (for example, triterpenes) (89, 169), indicating that the sites of synthesis of these lower terpene classes are compartmentalized and not as accessible as more "primary" biosynthetic processes. The morphology of many types of secretory structures does suggest a degree of isolation from the rest of the plant. The glandular epidermis of certain flowers is a conspicuous exception (158) and, in this case, very high rates of incorporation of exogenous precursors have been observed (114).

In certain instances, monoterpene and sesquiterpene synthesis is associated with different gland types such as the exocarp and endocarp glands, respectively, of *Poncirus trifoliata* L. fruit (134). Certain cell types may also exhibit such specialization, as in maritime pine, where monoterpene biosynthesis is restricted to immature epithelial cells of the resin ducts at the base of the needle, while sesquiterpene production takes place independent of cell age or location (29). In many other cases in which mono- and sesquiterpenes both occur in the glandular secretory cavity and where a similar locale of origin must be presumed, the evidence indicates that the sites of mono- and sesquiterpene biosynthesis are discrete, differing in their relative accessibility to exogenous precursors. Thus, incorporation of radioactive sugars and CO_2 into volatile terpenes of peppermint results in far greater labeling of monoterpenes than sesquiterpenes; the ratio is about 20:1, reflecting the approximate natural proportion of mono- and sesquiterpenes in the plant (69). Conversely, exogenous mevalonate is a far more efficient precursor of sesquiterpenes than of monoterpenes in this tissue (about 0.33 percent incorporation versus approximately 0.03 percent incorporation into monoterpenes) (88). Differential labeling of this type has been observed in other species (15, 158, 185) and is probably a general phenomenon. Thus, while the various secretory structures may be safely regarded as the primary sites of terpene biosynthesis and accumulation and the principal physical basis for certain compartmentalization phenomena, it is also clear that multiple types of biosynthetic sites exist among and within the secretory cells of these structures.

For most secretory organs, where the terpenoid substances are synthesized or in what manner they leave the protoplast is not exactly known (212). Based on evidence provided in an earlier review (158) and supported in general by subsequent studies (132), plant oil glands can be divided into 2 basic developmental types: one characterized by a highly developed endoplasmic reticulum and few plastids and the other by an abundance of plastids in the secretory cells. The endoplasmic reticulum-type cells may originate from the epidermis and the plastid-type secretory cells from the mesophyll. The possible roles of the ground plasm, endoplasmic reticulum, and plastids in terpenoid synthesis and secretion have been described (158). The secretory cells of resin ducts may represent a combination of the above types, and recent indirect evidence from studies with maritime pine (*Pinus pinaster* Ait.) suggests that monoterpene biosynthesis in the epithelial cells is associated with plastids (leucoplasts) while the elaboration of sesquiterpenes is associated with the endoplasmic reticulum (30).

Regardless of cell type, the terpenoid constituents first appear in cytoplasmic vacuoles and are transported in this vesicular form by a process generally termed "granular secretion" (108). The secretory process has been examined in most detail in resin duct systems (82) but whether the cell membrane envelops the oil droplet before release (51) or if a form of exocytosis (reverse pinocytosis) of the oil-filled vacuole occurs (28, 109) is not yet clear even here. An interesting feature of many secretory tissues is the presence of specialized cells at the interface where the secretory tissue borders ordinary tissue, such as the endodermis-like cells at the base of many secretory trichomes (1, 2, 34, 221). These cells have heavily cutinized or suberized lateral walls, to which the cytoplasm adheres, and presumably function during development as supporting structures and in allowing transport only through the symplast and preventing reverse-flow of secreted material via the apoplast.

The biosynthesis of terpenoids in glandular trichomes of herbaceous plants and resin canals of woody species has been the general subject of recent reviews (81, 82). An earlier review, emphasizing primarily *in vivo* studies, remains the only existing attempt to integrate the physiological and morphological aspects of lower terpene production (158).

III. BIOLOGICAL FUNCTION

The monoterpenes and sesquiterpenes traditionally have been regarded as functionless "metabolic waste products" (166, 172, 192), yet research over the years has indicated that these compounds can play rather varied and important roles in mediating the interactions of plants with their environments. The monoterpenes 1,8-cineol and camphor have been shown to inhibit the germination and growth of competitors and thus may act as allelopathic agents (144). There appear to be 2 basic types of plant-animal interactions: (1) attraction of animals that serve in pollination and as agents of seed dispersal (33, 151) and (2) defense mechanisms against phytophagous animals. Numerous lower terpenoid repellants and feeding deterrents to insects (154, 155, 164) as well as other herbivores (35, 110, 145) have been described. The involvement of Pinaceae monoterpenes in the preformed defense system and the induced response to attack by bark beetle-fungal complexes is well-known (31, 32, 52, 82, 199), as are a large number of sesquiterpenoid phytoalexins which accumulate as a consequence of infection or other stress (150, 204).

The lower terpenoids appear well-suited for such diverse ecological purposes. Volatility provides mobility, imparting the ability to influence another organism at some distance from the source plant. Complexity of composition and stereochemistry of the constituents confers the ability to communicate a selective biological message. A lipophilic nature allows for some persistence in the largely aqueous biosphere, while unusual structural features, such as cyclopropyl and furan groups, promote a degree of biological stability, with possible toxic consequences for other life forms. The highly specific location of terpenoids maintains these substances in concentrated form undiluted by distribution throughout the plant, and when sequestered in surface structures, such as glandular epidermis, ensures the necessary exposure to the atmosphere.

In most instances, ecological interactions are mediated by an individual terpenoid or simple mixture, and bulk physical properties of these compounds appear less critical [with the possible exceptions of the conifer wound response (82) and in the reduction of leaf transpiration and increased radiation reflectance (97)]. With the enormous number of compounds now known, to seek a role for every mono- and sesquiterpene produced in the plant kingdom seems unrealistic. As a class, however, the mono- and sesquiterpenes would appear, on the basis of the few examples cited here, to impart significant survival value to the plant. Adaptational interactions are quite complex, yet subtle and easily overlooked. Perhaps the time has come to discard the term "secondary compounds" in referring to the mono- and sesquiterpenes. "Natural products" is more suitable, avoiding a connotation of lesser value to the producing organism.

Although the role of lower terpenes as agents of chemical defense and communication by plants is gaining wide acceptance, no function for these compounds within the plant is obvious, and their sequestration in specialized glandular structures would seem to argue that no physiological function is likely. This classical perception of lower terpenoids as inert waste products permits a simple rationale for the diversity of terpenoid structures; i.e., the absence of a specific metabolic or physiological role allows random structural changes to occur with no disadvantage resulting to the plant. However, considerable evidence has demonstrated that monoterpenes and sesquiterpenes are by no means inert but are both rapidly synthesized and catabolized.

IV. GENERAL BIOCHEMICAL CONSIDERATIONS AND HYPOTHESES

The mono- and sesquiterpenes of the essential oils are most often cyclic, contain relatively few simple functional groups (such as hydroxyls, carbonyls, and double bonds), and commonly represent variations on a limited number of skeletal themes. As would be expected, the monoterpenes and sesquiterpenes exhibit a number of similar physical and chemical properties. The boiling point range increases with size and degree of functionality, accounting for the presence of monoterpenes and simple sesquiterpenes in the essential oils, and polyoxygenated sesquiterpenes and diterpenes in the nonvolatile fraction of resins. The monoterpenes (C_{10}) and sesquiterpenes (C_{15}) are but 2 groups of the isoprenoid family of compounds constructed in multiples of the branched C_5 (isoprene) unit and ranging in size from the "monomer" isoprene (considered a hemiterpene) to the high polymer rubber (molecular weight $\sim 10^6$). Early workers, notably Wallach (219), proposed that terpenoids could be hypothetically constructed by sequential condensations of isoprene (isopentane) units in a head-to-tail pattern (Figure 2), providing a degree of classification and the system of nomenclature in use today.

Even the small sampling of cyclohexanoid monoterpenes illustrated in Figure 3 makes it clear that the vast majority represent a relatively small number of skeletal themes multiplied by a range of simple derivatives, positional isomerism, and stereochemical variants. Representative sesquiterpenes of the essential oils are illustrated in Figure 4.

The first comprehensive proposal to rationalize the origin of the major structural types of monoterpenes was the "Biogenetic Isoprene Rule" formulated by Ruzicka in 1953 (189). This scheme, which focuses on cyclization processes without reference to the precise character of the acyclic biological precursor, is outlined in Figure 5. The essential features of this hypothesis (189) are the electrophilic attack by C-1 on the distal double bond to generate a monocyclic intermediate, which may undergo, via the cationic center, subsequent internal additions at the remaining double bond, hydride shifts, and Wagner-Meerwein rearrangements, thereby providing reasonable routes to most of the structural types encountered in nature. Termination of the cyclization reactions can be envisioned to involve transformation of the carbocation intermediates by proton loss, to yield the corresponding olefin, or by addition of a nucleophile (such as H_2O) to provide an alcohol of the corresponding skeletal type. Further modification of the parent cyclic compounds (via oxidation, reduction,

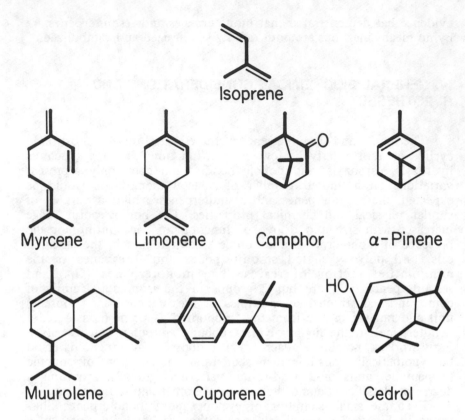

Figure 2. Some monoterpenes and sesquiterpenes and their division into isoprene units in a head-to-tail pattern.

isomerization, hydration, conjugation, and additional reactions) could thus lead to the vast array of individual monoterpenes.

The basic scheme for the cyclization to the various sesquiterpene skeleta is identical in concept but starts with a C_{15} (farnesyl) ion as precursor and includes the proviso that initial ring closure can involve attack at either the central or distal double bond (Figure 6). This and the above schemes have undergone refinement and extension over the years primarily by including additional skeletal types (58, 173) and with the modification that the acyclic precursor be the corresponding pyrophosphate ester (157, 214) derived more or less directly from mevalonic acid, the basic progenitor of all isoprenoids (203). The precise nature of cyclization intermediates in monoterpene and sesquiterpene biosynthesis has been the center of some controversy; however, this question is now essentially resolved.

Early attempts to deduce modes of cyclization and biosynthetic pathways were based largely on indirect approaches (such as struc-

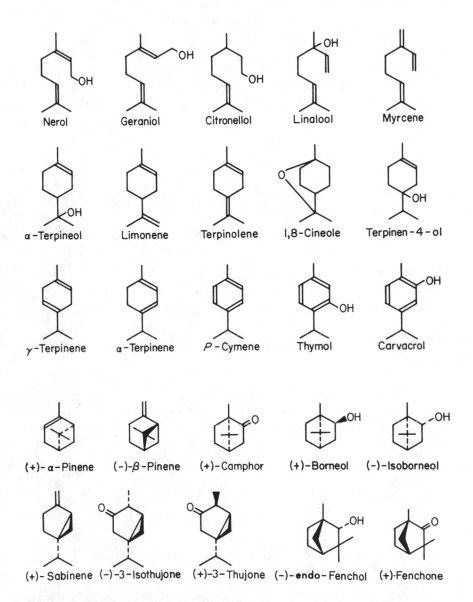

Figure 3. Representative monoterpenes.

tural and stereochemical correlations of co-occurring metabolites) and were followed by *in vivo* tracer studies using fundamental precursors such as acetate and mevalonate to determine labeling patterns and probable pathways based on time-course sequences. The latter approach proved to be unexpectedly difficult in practice because of

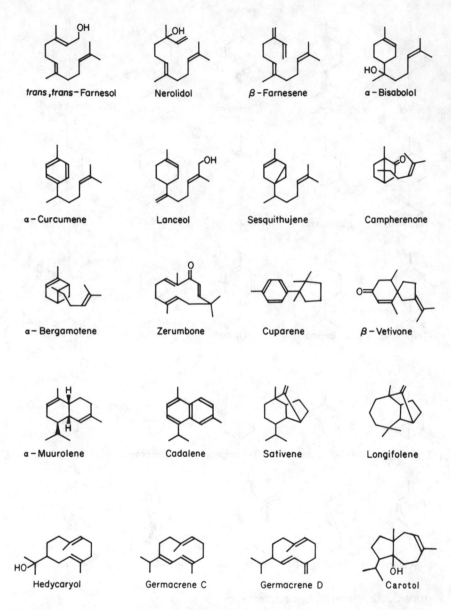

Figure 4. Representative sesquiterpenes.

frequently low and nonspecific incorporations resulting from compartmentalization effects (158). The methodology and limitations of such *in vivo* tracer studies have been described and a critical appraisal of this early work provided (12, 55, 60, 130). Current studies in this area have focused on biogenetic information gained from nuclear

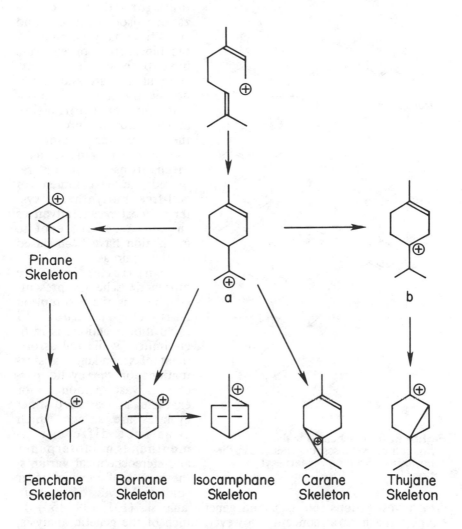

Figure 5. Ionic scheme for the formation of cyclic monoterpenes via the α-terpinyl cation (a) and the terpinen-4-yl cation (b).

magnetic resonance analysis of [13]C- and [2]H-labeled products generated from primary precursors (200, 205). Although this technique has, in many instances, superseded the more cumbersome use of ^{3}H/^{14}C double-labeled substrates followed by chemical degradation, the method has limitations and often suffers from the necessity of feeding simple precursors that may be too remote from the end-product analyzed to permit unambiguous conclusions (11, 46).

In spite of the shortcomings, and to the degree that tests have been made by labeling experiments with basic precursors such as

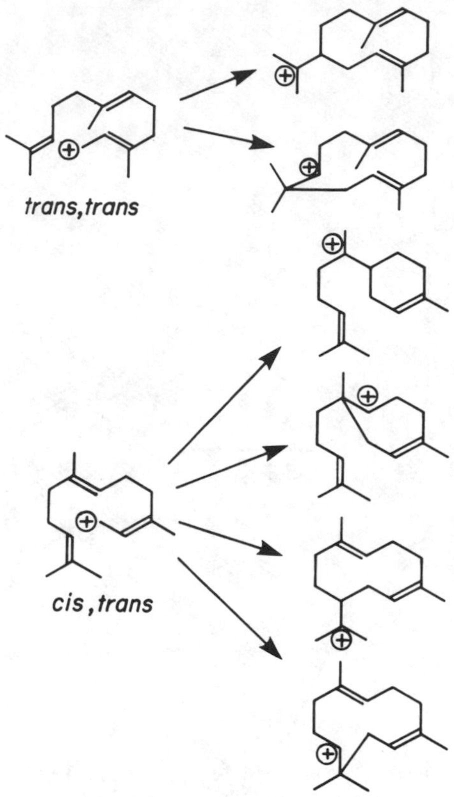

Figure 6. Ionic scheme for the formation of cyclic sesquiterpenes via the *trans, trans-* and *cis,trans-*farnesyl cations.

mevalonate, the cyclizations, isomerizations, and ring fissions predicted by the biogenetic isoprene rule have been confirmed. Exceptions are rare and of minor significance (15). To obtain further information about cyclization precursors, the number and nature of cyclase enzymes, and mechanisms of action required the development of cell-free biosynthetic systems. Most recent advances in the area of terpene cyclization have been based on this approach.

Implicit in the biogenetic schemes presented above is the assumption that the number of cyclization reactions is rather limited, while the assortment of secondary transformations of the cyclic parents is vast. Although, for example, at least 6 distinct cyclases are known which construct different *p*-menthane monoterpenes and stereochemical variants, the results of *in vivo* tracer studies (12, 42, 55, 60), *in vitro* investigations (66, 67), and genetic analyses (131, 139, 153) do support the general concept. However, much of the genetic analysis, while of great value in examining inheritance and relatedness, is sometimes flawed by accompanying biogenetic speculation drawn all too often without regard to the chemical plausibility and mechanistic feasibility of the proposed pathways.

V. EARLY BIOSYNTHETIC STEPS AND ACYCLIC PRECURSORS

All plants employ the general isoprenoid pathway in the synthesis of certain essential substances including phytol (C_{20}), carotenoids

(C_{40}), dolichol phosphate (C_{100}), steroids (C_{27}), prenylated quinones (plastoquinone), and plant hormones such as abscisic acid (C_{15}) and gibberellins (C_{20}). The mono- and sesquiterpenes are regarded as diverging at the C_{10} and C_{15} stages, respectively. This now well-known pathway begins with the condensation of 3 acetyl-CoA, in 2 steps, to form hydroxymethylglutaryl CoA, which is reduced to mevalonic acid, the committed precursor of all isoprenoids (Figure 7). A series of phosphorylations and decarboxylation with the elimination of the

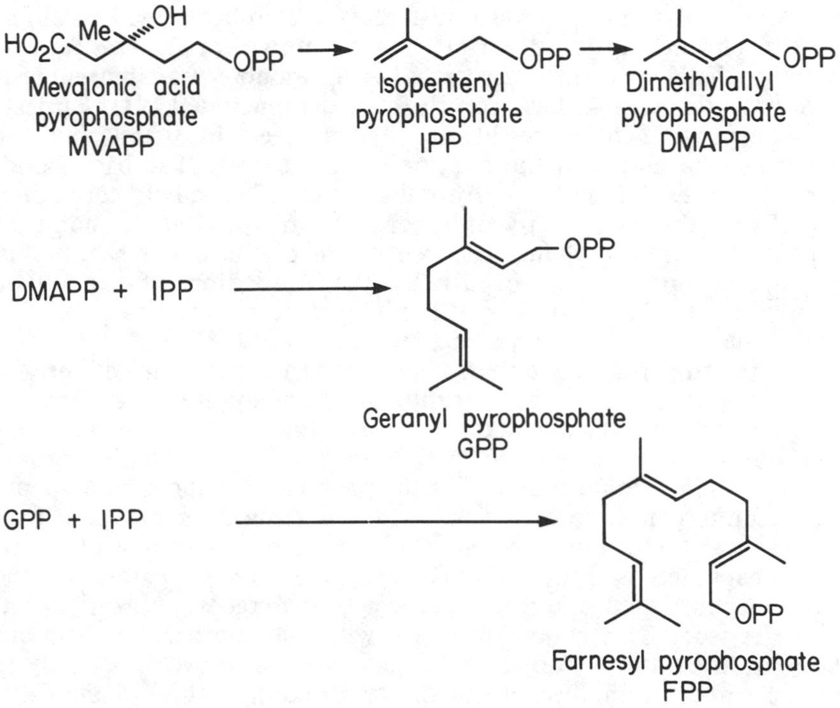

Figure 7. Outline of the early steps of the isoprenoid pathway leading from mevalonic acid pyrophosphate to the acyclic precursors of monoterpenes and sesquiterpenes.

C-3 oxygen function (as phosphate) yields isopentenyl pyrophosphate, the basic 5 carbon-containing isoprenoid condensing unit. While the details of the pathway have been worked out largely with microbial and animal systems (168, 184), each step has been demonstrated in plants and the general scheme described in the context of isoprenoid metabolism in these organisms (11, 159). The enzyme hydroxymethylglutaryl CoA reductase, which catalyzes the synthesis of mevalonate, has received considerable attention (101, 222) and is regarded as a key regulatory enzyme in terpenoid metabolism.

Isopentenyl pyrophosphate is isomerized to dimethylallyl pyrophosphate (183), the first allylic (prenyl) pyrophosphate of the pathway, which, with isopentenyl pyrophosphate as cosubstrate, condenses to yield the 10 carbon-containing intermediate, geranyl pyrophosphate (Figure 7). Another elongation cycle involving the addition of isopentenyl pyrophosphate forms the 15 carbon-containing intermediate, farnesyl pyrophosphate; the process thus continues to produce a series of homologous prenyl pyrophosphates differing in the number of isoprenoid units. The chain-lengthening steps are catalyzed by prenyl transferases, a number of which, differing in chain-length specificity, are known (183). A geranyl pyrophosphate synthetase associated with monoterpene biosynthesis in *Salvia officinalis* L. has recently been demonstrated (91). Farnesyl pyrophosphate synthetase has been examined in detail and the mechanism of action of the enzyme explored (183). The basic bond-forming process involves electrophilic attack of an allylic carbonium ion (from the prenyl pyrophosphate) on the double bond of isopentenyl pyrophosphate. The generation of the positive center in this alkylation reaction occurs by the ionization of the allylic pyrophosphate (183), a means of initiating carbon-carbon bond formation characteristic of terpenoid biochemistry (41).

With the realization of the fundamental role of prenyl pyrophosphates such as geranyl pyrophosphate and farnesyl pyrophosphate in the metabolism of essentially all isoprenoid compounds, it was natural to conclude that C_{10} and C_{15} prenyl pyrophosphates would function as the precursors of the monoterpenes and sesquiterpenes, respectively, a concept entirely compatible with hypothetical cyclization schemes. Although the central role of prenyl pyrophosphates is generally accepted, the precise nature of the pyrophosphorylated intermediate which undergoes cyclization has been at issue. The major difficulty with monoterpene cyclizations stems from geranyl pyrophosphate being unable to cyclize directly to the 6-membered ring because of the *trans-* configuration of the C-2 - C-3 double bond. For this reason, the earlier cyclization scheme (Figure 5) was formulated with the *cis* (neryl) cation as the acyclic precursor. Similarly, more recent proposals for monoterpene cyclizations have ascribed a key role as the acyclic precursor to neryl pyrophosphate (55, 157, 214) or to linalyl pyrophosphate (7) as there is no geometric obstruction in the cyclization of this tertiary isomer (structures of nerol and linalool are presented in Figure 3). However, numerous studies with partially purified enzymes have now proven that geranyl pyrophosphate is efficiently cyclized without formation of free intermediates such as neryl or linalyl pyrophosphate (61, 66).

Clearly, the monoterpene cyclases are capable of catalyzing both the required isomerization to a bound intermediate competent to cyclize and the cyclization reaction itself. The enzyme-bound intermediate is presumed to be the tertiary (linalyl) isomer. No compelling evidence exists for either free linalyl pyrophosphate or free neryl pyrophosphate as an obligate precursor of cyclic monoterpenes in any instance, and much of the earlier work supportive of such a role has been criticized (16, 55). Additionally, proposals for the direct formation of neryl pyrophosphate and linalyl pyrophosphate by direct coupling of C$_5$ units (8, 140) or for redox schemes for the *trans*-to-*cis* isomerization of geranyl pyrophosphate (17, 19, 55) either lack reliable evidence (37, 62, 66) or have been disproven (73, 208). A detailed summary of the arguments can be found elsewhere (67).

An identical steric impediment is encountered in the cyclization of *trans,trans*-farnesyl pyrophosphate to sesquiterpenes containing 6-member rings. Such cyclizations involving the central double bond are believed to occur by a mechanism completely analogous to that mediated by the monoterpene cyclases, with prior isomerization of the *trans*-allylic pyrophosphate most likely involving the corresponding tertiary allylic (nerolidyl) isomer (Figure 4) (5, 41, 42, 43, 44, 70). An isomerase which catalyzes the conversion of *trans,trans*-farnesyl pyrophosphate to nerolidyl pyrophosphate has, in fact, been demonstrated in extracts of the fungus *Gibberella fujikuroi* and the mechanism of this allylic transposition reaction studied in detail (45). Yet, the involvement of free nerolidyl pyrophosphate as an obligate intermediate in sesquiterpene cyclizations has not been explicitly demonstrated, and the possible intermediacy of *cis,trans*-farnesyl pyrophosphate in cyclization processes has not been rigorously defined experimentally. Proposals for redox-type *trans*-to-*cis* isomerization of the acyclic precursor (107, 171) have likewise been ruled out in the sesquiterpene series (4, 41, 48). The summary of the evidence, therefore, strongly suggests that monoterpenes and sesquiterpenes are derived, more or less directly, from the cyclization of one of the 2 normal acyclic isoprenoid precursors: geranyl pyrophosphate or farnesyl pyrophosphate (70).

The origin of the small group of acyclic monoterpenes and sesquiterpenes from their respective pyrophosphorylated precursors has received little experimental attention (42, 66), and the hydrolysis, dehydration, and redox processes involved are straightforward reactions. The origin of linalool, however, is of considerable interest in the context of monoterpene cyclization processes. Studies on the biosynthesis of linalool in *Cinnamomum camphora* Sieb. indicate that the allylic transposition reaction in the formation of linalyl pyrophosphate from geranyl pyrophosphate proceeds with exclusive syn stereochemistry (127, 207). The previously discussed farnesyl to nerolidyl rearrangement also takes place by a net suprafacial process (45). The proposed involvement of acyclic mono- and sesquiterpene olefins in the formation of cyclic compounds in *Pinus pinaster* (122, 123) has received no experimental support from studies with other biosynthetic systems.

VI. CYCLIZATION REACTIONS

The cyclization steps are at the core of mono- and sesquiterpene biosynthesis, determining the basic structural character of the terpenes a given organism is capable of producing. Thus, not surprisingly, cyclization processes have been a major focus of research. The key cyclization reactions, through which the parent monoterpene and sesquiterpene carbon skeletons are generated, are catalyzed by enzymes collectively known as cyclases. Multiple cyclases, each producing a different skeletal arrangement from the same acyclic precursor, often occur in higher plants, while single cyclases that synthesize a variety of related skeletal types are also known (84, 87, 116). Individual cyclases, each generating a simple derivative or positional isomer of the same skeletal type, have been described, as have distinct cyclases catalyzing the synthesis of enantiomeric products (67). The number of monoterpene and sesquiterpene cyclases in nature is presently uncertain, yet studies on the known examples from a limited number of plants and microorganisms (42, 66) suggest that the total is at least 200 to 300.

Cyclases, with the apparently rare exception of those isolated from certain conifers (30, 83), are operationally soluble enzymes possessing molecular weights in the 50,000 to 100,000 range. Based on relatively few examples from higher plant sources (116, 178), the cyclases appear to be rather hydrophobic, to possess relatively low pI values, and to operate optimally in the pH 6-7 range. The only cofactor required is a divalent metal ion, with $Mg^{2}+$ or $Mn^{2}+$ generally being preferred (61, 66, 186). Studies on the inhibition of cyclization reactions have been carried out with, for example, thiol-directed reagents, but results bearing on mechanistic features have been inconclusive (63, 66, 67).

All monoterpene cyclases can utilize geranyl pyrophosphate, and most can also utilize neryl pyrophosphate and linalyl pyrophosphate as acyclic precursors. Cyclization is accomplished without detectable interconversion among these 3 substrates or preliminary conversion to other free intermediates (61, 62, 66, 67). Assessment of the relative efficiency of cyclization of these isomeric allylic pyrophosphates is often hindered by the presence of competing phosphohydrolases, and the dangers in interpreting results obtained under such conditions have been described repeatedly (13, 61, 67, 87). Conclusions based on data in which this complication was ignored may be erroneous (206, 209, 210). In preparations of (+)-bornyl pyrophosphate cyclase from which phosphatases were removed, geranyl pyrophosphate was shown to be a more efficient substrate than neryl pyrophosphate, based on comparison of the V/Km ratios for each substrate (87). In pinene cyclase preparations, where corrections were made for substrate loss due to competing phosphatases, kinetic constants for the 3 acyclic precursors were roughly equivalent (116). Michaelis constants for all

3 substrates with all known cyclases are in the 1-20 μM range. Considerably less is known about sesquiterpene cyclases than monoterpene cyclases, since relatively few of the former enzymes have been examined in detail. The isolation, purification, and properties of a number of monoterpene and sesquiterpene cyclases have been described elsewhere (70).

The mechanism of cyclization of geranyl pyrophosphate is considered to involve initial ionization of the pyrophosphate moiety, in which the divalent cation is presumed to assist (218), followed by isomerization to a linalyl intermediate (linalyl pyrophosphate, the corresponding ion pair, or other bound equivalent), with rotation about the C-2 - C-3 single bond and subsequent cyclization of the cisoid conformer (41, 61, 66, 70). The proposed mechanism, which is completely consistent with the results of numerous model studies of terpenoid cyclizations (26, 128, 162, 181, 182) and with all evidence to date from studies on the cyclases, readily accounts for the direct cyclization of both linalyl pyrophosphate and the *cis*-isomer, neryl pyrophosphate. However, whether these latter acyclic precursors are, in fact, true enzyme-bound intermediates of the cyclization process or simply efficient substrate analogs is unclear.

A similar mechanistic scheme, consistent with model studies (5, 58, 152), can be applied to the cyclization of *trans,trans*-farnesyl pyrophosphate to any of the approximately 200 known sesquiterpene skeleta, with the additional variable that intramolecular electrophilic attack of the initially generated allylic cation may be directed toward either the central or distal double bond of the farnesyl chain. Formation of 6-membered rings is believed to occur by a mechanism completely analogous to that mediated by the monoterpene cyclases, with prior isomerization of the *trans*-allylic pyrophosphate most likely involving the corresponding tertiary allylic (nerolidyl) isomer (41, 45). Formation of 10- or 11-membered rings by initial electrophilic addition to the distal double bond of the farnesyl chain may or may not involve prior isomerization of the *trans*-2,3-bond, depending on the geometry of the eventually formed products. For example, cyclization of *trans, trans*-farnesyl pyrophosphate to the macrocyclic sesquiterpenes all-*trans*-humulene and caryophyllene by sage leaf extracts, apparently does not require initial double bond isomerization (see Figure 13) (78), whereas strong but indirect evidence has been advanced for the intermediacy of nerolidyl pyrophosphate in the formation of longifolene and sativene (see Figure 14) (6).

The monoterpenoid and sesquiterpenoid cyclases are unusual in that a small number of acyclic substrates, geranyl and farnesyl pyrophosphate, and presumably the corresponding tertiary allylic pyrophosphates serve as universal precursors of some 200 to 300 cyclized products under the catalysis of a nearly equal number of distinct enzymes. Not only the substrates, but the cyclization mechanisms as well, are believed to be universal. Before describing selected cyclizations, the relative importance of rate enhancement and product specificity in the context of the general cyclization models should be evaluated. It is now agreed that the cyclase catalyzes the initial ionization of the pyrophosphate moiety to generate an allylic cation in a manner completely analogous to the action of prenyl transferase (183). The subsequent course of the cyclization reaction critically depends upon the precise folding of the acyclic geranyl or farnesyl substrate. Stereoelectronic considerations dictate that the reacting double bonds of the precursor be aligned in roughly parallel planes to allow effective overlap of the appropriate 2p-orbitals.

By taking into account the conformational constraints imposed by the presence of 2 or 3 π-systems within a chain of only 8 or 12 carbon atoms, respectively, it is obvious that a small number of substrate conformations can account for the majority of known monoterpene and sesquiterpene skeletons. However, in what way the enzyme enforces the required conformation on the reacting substrate or what factors determine formation of distinct products arising from ostensibly identical substrate conformations is not known. Moreover, any model of substrate-catalyst interactions must take into account the substantial changes in charge distribution, hybridization, configuration, and bonding which characterize the cyclization process and its concomitant Wagner-Meerwein rearrangements, hydride migrations, and deprotonation-reprotonation events. Whether the enzyme actually lowers the ΔH of activation for any of these fundamental processes or simply directs the selection of a single reaction channel by precise control of substrate conformation and the positioning of counterions is not yet understood. These terpenoid cyclases, as with other cyclization and linear condensation enzymes, have the unusual ability to survive the transient generation at their active sites of highly reactive electrophilic species involving charge separations of perhaps up to 10 Å.

Studies on cyclizations leading to bicyclic monoterpenes of the bornane, pinane, and fenchane type (Figure 3) constitute the most detailed biochemical investigations in the monoterpene series thus far. While the general properties of the relevant cyclases resemble those of the monocyclic *p*-menthane series, the structural complexity of the bicyclic products lends itself to more detailed examination of the stereochemistry of cyclization processes.

Investigations of the enzymology and mechanism of camphor biosynthesis (Figure 8) have provided the most revealing information to date regarding a monoterpene cyclization process. The biosynthesis of (+)-camphor in sage has been shown to involve the conversion of geranyl pyrophosphate to (+)-bornyl pyrophosphate, which is subsequently hydrolyzed by a distinct pyrophosphatase to (+)-borneol, followed by the NAD-dependent dehydrogenation of the alcohol to the ketone (65, 80, 85, 86, 87). In tansy (*Tanacetum vulgare* L.) and rosemary (*Rosemarinus officinalis* L.), (–)-camphor is derived by a similar sequence of reactions (72, 85, 92).

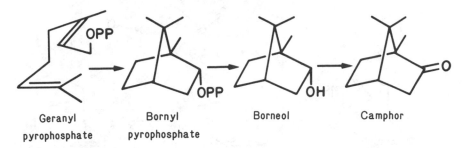

| Geranyl | Bornyl | Borneol | Camphor |
| pyrophosphate | pyrophosphate | | |

Figure 8. Pathway for the biosynthesis of camphor from geranyl pyrophosphate via bornyl pyrophosphate and borneol. Structures of the (–)-(1S,4S)-isomers are illustrated.

Studies on the biosynthesis of (+)-bornyl pyrophosphate were of particular significance in establishing, for the first time, that geranyl pyrophosphate is the preferred substrate for cyclization, that neryl pyrophosphate (although an alternate substrate for cyclization) is not a mandatory intermediate, and that the pyrophosphate moiety of the substrate is retained in the bicyclic product. This reaction type is thus far unique in the monoterpene series and has provided an unusual opportunity to examine the role of the pyrophosphate moiety in the coupled isomerization-cyclization process.

A scheme for the formation of (+)-bornyl pyrophosphate from geranyl pyrophosphate is presented in Figure 9. The first step is metal ion-assisted ionization with the generation of the tertiary allylic isomer now free to rotate about the C-2 - C-3 bond. Ionization of the tertiary intermediate, with backside addition to C-1 of the cisoid conformer by the neighboring double bond, generates the cyclohexanoid ring. Subsequent electrophilic attack on the newly created cyclohexene double bond and return of the pyrophosphate anion provides (+)-bornyl pyrophosphate with the correct stereochemistry. The isomerization to linalyl pyrophosphate with syn stereochemistry, and cyclization from the anti-endo conformation to the monocyclic α-terpinyl ion intermediate, are predicted features of many monoterpene cyclizations (70). One consequence of this scheme is that cyclization should proceed with net retention of configuration at C-1 of geranyl pyrophosphate and with inversion of configuration at C-1 of neryl pyrophosphate (the latter cyclization must occur without the attendant rotation at C-2 - C-3). These predictions were verified by the enzymatic generation of bornyl pyrophosphate from 1R- and 1S-^{3}H$_1$-labeled geranyl pyrophosphate and neryl pyrophosphate, followed by conversion to camphor and selective exchange of the *exo*-α-hydrogen of the derived ketone (67, 77).

An additional prediction of the cyclization scheme, dictated by the direction of approach of the pyrophosphate moiety, is the con-

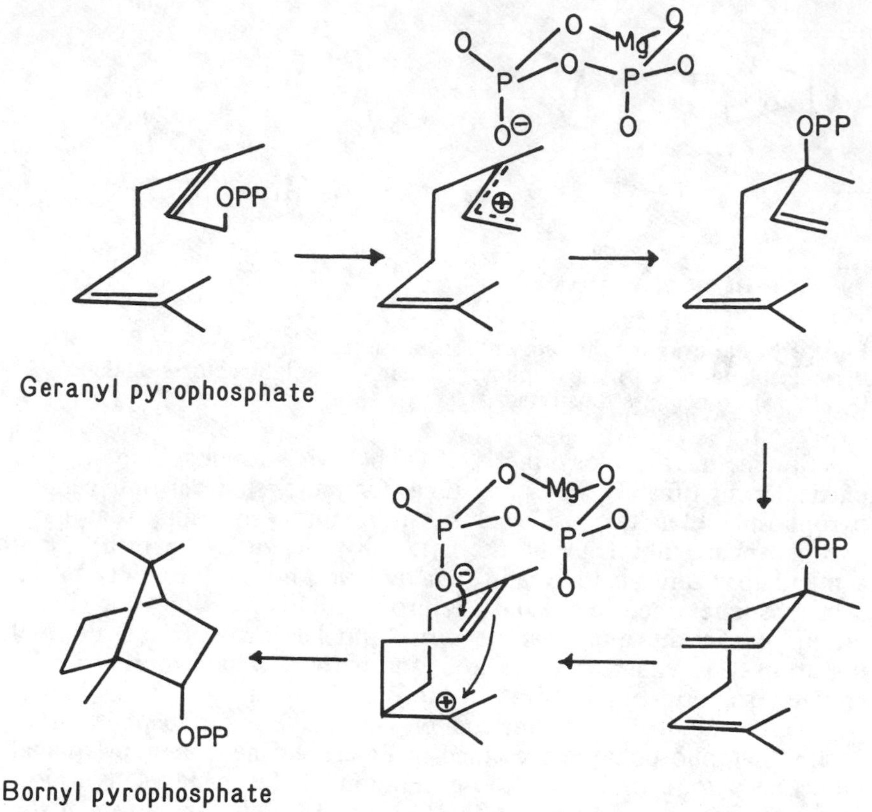

Geranyl pyrophosphate

Bornyl pyrophosphate

Figure 9. Proposed model for the cyclization of geranyl pyrophosphate to (+)-bornyl pyrophosphate via (–)-(3R)-linalyl pyrophosphate and the (4R)-α-terpinyl cation.

figuration of the presumptive linalyl pyrophosphate intermediate [(-)-3R-linalyl pyrophosphate in the case of (+)-bornyl pyrophosphate]. Since the bornyl pyrophosphate cyclase utilizes (±)-linalyl pyrophosphate as an alternate substrate, the question can, in principle, be addressed directly.

Recently, (±)-linalyl pyrophosphate was reexamined as a substrate with the (+)-bornyl pyrophosphate cyclase and the stereochemical composition of the product determined by chromatographic separation of diastereomeric derivatives. Although the enzyme synthesizes only (+)-bornyl pyrophosphate from geranyl pyrophosphate, the product generated from racemic linalyl pyrophosphate contained about 15 percent (–)-bornyl pyrophosphate. This result suggests that, when presented with the anomalous enantiomer of the racemic substrate, the (+)-bornyl pyrophosphate cyclase quite surprisingly is capable of synthesizing (–)-bornyl pyrophosphate as a minor product. The observation has yet to be verified directly with the optically pure linalyl pyrophosphates.

An examination of the role of the pyrophosphate moiety in the coupled isomerization-cyclization established, through the use of ^{32}P inorganic pyrophosphate, that exogenous pyrophosphate does not readily exchange with substrate-derived pyrophosphate (47). Several possible mechanisms (41, 45) for the interaction of the presumptive cationic intermediate with the anionic pyrophosphate partner have been explored. Experiments with ^{32}P-labeled substrates demonstrated that the 2 ends of the pyrophosphate moiety retained their identities during the cyclization to bornyl pyrophosphate. Thus, separate incubations of [1-^{3}H,α-^{32}P] and [1-^{3}H,β-^{32}P] geranyl pyrophosphate produced [^{3}H,^{32}P] bornyl pyrophosphates that were selectively hydrolyzed to the corresponding bornyl phosphates containing, respectively, all and none of the ^{32}P. Use of ^{18}O-labeled substrates subsequently revealed an unexpectedly tight coupling of the reaction partners at the active site of the cyclase. In this instance, incubations of [1-^{18}O] geranyl pyrophosphate with the enzyme yielded a product, analyzed by mass spectrometry of the derived benzoate, which indicated complete lack of positional oxygen isotope exchange during the cyclization, with the product having an ^{18}O enrichment essentially identical to that of the precursor (47).

This result, while implying great restriction in the motion of the pyrophosphate in relation to its terpenyl partner, could not distinguish between a 1,3-sigmatropic rearrangement or tight ion-pair with rotational restriction of the Pα-OP linkage, a 3,3-sigmatropic rearrangement involving a nonbridge oxygen and return of the formerly bridged oxygen, or processes involving bonding of the β-phosphate at the tertiary center. Studies in our laboratory with α-^{32}P- and β-^{32}P-labeled linalyl pyrophosphate have recently demonstrated that the 2 ends of the pyrophosphate moiety of this precursor retained their identity in the cyclization and that [1-^{18}O] linalyl pyrophosphate was converted to bornyl pyrophosphate without detectable oxygen isotope exchange. Thus, it is solely the pyrophosphate ester oxygen which is involved in all the critical bonding processes in the coupled isomerization-cyclization reaction. This situation is unlike that observed in the isomerization of farnesyl pyrophosphate to nerolidyl pyrophosphate by a fungal enzyme where complete scrambling of the 3 proximal phosphate oxygens occurs (45) but is reminiscent of an earlier report (161) that [1-^{18}O] geranyl pyrophosphate reisolated from incubations with prenyl transferase had not undergone detectable scrambling, in spite of strong evidence for the generation of the corresponding allylic cation at the active site of this enzyme. The observed lack of positional isotope exchange in the case of the bornyl pyrophosphate cyclase reaction is all the more remarkable when considering that the transient generation of the α-terpinyl cation-pyrophosphate anion pair must involve a charge separation of approximately 3 Å.

Each of the above experiments was carried out with the (+)-bornyl pyrophosphate cyclase (sage) and the results confirmed with the (–)-bornyl pyrophosphate cyclase (tansy); the availability of cyclases producing the enantiomeric products provides an exceedingly powerful probe of stereochemical and mechanistic questions.

The enzymes catalyzing the synthesis of α-pinene and β-pinene have been examined in partially purified preparations from *Citrus* fruit (57, 175) and sage leaves (115). Often, α-Pinene occurs naturally as a mixture of enantiomers [~70 percent (+)-isomer in sage], whereas β-pinene occurs almost exclusively as the (–)-isomer. Fractionation of sage leaf extracts by gel filtration produced 2 regions of pinene cyclase activity (cyclase I of molecular weight 96,000 and cyclase II of molecular weight 55,000) which catalyzed cyclizations of opposite enantiomeric specificity (116). Cyclase I catalyzed the conversion of geranyl pyrophosphate to (+)-α-pinene, to smaller quantities of (+)-limonene, and to the rearranged monoterpene (+)-camphene, whereas cyclase II transformed the acyclic precursor to (–)-α-pinene and (–)-β-pinene, as well as to (–)-camphene, (–)-limonene, and the acyclic olefin myrcene. Subsequent purification of each enzyme, as well as differential inactivation studies, provided strong evidence that each set of stereochemically related olefins was synthesized by a single cyclase, probably by a mechanism similar to that illustrated in Figure 10. The basic elements of this biosynthetic scheme are the same as those presented earlier. However, termination of the cationic reactions in this instance involves deprotonation to the olefins.

Neryl pyrophosphate and (±)-linalyl pyrophosphate can serve as alternate substrates for olefin synthesis by both cyclases, although in these cases the product distribution differs somewhat from the naturally occurring distribution in sage oil afforded with geranyl pyrophosphate as the precursor. Whether the anomalous enantiomer of linalyl pyrophosphate is an inhibitor of cyclization or may be functional as a substrate (as with bornyl pyrophosphate cyclases) is not yet clear; however, preliminary evidence suggests the latter. Future studies, perhaps involving enzyme modification or with suitably designed substrate analogs, may allow the product cascade generated by the pinene cyclases to be selectively derailed at each of the intermediate cyclization steps.

These same enzyme systems have been examined using the "noncyclizable" substrate analog 6,7-dihydrogeranyl pyrophosphate. One product of the enzymatic reaction has been tentatively identified as 6,7-dihydrolinalool, perhaps derived from dihydrolinalyl pyrophosphate or the equivalent ionic intermediate, and which may represent the uncoupling of the isomerization step from the subsequent cyclization reactions which are precluded in this instance.

The origin of the rearranged bicyclic monoterpene fenchone (Figure 3), derived from the corresponding alcohol *endo*-fenchol, presents another interesting cyclization. Partially purified extracts from *Foeniculum vulgare* L. convert $[1-^3H_2]$ geranyl pyrophosphate to

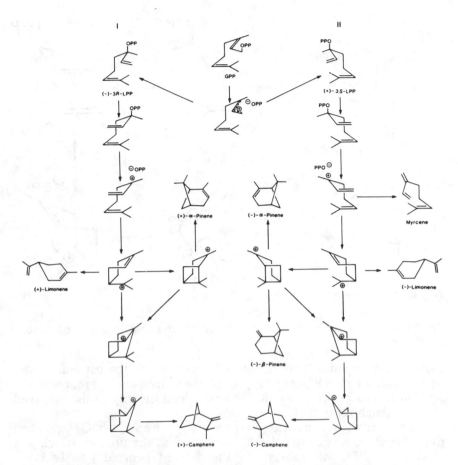

Figure 10. A scheme for the conversion of geranyl pyrophosphate (GPP) via linalyl pyrophosphate (LPP) to enantiomeric monoterpene olefins by pinene cyclase I (*left*) and pinene cyclase II (*right*).

(–)-*endo*-[7-³H] fenchol, establishing the course of the reaction to involve rearrangement of a pinyl intermediate (75, 76). All attempts to demonstrate the intermediacy of cyclic pyrophosphorylated intermediates in the formation to fenchol have been unsuccessful. The reason for this failure became apparent when the formation of (–)-*endo*-fenchol was analyzed in terms of the proposed stereochemical cyclization model (Figure 11). Cyclization of the initially generated 4*R*-α-terpinyl cation is expected to yield *exo*-2- pinyl pyrophosphate (or the corresponding ion-paired intermediate), and formation of the fenchyl skeleton from such an intermediate requires a 1,2-shift of the C-7 bridging carbon atom. The *endo*-face of the resulting 2-fenchyl cation is completely inaccessible to the

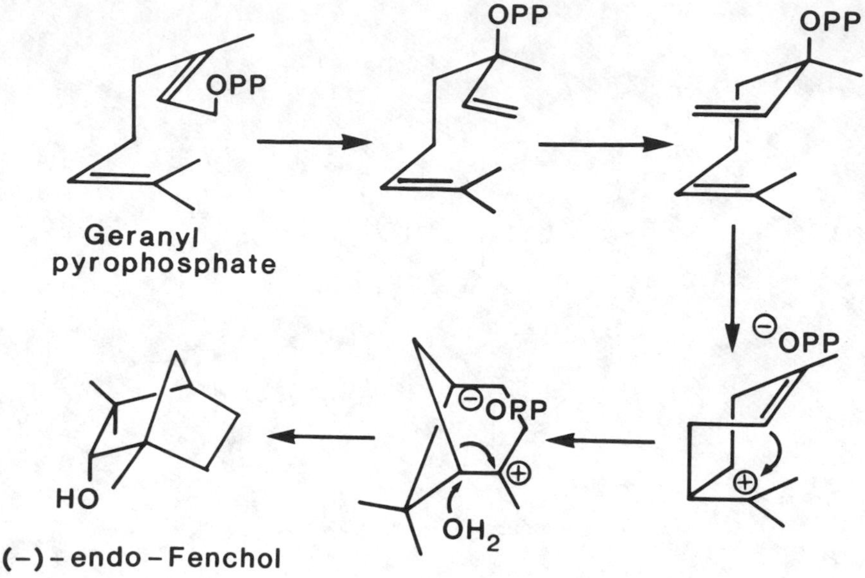

Figure 11. Proposed model for the cyclization of geranyl pyrophosphate to (–)-*endo*-fenchol.

pyrophosphate anion that is now situated *anti* to the cationic center as a result of the Wagner-Meerwein rearrangement. Capture of the fenchyl cation by water would, however, lead directly to the observed (–)-*endo*-fenchol product.

The prediction was borne out when [1-^{18}O] geranyl pyrophosphate was enzymatically converted to the product which was shown (by GLC-MS analysis of the derived benzoate) to be completely devoid of ^{18}O, thereby excluding fenchyl pyrophosphate as an intermediate (93). The manner by which the enzyme converts the pinyl intermediate to the fenchyl nucleus without concomitant formation of the favored bornane system is an example of the absolute control over Wagner-Meerwein rearrangements that is characteristic of terpene cyclizations but rarely observed in model reactions. A future challenge of research with these and related enzymes will be to distinguish the role of the catalyst in overall rate enhancement of the cyclization of geranyl pyrophosphate [rates are relatively slow, with K*m* values for geranyl pyrophosphate in the vM range (44, 61, 70)] from the ability to select a single reaction route from among several possibilities.

A number of other monoterpene cyclases have been examined in some detail, including those responsible for the synthesis of α-terpinene (141), γ-terpinene (178), and 1,8-cineole (84). The properties of these cyclases are much like those described above but, owing to the symmetry of the products, approaches to deducing the stereochemistry and mechanism of the cyclizations have been more limited. Additional cyclizations worthy of mention are the cyclization of geranyl pyrophosphate to limonene, the precursor of C-2 - and C-3 - oxygenated *p*-menthane monoterpenes in *Mentha* species (146), and the cyclization of geranyl pyrophosphate to sabinene, the precursor of C-3 - oxygenated thujane-type monoterpenes (143). The elucidation of the biosynthesis of thujane monoterpenes (such as 3-thujone) has followed a particularly circuitous path from initial hypotheses involving the photooxidation of sabinene, to the suggested involvement of α-terpineol and terpinen-4-ol (Figure 3) as intermediates, and to a proposal involving a series of 1,2-hydride shifts (55). Direct testing of [10-^{3}H] sabinene as well as other suggested intermediates in intact sage, tansy, and wormwood (*Artemisia abisinthium* L.) demonstrated that sabinene was the precursor of 3-thujone and 3-isothujone in these plants and eliminated all other cyclic compounds as possible precursors (143). Furthermore, cell-free preparations from each of these tissues convert geranyl pyrophosphate to sabinene as a major cyclic product.

Camphene and *endo*-fenchol are considered to be "irregular" monoterpenes in that they cannot be constructed by the simple head-to-tail joining of isoprene units. The studies outlined above indicate that these compounds are, however, derived via rearrangement of "regular" monoterpene precursors. There exists an additional class of irregular monoterpenes that are not readily derivable from regular structures but would appear instead to be constructed by an alternate means of joining 2 C$_5$ units quite unlike the classical 1'-4 condensation of dimethylallyl pyrophosphate and isopentenyl pyrophosphate that leads to geranyl pyrophosphate.

A survey of the naturally occurring irregular monoterpenes of the chrysanthemyl, santolinyl, artemisyl, and lavandulyl type, and critical analysis of the various biogenetic proposals led Epstein and Poulter (105) to elaborate an earlier suggestion (23) into an integrated scheme for the formation of these compounds (Figure 12). Numerous model studies have demonstrated the feasibility of the proposed biogenetic cleavages of the chrysanthemyl system to the artemisyl and santolinyl skeletons (58), and the various mechanistic and stereochemical features of these cyclopropyl carbinyl cation rearrangements have been explored in detail (179, 180). Although rupture of the C-2 - C-3 bond of the chrysanthemyl cyclopropane ring (*c,d,*-cleavage in Figure 12) leading to the lavandulanes has been suggested, mechanistic considerations favor direct coupling of dimethylallyl pyrophosphate to this skeleton (23, 105, 179). There is a highly developed theoretical framework for the construction of this group of irregular monoterpenes, yet biosynthetic investigations are meager (55, 66) and most questions regarding the origin of these compounds remain open to speculation.

Humulene and caryophyllene are among the most common sesquiterpenes found in the essential oils, and the cyclization of

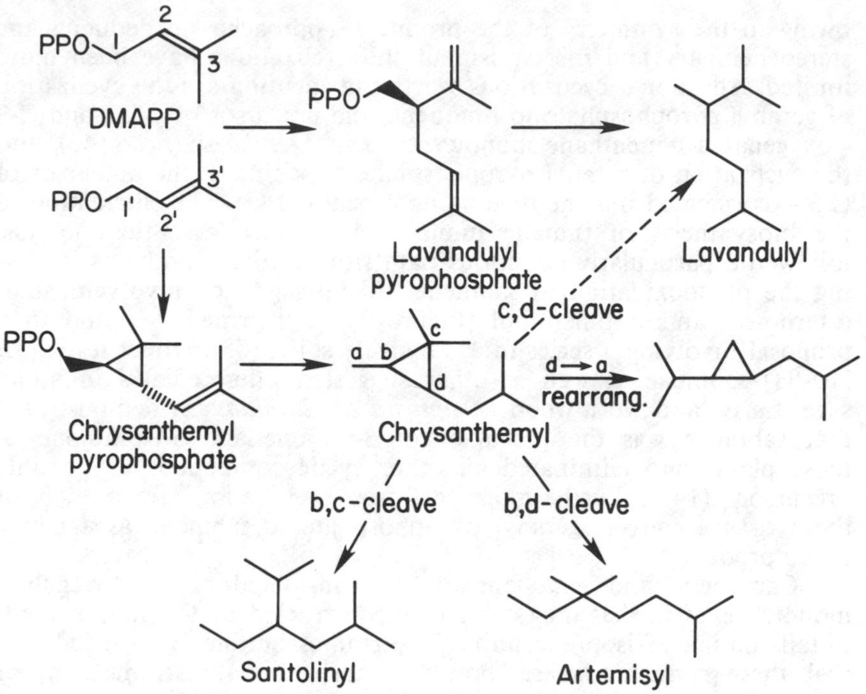

Figure 12. A unified scheme for the biosynthesis of irregular monoterpenes illustrating the condensation of dimethylallyl pyrophosphate (DMAPP) to chrysanthemyl pyrophosphate and lavandulyl pyrophosphate, and possible cleavages and rearrangements of the chrysanthemyl skeleton.

trans,trans-farnesyl pyrophosphate to both olefins has recently been demonstrated in cell-free preparations obtained from sage leaves (Figure 13) (78). In gross characteristics (such as pH optimum and cation requirement), the activity resembles that of monoterpene cyclases, but whether one or 2 enzyme(s) are responsible for the observed cyclizations is not yet known. Substrate specificity has not yet been examined, and this will be important in determining if nerolidyl pyrophosphate is cyclized and if *cis,trans*-farnesyl pyrophosphate is a functional substrate (as, for example, in the synthesis of *cis*-humulene).

The cyclization to humulene is of additional significance since humulene is considered to be the precursor (*via* reprotonation of the olefin) of a number of more complex polycyclic sesquiterpenes, including the illudoids, hirsutanoids, and pentalenoids (42). A particularly relevant example is the biosynthesis of pentalenene, the parent hydrocarbon of the pentalenolactone family of antibiotics in streptomyces (46, 49). Evidence was presented that pentalenene is derived from the olefin humulene *via* protonation of the conformational arrangement in which orbital overlap for the

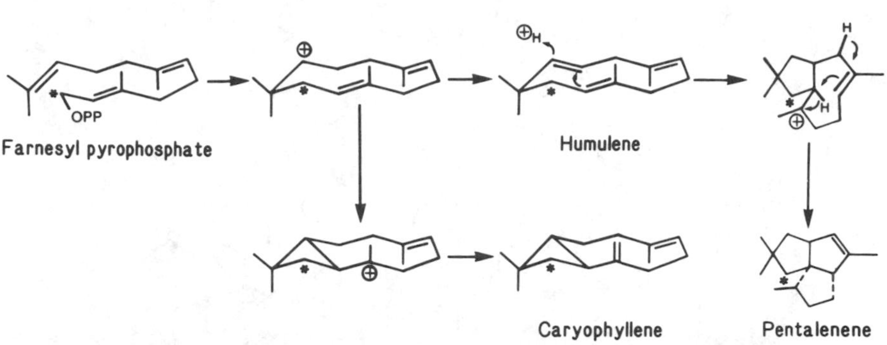

Figure 13. Cyclization of [1-³H] farnesyl pyrophosphate to (−)-caryophyllene and humulene and the conversion of humulene to pentalenene. The asterisks denote the position of tritium.

pentalenene cyclization was optimal (Figure 13). The alternative direct route from farnesyl pyrophosphate would require a 1,2-hydride shift from one secondary position to another of the humulyl cation, a step which is of no obvious preference to humulene formation followed by protonation. Although humulene could not be directly established as an intermediate in cell-free trapping experiments, indirect evidence favoring the intermediacy of this olefin has been described (43). The observation that humulene could not be trapped is best explained by the sequential cyclizations proceeding without release of intermediates from the enzyme surface. The application of bond-labeling methods and other stable isotope-nuclear magnetic resonance approaches to the biosynthesis of pentalenolactone and related sesquiterpenes derived from humulene has been described by Cane (42).

Another noteworthy cyclization, proceeding in this instance from a *cis*-humulyl cationic intermediate, is involved in the biosynthesis of longifolene in *Pinus ponderosa* Lawson (6). The indicated hydride shift in the humulyl cation (Figure 14) was demonstrated by feeding [5-³H₂,2-¹⁴C] mevalonate followed by chemical degradation to locate all 6 tritium atoms. This and related contributions led Arigoni (6) to suggest the importance of 1,3-hydride shifts to allylic cations and to advance a unified stereochemical theory to relate the folding and stereochemistry of the farnesyl pyrophosphate precursor to both the hydrogen transferred in the migration and the resulting absolute configuration of the sesquiterpene product.

Consistent with the hypothesis, a 1,3-hydride shift rather than 2 1,2-hydride shifts can be suggested in the transformation of the germacryl cation to a bicyclic intermediate and then to α-cubebene (Figure 14). Germacrene C (Figure 4) is a product of *trans,trans*-farnesyl pyrophosphate cyclization in cell-free extracts of *Kadsura japonica* Dunal seeds (165), but nothing is known about the responsi-

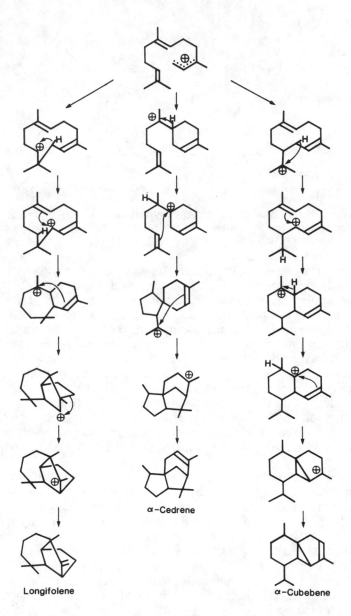

Figure 14. Hydride shifts in the biosynthesis of some tricyclic sesquiterpenes.

ble cyclase. As with humulene, reprotonation of germacrene C and related isomers is thought to lead to a variety of more complex polycyclic derivatives (42, 58, 188).

Of the 2 remaining simple cyclizations of farnesyl pyrophosphate involving electrophilic attack on the central double bond (Figure 6), those leading to the 7-membered ring are rare (as, for example, carotol [202] in Figure 4) while those leading to the 6-membered bisabolyl system are as common as the macrocyclic humulyl- and germacryl-type. Among the sesquiterpenes derived from the bisabolyl cation are the analogs of most common monoterpenes (65, 168, 211).

Although the mechanisms of cyclization of geranyl pyrophosphate and farnesyl pyrophosphate to the corresponding monoterpenes and sesquiterpenes are no doubt similar, the limited information available suggests that monoterpene and sesquiterpene cyclases are incapable of synthesizing the larger and smaller analogs when presented with the appropriate substrate (65). The cyclization of farnesyl pyrophosphate to γ-bisabolene has been demonstrated in cell-free extracts prepared from tissue cultures of *Andrographis paniculata* Del. (4, 171), but little is known of the cyclase involved. The conversion of [1,2-^{13}C$_2$] acetate to γ-bisabolene, and ultimately paniculide B, has also been explored in *Andrographis paniculata* tissue cultures (171). The ^{13}C NMR spectrum of the lactone exhibited 6 pairs of coupled doublets and 3 enhanced singlets (C-4, C-8, C-12), allowing the pathway to be readily deduced (Figure 15). Like the humulyl and germacryl systems,

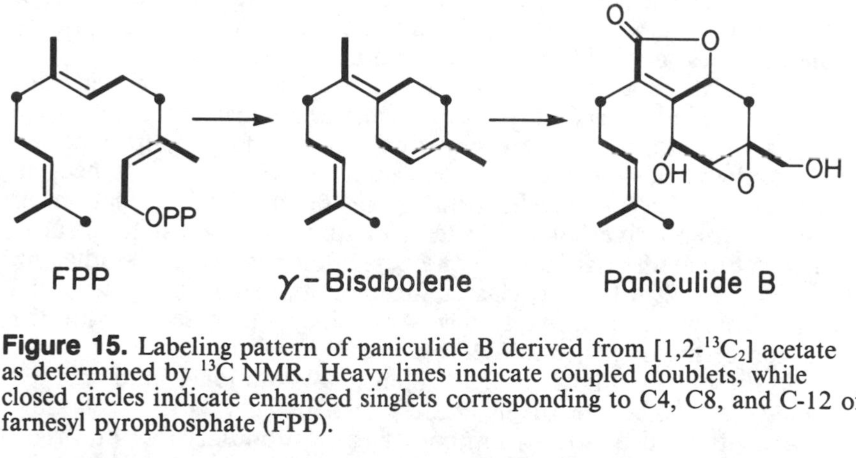

FPP   γ-Bisabolene   Paniculide B

Figure 15. Labeling pattern of paniculide B derived from [1,2-^{13}C$_2$] acetate as determined by ^{13}C NMR. Heavy lines indicate coupled doublets, while closed circles indicate enhanced singlets corresponding to C4, C8, and C-12 of farnesyl pyrophosphate (FPP).

the bisabolyl system may also undergo further cyclization and rearrangement to generate numerous other sesquiterpene skeleta. Of note in this regard are chemical simulations of the biogenesis of cedrene (Figure 14) and the spiranes and other polycyclics of vetiver oil (5).

VII. SECONDARY TRANSFORMATIONS

Whereas relatively few cyclases are thought to determine the basic structure of the monoterpenes and sesquiterpenes, any compendium of terpene compounds (99, 100, 120) will illustrate the very large number of derivatives of each skeletal type found in nature and give some appreciation of the large number of secondary enzymatic transformations presumed to occur among these terpenoid classes. Such modifications are generally responsible for imparting the biological function of many of these compounds. Although the metabolism of the lower terpenes encompasses a diverse assortment of biochemical transformations, the terpenoids of higher plants, especially those isolated from the essential oils, are commonly hydrocarbons or simple oxygenated derivatives. The co-occurrence of such structurally related compounds has led to considerable speculation concerning pathways and precursor-product relationships (11, 168), yet few of these proposals have actually been tested via *in vivo* tracer studies or with cell-free enzyme systems. Rather than attempting to compile these proposed reactions, most of which have ample biochemical precedent, 2 central and long-standing questions regarding secondary transformations are addressed (157). The first question deals with a general strategy for the oxidative metabolism of terpenoid olefins, while the second question deals with the specificity of the enzymes involved in these transformations.

Surveys of monoterpene and sesquiterpene cyclization reactions (42, 66, 70) indicate that there are relatively few cases in which oxygen is introduced in the cyclization step (as, for example, bornyl pyrophosphate, 1,8-cineole, and patchouliol) and many instances in which the product of cyclization is an olefin. The formation of oxygenated derivatives of the latter structural types must necessarily involve subsequent oxidation of the parent olefins. Recent studies on the origin of 2 different classes of monoterpenes have provided evidence for what is probably a general biosynthetic scheme for the formation of these oxygenated derivatives.

As shown in Figure 3, 3-thujone, 3-isothujone, and related thujane-type monoterpenes are widely distributed in the plant kingdom and often co-occur. A number of early proposals for the origin of these compounds (9, 10, 14, 18, 21, 22) were eliminated by demonstrating that the olefin sabinene administered exogenously served as the precursor of 3-thujone and/or 3-isothujone in *Artemisia absinthium* L., *Tanacetum vulgare* L., and *Salvia officinalis* L. (143). Additional *in vivo* studies, including the time-course of appearance of presumptive intermediates and isotopic dilution analysis (143), provided evidence to support the pathway illustrated (Figure 16).

From studies in our laboratory, the allylic hydroxylation of sabinene to *cis*-sabinol is virtually certain to be the first step in the

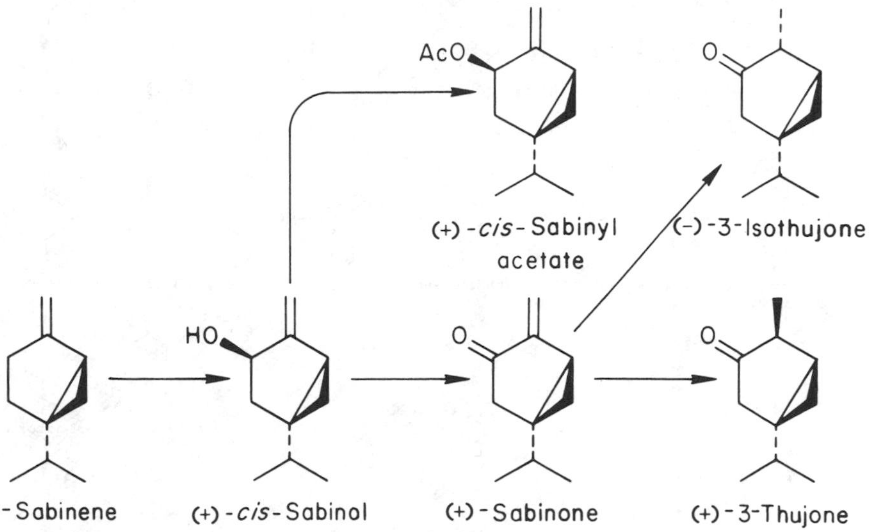

Figure 16. Proposed pathway for the biosynthesis of C-3-oxygenated thujane monoterpenes from sabinene.

transformation of the parent olefin to C-3 - oxygenated derivatives, and this conversion is carried out by a membranous, NADPH/O$_2$-dependent mixed function oxidase isolated from the relevant tissues. Subsequent steps in the synthesis of C(3)-oxygenated thujane monoterpenes have not yet been firmly established *in vitro,* but almost certainly involve, at some stage, oxidation to the α,β-unsaturated ketone and stereoselective double-bond reduction to afford either the thujone or isothujone series. The synthesis of monoterpenyl acetates via acetyl CoA acetyl transferases has been demonstrated (79).

Evidence for the allylic oxidation-conjugate reduction scheme in the metabolism of terpene olefins was also obtained from studies on the biosynthesis of oxygenated monoterpenes in *Mentha piperita* L. (Figure 17). The pathway from piperitenone to the menthol stereoisomers was deduced largely through the efforts of Loomis and associates (24, 25, 38, 39), who employed time-course studies and direct feeding experiments with labeled precursors. The sequential reduction of the conjugated double-bonds of piperitenone to the menthones in a cell-free system has subsequently been demonstrated (40) and affinity chromatography has been utilized to separate each of the positionally specific, NADPH-dependent reductases involved. Similar techniques have been employed to isolate and characterize the 2 stereospecific dehydrogenases responsible for the synthesis of (–)-menthol and (+)-neomenthol from (–)-menthone (148).

Although the pathway from piperitenone was well-accepted, until recently the origin of piperitenone was a point of contention, with

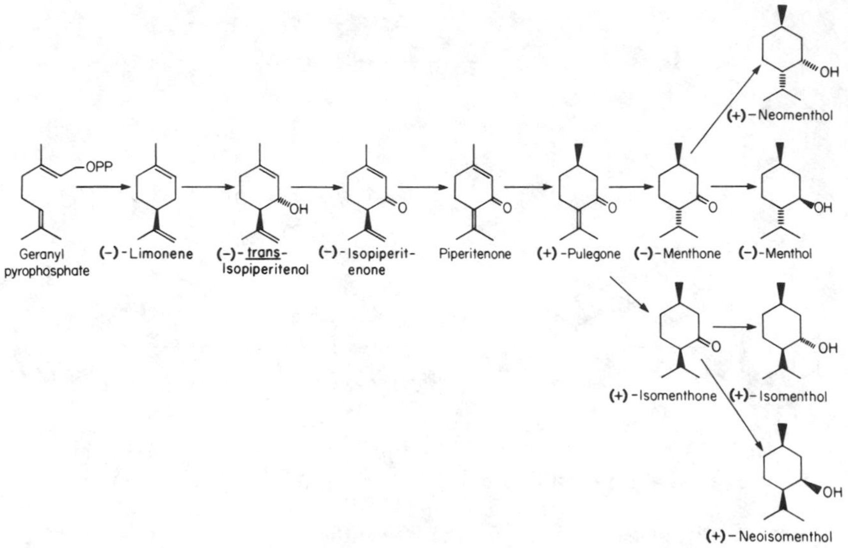

Figure 17. Proposed pathway for the conversion of geranyl pyrophosphate to C-3-oxygenated monoterpenes in peppermint (*Mentha piperita*).

some evidence available for either limonene or terpinolene as the most likely precursor. The problem was examined directly in *Mentha piperita* leaves using the appropriate labeled olefins (146). This and related *in vivo* studies proved conclusively that limonene was the precursor of the oxygenated monoterpenes in this species and in other *Mentha* species as well (146). It was also demonstrated that limonene [primarily the (-)-isomer] was the major cyclic product synthesized from geranyl pyrophosphate by cell-free homogenates of *Mentha piperita* leaf epidermis.

More recently, the hydroxylation of limonene to *trans*-isopiperitenol has been shown to be catalyzed by a microsomal mixed-function oxidase isolated from leaf homogenates, and both the isopiperitenol dehydrogenase and isopiperitenone isomerase have been partially purified and characterized (149). The mechanism of isomerization was shown to involve intramolecular hydrogen transfer. The summary of the evidence thus supports the direct synthesis of limonene from the acyclic precursor, the allylic oxidation of this olefin, the conversion of the product to a conjugated dienone, and the subsequent reduction of both conjugated double bonds (and eventually the carbonyl function) as the major features of monoterpene metabolism in *Mentha piperita*. An earlier review on the origin of menthol and its congeners can be found elsewhere (65).

The same allylic oxidation scheme can be applied to the synthesis of the myrtenyl and verbenyl series of derivatives from α-pinene (11) and to the synthesis of lanceol and zerumbone (Figure 4) from their respective sesquiterpene olefin precursors (168). However, in none of these examples is direct proof of the pathway presently available. Allylic hydroxylation probably gives rise directly to agerol (Figure 18), the endocyclic double bonds of which undergo epoxidation and subse-

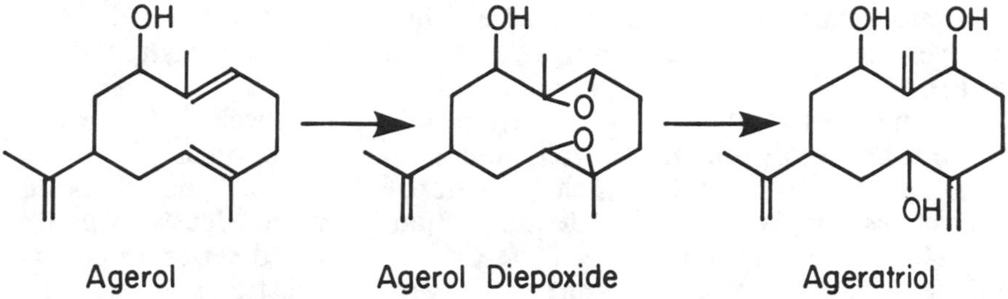

Agerol   Agerol Diepoxide   Ageratriol

Figure 18. Conversion of agerol to agerol diepoxide and ageratriol.

quent oxirane opening to afford ageratriol (27).

A novel mode of oxygenation is the iodoperoxidase-catalyzed conversion of α-terpinene to ascaridole (Figure 19), recently demonstrated in cell-free extracts of *Chenopodium ambrosioides* L. fruit

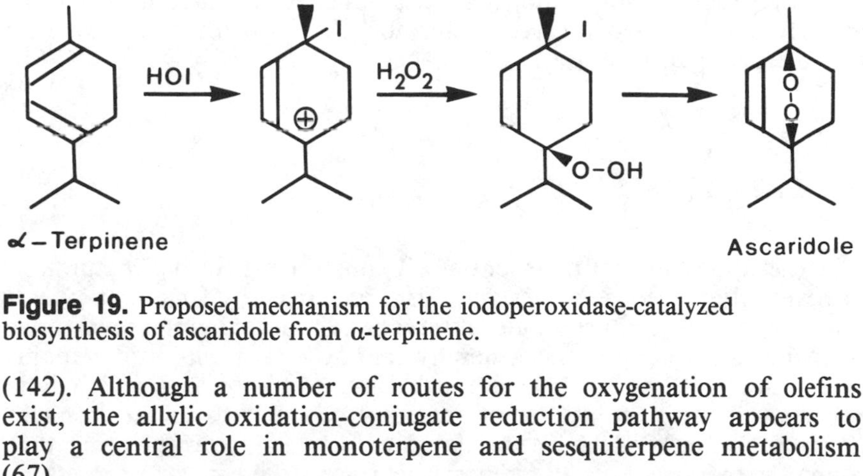

α–Terpinene   Ascaridole

Figure 19. Proposed mechanism for the iodoperoxidase-catalyzed biosynthesis of ascaridole from α-terpinene.

(142). Although a number of routes for the oxygenation of olefins exist, the allylic oxidation-conjugate reduction pathway appears to play a central role in monoterpene and sesquiterpene metabolism (67).

The aromatic monoterpenes (as, for example, *p*-cymene and thymol shown in Figure 3) are derived from γ-terpinene (177), with the parent olefin being the direct cyclization product of geranyl pyrophosphate (178). Aromatic sesquiterpenes such as α-curcumene and cuparene (Figure 4) are no doubt similarly derived by desaturation of the corresponding dienes, but such pathways have not been directly demonstrated.

As indicated above, a number of monoterpenol dehydrogenases, acetyl transferases, and double-bond reductases have been isolated from several essential oil-bearing species, and these enzymes are probably representative of the general types involved in secondary transformations of monoterpenes and sesquiterpenes. A question often raised with regard to monoterpene and sesquiterpene interconversions concerns the issue of whether these transformations are carried out by highly specific or relatively nonspecific enzymes. Too few examples have been studied thus far to allow a definitive answer; however, the enzyme systems that have been examined do exhibit a significant degree of substrate specificity. Thus a (+)-limonene reductase from *Citrus* specifically reduces the exocyclic double bond of this monocyclic diene, but (–)-limonene is not a substrate (176). Similarly, the previously described double-bond reductases involved in piperitenone metabolism in *Mentha piperita* (25, 40) act only on members of the C-3 - oxygenated series; members of the C-2 - oxygenated (carvone) series are not substrates.

Several types of evidence suggest that the monoterpenol dehydrogenases isolated from *Salvia officinalis* (80), *Tanacetum vulgare* and *Foeniculum vulgare* (72), and *Mentha piperita* (148, 149) [enzymes readily separated from alcohol (ethanol) dehydrogenase] can utilize a very limited range of substrates, specifically those monoterpenols produced by the respective species. By contrast to the enzymes involved in oxidative or reductive transformations, the enzymes responsible for conjugation reactions, such as acyl transferases and glycosyl transferases, are rather nonselective with regard to their monoterpenol cosubstrates.

VIII. CATABOLISM

The apparent loss of essential oil constituents during maturation of several herbaceous species was first recognized by Charabot (54) at the turn of the century. This observation, repeated numerous times over the intervening years, generally cannot be attributed to evaporative losses (157, 158, 213), although cases are known in which lytic processes lead to the release of secretory products to the atmosphere (216, 221). Rather, the accumulated evidence is overwhelming that monoterpenes and sesquiterpenes which are stored in, or exposed to, physiologically active tissues can undergo metabolic turnover. Summations of the supportive arguments are available (55, 66, 67, 81). Terpenes stored in essentially inactive tissue, such as wood resin ducts and heartwood, may be oxidized via endogenous peroxidases (102), but the isolation of these products from metabolically active tissue would seem to preclude extensive catabolism in this special circumstance (82). The once popular view that mono- and sesquiterpenes are metabolically inert waste products is no longer valid, whereas Charabot's (54) early (and widely ignored) contention that essential oil constituents are transported and consumed by the plant is remarkably accurate.

In metabolic turnover phenomena, 2 basic types can be distinguished. The first type represents a short-term effect (as, for example, measured by diurnal fluctuation or by the time-course of radiotracer incorporation), which is generally thought to involve metabolism of an active intracellular terpene pool and to be highly dependent on the balance between photosynthesis and utilization of photosynthate (158). The phenomenon is readily demonstrated in immature tissue where net synthesis greatly exceeds turnover and the terpenes therefore accumulate (68).

The second type of turnover occurs during late development and results in a net decrease in terpene content. The effect has been observed in numerous plants, especially among the Lamiaceae, and may exceed 50- percent terpene loss over the course of a few weeks (38, 39, 103, 104, 111, 136). Unlike the short-term effect, the longer-term permanent loss of terpenes necessarily represents the turnover of stored material, most of which is contained in extracellular compartments. The observed terpene turnover is commonly assumed to represent actual catabolism, as the conversion of terpenes to primary metabolites has been demonstrated in leaf tissue (21, 170). However, most claims for terpene turnover are based on simple measurements of terpene loss that may also represent conjugation and transport of terpenes derivatives out of the tissue being analyzed.

The most detailed studies on terpene catabolism have been carried out with peppermint (*Mentha piperita*) as a model system. Turnover of leaf oil in this species is greatly accelerated late in development (Figure 20), coincident with the conversion of (–)-menthone (the major monoterpene constituent) to (–)-menthol and to lesser quantities of (–)-menthyl acetate and (+)-neomenthol (38, 39, 90).

The most notable feature of monoterpene turnover in *Mentha piperita* is the large decrease in menthone content that accompanies the reductive metabolism of this ketone, a loss that cannot be accounted for by evaporation or by the increase in menthol or other volatile terpenoid constituents (38, 39, 90). Studies on the metabolism of (–)-[^{3}H] menthone in leaf discs revealed that menthone loss (not accounted for by volatile metabolites) was a result of the specific conversion of this ketone to (+)-neomenthyl-β-D- glucoside (90). Thus, menthone is reduced to roughly equal amounts of menthol and neomenthol, with the bulk of the menthol remaining in the volatile oil (as such or as the acetate ester) and the bulk of the neomenthol being converted to the glucoside. The pathways are highly specific with only menthyl acetate (with little neomenthyl acetate) and neomenthyl glucoside (with little menthyl glucoside) being formed (Figure 21).

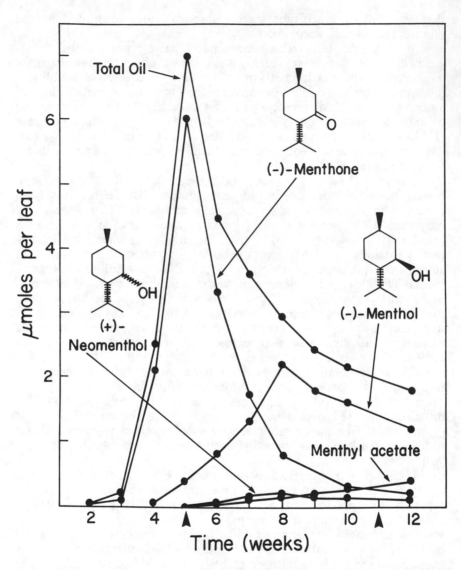

Figure 20. Monoterpene composition of midstem peppermint (*Mentha piperita*) leaves as a function of development. The first arrowhead on the time axis indicates the approximate time of floral initiation and the second arrowhead indicates the approximate time of full bloom.

Two possible explanations for such specificity seem evident; either the enzymes involved exhibit a high degree of selectivity or the 2 pathways are compartmentalized. Subsequent *in vivo* studies (160) with labeled menthone, menthol, neomenthol, and CO_2 indicated specificity was determined at the menthone reduction step, the sys-

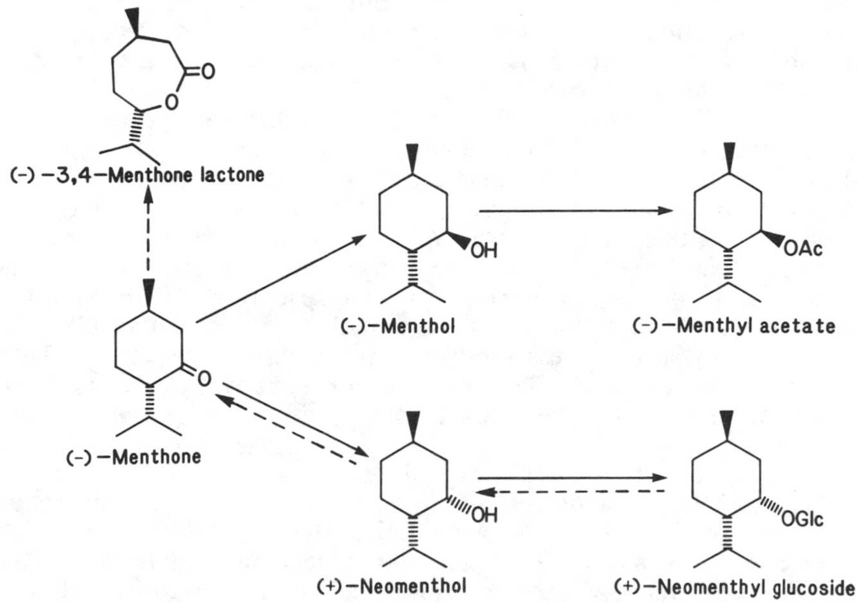

Figure 21. Pathways of (–)-menthone metabolism in peppermint (*Mentha piperita*) leaves (———) and of (+)-neomenthyl-β-D-glucoside metabolism in peppermint rhizomes (———).

tems were compartmentalized, and the transferases were not highly selective enzymes. The latter point was confirmed by isolating the acetyl CoA-dependent acetyl transferase (79) and the UDPG-dependent glucosyl transferase (160) and examining their specificity for monoterpenols. The 2 distinct, stereospecific dehydrogenases (both NADPH-dependent) were also isolated from *Mentha piperita* leaf extracts and characterized (148).

All of the evidence implicated compartmentalization of pathways as an essential feature of monoterpene metabolism in *Mentha piperita*. By separating the leaf epidermis from the mesophyll layer, the specific location of the neomenthol dehydrogenase and the glucosyl transferase in the mesophyll layer and the menthol dehydrogenase and the acetyl transferase in the epidermis (presumably in the epidermis oil glands) were demonstrated (96). Thus, the basis for compartmentalization of pathways was intercellular, not intracellular.

The fact that the water-soluble glucoside was not further metabolized in peppermint leaf discs (90) suggests a possible transport function (precluded in leaf disc experiments). By utilizing (–)-[³H] menthone as a tracer administered to leaves of intact flowering plants, the fate of the neomenthyl glucoside produced was explored

(90, 147). It was demonstrated that the glucoside was transported primarily to the developing rhizome with little transport to the flowers. Examination of the kinetics of metabolism and transport indicated that the process was sufficient to account for the observed decrease in leaf terpene content (95).

These results provided the first direct evidence supporting earlier suggestions (113, 138) that monoterpenyl glycosides are transport derivatives. They also demonstrated that catabolic transformations can take place at a site quite distant from the site of synthesis. Menthyl-β-D-glucoside has been reported in the rhizome of *Mentha arvensis* Hol. (190) and is presumed to be the foliar transport derivative in this species (191). Over the last several years, many other monoterpenyl glycosides have been found in a variety of species (71, 160), so the basic processes outlined for *Mentha piperita* may be a common phenomenon. The transport of terpenyl glycosides from leaves to flowers has been demonstrated in the essential oil rose (174).

More recent studies have focused on the metabolism of neomenthyl glucoside on reaching the rhizome (94, 95). The glucoside is hydrolyzed and the aglycone oxidized back to menthone, which undergoes oxygenation to 3,4-menthone lactone (Figure 21). This lactonization reaction accomplishes the crucial ring-opening step which allows subsequent β-oxidative degradation of the terpenoid chain (94). A similar lactonization reaction is probably involved in the metabolism of camphor in *Salvia officinalis* (71), and this overall strategy of oxidative ring-opened following by oxidative cleavage of the resulting chain has ample precedent in microorganisms that can utilize monoterpenes as the sole source of carbon and energy (50, 53, 59, 197, 198).

By employing (–)-[G-^{3}H] 3,4-menthone lactone and its progenitors as metabolic tracers with mint rhizomes, the probable pathway for the modified β-oxidation of the derived acyclic terpene skeleton (3,7-dimethyloctanoate) has been elucidated (94). Additionally, the metabolism of the [^{3}H]-labeled monoterpenes in rhizomes was shown to give rise to starch and soluble carbohydrates (via [^{3}H] pyridine nucleotides) as well as to acyl lipids and other isoprenoid lipids such as squalene and phytosterols (via either [^{3}H] acetyl CoA or [^{3}H] pyridine nucleotide) (94). While few details of the pathway are available, the conversion of [^{3}H] geranyl glucoside to waxes, organic acids, and other water-soluble products in rose petals has also been described (36), and similarity to the catabolism of menthone lactone in *Mentha piperita* would be expected.

The results outlined above suggest that, although monoterpenes and sesquiterpenes may have a primary function in ecological interactions, metabolic recycling allows utilization of the carbon and energy late in development at sites quite distant from the foliar site of synthesis.

IX. CONCLUDING REMARKS

A discussion of the regulation of monoterpene and sesquiterpene metabolism would be an appropriate conclusion. Unfortunately, in spite of much recent progress in this area of biochemistry, little has yet to be put forward regarding regulatory processes at the enzyme, cell, or whole organism level.

The broad outlines of the pathways involved in the biosynthesis of monoterpenes and sesquiterpenes have been clarified and, in the process, many previously proposed biogenetic schemes have been either discarded or placed on firm experimental footing. Much of what we know at the enzyme level relates to the catalysts of cyclization reactions, and such studies have testified to the fundamental soundness of the original biogenetic isoprene rule (189). General mechanistic models for monoterpene and sesquiterpene cyclizations have been proposed and, in a number of cases, detailed investigations have resulted in a fairly complete stereochemical description of the events surrounding the electrophilic cyclization of the prenyl pyrophosphate. Research on secondary transformations of the parent cyclic compounds has provided insights to the general strategies of metabolism and the gross properties of the responsible enzymes. Thus, the details of reaction pathways and some of the mechanistic and stereochemical features of the reactions catalyzed have begun to emerge from more extensive investigations. Otherwise, little is known about the enzymes as catalysts or as proteins. Molecular-level factors influencing rate enhancement and stereoselectivity are still conjectural, and the existence of classical regulatory features, such as allosterism, are as yet unknown. Preliminary studies have suggested developmental regulation of the enzymatic machinery dedicated to camphor biosynthesis (74), but whether control is exerted by manipulation of relevant enzyme level or activity per se is uncertain, as is the possibility of regulation of the enzymatic steps prior to the committed cyclizations.

Many features of mono- and sesquiterpene biosynthesis appear to be intimately related to the compartmentation of the biosynthetic sites within specialized secretory structures. Studies on the morphology of secretory structures have revealed considerable ultrastructural complexity and indicate the existence of a number of possible compartments bounded by membranes that arise from plastids or from endoplasmic reticulum. In a few instances (30, 124), monoterpene and sesquiterpene biosynthesis has been associated with a particular organelle. Yet, most enzymes of terpenoid metabolism examined thus far are operationally soluble, providing little clue to *in situ* organization or to the nature of the interaction between cytosol and membranous structures that must occur in the process of secretion.

Tissue and cell culture methods, of such great value in unraveling cellular processes in plants, have been of little use with regard to mono- and sesquiterpene biosynthesis. Such systems rarely produce terpenoids that either qualitatively or quantitatively resemble those accumulated by the intact plant (20, 56, 167, 220). This failure is generally attributed to the apparent requirement for tissue differentiation with formation of suitable storage structures, but the alternate explanation of the relevant terpenoids being produced and rapidly degraded has not been examined. Indeed, only recently has the degradation of lower terpenoids been appreciated and it understood that regulation must involve both biosynthetic and catabolic processes.

The reported effects of climate, nutrition, and various stresses on essential oil yield and composition are legion (112, 117, 156), yet our understanding of the bases of these effects is primitive and likely to remain this way until the gap between the genetic machinery and enzymatic expression can be bridged, and until the means by which these catalysts are controlled at the molecular level can be explained. More systematic studies of monoterpene and sesquiterpene biochemistry in relation to regulation at all levels are required. The experimental tools are at hand and, with the general background information now available, should facilitate such investigations. Exciting progress can be expected, both at the fundamental level and directed toward the solution of practical problems of plant protection and the cultivation of economically significant plants.

Acknowledgements

The work by the author and his colleagues cited herein has been supported by grants from the National Science Foundation, the National Institutes of Health, the Department of Energy, the Washington Mint Commission and Mint Industry Research Council, and the Haarmann and Reimer Corporation.

X. REFERENCES

1. Amelunxen, F. 1964. Elektronen mikroskopische untersuchungen an den drüsenhaaren von *Mentha piperita* L. Planta Med. 12:121–139.

2. Amelunxen, F. 1965. Elektronen mikroskopische untersuchungen an den drüsenschuppen von *Mentha piperita* L. Planta Med. 13:457–473.

3. Amelunxen, F., T. Wahlig, and H. Arbeiter. 1969. Über den Nachweis des ätherisches Öls in isolierten drüsenhaaren und drüsenschuppen von *Mentha piperita* L. Z. Pflanzenphysiol. 61:68–72.

4. Anastasis, P., I. Freer, C. Gilmore, H. Mackie, K. Overton, and S. Swanson. 1982. Cyclisation of farnesyl pyrophosphate to γ-bisabolene in tissue cultures of *Andrographis paniculata*. J. Chem. Soc. Chem. Commun. 268–270.

5. Andersen, N.H., Y. Ohta, and D.D. Syrdal. 1978. Studies in sesquiterpene biogenesis: Implications of absolute configuration, new structural types, and efficient chemical simulation of pathways. *In* E.E. van

Tamelen, ed. *Bioorganic Chemistry,* Vol. II. Academic Press, New York. pp. 1–37.

6. Arigoni, D. 1975. Stereochemical aspects of sesquiterpene biosynthesis. Pure Appl. Chem. 41:219–245.

7. Attaway, J.A., A.P. Pieringer, and L.J. Barabas. 1966. The origin of citrus flavor components I. The analysis of citrus leaf oils using gas-liquid chromatography, thin-layer chromatography and mass spectrometry. Phytochemistry 5:141–151.

8. Attaway, J.A., A.P. Pieringer, and L.J. Barabas. 1967. The origin of citrus flavor components. III. A study of the percentage variation in peel and leaf oil terpenes during one season. Phytochemistry 6:25–32.

9. Banthorpe, D.V. and D. Baxendale. 1973. Model systems for the biological oxidation of monoterpene hydrocarbons. Planta Med. 23:239–250.

10. Banthorpe, D.V., G.A. Bucknall, H.J. Doonan, S. Doonan, and M.G. Rowan. 1976. Biosynthesis of geraniol and nerol in cell-free extracts of *Tanacetum vulgare.* Phytochemistry 15:91–100.

11. Banthorpe, D.V. and B.V. Charlwood. 1980. The Isoprenoids. *In* E.A. Bell and B.V. Charlwood, eds. *Encyclopedia of Plant Physiology.* New series, Vol. 8 – Secondary plant products. Springer-Verlag, Berlin. pp. 185–220.

12. Banthorpe, D.V., B.V. Charlwood, and M.J.O. Francis. 1972. The biosynthesis of monoterpenes. Chem. Rev. 72:115–155.

13. Banthorpe, D.V., P.N. Christou, C.R. Pink, and D.G. Watson. 1983. Metabolism of linaloyl, neryl and geranyl pyrophosphates in *Artemisia annua.* Phytochemistry 22:2465–2468.

14. Banthorpe, D.V., H.J. Doonan, and A. Wirz-Justice. 1972. Terpene biosynthesis. Part V. Interconversions of some monoterpenes in higher plants and their possible role as precursors of carotenoids. J. Chem. Soc. Perkin Trans. I, 1764–1768.

15. Banthorpe, D.V. and O. Ekundayo. 1976. Biosynthesis of (+)-car-3-ene in *Pinus* species. Phytochemistry 15:109–112.

16. Banthorpe, D.V., O. Ekundayo, and M.G. Rowan. 1978. Evidence for geraniol as an obligatory precursor of isothujone. Phytochemistry 17:1111–1114.

17. Banthorpe, D.V., G.N.J. LePatourel, and M.J.O. Francis. 1972. Biosynthesis of geraniol and nerol and their β-D-glucosides in *Pelargonium graveolens* and *Rosa dilecta.* Biochem. J. 130:1045–1054.

18. Banthorpe, D.V., J. Mann, and I. Poots. 1977. 1,2-Hydrogen-shifts in the biosynthesis of the thujane skeleton. Phytochemistry 16:547–550.

19. Banthorpe, D.V., B.M. Modawai, I. Poots, and M.G. Rowan. 1978. Redox interconversions of geraniol and nerol in higher plants. Phytochemistry 17:1115–1118.

20. Banthorpe, D.V. and V.C.O. Njar. 1984. Light-dependent monoterpene synthesis in *Pinus radiata* cultures. Phytochemistry 23:295–299.

21. Banthorpe, D.V. and A. Wirz-Justice. 1969. Terpene biosynthesis. Part I. Preliminary tracer studies on terpeneoids and chlorophyll of *Tanacetum vulgare* L. J. Chem. Soc. (C):541–549.

22. Banthorpe, D.V. and A. Wirz-Justice. 1972. Terpene biosynthesis. Part VI. Monoterpenes and carotenoids from tissue cultures of *Tanacetum vulgare* L. J. Chem. Soc. Perkin Trans. I, 1769–1772.

23. Bates, R.B. and S.K. Paknikar. 1965. Terpenoids. IX. Biogenesis of some monoterpenoids not derived from a geranyl precursor. Tetrahedron Lett. (20), 1453–1455.

24. Battaile, J. and W.D. Loomis. 1961. Biosynthesis of terpenes. II. The site and sequence of terpene formation in peppermint. Biochim. Biophys. Acta 51:545–552.

25. Battaile, J., A.J. Burbott, and W.D. Loomis. 1968. Monoterpene interconversions: Metabolism of pulegone by a cell-free system from *Mentha piperita*. Phytochemistry 7:1159–1163.

26. Baxter, R.L., W.A. Laurie, and D. MacHale. 1978. Transformations of monoterpenoids in aqueous acid. The reaction of linalool, geraniol, nerol and their acetates in aqueous citric acid. Tetrahedron 34:2195–2199.

27. Bellesia, F., R. Grandi, A. Marchesini, U.M. Pagnoni, and R. Trave. 1975. Biosynthesis of the sesquiterpenoid ageratriol. Phytochemistry 14:1737–1740.

28. Benayoun, J. and A. Fahn. 1979. Intracellular transport and elimination of resin from epithelial duct-cells of *Pinus halepensis*. Ann. Bot. (London) 43:179–181.

29. Bernard-Dagan, C., J.P. Carde, and M. Gleizes. 1979. Etude des composés terpéniques au cours de la croissance des aiguilles du pin maritime: comparison de données biochemiques et ultrastructurales. Can. J. Bot. 57:255–263.

30. Bernard-Dagan, C., G. Pauly, A. Marpeau, M. Gleizes, J.-P. Carde, and P. Baradat. 1982. Control and compartmentation of terpene biosynthesis in leaves of *Pinus pinaster*. Physiol. Vég. 20:775–795.

31. Berryman, A.A. 1972. Resistance of conifers to invasion by bark beetle-fungal associations. BioScience 63:1194–1196.

32. Berryman, A.A. 1976. Theoretical explanations of mountain pine beetle dynamics in lodgepole pine forests. Environ. Entomol. 5:1225–1233.

33. Blum, M.S., R.M. Crewe, W.E. Kerr, L.H. Keith, A.W. Garrison, and M.M. Walker. 1970. Biologically active compounds in orchid fragrances. Science 164:1243–1249.

34. Bosabalidis, A. and I. Tsekos. 1982. Glandular scale development and essential oil secretion in *Origanum dictamnus* L. Planta 156:496–504.

35. Bryant, J.P. 1981. Phytochemical deterrence of snowshoe hare browsing by adventitious shoots of four Alaskan trees. Science 213:889–890.

36. Bugorskii, P.S. and M.N. Zaprometov. 1983. Catabolism of essential oil components (β-phenylethanol and geraniol) in rose petals. Fiziol. Biokhim. Kul't. Rast. 15:594–599.

37. Bunton, C.A. and O. Cori. 1978. Mechanistic aspects of terpenoid biochemistry: A cooperative basic research program. Interciencia 3:291–297.

38. Burbott, A.J. and W.D. Loomis. 1967. Effects of light and temperature on the monoterpenes of peppermint. Plant Physiol. 42:20–28.

39. Burbott, A.J. and W.D. Loomis. 1969. Evidence for metabolic turnover of monoterpenes in peppermint. Plant Physiol. 44:173–179.

40. Burbott, A.J. and W.D. Loomis. 1980. Monoterpene interconversions by cell-free enzymes from peppermint (*Mentha piperita*). Plant Physiol. 65 (suppl.):96.

41. Cane, D.E. 1980. The stereochemistry of allylic pyrophosphate metabolism. Tetrahedron 36:1109–1159.

42. Cane, D.E. 1981. Biosynthesis of sesquiterpenes. *In* J.W. Porter and S.L. Spurgeon, eds. *Biosynthesis of Isoprenoid Compounds.* Vol. 1. John Wiley and Sons, New York. pp. 283–374.

43. Cane, D.E. 1983. Cell-free studies of monoterpene and sesquiterpene biosynthesis. Biochem. Soc. Trans. 11:510–515. [*See also* Cane, D.E., C. Abell, and A.M. Tillman. 1984. Pentalenene biosynthesis and the enzymatic cyclization of farnesyl pyrophosphate: Proof that the cyclization is catalyzed by a single enzyme. Bioorg. Chem. 12:312–328.]

44. Cane, D.E. 1984. Enzyme-level studies of the biosynthesis of natural products. *In* C.J. Suckling, ed. *Enzyme Chemistry. Impact and Applications.* Chapman and Hall, London. pp 196–231.

45. Cane, D.E., R. Iyengar, and M.-S. Shiao. 1981. Cyclonerodiol biosynthesis and the enzymatic conversion of farnesyl to nerolidyl pyrophosphate. J. Am. Chem. Soc. 103:914–931.

46. Cane, D.E., T. Rossi, A.M. Tillman, and J.P. Pachlatko. 1981. Stereochemical studies of isoprenoid biosynthesis. Biosynthesis of pentalenolactone from [U-^{13}C$_6$] glucose and 6-^{2}H$_2$] glucose. J. Am. Chem. Soc. 103:1838–1843.

47. Cane, D.E., A. Saito, R. Croteau, J. Shashkus, and M. Felton. 1982. Enzymatic cyclization of geranyl pyrophosphate. Role of the pyrophosphate moiety. J. Am. Chem. Soc. 104:5831–5833.

48. Cane, D.E., S. Swanson, and P.N. Murthy. 1981. Trichodiene biosynthesis and the enzymatic cyclization of farnesyl pyrophosphate. J. Am. Chem. Soc. 103:2136–2138.

49. Cane, D.E. and A.M. Tillman. 1983. Pentalene biosynthesis and the enzymatic cyclization of farnesyl pyrophosphate. J. Am. Chem. Soc. 105:122–124.

50. Cantwell, S.G., E.P. Lau, D.S. Watt, and R.R. Fall. 1978. Biodegradation of acyclic isoprenoids by *Pseudomonas* species. J. Bacteriol. 135:324–333.

51. Carde, J.P., C. Bernard-Dagan, and M. Gleizes. 1980. Membrane systems involved in synthesis and transport of monoterpene hydrocarbons in pine leaves. *In* P. Mazliak, P. Benveniste, C. Costes, and R. Douce, eds. *Biogenesis and Function of Plant Lipids.* Elsevier, Amsterdam. pp 441–444.

52. Cates, R.G. and H. Alexander. 1982. Host resistance and susceptibility. *In* J.B. Mitton and K.B. Sturgeon, eds. *Bark Beetles in North American Conifers.* University of Texas Press, Austin. pp. 212–263.

53. Chapman, P.J., G. Meerman, and I.C. Gunsalus. 1965. The microbial transformation of fenchone. Biochem. Biophys. Res. Commun. 20:104–108.

54. Charabot, E., as described in E. Guenther. 1972. *The Essential Oils.* Vol. I. (reprinted). R.E. Krieger Publishing Co., Huntington, NY. pp. 69–72.

55. Charlwood, B.V. and D.V. Banthorpe. 1978. The biosynthesis of monoterpenes. *In* L. Reinhold, J.B. Harborne, and T. Swain, eds. *Progress in Phytochemistry,* Vol. 5. Pergamon Press, New York. pp. 65–125.

56. Charlwood, B.V. and K.A. Charlwood. 1983. The biosynthesis of mono- and sesquiterpenes in tissue culture. Biochem. Soc. Trans. 11:592–593.

57. Chayet, L., C. Rojas, E. Cardemil, A.M. Jabalquinto, R. Vicuña, and O. Cori. 1977. Biosynthesis of monoterpene hydrocarbons from [1-^{3}H] neryl pyrophosphate and [1-^{3}H] geranyl pyrophosphate by soluble enzymes from *Citrus limonum.* Arch. Biochem. Biophys. 180:318–327.

58. Coates, R. 1976. Biogenetic-type rearrangements of terpenes. *In* W. Herz, H. Grisebach, and G.W. Kirby, eds. *Progress in the Chemistry of Organic Natural Products,* Vol. 33. Springer-Verlag, Berlin. pp. 73–230.

59. Conrad, H.E., R. Dubus, M.J. Namtvedt, and I.C. Gunsalus. 1965. Mixed function oxidation II. Separation and properties of the enzymes catalyzing camphor lactonization. J. Biol. Chem. 240:495–503.

60. Cordell, G.A. 1976. Biosynthesis of sesquiterpenes. Chem. Rev. 76:425–460.

61. Cori, O. 1983. Enzymic aspects of the biosynthesis of monoterpenes in plants. Phytochemistry 22:331–341.

62. Cori, O., L. Chayet, M. De La Fuente, L.A. Fernandez, U. Hashagen, L. Pérez, G. Portilla, C. Rojas, G. Sanchez, and M.V. Vial. 1980. Stereochemical aspects of chain lengthening and cyclization processes in terpenoid biosynthesis. *In* F. Chapeville and A.-L. Haenni, eds. *Molecular Biology, Biochemistry and Biophysics,* Vol. 32. Springer-Verlag, Berlin. pp. 97–110.

63. Cori, O., L. Chayet, L.M. Perez, M.C. Rojas, G. Portilla, L. Holuigue, and L.A. Fernandez. 1981. Isoprenoid biosynthesis: Sulfhydryl groups in prenylsynthetase and carbocyclase from *Citrus flavedo.* Arch. Biol. Med. Exp. 14:129–137.

64. Croteau, R. 1977. Site of monoterpene biosynthesis in *Majorana hortensis* leaves. Plant Physiol. 59:519–520.

65. Croteau, R. 1980. The biosynthesis of terpene compounds. *In* R. Croteau, ed. *Fragrance and Flavor Substances.* D&PS Verlag, West Germany. pp. 13–36.

66. Croteau, R. 1981. Biosynthesis of Monoterpenes. *In* J.W. Porter and S.L. Spurgeon, eds. *Biosynthesis of Isoprenoid Compounds,* Vol. 1. John Wiley and Sons, New York. pp. 225–282.

67. Croteau, R. 1984. Biosynthesis and catabolism of monoterpenes. *In* W.D. Nes, G. Fuller, and L.-S. Tsai, eds. *Isopentenoids in Plants: Biochemistry and Function.* Marcel Dekker, New York. pp. 31–64.

68. Croteau, R., A.J. Burbott, and W.D. Loomis. 1972. Apparent energy deficiency in mono- and sesquiterpene biosynthesis in peppermint. Phytochemistry 11:2937–2948.

69. Croteau, R., A.J. Burbott, and W.D. Loomis. 1972. Biosynthesis of mono- and sesquiterpenes in peppermint from glucose-^{14}C and $^{14}CO_2$. Phytochemistry 11:2459–2467.

70. Croteau, R. and D.E. Cane. 1985. Monoterpene and sesquiterpene cyclases. *In* J.H. Law and H.C. Rilling, eds. *Methods in Enzymology,* Vol. 110, Academic Press, New York. pp. 383–405.

71. Croteau, R., H. El-Bialy, and S. El-Hindawi. 1984. Metabolism of monoterpenes: Lactonization of (+)-camphor and conversion of the corresponding hydroxy acid to the glucoside-glucose ester in sage (*Salvia officinalis*). Arch. Biochem. Biophys. 228:667–680.

72. Croteau, R. and M. Felton. 1980. Substrate specificity of monterpenol dehydrogenases from *Foeniculum vulgare* and *Tanacetum vulgare.* Phytochemistry 19:1343–1347.

73. Croteau, R. and M. Felton. 1981. Conversion of [1-^{3}H,G-^{14}C] geranyl pyrophosphate to cyclic monoterpenes without loss of tritium. Arch. Biochem. Biophys. 207:460–464.

74. Croteau, R., M. Felton, F. Karp, and R. Kjonaas. 1981. Relationship of camphor biosynthesis to leaf development in sage (*Salvia officinalis*). Plant Physiol. 67:820–824.

75. Croteau, R., M. Felton, and R.C. Ronald. 1980. Biosynthesis of monoterpenes: Conversion of the acyclic precursors geranyl pyrophosphate and neryl pyrophosphate to the rearranged monoterpenes fenchol and fenchone by a soluble enzyme preparation from fennel (*Foeniculum vulgare*). Arch. Biochem. Biophys. 200:524–533.

76. Croteau, R., M. Felton, and R.C. Ronald. 1980. Biosynthesis of monoterpenes: Preliminary characterization of *l-endo*-fenchol synthetase from fennel (*Foeniculum vulgare*) and evidence that no free intermediate is involved in the cyclization of geranyl pyrophosphate to the rearranged product. Arch. Biochem. Biophys. 200:534–546.

77. Croteau, R., M. Felton, and C.J. Wheeler. 1985. Stereochemistry at C-1 of geranyl pyrophosphate and neryl pyrophosphate in the enzymatic cyclization to (+)- and (–)-bornyl pyrophosphate, J. Biol. Chem. 260:5956–5962.

78. Croteau, R. and A. Gundy. 1984. Cyclization of farnesyl pyrophosphate to the sesquiterpene olefins humulene and caryophyllene by an enzyme system from sage (*Salvia officinalis*). Arch. Biochem. Biophys. 233:838–841.

79. Croteau, R. and C.L. Hooper. 1978. Metabolism of monoterpenes: Acetylation of (–)-menthol by a soluble enzyme preparation from peppermint. Plant Physiol. 61:737–742.

80. Croteau, R., C.L. Hooper, and M. Felton. 1978. Biosynthesis of monoterpenes: Partial purification and characterization of a bicyclic monoterpenol dehydrogenase from sage (*Salvia officinalis*). Arch. Biochem. Biophys. 188:182–193.

81. Croteau, R. and M.A. Johnson. 1984. Biosynthesis of terpenoids in glandular trichomes. *In* E. Rodriguez, P.L. Healey, and I. Mehta, eds. *Biology and Chemistry of Plant Trichomes*. Plenum Press, New York. pp. 133–185.

82. Croteau, R. and M.A. Johnson. 1984. Biosynthesis of terpenoid wood extractives. *In* T. Higuchi, ed. *Biosynthesis and Biodegradation of Wood Components*. Academic Press, New York. pp. 379–439.

83. Croteau, R. and F. Karp. 1976. Biosynthesis of monoterpenes: Enzymatic conversion of neryl pyrophosphate to 1,8-cineole, α-terpineol, and cyclic monoterpene hydrocarbons by a cell-free preparation from sage (*Salvia officinalis*). Arch. Biochem. Biophys. 176:734–746.

84. Croteau, R. and F. Karp. 1977. Biosynthesis of monoterpenes: Partial purification and characterization of 1,8-cineole synthetase from *Salvia officinalis*. Arch. Biochem. Biophys. 179:257–265.

85. Croteau, R. and F. Karp. 1977. Demonstration of a cyclic pyrophosphate intermediate in the enzymatic conversion of neryl pyrophosphate to borneol. Arch. Biochem. Biophys. 184:77–86.

86. Croteau, R. and F. Karp. 1979. Biosynthesis of monoterpenes: Hydrolysis of bornyl pyrophosphate, an essential step in camphor biosynthesis, and hydrolysis of geranyl pyrophosphate, the acyclic precursor of camphor, by enzymes from sage (*Salvia officinalis*). Arch. Biochem. Biophys. 198:523–532.

87. Croteau, R. and F. Karp. 1979. Biosynthesis of monoterpenes: Preliminary characterization of bornyl pyrophosphate synthetase from sage (*Salvia officinalis*) and demonstration that geranyl pyrophosphate is the preferred substrate for cyclization. Arch. Biochem. Biophys. 198:512–522.

88. Croteau, R. and W.D. Loomis. 1972. Biosynthesis of mono- and sesquiterpenes in peppermint from mevalonate-2-[14]C. Phytochemistry 11:1055–1066.

89. Croteau, R. and W.D. Loomis. 1973. Biosynthesis of squalene and other triterpenes in *Mentha piperita* from mevalonate-2-[14]C. Phytochemistry 12:1957–1965.

90. Croteau, R. and C. Martinkus. 1979. Metabolism of monoterpenes: Demonstration of (+)-neomenthyl-β-D-glucoside as a major metabolite of (–)-menthone in peppermint (*Mentha piperita*). Plant Physiol. 64:169–175.

91. Croteau, R., P. Purkett, and M. Felton. 1985. Geranyl pyrophosphate synthetase: Characterization of the enzyme and evidence that this chain-length specific prenyl transferase is associated with monoterpene biosynthesis in sage (*Salvia officinalis*), submitted.

92. Croteau, R. and J. Shaskus. 1985. Biosynthesis of monoterpenes: (–)-Bornyl pyrophosphate cyclase in soluble enzyme preparations from tansy (*Tanacetum vulgare*). Arch. Biochem. Biophys. 236:535–543.

93. Croteau, R., J. Shaskus, D.E. Cane, A. Saito, and C. Chang. 1984. Enzymatic cyclization of [1-^{18}O] geranyl pyrophosphate to *l-endo*-fenchol. J. Am. Chem. Soc. 106:1142–1143.

94. Croteau, R. and V.K. Sood. 1985. Metabolism of monoterpenes: Evidence for the function of monoterpenes catabolism in peppermint (*Mentha piperita*) rhizomes. Plant Physiol. 77:801–806.

95. Croteau, R., V.K. Sood, B. Renstrøm, and R. Bhushan. 1984. Metabolism of monoterpenes: Early steps in the metabolism of *d*-neomenthyl-β-D-glucoside in peppermint (*Mentha piperita*) rhizomes. Plant Physiol. 76:647–653.

96. Croteau, R. and J.N. Winters. 1982. Demonstration of the intercellular compartmentation of *l*-menthone metabolism in peppermint (*Mentha piperita*) leaves. Plant Physiol. 69:975–977.

97. Dell, B. 1977. Distribution and function of resins and glandular hairs in Western Australian plants. J. Proc. Royal Soc. West. Aust. 59:119–123.

98. Dell, D. and A.J. McComb. 1978. Plant resins--their formation, secretion and possible functions. *In* H. Woolhouse, ed. *Advances in Botanical Research*, Vol. 6. Academic Press, New York. pp. 227–316.

99. Dev, S., A.P.S. Narula, and J.S. Yadav. 1982. *Handbook of Terpenoids. Monoterpenoids.* Vol. I and II. CRC Press, Boca Raton, FL.

100. Devon, T.K. and A.I. Scott. 1972. *Handbook of Naturally Occurring Compounds*, Vol. II. *Terpenes.* Academic Press, New York. pp. 3–184.

101. Dugan, R.E. 1981. Regulation of HMG-CoA reductase. *In* J.W. Porter and C.L. Spurgeon, eds. *Biosynthesis of Isoprenoid Compounds*, Vol. 1. John Wiley and Sons, New York. pp. 95–159.

102. Ebermann, R. and K. Stich. 1982. Peroxidase and amylase isoenzymes in the sapwood and heartwood of trees. Phytochemistry 21:2401–2402.

103. Embong, M.B., D. Hadziyev, and S. Molnar. 1977. Essential oils from herbs and spices grown in Alberta. Sage oil, *Salvia officinalis*, L. (Labiatae). Can. Inst. Food Sci. Technol. J. 10:201–207.

104. Embong, M.B., L. Steele, D. Hadziyev, and S. Molnar. 1977. Essential oils from herbs and spices grown in Alberta. Peppermint oil, *Mentha piperia* var. Mitcham, L. Can. Inst. Food Sci. Technol. J. 10:247–256.

105. Epstein, W.W. and C.D. Poulter. 1973. A survey of some irregular monoterpenes and their biogenetic analogies to presqualene alcohol. Phytochemistry 12:737–747.

106. Erickson, R.E. 1976. The industrial importance of monoterpenes and essential oils. Lloydia 39:8–19.

107. Evans, R. and J.R. Hanson. 1976. Studies in terpenoid biosynthesis. Part XIV. Formation of the sesquiterpene trichodiene. J. Chem. Soc. Perkin Trans. I., 326–329.

108. Fahn, A. 1979. *Secretory Tissues in Plants.* Academic Press, New York. pp. 158–222.

109. Fahn, A. and J. Benayoun. 1976. Ultrastructure of resin ducts of *Pinus halepensis:* Development, possible sites of resin synthesis, and mode of its elimination from the protoplast. Ann. Bot. (London) 40:857–863.

110. Farentinos, R.C., P.J. Capretta, R.E. Kepner, and V.M. Littlefield. 1981. Selective herbivory in tassel-eared squirrels: Role of monoterpenes in ponderosa pines chosen as feeding trees. Science 213:1273–1275.

111. Firmage, D. and R. Irving. 1979. Effect of development on monoterpene composition of *Hedeoma Drummundii.* Phytochemistry 18:1827–1829.

112. Flück, H. 1963. Intrinsic and extrinsic factors affecting the production of secondary plant products. *In* T. Swain, ed. *Chemical Plant Taxonomy.* Academic Press, New York. pp. 167–186.

113. Francis, M.J.O. 1971. Monoterpene biosynthesis. *In* T.W. Goodwin, ed. *Aspects of Terpenoid Chemistry and Biochemistry.* Academic Press, New York. pp. 29–51.

114. Francis, M.J.O. and M. O'Connell. 1969. The incorporation of mevalonic acid into rose petal monoterpenes. Phytochemistry 8:1705–1708.

115. Gambliel, H. and R. Croteau. 1982. Biosynthesis of (±)-α-pinene and (−)-β-pinene from geranyl pyrophosphate by a soluble enzyme system from sage (*Salvia officinalis*). J. Biol. Chem. 257:2335–2342.

116. Gambliel, H. and R. Croteau. 1984. Pinene cyclases I and II. Two enzymes from sage (*Salvia officinalis*) which catalyze stereospecific cyclizations of geranyl pyrophosphate to monoterpene olefins of opposite configuration. J. Biol. Chem. 259:740–748.

117. Gershenzon, J. 1984. Changes in the levels of plant secondary metabolites under water and nutrient stress. *In* B.N. Timmermann, C. Steelink, and F.A. Loewus, eds. *Recent Advances in Phytochemistry,* Vol. 18. Plenum Press, New York. pp. 273–320.

118. Gibbs, R.D. 1974. *Chemotaxonomy of Flowering Plants,* Vol. II. McGill-Queen's University Press, Montreal, Canada. pp. 770–872.

119. Gildemeister, E. and F. Hoffman. 1955–1960. *Die ätherischen Öle.* 8 vols. Akademie Verlag, Berlin.

120. Glasby, J.S. 1982. *Encyclopaedia of the Terpenoids.* Wiley, New York. 2646 p.

121. Gleizes, M. 1978. Biosynthése des carbures terpéniques du pin maritime: Essai de localization. C.R. Acad. Sci. 286D:543–546.

122. Gleizes, M., A. Marpeau, G. Pauly, and C. Bernard-Dagan. 1982. Role of acyclic compounds in monoterpene biosynthesis in *Pinus pinaster.* Phytochemistry 21:2641–2644.

123. Gleizes, M., A. Marpeau, G. Pauly, and C. Bernard-Dagan. 1984. Sesquiterpene biosynthesis in maritime pine needles. Phytochemistry 23:1257–1259.

124. Gleizes, M., G. Pauly, J.-P. Carde, A. Marpeau, and C. Bernard-Dagan. 1983. Monoterpene hydrocarbon biosynthesis by isolated leucoplasts of *Citrofortunella mitis.* Planta 159:373–381.

125. Gogrof, G. 1957. The volatile oil, sesquiterpenes, and glandular trichomes of patchouli (*Pogostemon* species). Pharmazie 12:38–51.

126. Goodwin, T.W. and E.I. Mercer. 1972. *Introduction to Plant Biochemistry. Pergamon Press, Oxford. pp. 256–283.*

127. Gotfredsen, S.E. 1978. The biosynthesis of lagopodine A, B, and C, coccinol and linalool. Diss. ETH (Zurich), No. 6243. as cited in references 41 and 45.

128. Gotfredsen, S., J.P. Obrecht, and D. Arigoni. 1977. The cyclization of linalool to α-terpineol. Stereochemical course of the reaction. Chimia 31:62–63.

129. Guenther, E. 1972-1976. *The Essential Oils.* 6 vols. (reprinted), R.E. Krieger, Huntington, NY.

130. Hanson, J.R. 1970. The application of multiply-labelled mevalonate in terpene and steroid biosynthesis. Adv. Steroid. Biochem. Pharmacol. 7:51–96.

131. Hefendehl, F.W. and M.J. Murray. 1976. Genetic aspects of the biosynthesis of natural odors. Lloydia 39:39–51.

132. Heinrich, G. 1979. Zur Cytologie und Physiologie ätherische Öle erzeugender pflanzlicher Drüsenzellen. *In* K.H. Kubeczka, ed. *Vorkommen und Analytik ätherischer Öle.* Georg Thieme Verlag, Stuttgart. pp. 47–53.

133. Heinrich, G., W. Schultze, I. Pfab, and M. Böttger. 1983. The site of essential oil biosynthesis in *Poncirus trifoliata* and *Monarda fistulosa.* Physiol. Vég. 21:257–268.

134. Heinrich, G., W. Schultze, and R. Wegener. 1980. Zur Kompartimentierung der Synthese von Mono- und Sesqui-Terpenen des ätherischen Öls bei *Poncirus trifoliata.* Protoplasma 103:115–129.

135. Henderson, W., J.W. Hart, P. How, and J. Judge. 1970. Chemical and morphological studies on sites of sesquiterpene accumulation in *Pogostemon cablin* (Patchouli). Phytochemistry 9:1219–1228.

136. Hendricks, H. and F.H.L. Van Os. 1976. Essential oil of two chemotypes of *Mentha suaveolens* during ontogenesis. Phytochemistry 15:1127–1330.

137. Herout, V. 1971. Biochemistry of sesquiterpenoids. *In* T.W. Goodwin, ed. *Aspects of Terpenoid Chemistry and Biochemistry.* Academic Press, New York. pp. 53–94.

138. Horster, H. 1979. Monoterpenglykoside, eine Diskussion über ihre biologische Bedeutung und Möglichkeiten zur Synthese dieser Verbindungen. *In* K.H. Kubeczka, ed. *Vorkommen und Analytik ätherischer Öle.* Georg Thieme Verlag, Stuttgart. pp. 34–40.

139. Irving, R.S. and R.P. Adams. 1973. Genetic and biosynthetic relationships of monoterpenes. *In* V.C. Runeckles and T.J. Mabry, eds. *Recent Advances in Phytochemistry,* Vol. 6. Academic Press, New York. pp. 187–214.

140. Jedlicki, E., G. Jacob, F. Faini, O. Cori, and C.A. Bunton. 1972. Stereospecificity of isopentenyl pyrophosphate isomerase and prenyl transferase from *Pinus* and *Citrus.* Arch. Biochem. Biophys. 152:590–596.

141. Johnson, M.A. and R. Croteau. 1980. Cell-free biosynthesis and peroxidation of monoterpene hydrocarbons. Plant Physiol. 65 (suppl.):96.

142. Johnson, M.A. and R. Croteau. 1984. Biosynthesis of ascaridole: Iodide peroxidase-catalyzed synthesis of a monoterpene endoperoxide in soluble extracts of *Chenopodium ambrosioides* fruit. Arch. Biochem. Biophys. 235:254–266.

143. Karp, F. and R. Croteau. 1982. Evidence that sabinene is an essential precursor of C(3)-oxygenated thujane monoterpenes. Arch. Biochem. Biophys. 216:616–624.

144. Kelsey, R.G., G.W. Reynolds, and E. Rodriguez. 1984. Chemistry of biologically active constituents secreted and stored in plant glandular trichomes. *In* E. Rodriguez, P.L. Healey, and I. Mehta, eds. *Biology and Chemistry of Plant Trichomes.* Plenum Press, New York. pp. 187–241.

145. Kepner, R.E., B.O. Ellison, M. Breckenridge, G. Connolly, S.C. Madden, and C.J. Muller. 1974. Volatile terpenes in California bay foliage. Changes in composition during maturation. J. Agric. Food Chem. 22:781–784.

146. Kjonaas, R. and R. Croteau. 1983. Demonstration that limonene is the first cyclic intermediate in the biosynthesis of oxygenated *p*-menthane monoterpenes in *Mentha piperita* and other *Mentha* species. Arch. Biochem. Biophys. 220:79–89.

147. Kjonaas, R., C. Martinkus, and R. Croteau. 1980. Metabolism of *l*-menthone in peppermint. Plant Physiol. 65 (suppl.):96.

148. Kjonaas, R., C. Martinkus-Taylor, and R. Croteau. 1982. Metabolism of monoterpenes: Conversion of *l*-menthone to *l*-menthol and *d*-neomenthol by stereospecific dehydrogenases from peppermint (*Mentha piperita*) leaves. Plant Physiol. 69:1013–1017.

149. Kjonaas, R., K.V. Venkatachalam, and R. Croteau. 1985. Metabolism of monoterpenes: Oxidation of isopiperitenol to isopiperitenone, and subsequent isomerization to piperitenone by soluble enzyme preparations from peppermint (*Mentha piperita*) leaves. Arch. Biochem. Biophys. 238:49–60.

150. Kúc, J. and N. Lisker. 1978. Terpenoids and their role in wounded and infected plant storage tissue. *In* G. Kahl, ed. *Biochemistry of Wounded Plant Tissues.* de Gruyter, Berlin. pp. 203–242.

151. Kullenberg, G. and G. Bergström. 1975. Chemical communication between living organisms. Endeavor 34:59–66.

152. Larkin, J.P., D.C. Nonhebel, and H.C.S. Wood. 1976. Phosphate esters. Part 3. Formation of sesquiterpene hydrocarbons from *cis,trans* and *trans,trans*-farnesyl diphenyl phosphates. J. Chem. Soc. Perkin Trans. I, 2524–2528.

153. Lawrence, B.M. 1981. Monoterpene interrelationships in the *Mentha* genus: A biosynthestic discussion. *In* B.D. Mookherjee and C.J. Mussinan, eds. *Essential Oils.* Allured Publishing Corp., Wheaton, IL. pp. 1–81.

154. Levin, D.A. 1973. The role of trichomes in plant defense. Quart. Rev. Biol. 48:3–15.

155. Levin, D.A. 1976. The chemical defenses of plants to pathogens and herbivores. Annu. Rev. Ecol. Syst. 7:121–159.

156. Lincoln, D.E. and J.H. Langenheim. 1979. Effect of light and temperature on monoterpenoid yield and composition in *Satureja douglasii.* Biochem. Syst. Ecol. 6:21–32.

157. Loomis, W.D. 1967. Biosynthesis and metabolism of monoterpenes. *In* J.B. Pridham, ed. *Terpenoids in Plants.* Academic Press, New York. pp. 59–82.

158. Loomis, W.D. and R. Croteau. 1973. Biochemistry and physiology of lower terpenoids. *In* V.C. Runeckles and T.J. Mabry, eds. *Recent Advances in Phytochemistry,* Vol. 6. Academic Press, New York. pp. 147–186.

159. Loomis, W.D. and R. Croteau. 1980. Biochemistry of terpenoids. *In* P.K. Stumpf, ed. *The Biochemistry of Plants,* Vol. 4, Lipids. Academic Press, New York. pp. 363–418.

160. Martinkus, C. and R. Croteau. 1981. Metabolism of monoterpenes: Evidence for compartmentation of *l*-menthone metabolism in peppermint (*Mentha piperita*) leaves. Plant Physiol. 68:99–106.

161. Mash, E.A., G.M. Gurria, and C.D. Poulter. 1981. Farnesyl pyrophosphate synthetase. Evidence for a rigid geranyl cation-pyrophosphate anion pair. J. Am. Chem. Soc. 103:3927–3929.

162. McCormick, J.P. and D.L. Barton. 1978. Studies in 85 percent H_3PO_4. II. On the role of the α-terpinyl cation in cyclic monoterpene genesis. Tetrahedron 34:325–330.

163. Michie, M.J. and D.M. Reid. 1959. Biosynthesis of complex terpenoids in the leaf cuticle and trichomes of *Nicotiana tabacum.* Nature (London) 218:578.

164. Monaco, P., L. Previtera, and L. Mangoni. 1982. Terpenes in *Pistacia* plants: A possible defense role for monoterpenes against gall-forming aphids. Phytochemistry 21:2408–2410.

165. Morikawa, K. and Y. Hirose. Biosynthesis of germacrene C. Tetrahedron Letts., 1131–1132.

166. Mothes, K. 1973. Pflanze und Tier. Ein Vergleich auf der Ebene des Sekundärstoffwechsels. Sitzungsber. Österr Akad. Wiss. Math. Naturwiss. Kl. Sonderh. Abt. I 181:1–37.

167. Nabeta, K., Y. Ohnishi, T. Hirose, and H. Sugisawa. 1983. Monoterpene biosynthesis by callus tissues and suspension cells from *Perilla* species. Phytochemistry 22:423–425.

168. Nes, W.R. and M.L. McKean. 1977. *Biochemistry of Steroids and Other Isopentenoids.* University Park Press, Baltimore, MD. pp. 1–36, 147–170, 272–301.

169. Nicholas, H.J. 1962. Biosynthesis of β-sitosterol and certain terpenoid substances in *Ocimum basilicum* from mevalonic acid-2-^{14}C. J. Biol. Chem. 237:1485–1488.

170. Nicholas, H.J. 1964. Biosynthesis and metabolism of [^{14}C] sclareol. Biochim. Biophys. Acta 84:80–90.

171. Overton, K.H. and D.J. Picken. 1976. Biosynthesis of bisabolene by callus cultures of *Andrographis paniculata.* J. Chem. Soc. Chem. Commun. (3), 105–106.

172. Paech, K. 1950. *Biologie und Physiologie der Sekundaren Pflanzenstoffe.* Springer-Verlag, Berlin.

173. Parker, W., J.S. Roberts, and R. Ramage. 1967. Sesquiterpene biogenesis. Q. Rev. Chem. Soc. 21:331–363.

174. Pogorel'skaya, A.N., V.P. Kholodova, and S.A. Reznikova. 1980. Physiological aspects of essential oil accumulation in petals of the flowers of essential-oil rose. Fiziol. Rast. (Moscow) 27:356–362.

175. Portilla, G., M.C. Rojas, L. Chayet, and O. Cori. 1982. Synthesis of monoterpene hydrocarbons from [1-^{3}H] linalyl pyrophosphate by carbocyclase from *Citrus limonum*. Arch. Biochem. Biophys. 218:614–618.

176. Potty, V.H. and J.H. Bruemmer. 1970. Limonene reductase system in the orange. Phytochemistry 9:2319–2321.

177. Poulose, A.J. and R. Croteau. 1978. Biosynthesis of aromatic monoterpenes: Conversion of γ-terpinene to *p*-cymene and thymol in *Thymus vulgaris* L. Arch. Biochem. Biophys. 187:307–314.

178. Poulose, A.J. and R. Croteau. 1978. γ-Terpinene synthetase: A key enzyme in the biosynthesis of aromatic monoterpenes. Arch. Biochem. Biophys. 191:400–411.

179. Poulter, C.D. 1974. Model studies in terpene biosynthesis. J. Agric. Food Chem. 22:167–175.

180. Poulter, C.D. and J.M. Hughes. 1977. Model studies of the biosynthesis of non-head-to-tail terpenes. Stereochemistry of the head-to-head rearrangement. J. Am. Chem. Soc. 99:3830–3838.

181. Poulter, C.D. and C.-H.R. King. 1982. Model studies of terpene biosynthesis. A stepwise mechanism for cyclization of nerol to α-terpineol. J. Am. Chem. Soc. 104:1422–1424.

182. Poulter, C.D. and C.-H.R. King. 1982. Model studies of terpene biosynthesis. Stereospecific cyclization of *N*-methyl-(*S*)-4- ([1'-^{2}H] neryloxy) pyridinium methyl sulfate to α-terpineol. J. Am. Chem. Soc. 104:1420–1422.

183. Poulter, C.D. and H.C. Rilling. 1981. Prenyl transferases and isomerase. *In* J.W. Porter and S.L. Spurgeon, eds. *Biosynthesis of Isoprenoid Compounds,* Vol. 1. John Wiley and Sons, New York. pp. 161–224.

184. Qureshi, N. and J.W. Porter. 1981. Conversion of acetyl-Coenzyme A to isopentenyl pyrophosphate. *In* J.W. Porter and S.L. Spurgeon, eds. *Biosynthesis of Isoprenoid Compounds,* Vol. 1. John Wiley and Sons, New York. pp. 47–94.

185. Regnier, F.E., G.R. Waller, E.J. Eisenbraun, and H. Auda. 1968. The biosynthesis of methylcyclopentane monoterpenoids – II. Nepetalactone. Phytochemistry 7:221–230.

186. Rojas, M.C., L. Chayet, G. Portilla, and O. Cori. 1983. Substrate and metal specificity in the enzymic synthesis of cyclic monoterpenes from geranyl and neryl pyrophosphate. Arch. Biochem. Biophys. 222:389–396.

187. Royal Chemical Society (London). The previously published (1971–1983) periodic reviews on *Terpenoids and Steroids* and *Biosynthesis* have been superseded by *Natural Product Reports*.

188. Rücker, G. 1973. Sesquiterpenes. Angew. Chem. Int. Ed. Engl. 12:794–805.

189. Ruzicka, L., A. Eschenmoser, and H. Heusser. 1953. The isoprene rule and the biogenesis of terpenic compounds. Experientia 9:357–396.

190. Sakata, I. and K. Koshimizu. 1978. Occurrence of *l*-menthyl-β-D-glucoside and methyl palmitate in rhizoma of Japanese peppermint. Agric. Biol. Chem. 42:1959–1960.

191. Sakata, I. and K. Koshimizu. 1980. Seasonal variations in menthyl glucoside, menthol, menthone and related monoterpenes in developing Japanese peppermint. J. Agric. Chem. Soc. Jpn. 54:1037–1043.

192. Sandermann, W. 1962. Terpenoids: Structure and distribution. *In* M. Florkin and H.S. Mason, eds. *Comparative Biochemistry,* Vol. 3, Part A. Academic Press, New York. pp. 503–590.

193. Schery, R.W. 1972. *Plants for Man*, 2 ed. Prentice-Hall, Englewood Cliffs, NJ.

194. Schnepf, E. 1974. Gland cells. *In* A.W. Robards, ed. *Dynamic Aspects of Plant Ultrastructure.* McGraw-Hill, New York. pp. 331–357.

195. Scora, R.W. and C. Adams. 1973. Effect of oleocellosis, desiccation, and fungal infection upon the terpenes of individual oil glands in *Citrus latipes.* Phytochemistry 12:2347–2350.

196. Seigler, D.S. 1981. Terpenoids. *In* D.A. Young and D.S. Seigler, eds. *Phytochemistry and Angiosperm Phylogeny.* Praeger, New York. pp. 117–148.

197. Seubert, W. 1960. Degradation of isoprenoid compounds by Microorganisms. I. Isolation and characterization of an isoprenoid-degrading bacterium, *Pseudomonas citronellolis* n. sp. J. Bacteriol. 79:426–434.

198. Seubert, W. and E. Fass. 1964. Untersuchungen über den Bacteriellen abbau von Isoprenoiden. V. Der Mechanismus des Isoprenoidabbaues. Biochem. Z. 341:35–44.

199. Shrimpton, D.M. 1978. Resistance of lodgepole pine to mountain pine beetle infestations. *In* A.A. Berryman, G.D. Amman, R.W. Stark, and D.L. Kibbee, eds. *Theory and Practice of Mountain Pine Beetle Management in Lodgepole Pine Forests—A Symposium.* April. 25–27. College of Forest Resources, University of Idaho, Moscow.

200. Simpson, T.J. 1975. Carbon-13 nuclear magnetic resonance in biosynthetic studies. Chem. Soc. Rev. 4:497–522.

201. Smith, D.H. and R.E. Carhart. 1976. Structural isomerism of mono- and sesquiterpenoid skeletons. Tetrahedron 32:2513–2519.

202. Souček, M. 1962. On terpenes. CXLVIII. Biosynthesis of carotol in *Daucus carota* L. A contribution to configuration of carotol and daucol. Collect. Czech. Chem. Commun. 27:2929–2934.

203. Spurgeon, S.L. and J.W. Porter. 1981. Introduction. *In* J.W. Porter and S.L. Spurgeon, eds. *Biosynthesis of Isoprenoid Compounds,* Vol. 1. John Wiley and Sons, New York. pp. 1–46.

204. Stoessl, A. 1982. Biosynthesis of phytoalexins. *In* J.A. Bailey and J.W. Mansfield, eds. *Phytoalexins.* Halsted Press, New York. pp. 159–173.

205. Stothers, J.B. 1981. Sesquiterpenes—biosynthetic studies with ^{13}C and ^{3}H magnetic resonance—a synthetic approach via homoenolization. Pure Appl. Chem. 53:1241–1258.

206. Suga, T., T. Hirata, H. Okita, and K. Tsuji. 1983. Biosynthesis of cyclic monoterpenoids. The pivotal acyclic precursor for the cyclization leading to the formation of α-terpineol and limonene in *Mentha spicata* and *Citrus natsudaidai.* Chem. Lett., 1491–1494.

207. Suga, T., T. Shishibori, and M. Bukeo. 1972. Biosynthesis of linalool in *Cinnamomum camphora* var. linalooliferum. Bull. Chem. Soc. Jpn. 45:1480–1482.

208. Suga, T., T. Shishibori, and T. Hirata. 1977. Biosynthesis of cyclic monoterpenes in higher plants. The retention of the C-5 hydrogen atom of mevalonate during its incorporation into cyclic monoterpenes. Chem. Lett., 937–938.

209. Suga, T., T. Shishibori, and H. Morinaka. 1977. The intermediacy of linaloyl pyrophosphate in biosynthesis of cyclic monoterpenes by higher plants. Proc. Annu. Meet. Jpn. Biochem. Soc. Toyko, p. 1069.

210. Suga, T., T. Shishibori, and H. Morinaka. 1980. Preferential participation of linaloyl pyrophosphate rather than neryl pyrophosphate in biosyn-

thesis of cyclic monoterpenoids in higher plants. J. Chem. Soc. Chem. Commun., (4):167–168.

211. Terhune, S.J., J.W. Hogg, A.C. Bromstein, and B.M. Lawrence. 1975. Four new sesquiterpene analogs of common monoterpenes. Can. J. Chem. 53:3285–3293.

212. Thomson, W.W. and P.L. Healey. 1984. Cellular basis of trichome secretion. *In* E. Rodriguez, P.L. Healey, and I. Mehta, eds. *Biology and Chemistry of Plant Trichomes.* Plenum Press, New York. pp. 95–111.

213. Tyson, B.J., W.A. Dement, and H.A. Mooney. 1974. Volatilization of terpenes from *Salvia mellifera.* Nature (London) 252:119–120.

214. Valenzuela, P., E. Beytia, O. Cori, and A. Yudelevich. 1966. Phosphorylated intermediates of terpene biosynthesis in *Pinus radiata.* Arch. Biochem. Biophys. 113:536–539.

215. Venkatachalam, K.V., R. Kjonaas, and R. Croteau. 1984. Development and essential oil content of secretory glands of sage (*Salvia officinalis*). Plant Physiol. 76:148–150.

216. Vermeer, J. and R.L. Peterson. 1979. Glandular trichomes on the inflorescence of *Chrysanthemum morifolium* cv. Dramatic (Compositate). II. Ultrastructure and histochemistry. Can. J. Bot. 57:714–729 (and references therein).

217. Verzár-Petri, G. and M. Then. 1975. The study of the localization of volatile oil in the different parts of *Salvia sclarea* L. and *Salvia officinalis* L. by applying 2-^{14}C sodium acetate. Acta Botan. Scient. Hung. 21:189–205.

218. Vial, M.V., C. Rojas, G. Portilla, L. Chayet, L.M. Pérez, and O. Cori. 1981. Enhancement of the hydrolysis of geranyl pyrophosphate by bivalent metal ions. A model for enzymic biosynthesis of cyclic monoterpenes. Tetraderon 37:2351–2357.

219. Wallach, O. 1914. *Terpene und Camphor,* 2nd ed. Vit. Leipzig. [For recent accounts of the historical developments in isoprenoid chemistry, see references 168 and 203.]

220. Witte, L., J. Berlin, V. Wray, W. Schubert, W. Kohl, G. Höfle, and J. Hammer. 1983. Mono- and diterpenes from cell cultures of *Thuja occidentalis.* Planta Med. 49:216–221.

221. Wollenweber, E. and E. Schnepf. 1970. Vergleichende Untersuchungen über die flavonoiden Exkrete von "Mehl"- und "Öl"-Drüsen bei Primeln und die Feinstrucktur der Drüsenzellen. Z. Pflanzenphysiol. 62:216–227.

222. Wong, R.J., D.K. McCormack, and D.W. Russell. 1981. Plastid 3-hydroxy-3-methylglutaryl Coenzyme A reductase has distinctive kinetic and regulatory features: Properties of the enzyme and positive phytochrome control of activity in pea seedlings. Arch. Biochem. Biophys. 216:631–638.

The Biochemical Pharmacology of Plant Alkaloids

Trevor Robinson
Department of Biochemistry, University of Massachusetts, Amherst, MA 01003

CONTENTS

I. INTRODUCTION

Ever since prehistoric times, many plants have been used because of the physiological effects of alkaloids that they contain. Even now, when pure compounds are often preferred as drugs, some of the most valuable compounds are still isolated from plants rather than prepared synthetically. Since no perfectly satisfying definition of the term alkaloid is apparent, for the purposes of this review any compound that has been referred to in the literature as an alkaloid may be included.

A somewhat more specific orientation to the alkaloids is presented in Table 1, where skeletal structures for many common types of alkaloids and information about the metabolic precursors of these different alkaloid classes are shown. Amino acids and other common metabolites are the starting materials for alkaloid biosynthesis in alkaloid-containing plants; details of these metabolic transformations are available in other sources (117, 156, 213).

In spite of the long-term interest in physiological actions of alkaloids, only within the past 20 years or so has it become possible to understand some of these actions at a molecular level rather than in terms of behavioral or anatomical consequences. Aspects of alkaloid actions organized according to affected organ systems or according to plant sources can be found in texts of pharmacology or pharmacognosy (72, 204, 207). The approach in this review is subcellular and molecular, with alkaloid actions organized under the following categories:

A. Effects on subcellular structure components, such as membranes and cytoskeleton.
B. Effects on membrane transport processes.
C. Action at the receptors for endogenous chemical transmitters.
D. Effects on nucleic acids and protein synthesis components.
E. Inhibition and activation of enzymes.

There is some unavoidable overlap among these categories—for example, neuro-receptors and ion transporters are frequently closely linked to one another and to the activities of specific enzymes. Cross references will be given where appropriate. A greater complication is that often a single chemical has multiple actions, with one effect showing up prominently at one concentration and an entirely different type of effect showing up at another concentration. The literature is full of descriptions of effects of alkaloids on various purified systems that have little to do with the most striking pharmacological effect on an intact animal.

As an extreme point of view, one is probably safe in saying that, given a high enough concentration, *any* small molecule will undoubtedly have some kind of effect on *any* macromolecular system. Therefore, in examining reports of molecular effects of an alkaloid, it is necessary to ask what the concentrations were and whether these concentrations are consistent with what is attained when the alkaloid has an effect on a whole organism. This question leads to considerations of binding, transport, permeability, and degradation, which will be largely ignored in this review. Some of these matters as well as a more chemical point of view can be found elsewhere (156).

TABLE 1. The Most Important Classes of Alkaloids and Their Precursors.[a]

Class of alkaloid	Structural type (main precursor emphasized)	Biogenetic precursors
Pyrrolidine		Ornithine and Acetate
Pyrrolizidine		Ornithine
Tropane		Ornithine and Acetate
Piperidine Conium		Acetate
Punica, Sedum and Lobelia		Lysine, Acetate or Phenylalanine
Quinolizidine		Lysine
Isoquinoline		Phenylalanine or Tyrosine
Indole		Tryptophan
Rutaceae		Anthranilic acid
Terpene		Mevalonic acid

[a]Reprinted with permission from *Concise Encyclopedia of Biochemistry* (Berlin, New York: Walter de Gruyter, 1983), pp. 18–19.

II. EFFECTS ON SUBCELLULAR STRUCTURES

The physical disruption of membranes as distinguished from more specific actions on special components of membranes appears to account for the effects of a few alkaloids. This disruption leads to a general leakiness or even to lysis. The best-studied alkaloids having this mode of action are the steroid alkaloids of Solanaceae. For example, α-tomatine increases membrane permeability indiscriminately to many different solutes (158). The effect is antagonized by calcium ions (157). Studies with artificial liposomes suggest that tomatine interacts with membrane sterols to produce its effect (159).

Various ellipticine derivatives also disrupt erythrocyte and liposome membranes by a combination of ionic and hydrophobic interactions (59, 202). Vincristine associates with the lipid components of membranes (100). Other alkaloids affect membrane structure indirectly, not by attacking completed membranes, but by inhibiting the synthesis of membrane constituents. One of the myriad effects of colchicine falls into this category (120, 130), although colchicine may also interact directly with membrane proteins (7). Cepharanthine makes membranes more stable by inhibiting peroxidation of their lipids (176).

Colchicine from *Colchicum autumnale* L. has been known for a long time to stimulate formation of polyploid cells by blocking nuclear division while allowing chromosome duplication. The mechanism of this effect is now known to result from binding of the alkaloid to tubulin, the structural protein of microtubules. Tubulin from many different sources appears to be the same in essential features. It is a polymer based on 2 subunits—α and β—with a combined molecular weight of about 1.2×10^5 daltons (Figure 1). When one molecule of colchicine is bound per dimer, microtubule formation is inhibited because dimers bound to colchicine compete with unbound dimers in the process of assembling microtubules (118). Binding of colchicine occurs first at a low-affinity site; this initial binding changes the conformation of the dimer to expose a high-affinity binding site (69, 103). The study of structure-activity relationships suggests that the low-affinity binding site interacts with the methoxyl groups of ring A, while the high-affinity site binds ring C. The N-acetyl group has only slight importance.

Affinity constants for the 2 sites differ by about a thousandfold (18). The binding of colchicine to tubulin has a number of consequences in addition to affecting mitosis. In plants, for instance, straight growth (199), essential oil production (2), and haptonasty (134) may all be influenced by colchicine via its action on microtubule formation.

In a general sense, other alkaloids act similarly to colchicine, inhibiting the formation of microtubules, but by somewhat different

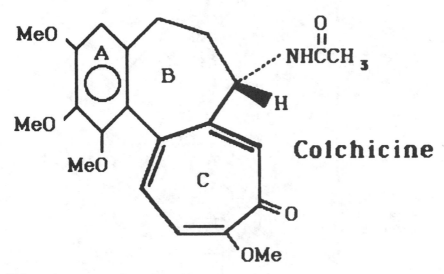

Figure 1. Colchicine.

detailed mechanisms. Vinblastine from *Catharanthus roseus* L. also binds to tubulin dimers in a 1:1 ratio and prevents microtubule formation. However, it is evident that the sites of binding for the 2 alkaloids are not identical. Two sites for vinblastine binding are available immediately, and there is no competition for sites between colchicine and vinblastine (27, 223). The dimeric structure of vinblastine is very important for binding to tubulin (Figure 2). The vindoline moiety has no activity by itself, and the catharanthine moiety has only about 1/1000 the activity of vinblastine (222). The methoxycarbonyl functional group is important, and the vindoline moiety cannot be replaced with a simpler indole (230). The acetyl group is not essential for binding and even decreases the activity (144).

Both colchicine and vinblastine have other effects on cellular metabolism that so far appear unrelated to microtubules. Some of these are cited in other sections of this review.

A third alkaloid that binds to tubuline is maytansine, but it has been studied much less than the other 2. There is apparently some overlap between the vinblastine and maytansine binding sites (112). Mescaline also binds to tubulin, most likely at the low affinity site (79).

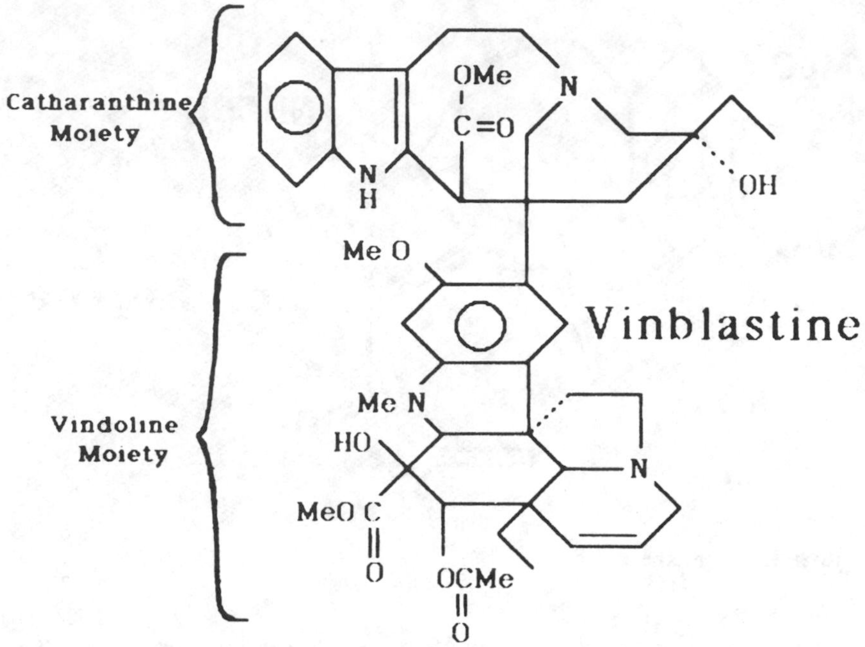

Figure 2. Vinblastine.

III. EFFECTS ON MEMBRANE TRANSPORT PROCESSES

The passage of both inorganic ions and organic molecules across cell membranes is an essential part of the activity of all cells, and many exquisite control mechanisms for these processes have been elucidated. Probably the most familiar modifiers of these processes are nonalkaloids, but several alkaloids can also be cited in this group.

A membrane-bound enzyme that catalyzes the hydrolysis of adenosine triphosphate (ATP) is present in many different animal cells. For activity, both sodium and potassium ions are required. The enzyme acts as a transmembrane "pump," moving Na^+ out of the cell and K^+ into the cell at the expense of energy derived from ATP hydrolysis. The high-affinity binding site for K^+ is at the outer end of the enzyme and for Na^+ is at the inner end of the enzyme. Detailed studies of this system have shown that Na^+ favors formation of a phosphorylated enzyme, while K^+ favors its dephosphorylation. The nonalkaloid inhibitor ouabain binds to the phosphorylated intermediate and inhibits dephosphorylation.

It is not yet entirely clear how various alkaloid inhibitors of sodium or potassium transport fit into the details of this mechanism, but there are probably several different mechanisms since even the chemically similar ouabain and digitoxin do not act identically (106). The alkaloid that is likely to act most similarly to ouabain is cassaine of *Erythrophleum guineense* G. Don (74). Harmaline and related β-carboline alkaloids from *Peganum harmala* L. interact at both the Na^+ and K^+ sites of the enzyme (168, 185).

Several protoberberine alkaloids inhibit Na^+ and K^+ transport but probably not by interaction at the cation sites. Berberine is competitive with the ATP substrate (126). Sanguinarine from many species of Papaveraceae is a potent inhibitor but not competitive either with the cations or with ATP (139, 167). This specific inhibition may account for some of the toxicity of sanguinarine-containing plant products (56). The entire (Na^+-K^+) ATPase story is complicated by the fact that imbalances in sodium and potassium concentrations produced by inhibition of this enzyme can lead, in turn, to secondary effects. For example, the elevation of intracellular sodium concentration can activate a sodium-calcium exchange system. Thus, inhibition of the ATPase may be followed by increased uptake of Ca^{++} (80).

Other systems are involved in sodium-potassium transport; for example, ion-specific pores in the membrane can be blocked or increased by various drugs, a few of which are alkaloids. The cyclopeptide alkaloid frangulanine from *Hovenia dulcis* Thunb. may act as an ionophore for K^+ (96).

Morphine and several related compounds induce permeability to K^+ in mitochondrial membranes (37), whereas quinine blocks K^+ conductance in islet cells (80). *Veratrum* alkaloids and aconitine cause increased permeability to Na^+ (39, 82, 149), whereas yohimbine acts to close sodium channels (11) and strychnine reverses the effect of veratridine (152). The molecular mechanisms for all these effects remain mostly unknown.

In addition to sodium and potassium ion transport, there are also mechanisms for transport of calcium across cell membranes. Alkaloids can affect these processes, but the effects are not as clear as for the Na^+ and K^+ ones. There is a membrane-bound Ca^{++}-ATPase analogous to the (Na^+-K^+)-ATPase, and some β-carboline alkaloids have been reported to act on it (20). Alkaloids that influence calcium uptake or release are quinine, caffeine, morphine, and papaverine (39, 60, 64, 205). Part of the pharmacological effect of cocaine (and related synthetic compounds such as procaine) can be explained by competition for calcium-binding sites on axonal membranes. Displacement of the Ca^{++} increases permeability and decreases the ability to initiate an action potential (40). This mechanism can account for the local anesthesia produced by cocaine but not its central effects.

Organic molecules must also be transported across membranes and, in a few instances, alkaloids have been reported to influence such transport. Harmaline and related alkaloids inhibit uptake of amino acids and choline by synaptosomes (168, 184, 196). Since some amino acids (e.g., γ-aminobutyric acid) are neurotransmitters and since choline is a precursor of the neurotransmitter acetylcholine, these effects may account for effects of harmala alkaloids on neural activity in addition to the alkaloid effects on (Na^+-K^+)-ATPase. Effects of alkaloids on release and uptake of catecholamines will be considered below.

IV. EFFECTS ON NEURORECEPTORS

A. Introduction

The concept of cell-surface receptor molecules on which both endogenous and exogenous small molecules act is a cornerstone in the explanation of many cell processes at the molecular level. Characterization of receptor molecules has been difficult because of their tight association with cellular structure and their low concentration but, even without detailed characterization of a purified receptor, the action of an alkaloid in many cases may be ascribed to an effect on a specific receptor.

In the animal nervous system alone, there are several dozen neuroregulators, each with specific receptors localized on certain cell types (192). Some of these receptors are certainly the sites where particular alkaloids exert their effects. Other receptors have been studied very little at this time but may well turn out to provide the explanation for presently not-understood alkaloid effects. For clarity, the neuroreceptor systems are considered in this order: cholinergic, adrenergic, opiate, serotonergic, purines, amino acid, and others.

B. Cholinergic System

Acetylcholine is the most widespread neurotransmitter. It functions in the peripheral autonomic system, in motor nerves to skeletal muscle, and in certain neurons of the central nervous system. Various drugs, including some alkaloids, can affect this cholinergic system at various points. Harmaline, by inhibiting uptake of choline, may decrease the amount of acetylcholine in synaptosomes (see Section III of this article). Several alkaloids weakly affect the release of acetylcholine, but the concentrations needed are probably too high to be pharmacologically relevant. A number of alkaloids ("agonists") mimic the effect of acetylcholine on its receptors, and different ones act preferentially on different types of acetylcholine receptors. Higher plant alkaloids that act as cholinergic agonists include nicotine, arecoline, pilocarpine, and some aconite alkaloids (1, 121, 135, 193). Some of these show mixed effects, mimicking acetylcholine at low concentration but blocking the receptor at high concentrations.

Several other alkaloids act only by blocking the acetylcholine receptor. The best known of these antagonists is d-tubocurarine. Close analysis of the action of d-tubocurarine suggests that it binds not only to the receptor *senso strictu* but also blocks the ion channel that is closely associated with, if not part of, the receptor (174). Other alkaloids that act as antagonists to acetylcholine are lobeline and several tropane alkaloids, for example (–)-hyoscyamine (102, 104). For a tropane alkaloid to be an antagonist, it must have tropic acid esterified with a tertiary amino alcohol. After acetylcholine has acted at its receptor, the compound is destroyed by the action of acetylcholinesterase. Several drugs that inhibit the esterase are well-known, and treatment with the drugs leads to continuous stimulation of the receptor. Most of the cholinesterase inhibitors are synthetic compounds, but they do include some alkaloids. The acetylcholinesterase has an anionic site containing negatively charged side-chains that bind the quaternary ammonium group of acetylcholine and an esteratic site containing side-chains of serine and histidine that binds the ester grouping (160). The alkaloid physostigmine (eserine) binds at both sites and generates a carbamylated serine residue, effectively destroying the enzyme's activity (155). Galanthamine acts similarly to physostigmine but reversibly (41).

Many other alkaloids show some inhibition of acetylcholinesterase because, being cations, they bind at the anionic site. Two of the more active of these are berberine and sempervirine; but it seems unlikely that any plants containing such alkaloids owe their pharmacological effects to inhibition of acetylcholinesterase (5, 63, 143, 208, 209). Many of these alkaloids have more important effects on other systems; for instance, several steroidal alkaloids that inhibit acetylcholinesterase also disrupt membranes, and some quaternary alkaloids inhibit ATPases (see Section II of this article).

C. Adrenergic System

The chemical transmitter in adrenergic synapses is norepinephrine (noradrenaline), a member of a larger class of compounds known as catecholamines (Figure 3). Four subtypes of receptors are recognized for norepinephrine and related compounds. However, the focus of this review precludes discussion of all the attendant complexities. In the best-studied case—vascular smooth muscle—the stimulation of α_1 receptors produces contraction, while stimulation of β receptors produces relaxation. Norepinephrine is much more active at α_1 receptors than at β receptors, although some related compounds demonstrate a reverse preference. The ratio of α_1 to β receptors also varies from tissue to tissue.

Drugs that act on adrenergic transmission show some analogies with those that act on cholinergic transmission. However, an important difference between the 2 systems is the lack of an enzyme

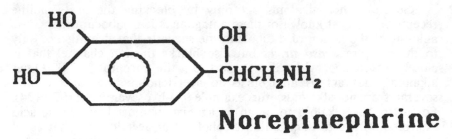

Figure 3. Norepinephrine.

analogous to acetylcholinesterase for destruction of the transmitter. Removal of norepinephrine from the junction occurs mostly by reuptake into the nerve terminal. Substances mimic the action of norepinephrine in one of 3 ways: stimulating release of endogenous norepinephrine, inhibiting its reuptake, or acting themselves as agonists at the receptor.

Some mimicking substances have more than one of these effects. Nicotine, ephedrine, and tyramine initiate release of norepinephrine, probably from storage vesicles (8). Cocaine inhibits the reuptake of norepinephrine (77). Reserpine has a complex action. It not only inhibits reuptake of norepinephrine but also of its precursor, dopamine, so that the long-term effect is a depletion of norepinephrine (70, 94).

Several alkaloids act as blockers of the α_1 receptor site with the result that endogenous transmitters can act only on β-sites, but norepinephrine is very inactive at β-sites (33). Yohimbine is an example of an alkaloid that blocks α_1 receptors yet is even more significant for blocking presynaptic α_2 receptors. Consequences of the presynaptic α_2 block are greater activity of adenyl cyclase and then release of more norepinephrine (71, 226). The structural features determining the types of action have been analyzed (65).

The enzyme monoamine oxidase (MAO) has a role in the overall activity of the adrenergic system, not because it is necessary to destroy excess norepinephrine, but because it acts as a scavenger for other amines that, if present, could stimulate the release of norepinephrine or mimic norepinephrine action at a receptor. Thus, inhibitors of monoamine oxidase, although not directly, stimulate adrenergic receptors. However, many compounds that act *in vitro* as inhibitors of MAO may have additional effects as well, so that the interpretation of a drug action as due primarily to inhibition of MAO is extraordinarily difficult. Most of the MAO inhibitors that are used as drugs are synthetic, but several naturally occurring alkaloids are also active in this way, for example, some of the harmala group (183) and some of the isoquinolines (125).

D. Opiate Receptors, Adenyl Cyclase

Neurons that respond to morphine and related alkaloids are widely distributed in animals, and it is now well established that the real, endogenous transmitters for these receptors are not alkaloids, but peptides (190, 191, 225, 231). Detailed work has revealed that there are probably at least 4 types of opiate receptors, differentially distributed and mediating different kinds of effects:

δ emotional
λ sedative
μ analgesic
σ psychotomimetic

To different degrees, a given opiate can stimulate all types of receptors (2, 181). The sequence of molecular events following the binding of an opiate to the receptor is still being vigorously investigated. There is clearly some involvement of 3',5'-cyclic adenosine monophosphate (cAMP) in the consequent reactions. Opiates decrease the activity of adenyl cyclase, perhaps by stimulating the hydrolysis of guanosine triphosphate (GTP), since the cyclase is activated by binding GTP to it (21, 36, 99). GTP also decreases the affinity of the receptor for opiate agonists (but not for antagonists). Sodium ions have effects similar to GTP (190, 191).

Several preparations of purified opiate receptor have been made and should prove useful in defining the structural requirements for binding (19, 38, 150, 163, 182). Many synthetic compounds have also been prepared in attempts to clarify the details of opiate-receptor binding (101, 150). When the structure of one of the endogenous peptide transmitters, Met[5]-enkephalin, is compared with the structure of morphine, some analogies can be seen (Figure 4).

The phenolic ring and nitrogen atom of morphine correspond to the tyrosine residue of the enkephalins, C-7 and C-8 of morphine correspond to the leucyl or methionyl side chains of enkephalins, and the 6-hydroxyl group corresponds to the carboxyl terminus (165). This alignment of functional groups is dependent on the enkephalins having a β-bend at the second glycine residue (123, 187). There is, however, some evidence that the binding site for enkephalins is not identical to the site for morphine (122, 161, 225). Even when clarification of the interaction of opiates with their receptors has been achieved, elucidation of the causal chain between opiate binding and the behavioral or physiological effects of an opiate seems likely to require much more research. Several other alkaloids not regarded as having opiate-like activity are known to stimulate membrane adenyl cyclases (220).

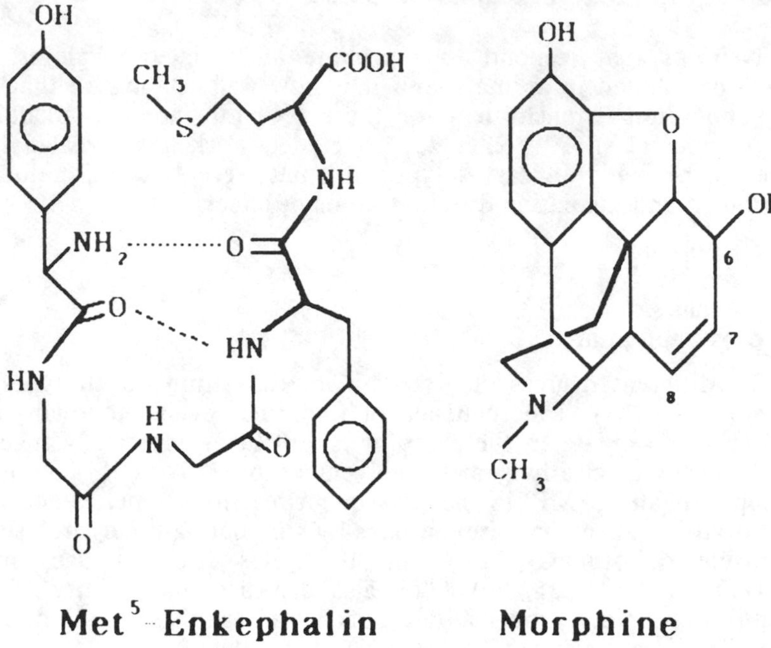

Met^5-Enkephalin   Morphine

Figure 4. Met^5-Enkephalin and Morphine.

E. Serotonergic Receptors

The properties of serotonin receptors are unclear even though these receptors are important presumptive sites for action of several hallucinogenic compounds, such as psilocin, bufotenine, harmine derivatives (3, 16, 28), and some of the ergot alkaloids. The partially synthetic ergot alkaloid lysergic acid diethylamide (LSD) is one of the most powerful of hallucinogenic drugs. The binding activity of these hallucinogenic compounds to brain membranes and their ability to displace serotonin correlates well with their pharmacological activity (34, 179). LSD, besides binding to postsynaptic serotonin receptors, also depresses the secretion of serotonin by serotonin-producing neurons, and it may also have effects on dopaminergic neurons.

Other hallucinogens do not have all of these additional activities of LSD (88). In fact, mescaline stimulates synthesis of serotonin, so that its hallucinogenic effect may come not from mimicking serotonin, but from providing more of it (175). Quinidine and reserpine depress the ability of blood platelets to accumulate serotonin, but this may not have anything to do with serotonergic neurons (25). Some structure-activity correlations for phenethylamine hallucinogens (e.g., mescaline) and serotonin have been attempted, but no completely clear relationships have been reported (13, 138). Some evidence exists that effects of cocaine on the central nervous system may be mediated by serotonergic neurons (154).

F. Purine Receptors

Accumulating evidence indicates widespread receptors for adenosine, but they are still much less known than other systems. Unlike other neurotransmitters, adenosine is evidently not restricted to a particular cell type (46). The action of adenosine is complex and concentration-dependent. Binding to a high-affinity receptor results in inhibition of adenyl cyclase, but binding to a low-affinity receptor activates the cyclase (47). In this way, the concentration of cAMP in the cell responds to the concentration of adenosine at the cell surface. Cyclic AMP has manifold functions, and it is not known what its specific significance in nerve cells may be. The alkaloids best known for their activity in this system are the methylated xanthines such as caffeine and theophylline. These 2 alkaloids appear to antagonize adenosine action at both types of receptors, and theophylline is more active than caffeine at both types.

Some synthetic purine derivatives show much greater differentiation between the 2 types of adenosine receptor (47). This same group of methyl xanthines is well-known to be inhibitory to the activity of cAMP phosphodiesterase; however, the concentration required for this inhibition is appreciably higher than the concentration needed to block adenosine receptors. Furthermore, these same methylxanthines may inhibit the escape of cAMP from cells (137). Thus, although most explanations for the action of caffeine and related alkaloids relate to effects on cyclic AMP levels, the mechanisms for achieving these effects are far from obvious. Later, physiological consequences of this adenosine system are on vasodilation and the release of other neurotransmitters (194).

Even less studied than adenosine receptors are other purine receptors, for instance, some that apparently respond to adenosine triphosphate and are blocked by quinidine. This group is apparently not involved with cAMP (30).

G. Amino Acid Receptors

Several amino acids are known to act as specific neurotransmitters in the central nervous system. Glycine, an inhibitory transmitter producing hyperpolarization of motoneurons of the spinal cord, is specifically antagonized by the complex alkaloid strychnine (195, 228, 229). Of course, the structures of glycine and strychnine are quite different, and this is a striking example of the difficulty in seeing structural similarity between 2 compounds that act at the same site.

Another inhibitory transmitter is the nonprotein amino acid γ-aminobutyric acid (GABA), which is present at significant concentrations in brain tissue (61, 116). Alkaloids that act as antagonists at GABA receptors are bicuculline (a benzyl-isoquinoline) as well as the pyridine alkaloids guvacine and arecaidine (17, 90). Bicuculline, which has been extensively studied, has been shown to compete with GABA for specific sites on synaptosomes (180). The *trans* conformation of GABA fits the structure of (+)-bicuculline (200) (Figure 5).

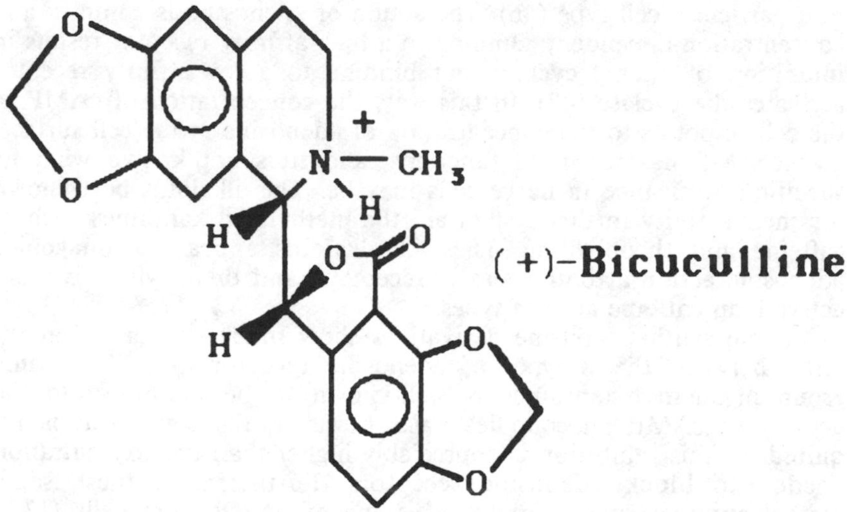

Figure 5. (+)-Bicuculline.

There is less convincing evidence for glutamic and aspartic acids as neurotransmitters in vertebrates, although they are present in the central nervous system, and their application to nerves is excitatory. Electrophysiological studies with the mealworm (*Tenebrio molitor*) have shown that L-glutamate is a transmitter and that it is antagonized by the alkaloid (+)-tubocurarine, which is well-known as an antagonist at the cholinergic receptor (227).

H. Other Neuroreceptors

In addition to the types of neuroreceptors discussed above, several others are less well-known or only postulated. The only one of these for which there appears to be information about its interaction with alkaloids is the dopamine receptor of certain brain cells and the pituitary gland. Tetrahydroisoquinoline alkaloids and some ergot alkaloids have been found to bind to these dopamine receptors (14, 26, 66).

V. EFFECTS ON NUCLEIC ACIDS AND PROTEIN SYNTHESIS COMPONENTS

Central events in the life of any cell are aimed at maintaining the integrity of its deoxyribonucleic acid (DNA), accurate replication of the DNA, transcription of the DNA to make ribonucleic acid (RNA), and translation of messenger RNA to manufacture all the proteins needed by the cell. In many parts of this system, interference by particular alkaloids has been found. While some of these interferences may have no physiological relevance, others may explain the behavioral or morphological effects of certain alkaloids.

Since nucleic acids are anions and many alkaloids are cations at physiological pH values, binding of alkaloids to nucleic acids often occurs. Of more interest than nonspecific electrostatic binding, though, is binding that occurs by insertion of alkaloids into the interior of the DNA double helix. This process, called "intercalation," is a high-affinity process that occurs with protoberberines (186), colchicine (31), ellipticine (197), quinacrine (136), quinine (62, 78), sanguinarine (115), and harman derivatives (6, 15, 55). Several other alkaloids, including steroidal diamines (164), caffeine (105), LSD (212), and quaternary trans-quinolizidines (45), bind to nucleic acids reversibly, but the mechanisms are not understood.

The consequences of alkaloid binding are not clearly known, but one result can be making the DNA more susceptible to damage by ultraviolet radiation. This photoactivation effect has been observed for dictamnine (148) and camptothecin (85). Absorption of UV energy may produce free radicals that lead to strand breakage. Camptothecin also induces an alkali-labile linkage in superhelical DNA (67).

Binding of an alkaloid could also affect the binding of another regulator to DNA. Caffeine and some other purines, for example, enhance the binding of the glucocorticoid receptor protein from rat liver cells to DNA (32). On the contrary, caffeine and theophylline inhibit the binding of the carcinogen dimethylbenz-(a)-anthracene to DNA of mouse cells (177). There is a confusing variety of findings about effects of caffeine on repair process for DNA. In some instances, it evidently inhibits the rejoining of broken strands or filling of gaps (22, 107, 142); in other instances, caffeine has been found to decrease the inhibition of thymidine incorporation caused by irradiation (166) or to counteract effects of ultraviolet damage (113).

A few alkaloids are recognized as alkylating agents that react to form covalent bonds with particular functional groups of nucleic acids and proteins with possibly mutagenic or carcinogenic results. Arecaidine (9) and several pyrrolizidine alkaloids are the best-known of this group (57, 87, 188). The most toxic pyrrolizidines are those with an unsaturated ring (pyrroles). These compounds can react with hydroxyl, amino, or thiol groups (86).

Although pyrrolizidines with saturated rings and pyrrolizidine-N-oxides are themselves not reactive, the N-oxides can be reduced by gut flora, and saturated rings can be dehydrogenated in the liver. Several plants used in herbal medicine contain pyrrolizidines (81) and, because of these metabolic transformations in the intestinal tract, oral use should be discouraged even if the compounds originally present in the plant are innocuous (23). Similarly, the active form of camptothecin appears to be an alkylating agent produced by a chain of metabolic transformations (133).

Several alkaloids have been found to inhibit DNA replication. An alkaloid mixture from *Narcissus tazetta* L. inhibits the activity of DNA polymerase by binding to the enzyme (146). By unknown mechanisms, mimosine (153, 169, 214), reserpine (76), and vinleurosine (42) inhibit the incorporation of nucleotides into DNA. The presence of caffeine or camptothecin in the culture medium causes tumor cells to make DNA of abnormally low molecular weight (84, 108). Harman inhibits the excision of pyrimidine dimers that are made during exposure to ultraviolet radiation (35). Many of the alkaloids cited in this paragraph have additional and quite different effects on other cell constituents, as cited in other parts of this review. Therefore, their effects on DNA may only partially explain their effects on whole organisms.

Several alkaloids are known to affect the overall process of transcription but whether, in any specific case, the effect is achieved by binding to the DNA template or to the RNA polymerase is usally obscure. Ellipticine is an inhibitor of purified RNA polymerase (172). Others that appear to be inhibitors of transcription as measured by ribonucleotide incorporation into the RNA of whole cells, or even intact organisms, may be acting only indirectly (43, 151). Reserpine (211) and colchicine (119) inhibit synthesis of particular messenger RNA molecules in, respectively, bacteria and cultured rat glial cells. In contrast, quinine applied to pea pods induces formation of messenger RNA for phenylalanine-ammonia lyase (78). The action of caffeine on transcription is confused, and it has been variously reported to have no effect (131), to be inhibitory (232), or to be stimulatory (140, 198).

Reverse transcription, making DNA from an RNA template, is a process catalyzed by the enzyme known as "reverse transcriptase" that occurs in the infection of mammalian cells with certain tumor-inducing viruses. Methylxanthines such as caffeine (198) and several benzophenanthridines (170, 171, 173) are inhibitors of reverse transcription, evidently interacting with the RNA primer.

Alkaloids can interfere with ribosomal protein formation at several different stages of the synthetic process. Mescaline treatment of isolated ribosomes or of the tissues from which ribosomes are isolated results in ribosomes that are less stable and less efficient in synthesis of proteins (48, 49, 50, 51, 52). Narciclasine inhibits protein synthesis on eukaryotic ribosomes by binding to the 60S subunit at the peptidyl transferase center so that access of the 3'-OH of the donor substrate is blocked and no peptide bond can be formed (12). The related alkaloid lycorine inhibits cell division and elongation, but it is not known whether these effects follow from an effect on protein synthesis (53).

Several alkaloids act similarly to the well-known inhibitor of eukaryotic protein synthesis, cycloheximide, by inhibiting translocation of the growing peptide chain from the A site to the P site of the ribosome. Alkaloids that act in this way belong to the ipecachuana, phenanthroquinolizidine, and phenathroindolizidine groups (54, 75, 91). Surprisingly, when whole animals are treated with these alkaloids, the activity of protein synthesis increases in ribosomes prepared from the animals (92). LSD can actually be incorporated into proteins during ribosomal translation, replacing a tryptophan unit and causing chain termination (224).

VI. INHIBITION OR ACTIVATION OF ENZYMES

As a general rule, alkaloids are chemically reactive molecules. Nucleophilic attack by the basic nitrogen atoms present in many alkaloid structures can be expected to modify functional groups on proteins and create changes in the activity of enzymes. Thus, while many effects of alkaloids on enzymatic activity have been observed, these effects may have no relationship to the effects of the alkaloids on whole organisms. In order to accept the explanation that the effect of an alkaloid on a whole animal is the result of a specific enzyme inhibition, information would have to be available showing that the alkaloid reached the postulated enzyme *in vivo* at a concentration sufficient to produce an effect, but this kind of information is not normally at hand.

The inhibition of phosphodiesterases is frequently invoked to explain the activity of methylated xanthine alkaloids such as caffeine and theophylline. Phosphodiesterases are important for their catalysis of the hydrolysis of cyclic-3',5'-adenosine monophosphate (cAMP). Since cAMP stimulates the catabolism of stored carbohydrate and fat, inhibition of the phosphodiesterase that destroys cAMP can have the effect of increasing the rate of breakdown of these storage compounds and raising levels of blood sugar and/or oxygen consumption. While this may provide a partial explanation for physiological action of the methylxanthines, complete acceptance of this explanation raises many problems, such as:

1. These alkaloids are known to affect other processes (95, 141, 189, 219).
2. Not all phosphodiesterases are equally sensitive (10).
3. The differential effects of different alkaloids on phosphodiesterase do not correlate completely with their larger physiological effects (215).
4. Effect of alkaloid is not reproduced exactly by increased concentration of cAMP (210).

Besides the methylxanthines, some other alkaloids are also inhibitors of phosphodiesterases--for example, papaverine (219), colchicine (215), and *Vinca* alkaloids (215).

Several alkaloids can be considered inhibitors of the oxidation processes that occur in mitochondria and microsomes. Known inhibitors of mitochondrial respiration include papaverine (127), tubocurarine, lasiocarpine, heliotrine (68), spegazzine (162), and several quinolines (4). Harman alkaloids are powerful inhibitors of mitochondrial monoamine oxidase (73). While a high concentration of reserpine can uncouple oxidative phosphorylation, this uncoupling is irrelevant to the psychoactive effects of reserpine (114, 217).

TABLE 2. Some Inhibitory Effects of Alkaloids on Enzymes.

Alkaloid	Enzyme Inhibited	Ref. No.
theophylline	alkaline phosphatase	44
protoberberines	liver alcohol dehydrogenase	145
cinchona alkaloids, lobeline	kidney diamine oxidase	147
colchiceine	various phosphatases	178
mimosine	pyridoxal phosphate enzymes	98, 124
quinidine	several glycolytic enzymes	83
isoquinolines	tyrosine hydroxylase	29, 218
d-tubocurarine	several dehydrogenases	201
indolizidines	α-mannosidase	93, 132
methylated xanthines	xanthine oxidase	97

The microsomal P-450 oxidase system is inhibited by emetine (89), nicotine (216), pilocarpine (206), pyrrolizidines (58), and derivatives of ellipticine (111, 203). The latter group has been studied extensively in this regard. It has been found that ellipticine itself is oxidized to 9-hydroxyellipticine by microsomes and that the derivative is an even stronger oxidase inhibitor than the parent compound (109). The structure-activity relationships for ellipticine derivatives have been elucidated and show the importance of the 5- and 11-methyl groups (110).

Feeding pyrrolizidine alkaloids from *Senecio jacobea* L. to rats is reported to lower the oxygenase activity in liver microsomes and to induce epoxide hydrolase activity (128, 221). These effects on microsomal enzymes might appear, at first glance, to be beneficial since they would result in polyaromatic procarcinogens being less converted to carcinogens if pyrrolizidine alkaloids were included in the diet. The drawback, of course, is that the pyrrolizidine alkaloids are themselves carcinogens (see Section V of this chapter). Oral administration of caffeine to rats has the opposite effect of increasing the oxidizing ability of liver microsomes (129). Several additional effects of alkaloids on enzyme activity are presented in Table 2.

VII. SUMMARY

Many medicinal plants owe their physiological activities to their content of alkaloids. More and more, it is becoming possible to understand these activities in terms of molecular interactions between alkaloid molecules and chemically defined components of the affected organism. Many of these effects are reviewed and categorized according to the type of biochemical system with which the alkaloid appears to interact. The major categories considered are subcellular structures, membrane transport, receptors, nucleic acids and protein synthesis, and enzyme effectors. Within each of these categories, examples are given of particular alkaloids or alkaloid types with as much detail as present knowledge permits of the structural features of the alkaloid molecule that are important for its activity.

In a few cases, it is evident that this kind of molecular mechanism can go a long way toward providing a satisfying explanation for some long-standing pharmacological questions. In many other cases, though, either molecular mechanisms are simply unknown or else the systems studied so far do not seem to be entirely relevant for explaining the larger effects of plant drugs on animal behavior or anatomy.

VIII. REFERENCES

1. Abood, L.G., D.T. Reynolds, and J.M. Bidlack. 1980. Stereospecific ^{3}H-nicotine binding to intact and solubilized rat brain membranes and evidence for its non-cholinergic nature. Life Sci. 23:1307–1314.

2. Adler, M.W. 1981. The *in vivo* differentiation of opiate receptors: Introduction. Life Sci. 28:1543–1545.

3. Aghajamian, G.K. and H.J. Haigler. 1978. LSD and other hallucinogenic indoleamines: Preferential action upon presynaptic serotonin receptors. Mod. Pharmacol-Toxicol. 13:101–120.

4. Akimenko, V.K., A.G. Kozlovsky, A.G. Medentsev, N.P. Golovchenko, and M.U. Arinbasarov. 1976. Mechanism of the effect of some quinoline alkaloids on the respiratory chain of mitochondria. Biokhimiya 41:2220–2228.

5. Alid, G., L.F. Valdés, and F.J. Orrego. 1974. Strychnine as an anticholinesterase. *In vitro* studies with rat brain enzymes. Experientia 30:266–268.

6. Allen, J.R.F. and B.R. Holmstedt. 1980. The simple β-carboline alkaloids. Phytochemistry 19:1573–1582.

7. Altstiel, L.D. and F.R. Landsberger. 1977. Interaction of colchicine with phosphatidylcholine membranes. Nature 269:70–71.

8. Arqueros, L., D. Naqira, and E. Zunino. 1978. Nicotine-induced release of catecholamines from rat hippocampus and striatum. Biochem. Pharmacol. 27:2667–2674.

9. Ashby, J., J.A. Styles, and E. Boyland. 1979. Betel nuts, arecaidine, and oral cancer. Lancet I:1112.

10. Ashton, A.R. and G.M. Polya. 1975. Higher plant cyclic nucleotide phosphodiesterases. Resolution, partial purification, and properties of three phosphodiesterases from potato. Biochem. J. 149:329–339.

11. Azuma, J., S. Vogel, I. Josephson, and N. Sperelakis. 1978. Yohimbine blockade of ionic channels in myocardial cells. Europ. J. Pharmacol. 51:109–119.

12. Baez, A. and D. Vazquez. 1978. Binding of [^{3}H] narciclasine to eukaryotic ribosomes. A study on a structure-activity relationship. Biochem. Biophys. Acta 518:95–103.

13. Baldwin, S., L.K. Kier, and D. Shillady. 1980. Approximate molecular potentials of mescaline analogs in a study of similarities to 5-hydroxytryptamine. Molec. Pharmacol. 18:455–460.

14. Banning, J.W., N.J. Uretsky, P.N. Patil, and J.L. Beal. 1980. Reticuline: A dopamine receptor blocker. Life Sci. 26:2083–2091.

15. Bassleer, R., J.M. Marnette, P. Wiliquet, M.C. DePauw-Gillet, M. Caprasse, and L.J.G. Angenot. 1983. Complementary study of the cytotoxic activity of melinonine F, an alkaloid derivative of β-carboline. Planta Med. 49:158–161.

16. Bennett, J.P., Jr. and S.H. Snyder. 1975. Stereospecific binding of D-lysergic acid diethylamide (LSD) to brain membranes. Relation to serotonin receptors. Brain Res. 94:523–544.

17. Bhattacharyya, A., K.M. Madyastha, P.K. Bhattacharyya, and M. S. Devanandan. 1981. Studies on bicuculline binding sites on neuronal membranes using fluorescent antibody techniques: Comparative binding of GABA and bicuculline. Biochem. Biophys. Res. Commun. 98:520–526.

18. Bhattacharyya, B. and J. Wolff. 1976. Anion-induced increases in the rate of colchicine binding to tubulin. Biochemistry 15:2283–2288.

19. Bidlack, J.M., L.G. Abood, P. Osei-Gyimah, and S. Archer. 1981. Purification of the opiate receptor from rat brain. Proc. Nat. Acad. Sci. U.S.A. 78:636–639.

20. Bloom, F., J. Barchas, M. Sandler, and E. Usdin. 1982. Beta-carbolines and tetrahydroisoquinolines. A.R. Liss, New York. 428 p.

21. Blume, A.J., D. Lichtstein, and G. Boone. 1979. Coupling of opiate receptors to adenylate cyclase: Requirement for sodium ion and GTP. Proc. Nat. Acad. Sci. U.S.A. 76:5626–5630.

22. Bowden, G.T. and N.E. Fusenig. 1980. Caffeine inhibition of postreplication repair of UV-damaged DNA in mouse epidermal cells. Chem. Biol. Interactions 33:101–113.

23. Brauchli, J., J. Luthy, U. Zweifel, and C. Schlatter. 1982. Pyrrolizidine alkaloids from *Symphytum officinale* L. and their percutaneous absorption in rats. Experientia 38:1085–1087.

24. Bricout, J., M.-J. Garcia-Rodriguez, and C. Paupardin. 1978. Effect of colchicine on the synthesis of essential oil by *Mentha piperita* plant tissues cultured *in vitro*. C. A. Acad. Sci. (D) 286:1585–1588.

25. Bridges, J.M. and M. Baldini. 1966. Effect of quinidine and related compounds on uptake and release of serotonin by blood platelets. Nature 210:1364–1365.

26. Britton, D.R., C. Rivier, T. Shier, F. Bloom, and W. Vale. 1982. *In-vivo* and *in-vitro* effects of tetrahydroisoquinolines and other alkaloids on rat pituitary function. Biochem. Pharmacol. 31:1205–1211.

27. Brodie, A.E., J. Potter, and D.J. Reed. 1979. Effects of vinblastine, oncodazole, procarbazine, chlorambucil, and bleomycin *in vivo* on colchicine binding activity of tubulin. Life Sci. 24:1547–1554.

28. Buckholtz, N.S. 1980. Neurobiology of tetrahydro-β-carbolines. Life Sci. 27:398–903.

29. Burke, W.J., M.P. Galloway, and C.J. Coscia. 1982. Tetrahydroisoquinolinecarboxylic acid and regulation of N-methyltransferase in cultured adrenal medulla. Biochem. Pharmacol. 31:3257–3260.

30. Burnstock, G. 1978. Basis for distinguishing two types of purinergic receptor. *In* R.W. Straub and L. Balis, eds. *Cell Membrane Receptors for Drugs and Hormones*. Raven Press, New York. pp. 107–118.

31. Busyman, E., T. Wilczak, B. Witman, and G. Siebert. 1977. Intercalation of colchicine with DNA molecules. Hoppe-Seylers Z. Physiol. Chem. 358:819–824.

32. Cake, M.H. and G. Litwack. 1978. Effect of methylxanthines on binding of the glucocorticoid receptor to DNA-cellulose and nuclei. Europ. J. Biochem. 82:97–103.

33. Caldwell, R.W., J.T. Elam, T.E. Mecca, and C.B. Nash. 1983. Vascular α-adrenergic blocking properties of quinidine. Europ. J. Pharmacol. 94:185–192.

34. Cascio, C.S. and K.J. Kellar. 1982. Tetrahydro-β-carbolines: affinities for tryptamine and serotonergic binding sites. Neuropharmacology 21:1219–1221.

35. Castellani, A. and R.B. Setlow. 1981. Harman inhibits the removal of pyrimidine dimers from the DNA of human cells. Biochem. Biophys. Res. Commun. 98:823–828.

36. Chang, K.-J., E. Hazum, A. Killian, and P. Cuatrecasas. 1981. Interactions of ligands with morphine and enkephalin receptors are differentially affected by guanine nucleotide. Molec. Pharmacol. 20:1–7.

37. Chistyakov, V.V. and G.P. Gegenava. 1980. Study of the mechanism of the opiate-induced permeability of mitochondrial membranes for potassium ions. Biokhimiya 45:492–497.

38. **Chow, T. and R.S. Zukin.** 1983. Solubilization and preliminary characterization of mu and kappa opiate receptor subtypes from rat brain. Molec. Pharmacol. 24:203–212.

39. **Couturier, E., A. Sener, K. Anjaneyulu, and W.J. Malaisse.** 1980. Inhibition by quinine of insulin release and calcium ionophoresis. Molec. Pharmacol. 18:243–246.

40. **Covino, B.G.** 1972. Local anesthesia. N. E. J. Med. 286:975–983, 1035–1042.

41. **Cozantis, D.A. and E. Toivakka.** 1978. Galanthamine. J. Am. Med. Assoc. 240:108.

42. **Creasey, W.A.** 1969. Biochemical effects of the *Vinca* alkaloids. IV. Vinleurosine. Biochem. Pharmacol. 18:227–232.

43. **Creasey, W.A.** 1979. Biochemical effects of berberine. Biochem. Pharmacol. 28:1081–1084.

44. **Croce, M.A., G.L. Kramer, and D.L. Garbers.** 1979. Inhibition of alkaline phosphatase by substituted xanthines. Biochem. Pharmacol. 28:1227–1231.

45. **Cushman, M., F.W. Dekow, and L.B. Jacobsen.** 1979. Conformations, DNA binding parameters, and antileukemic activity of certain cytotoxic protoberberine alkaloids. J. Med Chem. 22:331–333.

46. **Daly, J.W.** 1982. Adenosine receptors: Targets for future drugs. J. Med. Chem. 25:197–207.

47. **Daly, J.W., R.F. Bruns, and S.H. Snyder.** 1981. Adenosine receptors in the central nervous system: Relationship to the central nervous system of methyl xanthines. Life Sci. 28:2083–2097.

48. **Datta, R.K.** 1973. Mescaline-induced changes of brain cortex ribosomes. Effect of mescaline on tRNA and aminoacyl tRNA synthetase. Naunyn-Schmiedeberg's Arch. Pharmacol. 280:107–111.

49. **Datta, R.K., W. Antopol, and J.J. Ghosh.** 1971. Mescaline-induced changes of brain cortex ribosomes: Role of spermidine in counteracting the destabilizing effect of mescaline on brain cortex ribosomes. Biochem. J. 125:213–219.

50. **Datta, R.K. and J.J. Ghosh.** 1970. Mescaline-induced changes of brain-cortex ribosomes. Effect of mescaline on the hydrogen bonded structure of ribonucleic acid of brain-cortex ribosomes. Biochem. J. 117:969–980.

51. **Datta, R.K. and J.J. Ghosh.** 1970. Mescaline-induced changes of brain-cortex ribosomes. Effect of mescaline on the stability of brain-cortex ribosomes. Biochem. J. 117:961–968.

52. **Datta, R.K., J.J. Ghosh, and W. Antopol.** 1974. Mescaline-induced changes of brain cortex ribosomes. Effect of mescaline on the binding of aminoacyl-transfer ribonucleic acid to ribosomes of brain tissue. Biochem. Pharmacol. 23:1687–1692.

53. **De Leo, P., G. Dalessandro, A. De Santis, and O. Arrigoni.** 1973. Inhibitory effect of lycorine on cell division and elongation. Plant Cell Physiol. 14:487–496.

54. **Donaldson, G.R., M.R. Atkinson, and A.W. Murray.** 1968. Inhibition of protein synthesis in Ehrlisch ascites tumor cells by the phenanthrene alkaloids. Biochem. Biophys. Res. Commun. 31:104–109.

55. **Duportail, G. and H. Lami.** 1975. Interaction of the fluorophores harmine and harmaline with calf thymus DNA. Biochim. Biophys. Acta 402:20–30.

56. Dyke, S. 1978. Poppies and glaucoma. New Scientist 79:679–680.

57. Eastman, D.F., G.P. Dimenna, and H.J. Segall. 1982. Covalent binding of two pyrrolizidine alkaloids, senecionine and seneciphylline, to hepatic macromolecules and their distribution, excretion, and transfer into milk of lactating mice. Drug Metab. Dispos. 10:236–240.

58. Eastman, D.F. and H.J. Segall. 1980. The effect of pyrrolizidine alkaloids (*Senecio vulgaris*) on the liver mixed-function oxidase system. Toxicol Lett. 5:369–374.

59. El Mashak, E.-S.M. and J.-F. Tocanne. 1980. Effect of ellipticine and 9-methyoxyellipticine on the phase behavior of phosphatidylglycerols. A monolayer study. Europ. J.Biochem. 105:593–601.

60. End, D.W., R.A. Carchman, and W.L. Dewey. 1981. Interactions of narcotics with synaptosomal calcium transport. Biochem. Pharmacol. 30:674–676.

61. Enna, S.J., ed. 1983. *The GABA Receptor.* Humana Press, Clifton, NJ. 341 p.

62. Estensen, R.D., A.K. Krey, and F.E. Hahn. 1969. Deoxyribonucleic acid-quinine complex. Molec. Pharmacol. 5:532–541.

63. Faucher, A. and R. Monnet. 1967. Inhibition kinetics of horse serum cholinesterase by certain *Solanum* steroidal alkaloids. C.R. Acad. Sci. (D) 264:2247–2249.

64. Ferrari, M. 1974. Effects of papaverine on smooth muscle and their mechanisms. Pharmacol. Res. Commun. 6:97–115.

65. Ferry, N., M. Goodhardt, J. Hanoune, and T. Sevenet. 1983. Binding of yohimbine stereoisomers to α-adrenoreceptors in rat liver and human platelets. Brit. J. Pharmacol. 78:359–364.

66. Fluckiger, E. 1980. Recent advances in ergot pharmacology. *In* J.D. Phillipson and M.H. Zenk, eds. *Indoles and Biogenetically Related Alkaloids.* Academic Press, New York. pp. 283–291.

67. Fukada, M. 1980. Interaction between SV40 DNA and camptothecin, an antitumor alkaloid. J. Biochem. (Tokyo) 87:1089–1096.

68. Gallagher, C.H. 1968. Effects of neuromuscular blocking agents on mitochondria. IV. Effects of d-tubocurarine, pyrrolizidine alkaloids, and magnesium on oxidative phosphorylation. Biochem. Pharmacol. 17:533–538.

69. Garland, D.L. 1978. Kinetics and mechanism of colchicine binding to tubulin. Evidence for ligand-induced conformational changes. Biochemistry 17:4266–4272.

70. Giachetti, A. and P.A. Shore. 1978. The reserpine receptor. Life Sci. 23:89–92.

71. Goldberg, M.R. and D. Robertson. 1983. Yohimbine: A pharmacological probe for study of the α_2-adrenoreceptor. Pharmacol. Rev. 35:143–180.

72. Goodman, L.S. and A. Gilman. 1980. *The Pharmacological Basis of Therapeutics,* 6th ed. Bailliere Tindall, London. 1843 p.

73. Gorkin, V.Z. and L.V. Tatyanenko. 1967. Inhibition by harmine of oxidative deamination of biogenic monoamines. Life Sci. 6:791–795.

74. Gupta, R.S. 1981. Mutants of HeLa cells resistant to ouabain and cassaine: Evidence for the common site of action of cardiac glycosides and Erythrophleum alkaloids. Biochem. Pharmacol. 30:3039–3044.

75. Gupta, R.S., J.J. Krepinsky, and L. Siminovitch. 1980. Structural determinants responsible for biological activity of (–)-emetine,

(–)-cryptopleurine, and (–)-tylocrebine: Structure activity relationships among related compounds. Molec. Pharmacol. 18:136–143.

76. Hach, B., P. Mitznegg, and H. Heim. 1972. Influence of reserpine on incorporation of [³H]-thymidine in mouse liver DNA. Experientia 28:1418.

77. Hadfield, M.G., D.E.W. Mott, and J.A. Ismay. 1980. Cocaine: Effect of *in vivo* administration on synaptosomal uptake of norepinephrine. Biochem. Pharmacol. 29:1861–1863.

78. Hadwiger, L.A. and M.E. Schwochau. 1971. Specificity of deoxyribonucleic acid intercalating compounds in the control of phenylalanine ammonia lyase and pisatin levels. Plant Physiol. 47:346–351.

79. Harrison, C.M.H., B.M. Page, and H.M. Keir. 1976. Mescaline as a mitotic spindle inhibitor. Nature 260:138–139.

80. Herchuelez, A., P. Lebrum, A.R. Carpinelli, N. Thonnart, A. Sener, and W.J. Malaisse. 1981. Regulation of calcium fluxes in rat pancreatic islets. Biochem. Biophys. Acta 640:16–30.

81. Hirono, I., H. Mori, and M. Haga. 1978. Carcinogenic activity of *Symphytum officinale* L. J. Natl. Cancer Inst. 61:865–870.

82. Honerjager, P. 1983. Ceveratrum alkaloids: Progress in understanding their membrane and inotropic actions. Trends Pharmacol. Sci. 4:258–262.

83. Horn, R.S. 1968. The mechanism of inhibition of glycolysis by quinidine in heart tissue *in vivo*. Biochem. Pharmacol. 17:1717–1725.

84. Horwitz, S.B., C.-K. Chang, and A.P. Grollman. 1971. Camptothecin. I. Effects on nucleic acid and protein synthesis. Molec. Pharmacol. 7:632–644.

85. Hutchinson, C.R. 1981. Camptothecin: Chemistry, biogenesis, and medicinal chemistry. Tetrahedron 37: 1047–1065.

86. Huxtable, R.J. 1979. New aspects of the toxicology and pharmacology of pyrrolizidine alkaloids. Gen. Pharmacol. 10:159–167.

87. Huxtable, R.J. 1980. Problems with pyrrolizidines. Trends Pharmacol. Sci. 1:299–303.

88. Jacobs, B.L. and M.E. Trulson. 1979. Mechanisms of action of LSD. Amer. Sci. 67:396–404.

89. Johnson, R.K., P. Mazel, J.D. Donahue, and W.R. Jondorf. 1971. Factors involved in the inhibition of drug metabolism by (–)-emetine. Biochem. Pharmacol. 20:955–966.

90. Johnston, G.A.R., P. Krogsgaard-Larsen, and A. Stephanson. 1975. Betel nut constituents as inhibitors of γ-aminobutyric acid uptake. Nature 258:627–628.

91. Jondorf, W.R., J.D. Drassner, R.K. Johnson, and H.H. Miller. 1969. Effect of various compounds related to emetine on hepatic protein synthesis. Arch. Biochem. Biophys. 131:163–169.

92. Jondorf, W.R., R.K. Johnson, and J.D. Donahue. 1969. N-Methylemetine. Arch. Biochem. Biophys. 134:233–241.

93. Kang, M.S. and A.D. Elbein. 1983. Mechanism of inhibition of jack bean α-mannosidase by swainsonine. Plant Physiol. 71:551–554.

94. Kanner, B.I., H. Fishkes, R. Maron, I. Sharon, and S. Schuldiner. 1979. Reserpine as a competitive and reversible inhibitor of the catecholamine transporter of bovine chromaffin granules. FEBS Lett. 100:175–178.

95. Kasvinsky, P.J., S. Shechovsky, and R.J. Fletterick. 1978. Synergistic regulation of phosphorylase a by glucose and caffeine. J. Biol. Chem. 253:9102–9106.

96. Kawai, K., Y. Nozawa, and Y. Ogihara. 1977. Biochemical studies on peptide alkaloids: Induction of ion-selective mitochondrial swelling. Experientia 33:1454.

97. Kela, U., R. Vijayvargiya, and C.P. Trivedi. 1980. Inhibitory effects of methylxanthines on the activity of xanthine oxidase. Life Sci. 27:2109–2119.

98. Klosterman, H.J. 1974. Vitamin B₆ antagonists of natural origin. J. Agric. Food Chem. 22:13–16.

99. Koski, G. and W.A. Klee. 1981. Opiates inhibit adenylate cyclase by stimulating GTP hydrolysis. Proc. Nat. Acad. Sci. U.S.A. 78:4185–4189.

100. Kremmer, T. and L. Holczinger. 1980. Investigation of *Vinca* alkaloid-plasma membrane interactions by detergent gel chromatography. J. Chromatogr. 191:287–292.

101. Kullman, W. 1984. Design, synthesis, and binding characteristics of an opiate receptor mimetic peptide. J. Med. Chem. 27:106–115.

102. Kussaether, E. and J. Haase. 1972. Crystal and molecular structure of l-hyoscyamine hydrobromide. Acta Crystallog. Sect. B. 28:2896–2899.

103. Lambeir, A. and Y. Englcborghs. 1980. A quantitative analysis of tubuline-colchicine binding to microtubules. Europ. J. Biochem. 109:619–624.

104. Lambert, J.J., R.L. Volle, and E.G. Henderson. 1980. An attempt to distinguish between the actions of neuromuscular blocking drugs on the acetylcholine receptor and on its associated ionic channel. Proc. Nat. Acad. Sci. U.S.A. 77:5003–5007.

105. Lang, H. 1975. Model for repair inhibition by caffeine. Stud. Biophys. 50:213–221.

106. Langer, G.-A. 1981. Mechanism of action of the cardiac glycosides on the heart. Biochem. Pharmacol. 30:3261–3264.

107. Lau, C.C. and A.B. Pardee. 1982. Mechanism by which caffeine potentiates lethality of nitrogen mustard. Proc. Nat. Acad. Sci. U.S.A. 79:2942–2946.

108. Lehmann, A.R. 1972. Effect of caffeine on DNA synthesis in mammalian cells. Biophys. J. 12:1316–1325.

109. Lesca, P., P. Beaune, and B. Monsarrat. 1981. Ellipticines and human liver microsomes: Spectral interaction with cytochrome P-450 and hydroxylation. Inhibition of aryl hydrocarbon metabolism and mutagenicity. Chem.-Biol. Interactions 36:299–309.

110. Lesca, P., P. Lecointe, D. Pelaprat, D. Paoletti, and D. Mansuy. 1980. Structure-activity relationships in the inhibitory effects of ellipticines on benzo(a)pyrene hydroxylase activity and 3-methylcholanthrene mutagenicity. Biochem. Pharmacol. 29:3231–3237.

111. Lesca, P., E. Rofidinario, P. Lecointe, and D. Mansuy. 1979. A class of strong inhibitors of microsomal monooxygenases: The ellipticines. Chem.-Biol. Interactions 24:189–198.

112. Luduena, R.F. and M.C. Roach. 1981. Contrasting effects of maytansine and vinblastine on the alkylation of tubulin sulfhydryls. Arch. Biochem. Biophys. 210:498–504.

113. Lytle, C.D., A.L. Iacangelo, C.H. Lin, and J.G. Goddard. 1981. U.V.-enhanced reactivation in mammalian cells: Increase by caffeine. Photochem. Photobiol. 33:123–125.

114. Maina, G. 1974. Reserpine as an uncoupling agent. Biochim. Biophys. Acta 333:481–486.

115. Maiti, M., R. Nandi, and K. Chaudhuri. 1982. Sanguinarine: A monofunctional intercalating alkaloid. FEBS Lett. 142:280–284.

116. Mandel, P. and F. De Feudis. 1979. *GABA-Biochemistry and CNS Functions.* Plenum Press, New York. 517 p.

117. Mann, J. 1978. *Secondary Metabolism.* Oxford University Press, Oxford. 316 p.

118. Margolis, R.L., C.T. Rauch, and L. Wilson. 1980. Mechanism of colchicine-dimer addition to microtubule ends: The mechanism of substoichiometric colchicine poisoning. Biochemistry 19:5550–5557.

119. Marks, A., J.B. Mahony, and I.R. Brown. 1978. Colchicine inhibits the accumulation of messenger RNA for a brain-specific protein in rat glial cells. Biochem. Biophys. Res. Commun. 82:1306–1313.

120. Marks, A., J. Thibault, R.G. Whalen, J.B. Mahony, J. Law, and F. Gros. 1980. Selective action of colchicine on protein synthesis and release in a clonal line of rat glial cells. Biochimie 62:705–712.

121. Marks, M.J. and A.C. Collins. 1982. Characterization of nicotine-binding in mouse brain and comparison with the binding of α-bungarotoxin and quinuclidinyl benzilate. Molec. Pharmacol. 22:554–564.

122. Martin, W.R. 1981. Multiple opioid receptors. Life Sci. 28:1547–1554.

123. Maryanoff, B.E. and M.J. Zalesko. 1978. Stereochemical considerations in structural comparison of enkephalins and endorphins with exogenous opiate agents. J. Pharm. Sci. 67:590–591.

124. Mendoza, E.M.T. and L.L. Ilag. 1982. Biocidal properties of mimosine. Phillip. J. Biol. 11:235–244.

125. Meyerson, L.R., K.D. McMurtrey, and V.E. Davis. 1976. Neuroamine-derived alkaloids: Substrate-preferred inhibitors of rat brain monoamine oxidase *in vitro.* Biochem. Pharmacol. 25:1013–1020.

126. Meyerson, L.R., K.D. McMurtrey, and V.E. Davis. 1978. Isoquinoline alkaloids. Inhibitory actions on cation-dependent ATP-phosphohydrolases. Neurochem. Res. 3:239–257.

127. Michel, R. and A. Uzan. 1972. Action of papaverine, quinicine, and quinidine on oxidative phosphorylation by rat liver and heart mitochondria. J. Pharmacol. 3:265–277.

128. Miranda, C.L., P.R. Cheeke, and D.R. Buhler. 1980. Effect of pyrrolizidine alkaloids from tansy ragwort (*Senecio jacobaea*) on hepatic drug-metabolizing enzymes in male rats. Biochem. Pharmacol. 29:2645–2649.

129. Mitoma, C., T.J. Sorich, II, and S.E. Neubauer. 1968. Effect of caffeine on drug metabolism. Life Sci. 7:145–151.

130. Mitranic, M.M., J.M. Boggs, and M.A. Moscarello. 1981. An effect of colchicine on galactosyl- and sialyl-transferases of rat liver Golgi membrane. Biochim. Biophys. Acta 672:57–64.

131. Mitznegg, P., F. Heim, B. Hach, and M. Sabel. 1971. Effect of aging, caffeine-treatment, and ionizing radiation on nucleic acid synthesis in the mouse liver. Life Sci. II 10:1281–1292.

132. Molyneaux, R.J. and L.F. James. 1982. Loco intoxication: Indolizidine alkaloids of spotted locoweed (*Astragalus lentiginosus*). Science 216:190–191.

133. Moore, H.W. 1977. Bioactivation as a model for drug design bioreductive alkylation. Science 197:527–532.

134. Mukherjee, J. and S. Biswas. 1982. Tubulin from *Mimosa pudica* and its involvement in leaf movement. Phytochemistry 21:1881–1884.

135. Nambi Aiyar, V., M.H. Benn, T. Hanna, J.M. Jacyno, S.H. Roth, and J.L. Wilkens. 1979. The principal toxin of *Delphinium brownii* Rydb., and its mode of action. Experientia 35:1367–1368.

136. Nastasi, M., J.M. Morris, D.M. Rayner, V.L. Seligy, A.G. Szabo, D.F. Williams, R.E. Williams, and R.W. Yip. 1976. Structural implications of the electronic spectra of quinacrine-deoxyribonucleic acid complexes in the ultraviolet region (250–300 nm). J. Am. Chem. Soc. 98:3979–3986.

137. Nemecek, G.M., J.N. Wells, and R.W. Butcher. 1980. Inhibition of fibroblast cyclic AMP escape and cyclic nucleotide phosphodiesterase activities by xanthines. Molec. Pharmacol. 18:57–64.

138. Nichols, D.E. 1981. Structure-activity relationships of phenethylamine hallucinogens. J. Pharm. Sci. 70:839–849.

139. Nichols, J., K.D. Straub, and S. Abernathy. 1978. Effect of sanguinarine, a benzophenanthridine alkaloid, on frog skin potential difference and short circuit current. Biochim. Biophys. Acta 511:251–258.

140. Nishikawa, H. and I. Shiio. 1969. Effect of caffeine on adenylosuccinate lyase synthesis in *Bacillus subtilis*. J. Biochem. 65:523–529.

141. Nolan, L.L. and G.W. Kidder. 1979. Caffeine: Its action on purine metabolizing enzymes. Biochem. Biophys. Res. Commun. 91:253–262.

142. Ohnishi, T., K. Okaichi, Y. Ohashi, and K. Nozer. 1981. Effects of caffeine on DNA repair of UV-irradiated *Dictyostelium discoideum*. Photochem. Photobiol. 33:79–83.

143. Orgell, W.H. 1963. Inhibition of human plasma cholinesterase by alkaloids, glycosides, and other natural substances. Lloydia 26:36–43, 59–66.

144. Owellen, R.J., D.W. Donigian, C.A. Hartke, and F.O. Hains. 1977. Correlation of biologic data with physicochemical properties among the *Vinca* alkaloids and their congeners. Biochem. Pharmacol. 26:1213–1219.

145. Panelka, S. and J. Kovar. 1975. Interaction of liver alcohol hydrogenase with protoberberine alkaloids. Collect. Czech. Chem. Commun. 40:753–768.

146. Papas, T.S., L. Sandhaus, M.A. Chirigos, and E. Furusawa. 1973. Inhibition of DNA polymerase of avian myeloblastosis virus by an alkaloid extract from *Narcissus tazetta*. Biochem. Biophys. Res. Commun. 52:88–92.

147. Pec, P. and L. Macholan. 1976. Inhibition of diamine oxidase by cinchona alkaloids and lobeline. Collect. Czech. Chem. Commun. 41:3474–3481.

148. Pfyffer, G.E., I. Panfil, and G.H.N. Towers. 1982. Monofunctional covalent binding of dictamnine, a furoquinoline alkaloid, to DNA as target *in vitro*. Photochem. Photobiol. 35:63–68.

149. Pollard, H.B. and G.D. Pappas. 1979. Veratridine-activated release of adenosine-5'-triphosphate from synaptosomes: Evidence for calcium dependence and blockade by tetradotoxin. Biochem. Biophys. Res. Commun. 88:1315–1321.

150. Portoghese, P.S. 1978. Stereoisomeric ligands as opioid receptor probes. Accts. Chem. Res. 11:21–29.

151. Reddy, J., C. Harris, and D. Svoboda. 1968. Inhibition by lasiocarpine of RNA synthesis, RNA polymerase, and induction of pyrrolase activity. Nature 217:659–661.

152. Reiser, G., A. Gunther, and B. Hamprecht. 1982. Strychnine and local anesthetics block ion channels activated by veratridine in neuroblastoma x glioma hybrid cells. FEBS Lett. 143:306–310.

153. Reisner, A.H., C.A. Bucholtz, and K.A. Ward. 1979. Effects of the plant amino acid mimosine on cell division, DNA, RNA and protein synthesis in paramecium. Molec. Pharmacol. 16:278–286.

154. Reith, M.E.A., H. Sershen, D.L. Allan, and A. Lajtha. 1983. A portion of [^{3}H] cocaine binding in brain is associated with serotonergic neurons. Molec. Pharmacol. 23:600–606.

155. Robinson, B. 1971. Alkaloids of the calabar bean. *In* R.H. F. Manske, ed. *The Alkaloids* Vol. 13, Academic Press, New York. pp. 213–226.

156. Robinson, T. 1981. *The Biochemistry of Alkaloids,* 2d ed. Springer-Verlag, Berlin. 225 p.

157. Roddick, J.G. 1975. Effect of α-tomatine on the permeability of plant storage tissue. J. Exp. Bot. 26:221–227.

158. Roddick, J.G. 1978. Effect of α-tomatine on the integrity and biochemical activities of isolated plant organelles. J. Exp. Bot. 29:1371–1381.

159. Roddick, J.G. and R.B. Drysdale. 1984. Destabilization of liposome membranes by the steroidal glycoalkaloid α-tomatine. Phytochemistry 23:543–547.

160. Rosenberry, T.L. 1975. Acetylcholinesterase. Adv. Enzymol. 43:103–218.

161. Rothman, R.B. and T.C. Westfall. 1982. Allosteric coupling between morphine and enkephalin receptors *in vitro*. Molec. Pharmacol. 21:538–547.

162. Roveri, O.A. and R.H. Vallejos. 1974. Spegazzine, a new inhibitor of mitochondrial oxidative phosphorylation. Biochim. Biophys. Acta 333:187–194.

163. Ruegg, U.T., S. Cuenod, J.M. Hiller, T. Gioannini, R.D. Howells, and E.J. Simon. 1981. Characterization and partial purification of solubilized, active opiate receptors from toad brain. Proc. Nat. Acad. Sci. U.S.A. 78:4635–4638.

164. Saucier, J.-M., P. Lefresne, and C. Paoletti. 1968. Interaction of a diamino steroid, irehdiamine A, with deoxyribonucleic acid. C.R. Acad. Sci. (D) 266:731–734.

165. Schiller, P.M., C.F. Yam, and M. Lis. 1977. Evidence for topographical analogy between methionine-enkephalin and morphine derivatives. Biochemistry 16:1831–1838.

166. Schröder, E. and E. Magdon. 1975. Influence of caffeine on DNA synthesis and sedimentation behavior of normal and irradiated mammalian cells. Stud. Biophys. 51:209–214.

167. Seifen, E., R.J. Adams, and R.K. Riemer. 1979. Sanguinarine: A positive inotropic alkaloid which inhibits cardiac (Na^+–K^+)- activated ATPase. Europ. J. Pharmacol. 60:373–377.

168. Sepulveda, F.V. and J.W.L. Robinson. 1974. Harmaline, a potent inhibitor of sodium-dependent transport. Biochim. Biophys. Acta 373:527–531.

169. Serrano, E.P., L.L. Ilag, and E.M.T. Mendoza. 1983. Biochemical mechanisms of mimosine toxicity to *Sclerotium rolfsii* Sacc. Austral. J. Biol. Sci. 36:445–454.

170. Sethi, M.L. 1979. Inhibition of reverse transcriptase activity by benzophenanthridine alkaloids. J. Nat. Prod. 42:187–196.

171. Sethi, M.L. 1981. Screening of benzophenanthridine alkaloids for their inhibition of reverse transcriptase activity and preliminary report on the structure-activity relationships. Can. J. Pharm. Sci. 16:29–34.

172. Sethi, V.S. 1981. Inhibition of ribonucleic acid polymerase activity by ellipticine. Biochem. Pharmacol. 30:2026–2029.

173. Sethi, V.S. and M.L. Sethi. 1975. Inhibition of reverse transcriptase activity of RNA-tumor viruses by fagaronine. Biochem. Biophys. Res. Commun. 63:1070–1076.

174. Shaker, N., A. T. Eldefrawi, L.G. Aguayo, J.E. Warmick, E.X. Albuquerque, and M.E. Eldefrawi. 1982. Interactions of d-tubocurarine with the nicotinic acetylcholine receptor/channel molecule. J. Pharmacol. Exper. Ther. 220:172–177.

175. Shein, H.M., S. Wilson, F. Larin, and R.J. Wurtman. 1971. Stimulation of [^{14}C]-serotonin synthesis from [^{14}C]-tryptophan by mescaline in rat pineal organ cultures. Life Sci. II 10:273–282.

176. Shiraishi, N., T. Arima, K. Aono, B. Inouge, Y. Morimoto, and K. Utsumi. 1980. Inhibition by biscoclaurine alkaloid of lipid peroxidation in biological membranes. Physiol. Chem. Phys. 12:299–305.

177. Shoyab, M. 1979. Caffeine inhibits the binding of dimethylbenz(a)-anthracene to murine epidermal cells DNA in culture. Arch Biochem. Biophys. 196:307–310.

178. Siebert, G., M. Schonharting, M. Ott, and S. Surjana. 1975. Metabolic transformation of colchicine. III Inhibition of phosphatases by the metabolite O^{10}-demethylcolchicine (colchiceine) and their reactivation by divalent cations. Hoppe-Seyler's Z. Physiol. Chem. 356:855–860.

179. Silbergeld, E.K. and R.E. Hruska. 1979. Effects of ergot drugs on serotonergic function: Behavior and neurochemistry. Europ. J. Pharmacol. 58:1–10.

180. Simmonds, M.A. 1980. Evidence that bicuculline and picrotoxin act at separate sites to antagonize γ-aminobutyric acid in rat cuneate nucleus. Neuropharmacology 19:39–45.

181. Simon, E.J. 1981. Opiate receptors: Some recent developments. Trends Pharmacol. Sci. 2:155–158.

182. Simonds, W.F., G. Koski, R.A. Streaty, L.M. Hjelmeland, and W.A. Klee. 1980. Solubilization of active opiate receptors. Proc. Nat. Acad. Sci. U.S.A. 77:4623–4627.

183. Slotkin, T.A. and V. Di Stefano. 1970. Urinary metabolites of harmine in the rat and their inhibition of monoamine oxidase. Biochem. Pharmacol. 19:125–131.

184. Smart, L. 1981. Competitive inhibition of sodium-dependent high affinity choline uptake by harmala alkaloids. Europ. J. Pharmacol. 75:265–269.

185. Simonson, L.P. and J.S. Charnock. 1979. The *Harmala* alkaloids: Evidence for their complex inhibition of the K$^+$-acyl phosphate reaction of membranes. Molec. Pharmacol. 15:620–626.

186. Smékal, E. and N. Kubova. 1982. Interactions and DNA binding parameters of selected alkaloids of protoberberine group. Stud. Biophys. 92:73–81.

187. Smith, G.D. and J.F. Griffin. 1978. Conformation of [Leu^5]enkephalin from x-ray diffraction: Features important for recognition at opiate receptor. Science 199: 1214–1216.

188. Smith, L.W. and C.C.J. Culvenor. 1981. Plant sources of hepatotoxic pyrrolizidine alkaloids. J. Nat. Prod. 44:129–152.

189. Smith, P.A., F.F. Weight, and R.A. Lehne. 1979. Potentiation of calcium-dependent potassium activation by theophylline is independent of cyclic nucleotide elevation. Nature 280:400–402.

190. Snyder, S.H. 1979. Opiate receptors and morphine-like peptides. Harvey Lectures 73:291–314.

191. Snyder, S.H. 1980. Brain peptides as neurotransmitters. Science 209:976–983.

192. Snyder, S.H. 1984. Drug and neurotransmitter receptors in the brain. Science 224:22–31.

193. Snyder, S.H., K.J. Chang, M.J. Kuhar, and H.I. Yamamura. 1975. Biochemical identification of the mammalian muscarinic cholinergic receptor. Fed. Proc. 34:1915–1921.

194. Snyder, S.H., J.J. Katims, Z. Annau, R.F. Bruns, and J.W. Daly. 1981. Adenosine receptors and behavior actions of methylxanthines. Proc. Nat. Acad. Sci. U.S.A. 78:3260–3264.

195. Snyder, S.H., A.B. Young, J.P. Bennett, and A.H. Mulder. 1973. Synaptic binding of amino acids. Fed. Proc. 32:2039–2047.

196. Sokolove, P.G. and S.H. Roth. 1978. Effect of harmaline on the crayfish stretch receptor: Blockade at a GABA-mediated inhibitory synapse. Neuropharmacology 17:729–735.

197. Sorace, R.A. and B. Sheid. 1978. Characterization of ellipticine binding to native calf thymus DNA. Chem.-Biol. Interactions 23:379–386.

198. Srinivasan, A., E.P. Reddy, P.S. Sarma, and R.A. Schulz. 1979. Inhibition of RNA-dependent DNA polymerase activity of oncornaviruses by caffeine. Biochem. Biophys. Res. Commun. 91:239–246.

199. Steen, D.A. and A.V. Chadwick. 1981. Ethylene effects in pea stem tissue: Evidence of microtubule mediation. Plant Physiol. 67:460–466.

200. Sytinskii, I.A. 1978. Conformation of γ-aminobutyric acid and its receptors. Biokhimiya 43:771–781.

201. Szabo, P. 1966. Action of d-tubocurarine chloride on the metabolism of chick embryos. Naturwissenschaften 53: 109–110.

202. Terce, F., J. -F. Tocanne, and G. Laneelle. 1983. Localization of ellipticine derivatives interacting with membranes. A fluorescence-quenching study. Biochem. Pharmacol. 32:2189–2194.

203. Thal, C., M. Dufour, P. Potier, M. Jaouen, and D. Mansay. 1981. Rearrangement of vobasine to ervatamine-type alkaloids catalyzed by liver microsomes. J. Am. Chem. Soc. 103:4956–4957.

204. Trease, G.E. and W.C. Evans. 1978. *Pharmacognosy,* 11th ed., Baillière Tindall, London. 795 p.

205. Trotta, E.E. and G.L. Freire. 1980. Inhibition by caffeine of calcium uptake by brain microsomal vesicles. J. Pharmacol. 32:791–793.

206. Tsujimoto, A. and T. Dohi. 1977. A study of the nature of pilocarpine inhibition of hepatic drug-metabolizing enzymes. Biochem. Pharmacol. 26:2072–2074.

207. Tyler, V.E., Jr., L.R. Brady, and J.E. Robbers. 1981. *Pharmacognosy.* 8th ed. Lea and Febiger, Philadelphia, PA. 520 p.

208. Ulrichova, J., D. Walterova, V. Preininger, and V. Simanek. 1983. Inhibition of butyrylcholinesterase activity by some isoquinoline alkaloids. Planta Med. 48:174–177.

209. Ulrichova, J., D. Walterova, V. Preininger, J. Slavik, J. Lenfeld, M. Cushman, and V. Simanek. 1983. Isolation, chemistry, and biology of alkaloids from plants of the Papaveraceae. Part LXXXVI. Planta Med. 48:111–115.

210. Volpe, J.J. and J.C. Marasa. 1976. Long term regulation by theophylline of fatty acid synthetase, actyl-CoA carboxylase, and lipid synthesis in cultured glial cells. Biochim. Biophys. Acta 431:195–205.

211. Wacker, A., L. Trager, M. Maturova, and H. Beckmann. 1967. Inhibition of steroid-dependent enzyme induction in microorganisms by steroids and alkaloids. Naturwissenschaften 54:90.

212. Wagner, T.E. 1969. *In vitro* interaction of LSD with purified calf thymus DNA. Nature 222:1170–1172.

213. Waller, G.R. and O.C. Dermer. 1981. Enzymology of alkaloid metabolism in plants and microorganisms *In* E.E. Conn, ed. *The Biochemistry of Plants*. Vol. 7. Academic Press, New York. pp. 317–402.

214. Ward, K.A. and R.L.N. Harris. 1976. Inhibition of wool follicle DNA synthesis by mimosine and related 4(1H)-pyridones. Austral. J. Biol. Sci. 29:189–196.

215. Watanabe, K., E.F. Williams, J.S. Law, and W.L. West. 1981. Specific inhibition of a calcium dependent activation of brain cyclic AMP phosphodiesterase activity by vinblastine. Biochem. Pharmacol. 30:335–340.

216. Weber, R.P., J.M. Coon, and A.J. Triolo. 1974. Nicotine inhibition of the metabolism of 3,4-benzopyrene, a carcinogen in tobacco smoke. Science 184:1081–1083.

217. Weinbach, E.C., J.L. Costa, C.E. Claggett, D.D. Fay, and T. Hundal. 1983. Reserpine as an uncoupler of oxidative phosphorylation and the relevance to its psychoactive properties. Biochem. Pharmacol. 32:1371–1377.

218. Weiner, C.D. and M.A. Collins. 1978. Tetrahydroisoquinolines derived from catecholamines or DOPA. Effects on brain tyrosine hydroxylase activity. Biochem. Pharmacol. 27:2699–2703.

219. Weinryb, I. 1979. Cyclic AMP as an intracellular mediator of hormone action: Sutherland's criteria revisited. Persp. Biol. Med. 22:415–420.

220. Whetton, A.D. and M.D. Houslay. 1980. The effect of vinblastine on the glucagon, basal, and GTP-stimulated states of the adenyl cyclase from rat liver plasma membrane. FEBS Lett. 111:290–294.

221. Williams, D.E., C.L. Miranda, and D.R. Buhler. 1983. Pyrrolizidine alkaloid-induced alterations in benzo(a)pyrene metabolism and binding of benzo(a)pyrene metabolites to deoxyribonucleic acid. Biochem. Pharmacol. 32:2443–2447.

222. Wilson, L., J.R. Bamburg, S.B. Mizel, L.M. Gresham, and K.M. Creswell. 1974. Interaction of drugs with microtubule proteins. Fed. Proc. 33:158–166.

223. Wilson, L., K.M. Creswell, and K. Chin. 1975. Mechanism of action of vinblastine. Binding of acetyl-^{3}H-vinblastine to embryonic chick brain tubulin and tubulin from sea urchin sperm tail outer doublet microtubules. Biochemistry 14:5586–5592.

224. Winkelhake, J.L. and E.W. Voss, Jr. 1975. Mechanism of covalent incorporation of a lysergyl derivative to immunoglobulin peptides *in vitro*. J. Biol. Chem. 250:2164–2172.

225. Wolozin, B.L. and G.W. Pasternak. 1981. Classification of multiple morphine and enkephalin binding sites in the central nervous system. Proc. Nat. Acad. Sci. U.S.A. 78:6181–6185.

226. Woodcock, E.A. and C.I. Johnston. 1982. Characterization of adenylate cyclase-coupled α_2-adrenergic receptors in rat adrenal cortex using [^{3}H]-yohimbine. Molec. Pharmacol. 22:589–594.

227. Yamamoto, D. and H. Washio. 1979. Curare has a voltage-dependent blocking action on the glutamate synapse. Nature 281:372–373.

228. Young, A.B. and S.H. Snyder. 1973. Strychnine binding associated with glycine receptors of the central nervous system. Proc. Nat. Acad. Sci. U.S.A. 70:2832–2836.

229. Young, A.B. and S.H. Snyder. 1974. Glycine synaptic receptor. Evidence that strychnine binding is associated with the ionic conductance mechanism. Proc. Nat. Acad. Sci. U.S.A. 71:4002–4005.

230. Zavala, F., D. Guénard, and P. Potier. 1978. Interaction of vinblastine analogues with tubulin. Experientia 34:1497–1499.

231. Zhang, A.Z. and G.W. Pasternak. 1981. Opiatic and enkephalins. A common binding site mediates their analgesic actions in rats. Life Sci. 29:843–851.

232. Zuk, J. and Z. Swietlinska. 1973. Effect of caffeine on nucleic acids and protein synthesis in *Vicia faba*. Mutat. Res. 17:207–212.

Polyphenolic Compounds with Biological and Pharmacological Activity

T. Adzet
**Department of Pharmacognosy and Pharmacodynamics,
Faculty of Pharmacy, University of Barcelona,
Barcelona, Spain**

CONTENTS

I. INTRODUCTION

Polyphenolic compounds are present in most of the phanerogamic species. Included within this group of compounds are phenolic acids, flavonoids, anthocyanidins, and other related substances with an unsophisticated structure. For many years, the importance of these polyphenol compounds in general and the flavonoids in particular has been underestimated by pharmacologists, who have considered them as secondary products of vegetable metabolism with no specific physiological function. A radical change has occurred in the last 2 decades, however, following the discovery of numerous important pharmacological actions of these compounds (31, 60).

An initial important fact to be stressed is the general innocuous effect of the polyphenolic compounds to humans (59) despite the cytological and antimicrobial activity observed with certain flavones and flavonols, as well as the teratologic and mutagenetic capacity of flavonoids such as quercetin and kaempferol in preparations of hamster ovarian cells (16, 42, 47). Except for 2 cases of specific toxicity on the intestinal epithelial cells (15), a tannin-induced increase in fecal loss of endogenous nitrogen that inhibits growth (64), and a flavone-induced inhibition of diffusion of sugars (45), there is no evidence of any noticeable toxic effect on human tissues.

The polyphenol compounds generally present a tonifying action because of their natural antioxidant properties (98), as demonstrated *in vitro* (54). Other actions of polyphenolic compounds to be stressed are the stimulation of protein synthesis (4, 36) and the promotion of ammonia elimination (93). More specifically, the compounds cause a stabilizing of cell membrane components in cell organelles such as lysosomes (102) and, above all, a stabilizing of the plasmatic membranes of erythrocytes (17), mastocytes (51, 52), fibroblasts (35), hepatocytes (76, 77), and other similar cells.

II. PHARMACOKINETICS

The increasing interest in the pharmacological activity of the polyphenolic compounds has initiated many studies into their bioavailability (66). Their absorption rates are variable (19, 20), depending on the chemical structure of each polyphenolic compound. The union between plasmatic proteins (albumin) and flavonoids and polyphenol acids depends, to a great extent, on the existence of ortho-diphenol groups.

Studies on caffeic acid binding to bovine serum albumin demonstrated that there are 2 types of binding sites. The first binding site has a high affinity with little capacity and the second a low affinity with high capacity (1). Plotting the results of the equilibrium dialysis by the Scatchard method (84) indicates different slopes corresponding to the 2 different binding sites are obtained ($K_1 = 1740.36 \times 10^2$ M^{-1}; $n_1 = 0.27$; $K_2 = 59.15$ M^{-1}; $n_2 = 119.41$) (1).

Polyphenolic compounds can be detected in the gastrointestinal contents, lungs, kidneys, urine, blood, and expired CO_2 12 hours after they are administered to rats. In addition, the ingestion of polyphenolic acids initiates the appearance of a great number of metabolites of a polyphenol nature in the rat's urine. The polyphenolic acids appear to be affected by a variety of metabolic reactions, including hydrogenation, dehydrogenation, methylation, demethylation, B-oxidation of lateral chains, dehydroxylation of phenol hydrolysis products, and conjugation with glycine and glucuronic acid (14). Flavonoids administered to rats and guinea pigs lead to the presence of either free or glucurono-linked, phenol acid type, urinary metabolites (21, 25, 66, 83). Studies using radioactive-labeled carbon compounds producing high levels of $^{14}CO_2$ indicate a selective rupture of the A ring of flavonoids during metabolism (41). Further studies support biliary elimination as important in the excretion of intact molecules of flavonoids and their conjugates (5, 22, 89). However, the possibility of reabsorption of the biliary metabolites with the establishment of an enterohepatic cycle must be considered.

III. BIOLOGICAL AND PHARMACOLOGICAL ACTIVITY OF THE POLYPHENOL ACIDS

The administration of phenolic acids to experimental animals produces a wide range of biological manifestations. The more important biological effects are on serum levels of both gonadotrophin and prolactin from the pituitary gland, on the androgenic action in the rat prostate, on biliar secretion and hepatic metabolism, and on behavior.

Caffeic and oxidized rosmarinic acids inhibit the effects produced by human lutenizing hormone (LH) of chorionic origin and by an equal part mixture of LH and follicle-stimulating hormone (FSH) from the human hypophysis (69). An injection of ferulic acid induces the liberation of FSH from the pituitary and inhibits the liberation of prolactin (69); in this respect, ferulic acid can be considered analogous to the catecholamine metabolites.

Ferulic acid, whether of endogenous or exogenous origin, antagonizes the effect of androgens on the prostate of castrated rats (69). However, the acid has no effect on the seminal vesicles or the levator ani muscle of the male rat, and there is no appearance of oestrus in female rats and mice (69). It is probable that the mechanism of action of ferulic acid is through changes in amino acid uptake at the membrane level, since it does not hinder the linking of androgens to their receptors or the conversion of testosterone to 5 - dihydrotestosterone (69).

The acids 3,4-dihydroxphenylacetic, 3,4-dihydroxybenzoic, and caffeic (at concentrations of 5×10^{-5} to 5×10^{-3} M) have been observed as inhibitors of dihydroxyphenylalanine (dopa) receptor. Caffeic acid proved the most effective, giving 100-percent inhibition at 5×10^{-3} M (3). In addition, these acids are known to increase capillary resistance, to reduce capillary permeability, and to have antiseptic properties. The latter is especially useful in hospitals (36).

IV. PHARMACOLOGICAL ACTIVITY OF FLAVONOIDS

Flavonoids are known to inhibit the activation of polymorphonuclear leucocyte functions. Quercetin at a concentration of

10^{-5} to 10^{-4} M markedly inhibits the concanavalin A-induced enhancement of oxygen consumption without impairing leucocyte viability and concanavalin A binding. Concanavalin A-dependent cell secretion of lysozyme was also totally inhibited by 30 uM of quercetin.

Quercetin activation of leucocyte respiration appears to be stimulus-specific. Activity of the quercetin is exerted at specific sites of the plasma membrane of the leucocytes. As a mechanism of inhibitory action, this flavonoid appears to either interfere with the formation of microaggregates of membrane constituents (the first step of the respiratory stimulus) or affect the generation of signals such as changes in ion permeability caused by the association of membrane constituents (11).

Quercetin is an effective inhibitor of ragweed antigen-induced histamine release from the basophils of subjects with hay fever but has no effect on nonantigen-stimulated basophils. The stereochemistry of the gamma-pyrone ring system appears to be important in determining inhibitory activity of the quercetin. The hydroxyl in C_3 position is not essential for this activity but enhances it like the C_4-keto-5-OH couplet. The compounds with B ring hydroxylation at 3' and 4' position are more active (27, 63).

Some flavonoids exhibit anti inflammatory activity. Application of taxifolin and a mixture of naringenin-5-glucoside, isohelicrysin, apigenin, luteolin, kaempferol, and quercetin proved to have potent anti inflammatory action on exudative and proliferative phases of inflammation (38). Taxifolin prevented the increase in serum alanine aminotransferase and aspartate aminotransferase activities during inflammation, being one-eighth as active as hydrocortisone. In addition, taxifolin increases the liver's ATP phosphohydrolase activity (74, 108).

Spasmolytic actions have been demonstrated to be respondent to some flavonoids. Kaempferol, quercetin, and their 3-glycosides decrease the contraction tonus and amplitude of intestinal and uterine segments inhibiting barium chloride-, acethylcholine- or histamine-induced contractions (49, 58, 103, 104).

Flavonoids have been connected with several biochemical reactions. Some flavonoids and related compounds such as lignins have a significant inhibitory effect on protein synthesis when added to rat bone marrow cell cultures (113). The addition of quercetin and flavones to liver homogenates or adipose tissue extracts play a role in biological reduction-oxidation reactions by retarding the oxidation of lipids (54). The flavonoids produce a clear increase in vitamin E and a moderate accumulation of vitamin A and carotenoids in the liver (90).

An extract containing myricetin, quercetin, kaempferol, gallic acid, and tannins decreases the total level of lipids and creates a displacement in the level of individual lipid fractions in the blood and liver of rats (44, 91). Moreover, an increase in serum cholesterol level and capillary resistance has been retarded by ingestion of flavonoids. However, flavonoids are not known to affect changes in the aorta surface or the aorta lipid content caused by atherogenesis in animals fed a feed deficient in flavones (95, 105). Experimental studies on atherosclerosis have indicated that a subcutaneous injection of a mixture of quercetin and kaempferol at 8 mg/kg for 20 days will produce a hypocholesteremic effect with a normal recovery of the cholesterol phospholipid ratio (57). Treatment with the heterosides are less effective (23, 24, 53, 55, 56).

The interaction of flavonoids with amino acids is related to vitamin content of tissue (34, 118, 119, 120, 121, 122). It has been observed that the tea catechols [(–)epicatechol, (–)epigallocatechol, (–)epicatechol gallate, and (–)epigallocatechol gallate] inhibit the enzymatic transformation of L-tyrosine when added to rat liver homogenates in combination with the tyrosine. Rutin, quercetin, hesperidin, protocatechic acid, and homovanillic acid have similar effects, but only at much higher concentrations (9). The oxidation of L-proline by liver homogenate from starving rats is strongly enhanced by pure tea catechols, alone or in mixture with ascorbic acid (10).

Experiments with quercetin indicate that it inhibits the (Na^+, K^+) adenosine triphosphatase (ATP). The flavonoid interrupts the formation of E_2-P from either Pi or E_1-P, as well as the hydrolysis of the phosphoenzyme. This mode of action is different than that of other inhibitors of this triphosphatase enzyme (26, 48, 96, 97). At low concentrations, quercetin inhibits both soluble and particulate mitochondrial ATPase with the hydroxyl groups at the 3' and perhaps the 3 position important for the inhibition. The proposed mechanism of action is a blocking of the undesirable hydrolysis of ATP catalyzed by the coupling factor F_1 (48). Quercetin inhibits the ATP-driven reduction of NAD^+ by succinate in mitochondrial particles under conditions where a protein inhibitor is ineffective (50). The compound has no effect on oxidative phosphorylation in submitochondrial particles.

Studies of the effects of a combination of coumarin and rutin sulfate on the stimulated exocrine secretion of the pancreas and on changes of pancreatic enzymes in the thoracic duct lymph have been conducted. This combination of components has no direct effect on the exocrine function of the pancreas but, following the administration of the compounds, amylase and lipase activities in the lymph of thoracic duct increase temporarily. The increase in enzyme activity is probably a consequence of increased outflow of interstitial liquid (high in enzyme content) from the pancreas to the thoractic duct with the levels of pancreatic enzymes in the lymph thus also increasing (6). Benzopyrones are known to potentiate the contractibility of lymphatic vessels (with the increased flow of interstitial fluid from the pancreas).

Certain flavonoids of *Cannabis sativa* L. (flavocannabiside and flavosativaside) are weak inhibitors of lens aldose reductase, an enzyme implicated in the pathogenesis of cataracts in humans suffering from diabetes and galactosemia. Other flavonoids, such as quercitrin, quercetin, myricetin, and oneritin, are reported to be more potent inhibitors of the reductase (70, 88).

Flavonoids can inhibit cathepsin activity in the cortical layer of the pig kidney. The addition of ascorbic acid increases the inhibitory activity of the flavonoid, especially when the ascorbic acid content of the complex is high. Ascorbic acid and flavonoids appear to have synergistic properties in a mixture (121).

For several years, both biochemists and pharmacologists have shown great interest in calcium action (28). Kozawa (46) has experimented on the action of extracts of "Qian-Hu," prepared from the roots of *Peudanum praeruptorum* Dunn., which contain coumarins such as (±)-praemptorin A, (+)-anomalin and (+)-3' (5)-angeroyloxy-4' (5)-isovaleryloxy-3'-4'-dishydro-seselin. The most effective coumarin for antagonizing the action of acetylcholine noncompetitively on the small intestine was (±)-praemptorin A. This compound suppresses the contraction of potassium ion depolarized smooth muscle that is induced by the influx of extracellular calcium ions. For this reason, (±)-praemptorin should be effective in relieving angina. Anomalin and seselin do not significantly affect contraction of the smooth muscle (46).

The aerobic oxidation of ascorbic acid in neutral or alkaline solutions is catalyzed by copper (II) ions and thought to proceed through a free-radical mechanism. The ability of flavonoids to inhibit aerobic oxidation has been attributed to their ability to act as free-radical acceptors and to remove catalytic metal ions through formation of complexes with the metal. The effectiveness of flavonoid to form complexes with metal are undoubtedly influenced by pH of the system (98).

As an experimental development, studies on the action of the flavonoids on the vascular wall are probably the most historically important (30, 116). Anthocyanosides produce a protective effect on pathologically altered capillaries. The hypothesis for explaining this protective action involves phospholipids and mucopolysaccharides (62). In addition, there may be a membrane-stabilizing effect as escinol, esculetin, glyvenol, rutin, and escin have been shown to stabilize the membranes of erythrocytes subjected to hypotonic hemolysis. Laboratory experiments indicate that glyvenol is the most effective membrane stabilizer (17).

Flavonoids also affect capillary resistance. The *ortho*-diphenolic flavonoids are metabolized by the catechol O-methyltransferase, and thereby compete with the catecholamines for this enzyme. Thus, the flavonoids prolong the life of the amines, leading to an increase in their action on the precapillary sphincters. In this way, activity of *ortho*-diphenolic flavonoids on capillary resistance is a consequence of indirect adrenalitic action.

The *ortho*-diphenolic flavonols have the same mechanism of action as the flavonoids, but they provoke a second increase in capillary resistance motivated by increasing the reduction rate of dehydroascorbic acid to ascorbic acid by other flavonols (12, 13, 32, 75). The flavonoids also exert an effect at the endothelial cell membrane level, reinforcing the lecithinic molecular system (33).

Another pharmacological action is the protector effect on carcinogenesis. Naturally occurring food constituents, particularly those in vegetables and fruits, have been found to inhibit the neoplasic effects of chemical carcinogens. Among the inhibitory compounds, coumarin, p-coumaric acid, tangeretin, nobiletin, and B-naphthoflavine are very abundant in cruciferous plants. Although no definitive information on the mechanism exists, there is an inverse correlation between cruciferous intake and its incidence on colon, lung, and stomach cancer. Any conjectures are premature, but it is possible that their activity as antioxidants on microsomal mono-oxygenase promotes a detoxifying action with an antineoplasic effect (115).

The germicidal effect of some flavonic compounds is unspecific and includes many bacteria and microscopic mushrooms. Experiments with the *Pseudomona fluorescens* cultures have revealed that (+) catechol induces changes at the microorganism protein metabolism level (36, 43).

V. PHARMACOLOGICAL ACTIONS AT HEPATIC LEVEL

The isolation of silymarin from the seeds of the milk thistle, *Silybum marianum* (L.) Gaertn., has given a scientific basis to antihepatotoxic therapeutics that were formerly conducted with undefined preparations of the plant material (39, 110, 111). Initial pharmacological studies indicated silymarin to be a useful antagonist to carbon tetrachloride, thioacetamide, and phalloidine liver toxicants. Although originally classified in the flavonol group (according to the methodology then in use), silymarin is now known to be a complex substance consisting of silybin, silydianin, and silycristin. These substances belong to the 2-phenylchromanone group of the taxifolinic type and contain a molecule of coniferyl-alcohol in an oxidative link. Taxifolin is also found among the components of the milk thistle seeds (18, 78, 109, 114).

One of the obstacles in the introduction of antihepatotoxic therapeutics with silymarin has been the shortage of pure amanita toxins. With the availability of sufficient quantities of α-amanitine and phalloidine in recent years, experiments on the antagonism of silymarin against lethal and nonlethal intoxications of both toxins have been conducted. Both silymarin (the mixture) and its various components have great activity in a preventive and curative sense against α-amanitine and phalloidine in the isolated and perfused rat liver (94, 99). Mice intoxicated with phalloidine die in 2 to 3 hours with acute haemorrhagic hepatic dystrophy while animals treated with silymarin at a dosage of 15 mg/kg intravenously survive the hepatic lesion caused by phalloidine (112). A curative treatment of 100 mg/kg of silymarin intravenously 10 minutes after phalloidine intoxication will also protect mice from the lethal action. The protective activity of silymarin diminishes when it is administered 20 minutes after the phalloidine, and no protective activity exists when treatment begins at 30 minutes, as the liver is too damaged to enable restoration of function.

In a test of silymarin against the toxic action of α-amanitine, 79 percent of the test animals died in the 14 days following an intraperitoneal administration of the toxin at a dosage of 0.5 mg/kg. Silymarin administered at dosages of 100 mg/kg intravenously one hour before the intoxication and at various time intervals (10, 19, 30 minutes) after intoxication reduced mortality in the animals by 100 percent in the case of preventive treatment and by 85 percent in the curative one carried out 10 minutes after the administration of the toxic.

Other experiments also support the evidence of silymarin as a protective agent against lesions of the liver. In rats pretreated with sodium phenobarbital in their drinking water to stimulate the microsomal system of the liver, intravenous injection with 100 mg/kg of silymarin reduced the severity of lesions induced by treatment with carbon tetrachloride (65). Observations of test animals with a carbon tetrachloride-induced hepatic lesion that had been treated with an intravenous injection of sodium hexobarbital indicated that the duration of sleep is shortened 50 percent by treatment with silymarin (65). A highly significant reduction in the glutamic oxalacetic transaminase (GOT), glutamic pyruvic transaminase (GPT), succinate dihyodrogenase (SDH), and other plasmatic parameters pathologically increased by the lesion was observed after treatment with silymarin.

Other experimental models of hepatic lesion in the rat, such as those produced by galactosamine or by praseodymium nitrate, are similarly opposed by silymarin (101). Although results from experiments with barbiturates and carbon tetrachloride suggest a protective enzyme induction attributable to silymarin, necropsy studies on the livers of test animals have demonstrated that silymarin does not act by means of enzyme induction (61).

Of all the studied models of liver lesion, silymarin treatment immediately following the intoxication with α-amanitine or phalloidine provides the greatest safety margin. If the silymarin is administered more than 20 minutes after intoxication, the action is not effective. Antiphalloidinic activity is also evident *in vitro* where addition of silymarin to the perfusion liquid of an already intoxicated liver (or the transference of the toxin to a perfusion medium containing silymarin) and the administering of phalloidine and silymarin to a live animal with subsequent perfusion will inhibit formation of liver lesions. The mechanisms involved in the anti-α-amanitine and antiphalloidine action are unknown.

Experiments on isolated and artificially perfused livers indicate the primary action of phalloidine as being upon the hepatocyte membrane where the phalloidine attaches itself and on which it acts, destroying the membrane (99). The α-amanitine penetrates into the cell and then acts, by means of the inhibition of RNA synthesis. A competitive antagonism between the silymarin and the amanita toxins appears to exist, although pharmacologically speaking, neither substance behaves in the sense of a true competitor. If the cell membrane is occupied by silymarin, the amanita toxins can neither attach themselves to the hepatocyte membrane nor penetrate into the cell (117). Silymarin, even when administered in very high doses, is not capable of displacing amanita toxins from receptors once the latter are attached.

From all of the available information, it seems that silymarin acts primarily as a preventive of toxicant action on the liver. The high effectiveness of silymarin in anti-amanita activity raises the question of its specificity. Under appropriate conditions, a multiple of the LD_{100} of phalloidine or α-amanitine can be converted to the LD_0 by treatment of the test animal with silymarin, suggesting great specificity of action. Silymarin can completely antagonize the action of praseodymium nitrate and partially antagonize the action of carbon tetrachloride, galactosamine, thioacetamide, and ethionine in induction of hepatic lesions (83).

Although there seems to be no solid evidence, one hypothesis on silymarin action proposes that the anticarbon tetrachloride and antitetrachloride metabolite action is related to an effect of silymarin on the catabolizing enzyme system. Following subchronic treatment of rats with silymarin there was no variation in the average time span of antipyrine in plasma, in hepatic weight, or in the hepatic weight-body weight ratio. Subchronic treatment with silymarin also did not affect the concentrations of cytochrome P_{450}, ethylmorphine-N-demethylase, or glucuronyltransferase in the liver (107).

The number of substances that play a preventive or curative role in acute, subchronic, and chronic intoxication by carbon tetrachloride is so large and their chemical nature so different that it is virtually impossible to explain all of the anticarbon tetrachloride actions in a uniform way. Vitamins and related substances such as nicotinic acid and derivatives, vitamin E (tocopherol), ascorbic acid and vitamins of the B complex, and poly-2-vinylpyridine-N-oxide (PVNO) can almost certainly act in an anticarbon tetrachloride manner. Even pretreatment of rats with small doses of carbon tetrachloride protects the animals for 24 hours or more from another lethal dose of this toxin (79, 80, 81, 82, 92).

Protective activity of silymarin against lesions caused by galactosamine appears only when the intoxication is in small doses

(106). The hepatotoxic action of praseodymium (formation of an adipose liver with necrotization of the central lobes) is totally antagonized by silymarin both in preventive and curative treatments (94). The increase in hepatic triglycerides, produced by intoxication with ethionine, is antagonized by silymarin. Silymarin also inhibits the increase in enzymatic activity of fumarase, malate-dehydrogenase, and succinate cytochrome C-reductase induced by ethionine.

Silymarin is capable of prolonging survival significantly and slowing down weight loss in animals treated with thioacetamide, an active hepatotoxic substance (37). A single parenteral dose of silymarin an hour before treatment with thioacetamide inhibits the pathological reactions, and it can be concluded that silymarin is one of the substances that can have a favorable influence in acute and chronic hepatic lesions produced by thioacetamide (87).

Because of the widespread ethanol consumption and the fact that ethanol is degraded almost exclusively in the liver, lesions of the liver induced by alcohol are of great interest. The mitochondrial changes that occur following development of an alcoholic lesion in the rat can be almost completely avoided by treatment with silymarin, and there is even a partial protective effect on lysosomal metabolism (72).

The question of whether the flavonic compounds in general and silymarin in particular act only in the preventive or curative field is demonstrated by the model of intoxication by amanita toxins. As silymarin occupies the cell membrane of the hepatocytes and prevents the α-amanitine from reacting and penetrating the cells, no toxic effect develops. Amanita toxins attached to the cell membrane cannot be displaced by silymarin but, on the other hand, the toxins cannot penetrate the cell when the membrane is occupied by silymarin.

The probability of these hypotheses being correct is deduced from the temporary course of the curative action of silymarin, both on phalloidine and on α-amanitine (71). Thus, in the sense of the action mechanism, the molecular pharmacology, or the pharmacodynamics, silymarin is a hepatoprotector that prevents the penetration of the amanita toxins. When, under experimental conditions, a situation exists where some of the receptors are occupied by the toxins while others are blocked due to silymarin, there will be a failure in one part of the hepatocyte parenchyma. The death or survival of the experimental animal will be decided according to the quantity of hepatocytes either necrosized or protected (100).

As already known, the extirpation of up to two-thirds of the liver is compatible with life; it can therefore be supposed that up to two-thirds of the hepatocytes can yield under the action of toxins. The action of silymarin or other flavonic compounds as a hepatoprotector can be considered clinically curative when the remaining protected hepatocytes of the test animals are able to regenerate after toxicant treatment.

The clinical curative action in the human being must also be understood as described above. One cannot assume that, in all cases of hepatopathy, all areas of the liver are at the same stage of lesion as some hepatocytes may be necrotic while others are still intact. Since the silymarin prevents the penetration by toxins, it can be deduced that the intact hepatocytes will be protected and will allow regeneration of the organ; the preventive action, from a pharmacodynamic point of view, becomes a clinically curative action. The hepatocellular field offers hopeful signs for therapeutics, using flavonic compounds and polyphenolic structures in general (2, 7, 8, 29, 40, 68, 73, 86).

VI. REFERENCES

1. Adzet, T., J. Camarasa, E. Escubedo, and M. Merlos. 1984. Estudio *in vitro* de la interaccion polifenol-proteina. Proc. 2nd. Congress Europeen Biopharm. et Pharmacocin. Salamanca. In press.

2. Alcala-Santaella, R., A. Cos, G. Garcia, G. Lara, S. Torres, and J.L. Velo-Bellver. 1973. Hepatopatias cronicas activas, nuevo tratamiento. Muench. Med. Wochenschr. 3.

3. Andary, C., G. Privat, P. Chevallet, H. Orzalesi, J. Serrano, and M. Boucard. 1980. Etude chimique et pharmacodynamique d'esters heterosidiques de l'acide caffeique isoles d'Orbanche rapum-genistae. Farmaco, Ed. Sci. 35:1–30.

4. Anisimov, M., N. Suprunov, and N. Prokof'eva. 1972. Effect of compounds isolated from araliaceae family plants on the *in vitro* biosynthesis of protein. Rastit. Resur. 8:378–380.

5. Barrow, A. and L. Griffiths. 1971. Biliary excretion of hydroxyethyl rutosides and other flavonoids in the rat. Biochem. J. 125:24–25.

6. Bartos, V. and V. Brzek. 1979. Exocrine secretion of the pancreas and enzymes in the lymph after administration of a combination of coumarin and rutin sulphate. Arzneim. Forsch. 29:548–549.

7. Bataller, R., R. Gil, V. Olaso, P. Puche, and E. Pamies. 1974. Analisis del efecto de la silimarina sobre los valores quimico-funcionales de enfermos hepaticos cronicos compensados. Clin. Med. 151:111–116.

8. Benda, L. and W. Zenz. 1973. Silymarin bei leberzirrhose. Wein. Med. Wochenschr. 123:34–36.

9. Berezovskaya, N. 1967. Effect of bioflavonoids and ascorbic acid on tyrosine metabolism. Vop. Pitan. 26:41–53.

10. Berezovskaya, N. 1968. Effect of bioflavonoids and ascorbic acid on the enzymic oxidation of proline and hydroxyproline in animals. Fenol'nye Soedin. Ikh Biol. Funkts. Mater. Vses. Simp. 1st. pp. 383–388.

11. Berton, G., C. Schneider, and D. Romeo. 1980. Inhibition by quercetin of activation of polymorphonuclear leucocyte functions, stimulus specific effects. Biochim. Biophys. Acta 595:47–55.

12. Bettini, V., S. Baraldi, A. Calcagno, E. Legranzi, F. Mayellaro, and R. Martino. 1981. Influenza del 4-metilesculetolo sulle risposte di segmenti di arterie coronarie isolate all'adrenalina, in presenza di pirogallolo. Acta Vitaminol. et Enzymol. 3:236–243.

13. Bettini, V., E. Legrenzi, C. Dalla Valle, and C. Petrella. 1977. Influenza di un flavonoide (4-metilesculetolo) sulle risposte di segmenti di

arterie coronarie isolate all adrenalina. Boll. Soc. Ital. Biol. Sper. 53:2027–2030.

14. Booth, A., D. Emerson, F. Jones, and F. DeEds. 1957. Urinary metabolites of caffeic and chlorogenic acids. J. Biol. Chem. 229:51–59.

15. Brown, J., P. Dietrich, and R. Brown. 1977. Frameshift mutagenicity of certain naturally occurring phenolic compounds in the *Salmonella* microsome test: Activation of anthraquinone and flavonol glycosides by gut bacterial enzymes. Biochem. Soc. Trans. 5:1489–1492.

16. Carver, J., A. Carrano, and J. McGregor. 1983. Genetic effects of the flavonols quercetin, kaempferol, and galangin on Chinese hamster ovary cells *in vitro.* Mutat. Res. 113:45–60.

17. Chaika, L. and Ya.I. Khdzai. 1977. Membrane-stabilizing effect on drugs used in treating venous insufficiency. Farmakol. Toksikol. 40: 306–309.

18. Corvallini, L., A. Bindoli, and N. Siliprandi. 1978. Comparative evaluation of antiperoxidative action of silymarin and other flavonoids. Pharmacol. Res. Commun. 10:133–136.

19. Crevoisier, C., P. Buri, and J. Boucherat. 1975. Etude du transport de trois flavonoides a travers des membranes artificielles et biologiques. Etude du transport *in situ* a travers l'intestin grele du rat. Pharma. Acta Helv. 50:231–236.

20. Crevoisier, C., P. Buri, and J. Boucherat. 1975. Etude du transport de trois flavonoides a travers des membranes artificielles et biologiques. Etude du transport *in vitro* a travers des membranes lipidiques composees. Pharma. Acta Helv. 50:103–108.

21. Das, N. and L. Griffiths. 1969. Flavonoid metabolism. Metabolism of (+) catechol in the rat and guinea pig. Biochem. J. 115:831–836.

22. Das, N. and S. Sothy. 1971. Flavonoid metabolism. Biliary and urinary excretion of metabolites of (+)-[U-^{14}C] catechin. Biochem. J. 125:417–423.

23. Dorofeenko, G., A. Shinkarenko, L. Lisevitskaya, A. Kazakov, A. Pyshchev, and V. Mezheritskii. 1974. Synthesis of isoflavones with hypocholesteremic activity. Khim. Geterotsikl. Soedin. (6) 875.

24. Dorofeenko, G., A. Shinkarenko, L. Lisevitskaya, V. Mezheritskii, A. Kazakov, and Yu. Zhdanov. 1975. Effect of isoflavones on lipid metabolism under experimental hypercholesteremia. Biol. Nauki. 18:35–38.

25. Fedurov, V. 1966. Metabolism of bioflavonoids in animals. Fenol'nye Soedin. Ikh. Biol. Funkts. Mater. Vses. Simp. 1st. p. 371–377.

26. Fedurov, V. 1969. Mechanism of the effect of flavonoids on respiration and oxidative phosphorilation of rat liver mitochondria. Ukr. Biokhim. Zh. 41:489–492.

27. Fewtrell, C. and B. Gomperts. 1977. Effect of flavone inhibitors of transport ATPases on histamine secretion from rat mast cells. Nature 265:635–636.

28. Fewtrell, C. and B. Gomperts. 1977. Quercetin: A novel inhibitor of a Ca^{2+} influx and exocytosis in rat peritoneal mast cells. Biochim. Biophys. Acta 469:52–60.

29. Fintelmann, V. 1974. Terapeutica de las hepatosis toxico-metabolicas. Lecc. Med. 145.

30. Gabor, M. 1973. L'influence des flavonoides sur la resistance vasculaire. Possibilites et problemes. Bull. Liaison, Groupe Polyphenols 4.

31. Gabor, M. 1974. Les perspectives dans la recherche pharmacologique sur les flavonoides. Bull. Liaison, Groupe Polyphenols 5(4):14.

32. Gazabe, J. 1973. Interference des polyphenols dans le catabolisme des catecholamines. Bull. Liaison, Groupe Polyphenols 4.

33. Gazabe, J., C. Roger, M. Achard, and J. Parrot. 1974. Polyphenols et resistance capillaire. Bull. Liaison, Groupe Polyphenols 5(5):8.

34. Golovkina, M., V. Ledova, and N. Novotel'nov. 1968. Effect of the ascorbic acid-flavonoid system on proteolytic enzyme activity. Myas. Ind. Lud. 39:36–38.

35. Gotzos, V., A. Spreca, and G. Conti. 1971. Action de O–(B-hydroxyethyl)-rutoside sur les fibroblastes de l'embryon de poulet cultives *in vitro*. Arc. Anat. Microsc. Morphol. Exp. 60:133–146.

36. Greppin, H. and R. Horn. 1969. Action of (+)-catechol on *Pseudomones fluorescens*. Experientia 25:429–430.

37. Guemes, F., C. Perez, J. Sallent, and E. Arias. 1974. Estudio clinico experimental con silimarina en el tratamiento de las hepatopatias difusas de caracter potencialmente reversible. Rev. Clin. Esp. 132:263–268.

38. Gupta, M., T. Bhorlla, G. Gupta, C. Mitra, and K. Bhargawa. 1971. Anti-inflammatory activity of taxifolin. Jpn. J. Pharmacol. 21:377–382.

39. Hahn, G., H. Lehman, M. Kurten, H. Uebel, and G. Vogel. 1968. Pharmacology and toxicology of silymarin, antihepatotoxic compound from *Silybum marianum*. Arzneim. Forsch. 13:698–704.

40. Hammerl, H., O. Pichler, and M. Studlar. 1971. Uber die objektivierung der silymarinwirkung bei lebererkrankungen. Med. Klin. 66:1204–1208.

41. Harborne, J.B. and T.J. Mabry. 1982. *The Flavonoids: Advances in Research.* Chapman and Hall Ltd., London.

42. Ho, R., H. Kawamura, Y. Tokoro, K. Tosaka, S. Nakayama, S. Toida, S. Matsura, M. Ozaki, and T. Hiyawa. 1972. Toxicity and teratogenicity of 1,3-dimethylxanthine-7-acetic acid-7-[(2-dimethylamino)ethoxy] flavone (perflavone). Toho Igakkai Zasshi 19:116–118.

43. Hufford, Ch. and W. Lasswell. 1978. Antimicrobial activities of constituents of *Uvaria chamae*. J. Nat. Prod. 41:156–160.

44. Kadykow, M., L. Samochowiec, and J. Wojcicki. 1973. Influence of bioflavonoids on serum lipid levels in rats. Acta Med. Pol. 14:173–176.

45. Kimmich, G. and J. Randles. 1978. Phloretin-like action of bioflavonoids on sugar accumulation capability of isolated intestinal cells. Membr. Biochem. 1:221–237.

46. Kozawa, T., K. Sakai, M. Uchida, T. Okuyawa, and S. Shibata. 1981. Calcium antagonistic action of a coumarin isolated from "quian-hu" a Chinese traditional medicine. J. Pharm. Pharmacol. 33:317–320.

47. Kupchan, S., C. Sigel, R. Hemingway, J. Knox, and M. Udayamurthy. 1979. Cytotoxic flavones from *Eupatorium* species. Tetrahedron 25:1603–1615.

48. Kuriki, Y. and E. Raker. 1976. Inhibition of (Na^+, K^+) adenosine triphosphatase and its partial reactions by quercetin. Biochemistry 15:4951–4956.

49. Lallement-Guilbert, N. and L. Bezanger-Beauquesne. 1970. Recherches sur les flavonoides de quelques labiees medicinales. Plant. Med. Phytother. 4:92–107.

50. Lang, D. and E. Racker. 1974. Effects of quercetin and F_1 inhibitor on mitochondrial ATPase and energy-linked reactions in submitochondrial particles. Biochim. Biophys. Acta 333:180–186.

51. Lecomte, J. 1975. Pharmacological properties of silybine and silymarin in the rat. Arch. Int. Pharmacodyn. Ther. 214:165–176.

52. Lecomte, J. and J. Damas. 1974. Mast cell protection against dextran induced by silybin. C.R. Seances Soc. Biol. Ses. Fil. 168: 1449–1451.

53. Leont'eva, T., A. Kazakov, and V. Ryzhenkov. 1979. Effect of total flavonoid from red clover and common gram on the content of lipids in rat liver tissue and blood. Vopr. Med. Khim. 25:444–447.

54. Letan, A. 1967. The possible transference of flavonol antioxidants from the diet to the tissue lipids of rats. Brit. J. Nutr. 21:315–323.

55. Lisevitskaya, L., L. Shinkarenko, V. Bandyukova, and V. Makarov. 1968. Flavonol substances during experimental atherosclerosis. Aktual. Vopr. Farm. 176–177.

56. Lisevitskaya, L., L. Shinkarenko, and E. Oganesyan. 1968. Action of quercetin and flavonoid preparations from pontic azalea (*Rhododendron luteum*) and caucasian rhododendron (*R. caucasicum*) on some indexes of cholesterol metabolism in white rats with experimental hypercholesteremia. Biol. Nauki. 12:50–52.

57. Lisevitskaya, L., L. Shinkarenko, G. Zemtsova, and V. Kampantsev. 1968. Effect of luteoline and luteoline-7-glycoside on lipid metabolism during experimental atherosclerosis. Aktual. Vopr. Farm. 178–179.

58. Makarov, V. 1968. Spasmolytic and antitonic action of *Prunus spinosa* flavonoids. Aktual. Vopr. Farm. 188–190.

59. Masquelier, J., J. Michaud, J. Laparra, and M. Dumou. 1979. Flavonoides et pycnogenols. Int. J. Vit. Nutr. Res. 49:307–311.

60. Masquelier, J., J. Michaud, J. Laparra, and M. Dumou. 1979. Pycnogenols: un nouvel essor therapeutique des derives catechiques. Bull. Soc. Pharm. Bordeaux 118:95–108.

61. Meib, R., V. Heinrich, H. Robeneck, and H. Themann. 1982. Effect of silybin on hepatic cell membranes after damage by polycyclic aromatic hydrocarbons. Agents Actions 12:1–2.

62. Mian, E., S. Curri, A. Lietti, and E. Bombardelli. 1977. Anthocyanosids and the microvascular wall. New finding in syndrome due to abnormal capillary fragility. Minerva Med. 68:3565–3581.

63. Middleton, E. and G. Drzewiecki. 1982. Effects of flavonoids and transitional metal cations on antigen-induced histamine release from human basophils. Biochem. Pharmacol. 31:1449–1453.

64. Mitjavcha, S. 1973. Effect de l'acide tannique sur la perte d'azote fecal endogene chez le rat. Bull. Liaison, Groupe Polyphenols 4.

65. Monfort-Albelda, R., J. Alemany, F. Sanchez de la Cuesta de Alarcon, and J. Aznar-Lopez. 1972. Influencia de la silimarina sobre los efectos del tetracloruro de carbono en la actividad diamino-oxidasa del higado de ratas. Acta Med. Nov.:1–7.

66. Mosser, J., M. Trouilloud, V. Vergely, F. Fauran, and J. Cros. 1974. Pharmacologie des flavonoides: Aspects pharmacocinetiques. Bull. Liaison, Groupe Polyphenols 5(12):13.

67. Nakagawa, Y., M. Shetlar, and S. Wender. 1965. Urinary products from quercetin in neomycin-treated rats. Biochim. Biophys. Acta 97:233–241.

68. Neumaier, W. 1970. Enjuiciamiento critico de los valores de laboratorio durante una nueva hepatoterapia. Arzt. Praxis. 21:3637–3639.

69. Okamoto, R., S. Sakamoto, K. Noguchi, Y. Kobayashi, T. Suzuki, and Y. Torii. 1976. Effects of ferulic acid on FSH, LH and Prolactin levels in serum and pituitary tissue of male rats. Proc. Jpn. Acad. 52:264–267.

70. Okuda, J., I. Miwa, K. Inagaki, T. Horie, and M. Nakayama. 1982. Inhibition of aldose reductases from rat and bovine lenses by flavonoids. Biochem. Pharmacol. 31:3807–3822.

71. Paris, J., M. Heraud, and J. Andre. 1975. Appreciation de l'effect de la silymarine en pathologie hepatique. M.P. Juin.

72. Platt, V. and B. Sdenorr. 1971. Biochemical and electronoptic studies on the possible influence of silymarin on hepatic damage induced by ethanol in rats. Arzneim. Forsch. 21:1206–1208.

73. Poser, G. 1971. Experiencias con silimarina en el tratamiento de las hepatopatias cronicas. Arzneim. Forsch. 21:1209–1212.

74. Prokopenko, O., V. Spiridonov, V. Litvinenko, V. Chornobai, G. Obolentseva, Ya. Khadzhai, and Z. Tatarko. 1972. Phenol compounds of *Helichrysum* and their biological activity. Farm. Zh. 27:3–7.

75. Raineri, A., M. Palazzoadriano, and A. Battaglia. 1966. Effetti dil bioflavonoidi e della strofantina sulla O-metiltransferasi e analisi dell'interazione. Boll. Soc. Ital. Biol. Sper. 43:401–404.

76. Ramellini, G. and J. Meldolesi. 1974. Stabilization of isolated rat liver plasma membranes by treatment *in vitro* with silymarin. Arzneim. Forsch. 24:806–808.

77. Ramellini, G. and J. Meldolesi. 1976. Liver protection by silymarin: *In vitro* effect on associated rat hepatocytes. Arzneim. Forsch. 26:69–73.

78. Rauen, H. and H. Schriewer. 1971. The antihepatotoxic effect of silymarin on liver damage in rats induced by carbon-tetrachloride, d-galactosamine and allyl-alcohol. Arzneim. Forsch. 21:1194–1201.

79. Rauen, H., H. Schriewer, and H. Fels. 1973. Die antihepatotoxisch wirkung aliphatischer und heterozyklischer mercaptoverbindungen bei der leberschadigung der ratte durch CCl₄. I. Arzneim. Forsch. 23:136–140.

80. Rauen, H., H. Schriewer, and H. Fels. 1973. Die antihepatotoxische wirkung aliphatischer und heterozyklischer mercaptoverbindungen bei der leberschadidung der ratte durch CCl₄. II. Arzneim. Forsch. 23:141–145.

81. Rauen, H., H. Schriewer, B. Gebauer, and M. Abu Tair. 1973. Die wirkung essentieller phospholipide bei der akuten experimentellen leberschadidung durch CCl₄. Arzneim. Forsch. 23:1332–1334.

82. Rauen, H., H. Schriewer, U. Tegtbauer, and J. Lasana. 1973. Die wirkung aliphatischer und heterozyklischer mercaptoverbindungen auf die lipidperoxidation bei der leberschadidung der ratte durch CCl₄. Arzneim. Forsch. 23:145–148.

83. Rauen, H., H. Schriewer, U. Tegtbauer, and J. Lasana. 1973. Silymarin verhindert die lipidpreoxidation bei der CCl₄- leberschadigung. Experientia 29:1372.

84. Scatchard, G. 1949. The attraction of proteins for small molecules and ions. Ann. N.Y. Acad. Sci. 51:660–667.

85. Scheline, R. 1970. The metabolism of (+)-catechin to hydroxypheny-valeric acids by the intestinal micronflora. Biochim. Biophys. Acta 222:228–230.

86. Schilder, M. 1970. La silimarine en el ensayo clinico. Therapiewoche. 20:3446.

87. Schriewer, H., R. Badde, F. Roth, and H.M. Rauen. 1973. Die antihepatotoxische wirkung des silymarins bei der liberschadigung durch thioacetamid. Arzneim. Forsch. 23(1a):157–158.

88. Segelman, A., F. Segelman, S. Varma, H. Wagner, and O. Seligmann. 1977. *Cannabis sativa* L. (marijuana). IX: Lens aldose reductase inhibitory activity of marijuana flavone C-glycosides. J. Pharm. Sci. 66:1358–1359.

89. Shaw, I. and L. Griffiths. 1980. Identification of the major biliary metabolites of (+)-catechin in the rat. Xenobiotica 10:905–911.

90. Shipochliev, I., G. Petkov, S. Dimitrov, P. Stoyanov, V. Ivanov, and N. Kikolov. 1970. Effect of the flavonoids of the oil-bearing rose (*Rosa damascena*) on the accumulation of vitamins A and E and carotenoids in the liver of broilers. Vet. Med. Nauki. 7:99–104.

91. Shnyakina, G. and N. Murzina. 1974. Phenol compounds of some *Sedum* species of the Soviet far east and effects of their leaf extracts on the lipid metabolism of rats. Rastit. Resur. 10:358–362.

92. Siegers, C., M. Volpel, G. Seheel, and M. Yames. 1982. Effects of dithiocarb and (+)-catechin against carbon tetrachloride-alcohol induced liver fibrosis. Agents Actions 12:743–748.

93. Sokolova, V. and L. Lynbartseva. 1979. Effect of flavonoids on some nitrogen metabolic pathways in experimental uremia. Vopr. Med. Khim. 25:379–382.

94. Strubelt, O., C. Siegers, and M. Yames. 1980. The influence of silybin on the hepatotoxic and hypoglycemic effects of praseodymium and other lantanides. Arzneim. Forsch. 30:1690–1694.

95. Szabo, R., A. Antal, A. Rednik, K. Liptak, I. Gyori, M. Gabor, and S. Benko. 1971. Lipid content of the aorta and changes in its internal membrane in rats on a flavone-free diet during atherogenesis. Kiserl. Orvostud. 23:154–163.

96. Teras, L. 1966. Effect of bioflavonoids upon the adenosine triphosphatase activity in liver mitochondria. Eesti NSV Teaduste Akad. Toimetised. Biol. Seer. 15:587–592.

97. Teras, L. 1967. The effects of bioflavonoids on oxidative phosphorylation in rat liver mitochondria. Vopr. Med. Khim. 13:573–578.

98. Thompson, M. and C. Williams. 1976. Stability of flavonoid complexes of cooper-II and flavonoid antioxidant activity. Anal. Chim. Acta 85:375–381.

99. Trost, W. and G. Halbach. 1978. Anti-phalloidine and anti-amanitine action of silybin in comparison with compounds similar to estructural parts of silybin. Experientia 34:1051–1052.

100. Tuchweber, B., W. Trost, M. Salas, and R. Sieck. 1976. Prevention of praseodymium-induced hepatotoxicity by silybin. Toxicol. Appl. Pharmacol. 38:559–570.

101. Tyntyulkova, N., S. Tuneva, U. Gorantcheva, G. Taner, V. Zhivkov, H. Chelibonova, and S. Bozhkov. 1981. Hepatoprotective effect of silymarin on liver of d-galactosamine-treated rats: Biochemical and morphological investigations. Methods Find. Exp. Clin. Pharmacol. 3:71–77.

102. Van Caneghem, P. 1972. Influence of some hydrosoluble substances with vitamin P activity on the fragility of lysosomes *in vitro*. Biochem. Pharmacol. 21:1543–1548.

103. Van der Broncke, C. 1982. Chemisch en farmakologisch onderzoek van *Origanum compactum, Thymus satureioides* en enkeleandere thymussorrten. Thesis. Leuven.

104. Van der Broncke, C., J. Lemli, and J. Lamy. 1982. Action spasmolytique des flavones de differentes especes de *Thymus.* Plant. Med. Phytother. 16:310–317.

105. Vasilenko, Yu., G. Dorofeenko, A. Nazakov, L. Lisevitskaya, T. Leont'eva, U. Mezheritski, E. Parfent'eva, and A. Shinkarenko. 1978. Effect of red clover flavonoids and some of their synthetic analogs on lipid metabolism indexes in animals with experimental atherosclerosis. Izv. Sev.-Kauk. Nauchn. Tsentra Vyssh. Skh. Estestv. Nauki. 6:99–101.

106. Vazquez, J. 1974. Estudios experimentales con silimarina. I. Estudio comparado de actividades enzimaticas mitocondriales de higado de ratas tratadas con etionina y con etionina mas silimarina. Med. Clin. (Barcelona) 62:28–30.

107. Vazquez, J. 1974. Estudios experimentales con silimarina. II. Efectos de la silimarina sobre el higado graso producido en ratas por la intoxicacion alcoholica aguda. Med. Clin. (Barcelona) 62:117–118.

108. Villar, A., J. Esplugues, and M. Alcaraz. 1982. Acute anti-inflammatory activity of *Sideritis mugronensis* flavonoid. Arch. Farmacol. Toxicol. 8:99–105.

109. Vogel, G. 1968. Silymarin, antihepatotoxic principle from *Silybum marianum* L. as antagonist of the effect of phalloidine. Arzneim. Forsch. 18:1063–1064.

110. Vogel, G. 1977. *Natural Substances with Effects on the Liver.* Springer-Verlag, Berlin.

111. Vogel, G., W. Trost, R. Braatz, K. Odenthal, G. Brusewitz, H. Antweiler, and R. Seeger. 1975. Untersuchungen zur pharmakodynamik, angriffspunkt und wirkungsmechanismus von silymarin, dem antihapatotoxischen prinzip aus *Silybum marianum.* Arzneim. Forsch. 25:82–89.

112. Vogel, G., W. Trost, and G. Halbach. 1974. Etude de l'action protectrice de la silymarine vis-a-vis de l'intoxication par la phalloidine chez la souris. Agressologie 15:263–270.

113. Vonder, M. 1973. Polyphenols (flavonoides) et effects biochimiques. Bull. Liaison, Groupe Polyphenols 4(20):22.

114. Wagner, H. 1974. The chemistry and pharmacology of the flavonolignans of *Silybum marianum.* Bull. Liaison, Groupe Polyphenols 5(1):24.

115. Wattenberg, L. and L. Lam. 1981. Inhibition of chemical carcinogenesis by phenols, coumarins, aromatic isothiocyanates, flavones and indoles. *In* M. Zedeck, ed. *Inhibition of Tumor Induction and Development.* Plenum Press, New York. pp. 1–19.

116. Weibel, I., M. Comte, and R. Horn. 1973. Metabolisme du glucose dans le tissue veineux. Influence *in vitro* de quelques polyphenols. Bull. Liaison, Groupe Polyphenols 4(21):15.

117. Weil, G. and M. Frimmer. 1970. Effect of silymarin on the isolated perfused rat liver poisoned by phalloidine. Arzneim. Forsch. 20:862–863.

118. Wilson, H., C. Price-Jones, and R. Hughs. 1976. The influence of an extract of orange peel on the growth and ascorbic acid metabolism of young guinea pigs. J. Sci. Food Agric. 27:661–666.

119. Zloch, Z. 1969. Influence of quercetin and epicatechol on biochemical changes in guinea pigs during experimental C-hypovitaminosis. Int. Z. Vitaminforsch. 39:269–280.

120. Zloch, Z. 1973. Influence of bioflavonoids on the vitamin C value of crystaline dehydro-L-ascorbic acid. Int. J. Vit. Nutr. Res. 43:378–386.

121. Zloch, Z. 1974. Effect of regulated peroral doses of dehydroascorbic acid and bioflavonoids on several biochemical functions of vitamin C. Int. J. Vitam. Nutr. Res. 44:466–476.

122. Zloch, Z. 1977. The influence of bioflavonoids on the metabolism of vitamin C. Flavonoids Bioflavonoids, Proc. Hung. Bioflavonoid Symp. 5th. pp. 445–459.

Production Ecology of Secondary Plant Products

Jenő Bernáth
Research Institute for Medicinal Plants, H-2011
Budakalasz, P.O. Box 11, Hungary

CONTENTS

I. SECONDARY PLANT PRODUCTS IN THE ECOLOGICAL SYSTEM

As more and more attention in recent years has been given to enlarging yields through increased biomass production, extending and merging ecological analyses with up-to-date techniques has assumed more importance (46, 78, 116, 159). Although considerable information on model production systems has been published (80), the principles and practices characterizing and describing primary plant production cannot be directly adapted to the production of secondary plant products. Namely, the "appearance" of a special product in the ecological system postulates the presence of special circumstances beyond general production regularities. For instance, much of the evidence indicates that many secondary products are produced to regulate production of neighboring organisms (61). Whether secondary products are regarded as compounds which serve a defensive or attractant role, their very production presumes a special adaptation to physiological and ecological phenomena.

The establishment of production-ecological principles for secondary products would be no more than illusion if the biological and taxonomical knowledge accumulated in the last 3 decades was not available. Almost all summary works concerning the biosynthesis of secondary products (9, 105, 112, 119, 122, 158) indicate that, for the accumulation, the influence of ecological factors must be considered. This differs from the majority of chemotaxonomic studies that deal with ecological connections and ecological implications (64).

Discovery of effective primary-secondary production relationships depends on the introduction of modern physio-ecological methods. Observations (50, 110) can only be confirmed or rejected, and effective environmental influences can only be responsibly explored by up-to-date hypotheses and methodologies.

In agreement with the general research strategy of modern ecology (81), the starting point for exploring work on secondary plant products is the study of the overall production system. The regulatory techniques developed depend, to a great extent, on the ecosystem where the plant will be grown. For the production of secondary plant products we can define natural or quasinatural ecosystems, which are partially under human influence, and agricultural ecosystems, which produce secondary products.

In a natural ecosystem, species separated on the basis of their secondary product contribute to the development or modification of the existing ecological balance. However, for a full understanding of their production processes, a detailed analysis of the occurrences and the possible exact circumscription of their role in the phytocenosis, as revealed by studies on geographical distribution of the secondary products, is required (10, 25, 36, 98, 120, 132, 141).

Investigations on phytocenosis and on the ecological demand of species producing secondary compounds indicate required production conditions. Some investigations of this kind are available, and analyses based on similar principles have yielded results (22, 58, 92, 93, 99, 117, 143). However, the efforts to discover regulatory mechanisms in the natural systems producing secondary products cannot be regarded as satisfactory. In many countries, the declaration of some medicinal plants as "protected" calls attention to the lack of wide-ranging ecological investigations. For instance, out of approximately 200 wild-growing medicinal plants in Hungary, several (*Adonis vernalis, Valeriana sambucifolia, Gentiana* spp., *Pulmonaria* spp.) have been declared protected to prevent their extermination.

Investigations on agricultural ecosystems producing secondary compounds need to analyze production processes to aid in developing new production systems. With such knowledge, new artificial systems can be created to approach the physiological demand of the plant species. Production-biological studies must ensure maximal exploitation of ecological potentials of a given habitat with the goal of ecological optimization of secondary compound production, not a general increase in production.

II. ENVIRONMENTAL CONTROL OF THE FORMATION OF SECONDARY PRODUCTS

The close connection between the formation of primary and secondary products (9) presumes that the factors acting on processes are influencing, to a decisive extent, synthesis as well as accumulation of secondary compounds. In this case, the starting point is primary production, since the processes of formation and accumulation of secondary products do not separate from the full phytomass, but represent its productive ratio. The task of experimental and evaluative work is to discover the effects a given environmental stress has on universal and special processes within the plant. As outlined in Figure 1, the production of secondary compounds may be modified by:

- Influencing the dry-matter production.
- Changing the proportions of organs.
- Modifying the accumulation level.

A. Relationship between Dry-Matter and Secondary Production

Nowinski (110) has concluded that increasing secondary product yield of medicinal plants and volatile oil-yielding plants by increasing dry-matter production is 2 to 3 times more effective than any direct effect on special products. This hypothesis reflects a general, practical

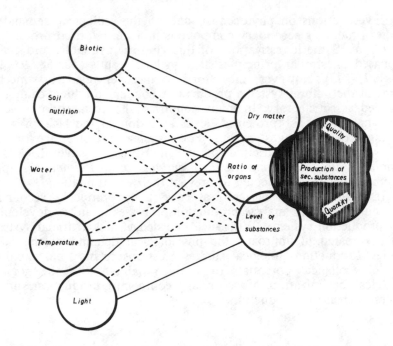

Figure 1. The Factors Affecting Accumulation of Secondary Compounds in Plants. The quality and quantity of production can be regulated by environmental factors modifying dry-matter production, ratio of organs, and level of active substances. Data of Bernáth and Tétényi (16).

view, but its incompleteness diverts attention from the fact that an increase in dry-matter production might vary secondary product accumulation.

1. Linearlike Equation

The most general of productive connections states that, in the increasing range of the optimum curve, the unit growth of dry matter production will nearly produce a unit accumulation of secondary product. Among others, a good example for this is the development of steroid alkaloids as related to nutrient supply. According to Flück (50), the first influence of increased nutrient supply in species of the Solanaceae family is increased dry-matter production, resulting in increased alkaloid production. *Solanum laciniatum* and *Solanum dulcamara* have been investigated along these lines in the utmost detail by several investigators (26, 56, 70, 77, 147) with similar results. Our investigations also demonstrate that dry-matter production will be modified by nutrient supply with corresponding unchanged levels of alkaloid (Figure 2). Thus, the production of steroid alkaloids (Y) is basically determined by the quantity of dry matter

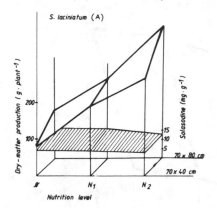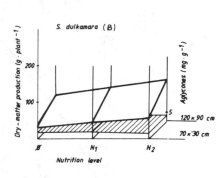

Figure 2. Production as Affected by Nutrition and Plant Spacing. A = *Solanum laciniatum*, B = *Solanum dulcamara*. Aglycone concentration (solasodine, tomatidenol, soladulcidine) remained relatively stable in both species as total dry-matter production increased with increases in nutrition and spacing.

developed (X); the connection of both can be approached by a linear equation for *Solanum dulcamara*:

Y = – 0.72 + 3.14 X (on growing area 70 x 30 cm)

Y =   44.80 + 2.70 X (on growing area 120 x 90 cm)

and for *Solanum laciniatum*:

Y = 353.7 + 12.3 X (on growing area 70 x 40 cm)

Y = 677.1 + 12.0 X (on growing area 70 x 80 cm)

Apart from extreme stress effects, an approximately linear connection exists between alkaloid production in poppy-heads of *Papaver somniferum* and yields of dry matter as adjusted for water supply (87, 129, 148, 162). Under controlled conditions, Bernáth and Tétényi (20) have reported that improvement of water supply increases overall plant production with no change in the intensity of alkaloid accumulation. Consequently, the production of alkaloids (Y) is proportional with the change in yield of dry matter (X) and can be described under controlled conditions as Y = 0.16 + 0.56 X.

Similar relationships exist in volatile oil-yielding plants (Figure 3) (4). An increase in nitrogen to *Mentha arvensis* induces an increase in development of fresh plant mass. Since the volatile oil level per unit biomass has remained practically the same, the total production of volatile oil has proportionally increased with the change in yield of plant matter.

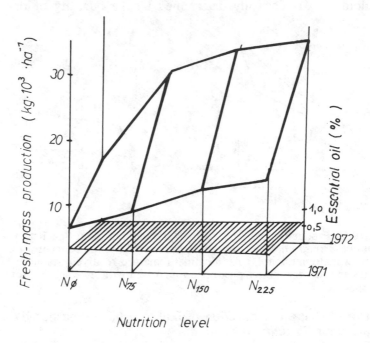

Figure 3. Production of *Mentha arvensis* as Affected by Nutrition and Growth Year. The level of essential oil was relatively stable as total fresh-mass production increased with increases in the nutritional level and the growth year. Data of Bains *et al.* (4).

2. Relation Approached by Power Function

In several cases, however, the production relationship between primary and secondary products is not characterized by a linear function. In this situation, the quantitative accumulation of secondary compounds is greater than the value which can be expected on the basis of an increase in dry-matter production. This is exemplified by alkaloid production of *Papaver somniferum* under changes in light levels (17). As indicated by data in Figure 4, an increase in light level promotes dry-matter production along a sigmoidal curve. Intensive growth is within the interval of 8 and 16 kilolux (klx) and light saturation is near 32 klx, similar to other species of C_3 plants (81). Simultaneous with an increase in dry-matter production is intensive alkaloid accumulation per unit dry matter. The alkaloid production (Y) increases more than the accumulation of dry matter (X) with higher light levels, and the relationship is approached by the power function $Y = 0.0077 \, X^{3.06}$.

Similarly, the change in production of C-glycoside of *Digitalis lanata* with change in nitrogen supply can be characterized by a

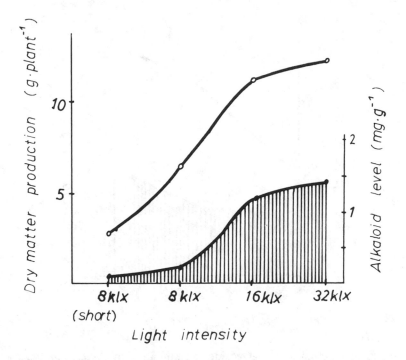

Figure 4. Production and Alkaloid Accumulation in *Papaver somniferum* as Affected by Light. The increase in alkaloids (●) was accompanied by a more characteristic appearance of morphinanes (increase of 1.57 percent) in plant dry matter (o). Data of Bernáth and Tétényi (17).

power function (Figure 5). On the basis of investigations carried out under controlled conditions, a threefold increase in nitrogen results in a nearly doubling of the dry-matter production (X) but an even greater accumulation of C-glycosides (Y) as described by $Y = 1.1134$ $X^{1.63}$. However, the change is smaller than the effect of light noted on *Papaver somniferum* and may be attributable to effects of nitrogen under field conditions.

In a summary, Singh (133) also mentions the increased production effects of nutrient supply on *Digitalis lanata*. While noting the increased production effect of soil nutrients, Balbaa *et al.* (6) could detect no changes in glycoside levels. In water culture experiments, Milletti and Frenguelli (103) also observed that variations in nitrogen, phosphorous, and potassium supply significantly influenced dry-matter production but not glycoside content.

In experiments with *Mentha piperita*, Hornok (67) detected, among the volatile oil-yielding plants, a power function relationship between nutrients and product which contrasts with the linear relationship reported by Bains *et al.* (4). Application of nitrogen fertilizer resulted in an increase in all primary productions up to the 2 highest

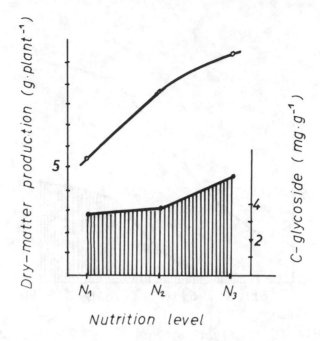

Figure 5. Production and C-glycoside Accumulation in *Digitalis lanata* as Affected by Nutrition. An increase in dry-matter production (o) with increases in nutritional level is accompanied by more intensive accumulation of C-glycoside (●).

treatment levels tested where the probable optimum range for primary production was reached. Parallel with the increase in production of plant matter, the volatile oil-level-per-unit dry matter increased from 0.911 percent to 1.528 percent, indicating that the proportion of dry matter and secondary products was shifting to increased levels of secondary products with the volatile oil yield production rate characteristic of a power function.

3. Relation Approached by Orthogonal Polynomial

Another characteristic type of change, perhaps the least known, consists of reductions in formation of secondary compounds with intensive increases in dry-matter production. Such a change is obvious when growing *Digitalis lanata* in a phytotron at different irradiance levels (23). At an illumination level of 8 klx, a relatively low dry-matter production [similar to the results of Balbaa (6)], and a relatively high C-glycoside level can be seen (Figure 6). Increasing the irradiance to 16 klx signficantly increased dry-matter production, but accumulation of C-glycoside-content was not stimulated, resulting in a positive high light effect on dry-matter production and a negative high light effect on C-glycoside production. The response of the

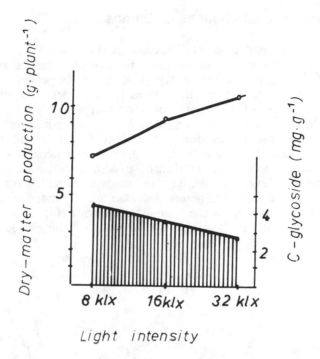

Figure 6. Production and C-glycoside Accumulation in *Digitalis lanata* as Affected by Light Intensity. Increased dry-matter production (o) with increases in light level is accompanied by less accumulation of glycosides (●). Data of Bernáth *et al.* (23).

primary and secondary processes in *Digitalis lanata* were to different external effects, and the maxima of their accumulation ensued at different effect intervals. Accordingly, the relationship of the primary and secondary production can be interpolated into an orthogonal polynomial: $Y = 120.21 - 39.9X + 5.7X^2 - 0.3X^3$.

This orthogonol relationship is perhaps best known in volatile oil-yielding species. According to the investigation of Vágújfalvi (151), shoot and flower production of *Matricaria chamomilla* varies with applied nitrogen levels. While dry-matter production increases with application of nitrogen, the content of the volatile oil begins to decline at the beginning of intensive dry-matter production.

The same results were obtained by Singh (133) in India, establishing that a nitrogen level which doubled the biomass production of *Matricaria chamomilla* decreased the volatile oil content from 0.64 percent to 0.59 percent per unit dry matter. Similar changes based on the influence of irrigation are also reported for *Matricaria chamomilla* by Kerekes (74). In addition, Hornok (67) has indicated a similar response to increasing nitrogen supply in *Anethum graveolens*.

B. The Proportional Changes of Organs

Factors that lead to a modification in the ratios of plant organs to whole plants (with consideration for localization of secondary products) also influence secondary production. Expected accumulation of secondary products will alter as the number of accumulating organs, the place of synthesis, or the proportion of both shifts. Among others, an obvious example is *Solanum laciniatum* where an increase in alkaloid production is promoted by the accumulation of more berries, each with an alkaloid content of 3 percent (12). As a further illustration, an examination of growth in *Solanum laciniatum* under increased levels of nitrogen indicates a linear increase in the mass of leaves, a power function increase in the mass of the stem, and almost no increase in the amount of berries (Figure 7). While a large nutrient dose is favorable for growth of the whole plant, a

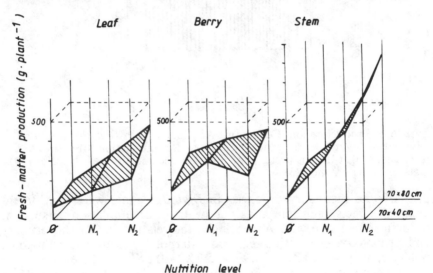

Figure 7. The Effect of Soil Nutrition and Spacing on Leaf, Berry, and Stem Production in *Solanum laciniatum*. The increase in leaf tissue (containing 1.5 to 1.7 percent solasodine) is linear with increases in nutrition and spacing, the increase in berry tissue (3.0 to 3.5 percent solasodine) is maximum at a medium nutrition level, and the increase in stem tissue (containing 0.2 percent solasodine) appears to increase exponentially with increases in nutrition level. Data of Bernáth and Tétényi (16).

decrease in berry production results in a decrease in alkaloid yield per plant.

According to our investigations (17), another alkaloidal species, *Papaver somniferum,* produces different proportions of organic constituents, depending upon environmental factors. Under short-day conditions and at low light level, the European species is in a characteristically vegetative form with the production of stems and leaves about 22 times greater than capsule yield. Under long-day conditions and at low light levels, the amount of vegetative material in the plant is only 3 times greater than capsule yield. The ratio of capsule to vegetative production becomes greatest as light levels are raised to 16 klx with a decrease in the capsule to vegetative ratio if the light level is increased to yet a higher level.

With regard to the volatile oil-yielding species, Vágújfalvi (151) has drawn attention to a reduction in flower yield of *Matricaria chamomilla* if nitrogen supply levels are increased beyond a certain limit. The flower-to-shoot ratio of about 1.5, measured at the optimum nitrogen level, can be diminished to below one. Hornok (67) reports that in *Anethum graveolens,* increasing the vegetative mass decreases the amount of seeds.

From a methodical point of view, the production of *Valeriana officinalis* raises an interesting question (in contrast to earlier examples) as the accumulation of secondary products is in the roots and changes in the ratio between the underground and above-ground parts will influence the accumulation of secondary products (11, 44, 137). According to our investigations (13), the ratio between root and shoot will change with the addition of soil nutrients. By increasing the nitrogen supply, the root-to-shoot ratio can be diminished from 1.356 to 0.696 and the root surface area decreased from 0.4417 m^2 to 0.1009 m^2 (a thick root system with a relatively small surface area develops). A change in phosphorous supply produces an analogous effect. The interaction of 2 elements (Figure 8), indicates that a high nutrient level is a marked production-limiting factor. Although the amount of shoot mass is increased at the high nutrient level, production of root mass is optimum at a medium nutrient level.

C. Accumulation Level of Secondary Products

An understanding of biosynthetic pathways for secondary products makes it evident that environmental influences on the special processes can be indirectly realized by modification of primary processes. In examining the relationship of light levels and production of secondary compounds, consideration must be given to the fact that plant response is through a complex biochemical system. The measured changes may result from changes in enzyme activity or quantity, precursor formation or flow, and accumulation and degradation of compounds. For example, a decreased level of product accumulation could present itself through inhibition of precursor flow or by the degradation of the accumulated product. Thus, it is advisable to also consider degradation possibilities with any interpretation in the majority of literature dealing with accumulation. In interpreting data of field tests, special note should be made of the environmental

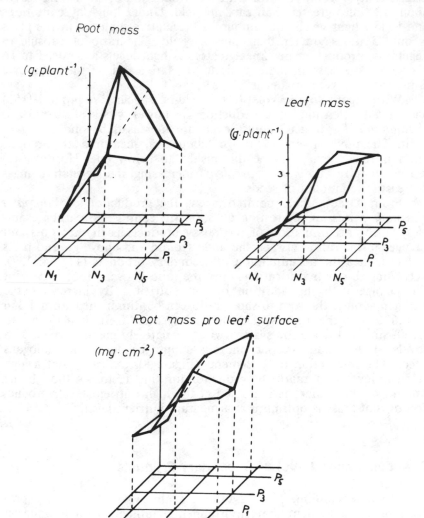

Figure 8. Interaction of Nitrogen and Phosphorus in Growth of *Valeriana officinalis*. Root production was highest at medium level of nitrogen and phosphorus. Leaf production was highest at the higher nitrogen and phosphorus levels. The amount of root tissue per area of leaf tissue (mg/cm^2) was increased by application of nitrogen and phosphorus. Data of Bernáth *et al.* (14).

complex that is especially rich in complicated interrelationships regulating synthesis systems within the plant.

1. Physio-Ecological Background of the Accumulation of Secondary Compounds

a. Morphology - chemosyndrome - chemism

A fundamental condition of investigations on production ecology is to have available well-defined plant material. The "classic" characterization of plant species and populations is insufficient. The situation is relatively simple only when the presence of a secondary product is effectively linked to a morphological structure. For example, there is a connection between the presence of flavonoid pigments and the color of flower and fruit (62), and even changes in the ratio of components result in different color forms (60).

The presence of betalaines also presents itself in several cases as an expressed morphologic feature (91). The existence of such a connection is also known to be bound to micromorphologic structures (8, 42) where the secondary product and the presence of the given morphologic feature are functionally connected. To relate special products to their morphologic appearance becomes ambiguous when the appearance of the morphologic quality is not closely connected to a metabolic process due to either the lack of a biosynthesis-morphological relationship or to a failure to recognize any relationship. Systematic work in a survey of *Solanum dulcamara* (16, 68, 156) provides an example. In estimating the occurrence of the species in Hungary, a close connection between the grade of hairiness and the qualitative presence (differentiated on the basis of saturation and epimer character) of the alkaloid aglycones could be established (Figure 9).

Solasodine content appears connected with the hairless phenotype. The presence of mixed unsaturated aglycone (solasodine + tomatidenol in a ratio of 2 to 3 with soladulcidine) was also more frequent in nonhairy plants. As the extent of hairiness increased, the ratio of saturated aglycones increased. However, this coincidence is not functional and, at the same time, is not exclusive since the saturated aglycone may be present in individuals with fewer hairs.

Apparently, the extent of hairiness and the level of saturation of the alkaloids have an analogous adaptation parallel with the strengthening of continentality. Similar proofs are available in relation to alkaloid composition (96). From this, depending on the number and method of sampling in a given situation, either positive or negative relationships between morphological features and chemical composition could be proved. Since the connection of both factors is not functional with one another, their relationship is occasional and, under changing selective pressure of the environment, they will certainly separate.

However, morphologic characterization cannot be fundamentally neglected because of the above, as full knowledge on qualitative and

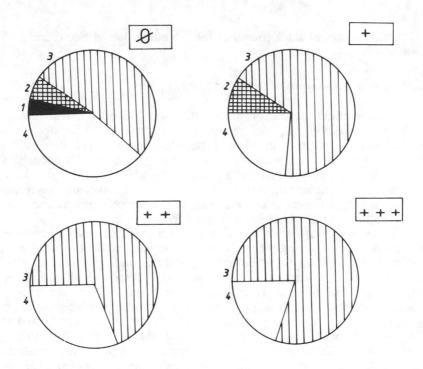

Figure 9. The Relationship between Morphology and Chemical Character in *Solanum dulcamara* of Hungary. Among hairless plants (0), chemotaxa of solasodine (1), of mixed-unsaturated type (2), of mixed-saturated type (3), and of soladulicidine type (4) were present. With increasing hairy character (+, ++, and +++), saturated aglycones (3) become more dominant. Data of Vo Hong Nga *et al.* (156).

quantitative characteristics of the secondary plant product are needed to completely determine relationships. For this, up-to-date chemotaxonomic data (55, 63, 64, 66, 135, 139, 141) provide the best aid. The strengthening of ecological views can be expected as Smith (135) conceives:

> "It is axiomatic that further research in biochemical ecology will inform and encourage the application of chemical data in taxonomy. Taxonomists must be as mindful of ecological research in the future as they have been in the past."

From the collection of knowledge accumulated so far, it seems unavoidable to interpret 2 concepts: chemism and chemosyndrome. Chemism is a generally accepted category and the chemosyndrome, based on the reports of Culberson and Culberson (38) and Hertel (65), is accepted for demonstration of chemical differentiation among lichenous species. The chemosyndrome character is developed by enzyme activity on specific substrates.

However, the chemosyndrome can hardly be considered an unambiguous constant spectre. In generalizing the symptomatic character of the chemosyndrome concept to higher plants, one must emphasize and conceive it as the reflection of special metabolic processes measurable in a given time. Accordingly, chemism as genetically fixed biosynthetic pathways can be characterized by the chemosyndrome at a specific instant.

These concepts describe the unity of content and form, the discrepancy between them, and the mutual dependence of each in the occurrence of secondary products in the flora. The chemosyndrome, as a "fingerprint," describes both the chemism in a theoretically infinite number of possibilities and the "phenotypic" appearance. In addition to ontogenetic predetermined variations, even the influence of ecological factors may be significant in the change of chemosyndrome notions.

b. Ontogenetic changes in the formation of secondary products

In an arbitrarily selected time and spatial dimension, unlimited options of the chemosyndrome series can theoretically characterize a variety, a species, and a chemovariety. For the sake of screening, ontogenetic changes in formation of secondary products and organic differentiation of localization have to be separated from the role of ecological factors.

The fundamental conditions for localization are a structural appearance at the place of biosynthesis and a system of cells, tissues, and organs able to accumulate the product. In this respect, species-accumulating secondary products differ. While the root is the main location for synthesis of the alkaloids in the Solanaceae family, the above-ground organs take part in accumulation and transformation (158). On the other hand, the development of *Papaver* alkaloids takes place in the leaf (2, 30, 118). An extreme example is *Ricinus communis,* where almost all organs are capable of converting nicotinic acid to ricin (158). Investigations with *Mentha* indicate the volatile oil-yielding plants have a similar structure for development and accumulation (89).

In ontogenesis, a reckoning with the appearance, accumulation, and occasional metabolism of secondary products begins with germination. In the alkaloidal (48, 127, 128, 134, 152) and glycosidic species (47), the secondary compounds may occupy an important physiological part in the early developmental phase even if an effect on further development is unknown.

The number of investigations related to developmental phases following germination is extraordinarily great. Waller and Nowacki (158) have recently summarized numerous examples indicating changes in the secondary products of *Coffea arabica, Atropa belladonna, Delphinium ajacis, Festuca arundinaces,* and *Ricinus communis.* At the 4th Symposium of ISHS in Angers (1983), the ontogenetic change in the inner content of the volatile oil-yielding *Pelargonium graveolens* and *Origanum vulgare* was discussed. In several cases, interpretations of the results are encumbered since separating changes depending on ontogenesis from those of ecological origin is extraordinarily difficult.

The qualitative and quantitative changes of alkaloids in *Papaver somniferum* are closely connected with growth and development of the plant. Field tests indicate that the quantity of alkaloids of the morphine group and the proportion of alkaloid components change during development (141, 144, 155). Although the investigators have stated that modifying effects of environmental factors might be significant, the reported developmental changes are supported by our investigations under controlled environmental conditions (Figure 10). The quantity of morphine, codeine, and thebaine in an English variety ('Reading') and a Hungarian variety ('Kompolti M') of poppy increases at the end of the rosette state and following flowering. At the same time, there is an increase in the proportion of morphine.

The differences between varieties can be explained by the fact that, although the character of the change is the same in both varieties, the extent of change depends upon both the genetic makeup of the plant and the environment. The more moderate accumulation of alkaloids under a low light level reduces the changes associated with development.

A functional relationship between ontogenetic change and development and between development and accumulation of secondary products has also been verified for several of the volatile oil-yielding species. Thus, the characteristic volatile oil content of *Matricaria chamomilla* is even connected to a definitive level of differentiation within the development of inflorescence (67). A well-known phenomenon is the linalool and geraniol and geraniol-acetate content of the fruit of *Coriandrum sativum* following pollination (67). The leaf of *Anethum graveolens* contains d-carvone and d-phellandrene while the fruit is 20 to 28 percent d-limonene. Proportionally, *Mentha piperita* contains more menthol in the leaf and more menthofuran in the inflorescence (67).

In contrast, the qualitative connection between the development of secondary products and the phase differentiation following the cotyledonous stage cannot be proved in numerous cases. As a classic example of this lack of association, the accumulation of steroid glyco-alkaloids in the growth season could be mentioned. Muravjeva *et al.* (106) and Tóth (146) have attempted to coordinate the solasodine content in the leaf of *Solanum laciniatum* with a phenophase. While maximum values of solasodine are found in the flowering period, this appears not to be connected with development, but rather with changes in temperature.

The beginning of flowering at the first branch level can be associated with high average temperatures characteristic of the inves-

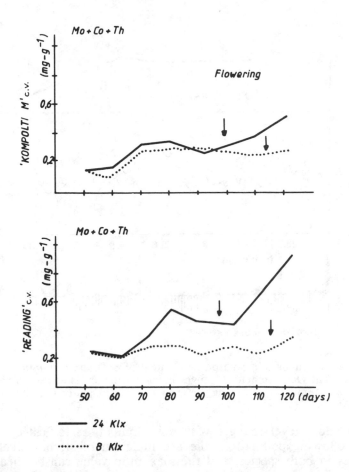

Figure 10. The Effect of Light on Morphinan Alkaloid Accumulation of Poppy Leaves. Alkaloid accumulation was affected by early growth and flower development. Arrows indicate time of flowering. Data of Bernáth and Tétényi (20).

tigation zone (Figure 11). The drastic reduction in solasodine content characteristic of the second half of the growth season can be avoided by covering the foliage with plastic foil to maintain warmer temperatures (13) and thus, the change in solasodine content during the growth season must be attributed to ecological effects.

Synthesis of steroid glyco-alkaloids can also be connected to growth in *Solanum dulcamara,* but the relationship of growth and development to secondary product synthesis becomes more complex as the deviations within organs of 2 different species of *Solanum* are considered. In accordance with several investigations (94, 125, 161), the alkaloid content of the berry is of decisive significance. However,

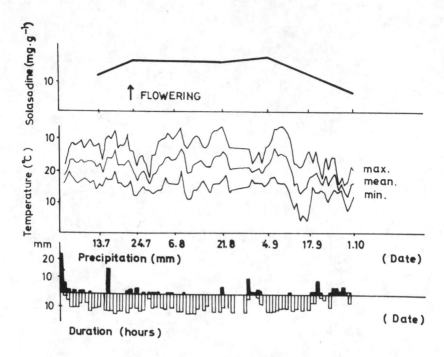

Figure 11. Changes in Solasodine Content of *Solanum laciniatum* Leaves during Plant Development. Changes in solasodine levels appear to parallel changes in temperature during the growth period. Data of Bernáth and Tétényi (16).

the alkaloid level changes with development, as indicated in Figure 12. Following pollination, the accumulation of steroid alkaloids increases in both species, and the maximum value can be measured at the medium berry size within either species. Further growth of the berry contributes to dilution of the alkaloid content and then to transformation processes associated with ripening that can lead in the direction of other steroids (125).

A similar differentiation can be revealed for nearly all species synthesizing a secondary product. For volatile oils, a qualitative gradient theory has been elaborated as an explanation of differentiation of the ligneous plants (142). Luckner and Diettrich (90) have also demonstrated variation in glycoside content within the leaf of *Digitalis lanata* by using the RIA-method.

On the basis of the examples presented above, the development and accumulation of secondary products is a process connected to development and/or growth. The chemosyndrome notation, measurable in a given time, is influenced to a great extent by the ontogenetic changes. In this case, the connection of growth and development to secondary products can be considered a dialectical interaction. Name-

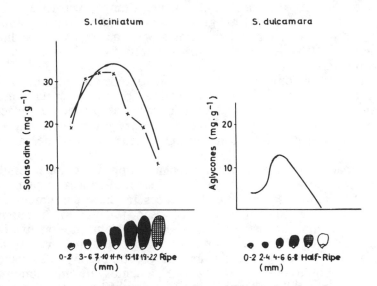

Figure 12. Accumulation of Aglycones during Berry Development.
Maximum aglycone (solasodine, soladulcidine, and tomatidenole)
concentrations were measured in a medium-sized berry of both *Solanum
laciniatum* and *Solanum dulcamara*.

ly, the accumulation of a secondary product is associated with a
growth process following a differentiation in development.

All differentiation points induce qualitative new growth processes
and this, in addition to universal metabolism, may also be reflected
(but not necessarily) by the formation of secondary products. A
significant change in the accumulation of secondary products can be
expected when some kind of biological connection exists between the
new type of growth and the formation of the given secondary product.

c. Flexibility in the formation of secondary products

Several questions on the extent of environmental controls of
secondary product formation and accumulation during changes in
plant development arise. When are 2 chemosyndrome notions, measured in different times, a uniform chemism (chemotaxon), and what
are the extreme values limiting a new chemotaxon? How can it be
determined whether different chemosyndrome notions and secondary
product formation of individuals separated by habitat are a differentiation based on real chemism or a different physiological deviation of
state (attributable to ontogenetic or environmental change)?

In this respect, valuable information comes from investigations
on species of different origin planted in the same habitat. Sárkány
(126) and Máthé *et al.* (100) report that in an original habitat, the

vincamine content of *Vinca minor* plants changes within a broad interval (between 1.1 to 3.3 mg/g). During cultivation, the vincamine content levels off at about 3.0 milligrams per gram of tissue. Nicholls and Bohm (108) have reported similar results for the flavonoids of *Lupinus sericeus.*

In other more complete works with flavonoids (36, 85, 102, 132), significantly different orientine-isoorientine content of species measured in an original habitat was similar when the plants were placed under cultivation. Thus, the different secondary product content and composition measured within each habitat reflect environmental factor(s).

Genetically, all *Lupinus sericeus* plants appear to have similar capacities for the accumulation of orientine. Differences in plants in content of orientine come from differences in the environment and thus the orientine content cannot be used to support taxonomic distinctions within the species. The chemosyndrome notion of samples collected from habitats with different potentialities reflects not the deviations due to the chemism but the taxon-physio-ecological flexibility. In some species (94, 141), the chemosyndrome notion of individuals either collected or planted in different habitats has a good congruency. In this case, the separation according to habitat coincides with a differentiation based upon chemism.

Contrary to field investigations, application of controlled plant growth conditions represents an important advantage (24). Chemical differentiation can be limited, and the extent of ecological flexibility and change of direction can be limited. In work at the phytotron in Gif-sur-Yvette (31, 32, 33, 34), elements of the ecophysiological concept have been developed with an attempt to check traditional chemotaxa. Scopolamine and hyoscyamine accumulation of *Datura metel* and *Datura tatula* were affected by both the day length and light levels. In *Duboisia myoporoides,* alkaloid synthesis reacts to a change in length of day, light level, and temperature (34). In investigations on other plants, variability in *Papaver somniferum* alkaloids has been noted with attempts to relate differences to field conditions (141, 144).

The differentiation in physiological character and alkaloid composition due to the wide range of the plant species (43) makes it extremely difficult to screen for any ecological flexibility in an inhomogeneous environmental system. The unknown character of the environment has become a limiting factor, and the United Nations Narcotics Laboratory (150) has published research recommendations for exploring environmental effects.

Initial research (145) under controlled conditions has indicated the necessity of associating environmental conditions with changes in synthesis and accumulation of alkaloids. Total alkaloid content of 3 investigated cultivars was maximal at a light level of 32 klx as compared with light levels of 16 klx and 8 klx (Table 1)(17, 20).

However, the relative light level can affect the 3 main alkaloid groups

TABLE 1. The Effect of Light and Temperature on Poppy Alkaloids.

			Main Alkaloid Groups				
	Light/Temperature Treatment		morphinan			phthalide- and benzyl isoquinoline	
Cultivar	before	after	morphine	codeine	thebaine	narcotine + narcotoline	laudanine + papaverine
	(light in klx)		(mg/g dry wt)			(mg/g dry wt)	
Kek Duna	16	32	6.80	0.55	0.35	2.44	0.13
	16	16	6.00	0.13	0.01	1.69	0.06
	8	8	1.95	0.00	0.00	0.01	0.03
	8	short day	2.00	0.00	0.00	0.00	0.00
Kompolti M	16	32	7.51	0.75	0.80	4.43	0.97
	16	16	5.25	0.32	0.10	3.00	0.04
	8	8	2.50	0.00	0.00	3.00	trace
	8	short day	-	-	-	-	-
Reading	16	32	3.50	5.68	0.25	2.81	5.15
	16	16	2.75	4.60	0.02	3.08	4.33
	8	8	2.50	0.28	0.00	0.62	3.63
	8	short day	3.07	0.83	0.00	0.50	3.10
	(relative temperature)[a]						
Kompolti M	low		5.36	0.21	0.08	2.07	0.15
	high		5.91	0.62	0.34	2.72	0.15
Reading	low		4.61	0.23	0.00	1.31	2.48
	high		2.98	3.92	0.16	2.25	4.74

[a] At fixed light of 16 klx.

of the cultivar in different proportions. The morphinan group in the variety 'Kek Duna,' the morphinan and phthalide isoquinoline in the variety 'Kompolti M' and all 3 alkaloid groups in the variety 'Reading' (of British origin) remain relatively stable as the light level is changed. Varying the light supply, however, modified the proportion of alkaloid components within the main morphinan alkaloid group.

A universal effect seems to be that, under low illumination, the proportion of higher methylation components, as indicated by a change in the morphinan group, is reduced. Yet, this response is species-dependent for the proportion of morphine, codeine, and thebaine at a given illumination level. Similarly, a change in temperature results in both qualitative and quantitative variations in secondary components, although to a smaller value than the influence of light intensity. A high-temperature growth program increases the development and accumulation of alkaloids and, at the same time, produces a higher ratio of methylated alkaloids (codeine, thebaine).

The flexibility of the chemosyndrome notion developing in response to the effect of light and temperature can be easily interpreted on the basis of known biosynthesis. According to the biosynthetic scheme illustrated in Figure 13 [based on the assumption of Nowacki *et al.* (109)], a restricted flow of mutual precursors of alkaloids and

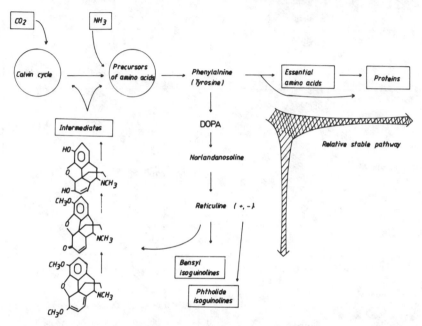

Figure 13. The Relationship of Primary and Secondary Synthesis Processes in Poppy Alkaloid Formation. The amino acids (phenyamine and tyrosine) are precursors for both protein and alkaloid biosynthesis. Protein formation was more stable and preferred under unsuitable conditions [Data of Nowacki *et al.* (109)]. Alkaloid formation was regulated by the availability of precursors. Data of Bernáth and Tétényi (17, 20).

proteins blocks biosynthesis at low light levels and low temperatures. The formation of essential amino acids pushes biosynthesis of alkaloids into the background. Even the probability of metabolism of already-accumulated alkaloids and their return into general plant metabolism is imaginable (48, 115).

In contrast, under favorable conditions, the equilibrium would shift toward the biosynthesis of alkaloids since the surplus flow of amino acid precursor causes a super-abundance of amino acid synthesis. The plant is able to store the alkaloid in a relatively large quantity but the possibility of storage as amino acids is limited. Reticuline is the first key compound in the formation of alkaloid groups. The proportions of alternate pathways (morphinanes, benzylisoquinolines, and phthalideisoquinolines) can be equally modified by species chemism and by environmental influences.

Enzymatic demethylation within the morphinan group possibly represents a recent alternate accumulation mechanism modifying the chemosyndrome notion. In this manner, conversion to the thebaine-codeine-morphine pathways takes place undisturbed in the presence of the limited quantity of precursors found at low light levels and cold temperatures. The thebaine and codeine are continually demethylated without accumulation and only the presence of morphine can be proved. With intensive precursor flow, a saturation level of morphine is reached; at that point, first codeine and then thebaine accumulate to a significant extent. Demethylation presents such a restricted biosynthetic pathway that the acceptance of precursors is limited and the increasing levels of higher methylated compounds are accumulated.

The accumulation of morphine-codeine-thebaine is an enzymatically regulated process. Expressed differences in species and chemotaxonomical differences are reported (17). Certain species (chemotaxons), such as the 'Kek Duna' and 'Kompolti M,' are able to flexibly increase their demethylating processes while in other species like 'Reading,' this possibility is limited.

An interpretation of physio-ecological flexibility is provided by the investigations of Bazzaz *et al.* (7) on *Cannabis sativa*. Plants originating from extremely different localities were grown under day-night temperatures of 32 and 23°C, respectively. Results of these experiments indicate a deviating chemosyndrome notion dependent upon temperature (Figure 14). There is an effective differentiation in accumulation of secondary product under cold conditions. Plants of Jamaican and Nepalese origin (the chemotaxon) increase their Δ^1-tetrahydrocannabinol content a great deal under cold circumstances, while the Panamian ecotype increases synthesis slightly and plants originating from Illinois only minimally.

Culberson *et al.* (39) demonstrated that differences in the formation of phenolic acids of *Cladonia cristatella* are explainable by physio-ecological flexibility. The relative activity of both barbatic and didymic acid pathways undergoes a modification with changing environmental conditions. In the cold, the quantity of product developing along the barbatic acid pathway increases. In high light levels, the accumulation of depsides is stimulated. The bioconversion of the same precursor to phenolic acids may continue by 2 alternate pathways partly under environmental control.

Loomis (89) has proved interpretations on the flexibility of the chemosyndrome notion by investigating the volatile oil-yielding species *Mentha piperita*. A characteristic pulegone accumulation is obvious under an illumination cycle of 14 hours and at a day and night air temperature of 25°C. The quantity of pulegone formed under the above conditions was nearly twice that of menthone and menthofuran. However, by reducing the night temperature to 8°C,

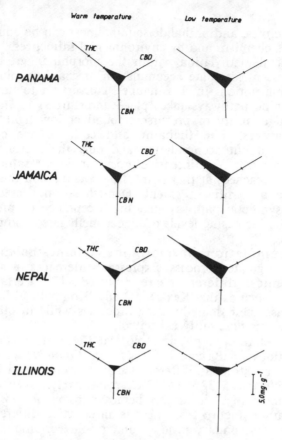

Figure 14. The Effect of Temperature on Secondary Product Formation in *Cannabis sativa*. Measured 1-tetrahidrocannabinol (THC), cannabidiol (CBD), and cannabinol (CBN) content in biochemical ecotypes. Data of Bazzaz *et al.* (7).

menthone becomes dominant. If the illumination cycle is extended to 18 hours, the role of the night temperature becomes secondary.

With great probability, the expressed biosynthetic changes can be attributed to the relationship of photosynthesis and respiration to modified ratios in the oxidation-reduction processes. From this point of view, investigations on different chemotaxa of *Satureja douglasii*, among the volatile oil-yielding plants, has yielded valuable results (86, 117). Cultivation of populations with different chemism under different light and temperature circumstances verified the existence of 4 types and, at the same time, gave an estimate of the extent of flexibility. The characteristic share of isomenthone type, which is 15.8 to 21.2 percent at low temperature, decreases to 2.4 to 7.0 percent under warm conditions. Analytically, the quantity of carvone in the carvone type was reduced from between 37.7 to 45.9 percent to between 28.7 to 31.7 percent.

Similarly, Lavigne *et al.* (83) and Firmage (49) have verified in *Jasminum grandiflorum* and *Hedeoma drummondii*, respectively, the existence of flexibility in volatile oil yield under controlled conditions. The data obtained on the chemical composition of *Hedeoma drummondii* (Figure 15) indicate the unambiguous physio-ecological

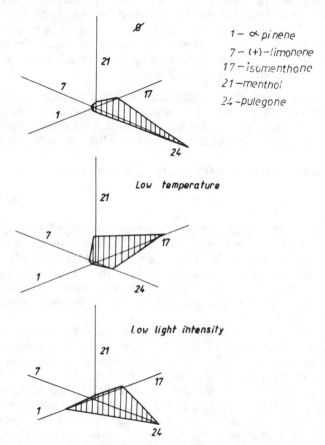

1 – α pinene
7 – (+)-limonene
17 – isomenthone
21 – menthol
24 – pulegone

Figure 15. The Effect of Light Level and Temperature on Composition of *Hedeoma drummondii* Leaves. Ø = Composition of unstressed control plants. Isomenthone accumulation was promoted by low temperatures. α-pulegone was promoted by low light levels. Data of Firmage (49).

flexibility of the secondary products. Like the results discussed previously, the shift in the ratio of photosynthesis to respiration in the direction of respiration enables the accumulation of pulegone at a low light intensity. Under cold temperatures and as a result of a contradictory process, isomenthone becomes one of the main components.

On the basis of the examples mentioned above, flexibility can be summarily characterized by the quantitative accumulation of secondary products, by the proportional change in components, and, in several cases, by the parallel development of quantitative and qualitative differences. The appearance of flexibility then comes from:

- An ontogenetic differentiation in biosynthetic pathways of secondary products leading to the potential formation of products characteristic for the chemism of the species.
- The flow of precursors, the enzymolitic processes, and the metabolism of developed secondary products being influenced by the environment with "minimal" chemosyndrome notions originating in inhibition.

The conditions optimizing accumulation have contradictory effects. Thus, in relation to a concrete product, the amplitude of flexibility is theoretically limited by the absence and by the maximal quantity that can be accumulated structurally, physiologically, and biochemically.

2. Influence of Environmental Factors on Accumulation

a. Influence of light

Since the precursors produced during photosynthesis also form the backbone for the synthesis of secondary compounds, a relatively close connection between light and special product formation can be rightly postulated. Within this framework, the physio-ecological role of light is fundamental, and the response of plants synthesizing special products under different irradiances may be extraordinarily diversified.

In *Nicotiana tabacum,* a light reaction may be already measured during germination. Weeks (160), corroborating earlier investigations, demonstrated that a significantly higher quantity of nicotine is accumulated by seeds germinating in darkness than in etiolated juvenile plants. As an explanation, Waller and Nowacki (158) have suggested that greater quantities of storage carbohydrates are used in respiration by plants germinating in darkness and, in this process, amino acids are released from reserve proteins. A part of the amino acids are then utilized in the biosynthesis of nicotine. There is a similar accumulation of ricin in etiolated plants of *Ricinus communis* (158).

A contradictory example is synthesis of steroid glyco-alkaloids in the Solanaceae family. In tubers of *Solanum tuberosum,* alkaloid accumulation begins exclusively upon exposure of tissue to light. Rowson (121) has reported six- to eightfold decreases in alkaloids of *Datura* species and *Atropa belladonna* plants growing in shade.

Indirectly, the effect of light can be supported by a comparison of latitudes differing in light conditions. According to Waller and Nowacki (158), *Scopolia carniolica* accumulates one percent alkaloid in the Caucasus and 0.3 percent in Sweden; the *Atropa belladonna* has an alkaloid content of 1.3 percent in the Crimean Peninsula and 0.4 to 0.6 percent in Leningrad. Similar results have been obtained with *Datura strammonium, Hyoscyamus niger,* and *Anisodus luridus.* Obviously, the results must be accepted carefully as light is probably just one of numerous influential factors in the different habitats.

Our investigations tend to prove a relationship between irradiance level and the formation of steroid glyco-alkaloids (21). In *Solanum dulcamara* and *Solanum laciniatum,* the light synthesis relationship depends on light demand and ecological adaptability of the species (Figure 16). An increase in light level stimulates the synthesis and accumulation of alkaloids in poppy (*Papaver*) to a greater extent than primary processes are stimulated by increases in light (17).

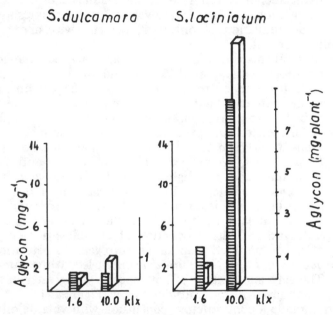

Figure 16. The Effect of Light Level on Aglycone Production in *Solanum dulcamara* and *Solanum laciniatum. Solanum laciniatum* was more light-sensitive than *Solanum dulcamara.* Aglycones (aglycon) are expressed on both a dry weight and per plant basis as related to kilolux (klx) of light. Data of Bernáth and Tétényi (16).

The role of light levels in terpenoid accumulation has also been investigated. According to Croteau *et al.* (37), the synthesis of monoterpenes is closely connected with processes favorable to the accumulation of sucrose or photosynthetic analogs. An increase in photosynthesis enables the formation of terpenoids and inhibits their metabolic decomposition.

On the basis of investigations carried out under controlled conditions, Lincoln and Langenheim (86) have reported that light levels scarcely influence monoterpenoid content of *Satureja douglasii* but significantly affect component composition. Supporting the assumption of Croteau *et al.* (37), Firmage (49) reports that the volatile oil content of *Hedeoma drummondii* is reduced nearly 50 percent under low light levels in the phytotron. In addition, significant changes in composition occur with significant increases in the proportions of α-pinene. Observations by Hornok (67) indicate that shade significantly reduces the volatile oil content of *Mentha piperita* from 1.43 percent to 1.09 percent. Parallel with the reduction in oil, composition is modified, with menthol content reduced from 61.8 percent to 57.5 percent. Under controlled conditions, Saleh (124) has measured an analogous change in the volatile oil content of *Matricaria chamomilla*. While a volatile oil content of 0.88 percent (with 8.4 percent chamazulene) is reported at an irradiance of 9.5×10^4 erg m^2/sec, a reduction in the light level by two-thirds resulted in a volatile oil accumulation of only 0.40 percent, with about half the chamazulene content.

The spectral distribution of light can only be studied under natural conditions with great difficulty and by accepting numerous compromises. In spite of this, light needs to be examined within ecosystems as different light environments may be expected and differences in biological responses may occur (72, 153). A favorable effect of green light on *Datura strammonium* in contrast to *Digitalis glykosides* has been reported. Kuznyecova and Hazanov (79) cultivated *Stephania glabra, Rauvolfia canescens,* and *Solanum laciniatum* in blue and red light under controlled conditions and report that, under long-term blue light treatment, more pigments develop, leaves become thicker with greater light absorption capacity, and alkaloid accumulation increases. Red light treatment reduced the rate of photosynthesis, the production of alkaloids, and, in general, the formation of products containing nitrogen. Investigations with *Solanum laciniatum* and *Solanum dulcamara* led to the same results (21, 22). The aglycone-content of both species was greater in blue and green light and lower in red and violet light (Figure 17).

Having made a contradictory conclusion with volatile oil-yielding species, Pavlov and Ilieva (111) and Saleh (124) have stressed the unfavorable effect of the short wavelength radiation and a stimulatory effect on formation of special products in plants growing in red-colored light. The difference in light response between alkaloid and volatile oil biosynthesis is probably related to the encouragement of amino acid synthesis under short wavelengths, leading to alkaloid synthesis and the increased accumulation of carbohydrates under red-colored light, leading to increased volatile oil synthesis.

Photoperiod plays a fundamental role in regulation of the growth and development processes of a species. While much is already known about the physiological and physio-ecological regularities of photoperiodism, an effect on secondary metabolic processes can only be proved on the basis of examples. Tso (149), studying alkaloid accumulation in *Nicotiana tabacum* under long-day (16 hours of illumination) and short-day (8 hours of illumination) conditions, discovered significantly more nicotine accumulated under longer days. A

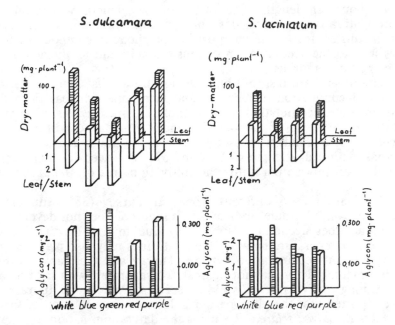

Figure 17. The Effect of Light-Color on Biomass and Aglycone Production in *Solanum dulcamara* and *Solanum laciniatum*. Shorter wavelengths of light appeared to increase the concentration of aglycones (aglycon) in tissue. Total aglycone production was dependent upon dry matter production. Data of Bernáth *et al.* (21).

red-light interruption of 5 minutes' duration in the dark period will successfully stimulate intensive alkaloid formation. A light treatment of 16 hours stimulates the accumulation of scopolamine as opposed to hyoscyamine in *Datura tatula* (32). The effect of a short-day (9 hours) treatment is only partially (or not at all) cancelled by a light interruption of 7 hours.

Investigations with *Datura metel* (31) produced similar results with light-induced formation of scopolamine inhibited by low levels of light, even under long-day conditions, verifying the presumable light-level, day-length interaction. Investigations with *Papaver somniferum* have demonstrated that short days inhibit alkaloid formation (17). A short day is analogous with low light levels and universally inhibits the accumulation of poppy alkaloids.

Akahori *et al.* (1) have studied the connection between plant development and the length of day as related to the promotion of sapogenin steroid synthesis in *Dioscorea tokoro* under long days. A study on the photoperiodic response of *Dioscorea deltoidea* by Karnick (73) provided similar results. Plants cultivated under short-day conditions of 6 hours in length have only one-half the sapogenin accumulation in the bulb as plants grown under long-day conditions of 18 hours in length. The effect of day length was similar in accumulation of the glycosides and phenolic compounds, with a significant difference in the composition of phenolic compounds. Short days lead to the accumulation of mustard acid and ferulic acid in the tuber within 9 months.

Grahle and Höltzel (59) have demonstrated that long days stimulate the accumulation of menthol and menthone, whereas short days lead to the accumulation of menthofuran in *Mentha piperita*. A volatile oil content of 1.4 percent under long-day conditions is reduced about one-half with a day length of 10 hours and to less than one-half with a day length of 8 hours (67). The need for long days to stimulate oil production limits the cultivation area of *Mentha piperita* (52).

Cultivation of 6 different clones in Turkey (38° latitude) and Germany (48.5° latitude) indicates that menthol does not develop, but menthone does accumulate in Turkey due to day length. The difference in temperature between the 2 latitudes may also play a part in changes in oil accumulation between Turkey and Germany, as the 2 environmental factors cannot be analyzed separately with field data.

Among the volatile oil-yielding species, Pavlov and Ilieva (111) have reported that the photoperiod influences accumulation of special products in *Salvea sclarea*. Reducing the daily illumination to 9 hours reduces accumulation of total nitrogen, protein nitrogen, free amino acids, and sucrose. The addition of red light, but not blue or green light, increases the accumulation of nitrogen compounds.

b. Influence of temperature

A relationship between temperature and secondary product synthesis is clearly noticeable during germination (158). In *Nicotiana tabacum,* the nicotine content of plants from seed germinating at a temperature of 27°C is 2 to 3 times higher than that of plants from seed germinating at a temperature of 16 to 21°C. Of the total alkaloids in the plant, the highest proportion of nicotine is developed under warm conditions. Warm weather favors the formation of alkaloids in other Solanaceae species (121). A similar relationship between the alkaloid content of *Atropa belladonna* and the mean temperature of the growth season has been reported (154). An effect of temperature on development of steroid glyco-alkaloids in *Solanum laciniatum* has been demonstrated in field experiments (13) and confirmed under controlled conditions (16).

Although *Solanum laciniatum* and *Solanum dulcamara* accumulate partially analogous aglycones, the *Solanum laciniatum* requires higher temperatures for maximizing synthesis (Figure 18). The quantity of solasodine increases proportionally to increases in air temperature, with a significant reduction in solasodine only observed with a generally appearing heat injury to the plant at a temperature above 26°C.

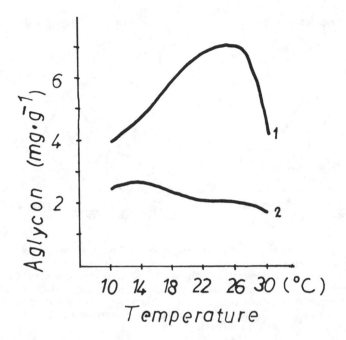

Figure 18. Leaf Concentration of Aglycones as Affected by Temperature. There was an intensive change in aglycone (aglycon) concentration of *Solanum laciniatum* (1) associated with a rise in temperature. A change in temperature had little effect on aglycone (aglycon) formation in *Solanum dulcamara* (2). Data of Bernáth and Tétényi (16).

Tétényi (141) has called attention to the environment as causing variability of alkaloid content in poppy. Under rainy, cold weather conditions, the morphine content of tissue does not rise above 0.4 percent. Investigations in Poland (158) indicate that under cold conditions, the usual 0.41 percent morphine content of the Hungarian species is never greater than 0.36 percent. Studies in the Soviet Union (27, 71) support an alkaloid content-temperature relationship. In contrast, the morphine level measured in opium apparently increases when the plant is grown in cold temperatures (40, 84).

Investigations carried out under controlled conditions provide an explanation for the above contradiction (18, 19). An increasing light level increases the development and accumulation of alkaloids under both cold and warm conditions (Figure 19). However, the proportional level of different methylated components is characteristically dependent upon temperature. The saturation curves interpolated with codeine (Y) values indicate the change with temperature (X)

at low temperature:

$$Y = 0.5(1 - e^{\,0.69269 - 0.000076\,X})$$

Low temperature program   High temperature program

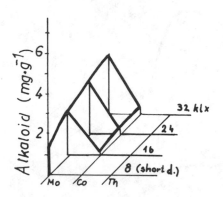 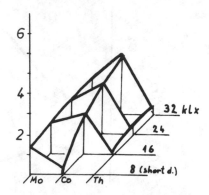

Figure 19. The Accumulation of Morphinanes in Poppy Capsules as Affected by Light and Temperature. Morphine (Mo) accumulation was promoted by higher light levels in both warm and cold temperatures. Codeine (Co) and thebaine (Th) accumulation were promoted by higher light levels at warmer temperatures but not colder temperatures. At a low temperature, the demethylation processes (to morphine) are the dominant biochemical reactions. Data of Bernáth and Tétényi (19).

at high temperature:

$$Y = 6.0(1 - e^{\,0.92604 \,-\, 0.000129\; X})$$

It can be postulated that temperature exerts its effect via regulation of methylation processes, speeding up or slowing down transformation among components and modifying the accumulation ratio of components. The above hypothesis explains inconsistencies in literature data as, in general, a low temperature is unfavorable for accumulation of alkaloids. Yet, considering the ratio of morphine to other components, the low temperature effect is seemingly positive.

Although the existence of a relationship between temperature and monoterpenes has also been demonstrated under controlled conditions (89), the conception of a temperature-product association is sometimes ambiguous. The volatile oil content of *Matricaria chamomilla* is stable (for both quantity and quality) under an extreme range of natural conditions (138). Large quantities of volatile oil are produced by *Matricaria chamomilla* in a phytotron at a constant temperature of 25°C or with a night temperature of 15°C, but the proportion of chamazulene in the oil is highest with the 15°C temperature (123). According to Hotyn (69), the volatile oil content of *Mentha piperita* increases proportionally with an increase in the daily mean temperature during the intensive growth phase. An increase in the mean temperature of 2 to 3°C on the days prior to harvesting significantly increases the volatile oil content. At the same time,

Hotyn (69) has drawn attention to a reduction in menthol content parallel with an increase in temperature.

The heat response of *Jasminum grandiflorum* has been investigated and significant differences are noted between the volatile oil content and composition of plants grown under field conditions and those grown under controlled conditions (83). On the basis of investigation of *Satureja douglasii,* the importance of the genetic contribution has been recognized along with the influence of environment (86). Firmage (49) has revealed regularities in the volatile oil content and composition of *Hedeoma drummondii* under controlled conditions. In a cold system, the quantity of pulegone is reduced and the proportion of (+) limonene and α pinene is increased. The development of the reduced monoterpenes is also increased. Thus, similar to observations with *Mentha* (28), cold temperatures assist synthesis of reduced compounds; this temperature effect may be attributed to reduced respiration and the resulting enrichment of tissue with photosynthetic products.

c. Water supply

Numerous forms of plant adaptation to water supply are known and, in accordance with this, the metabolic water supply relationships strongly depend on ecotype. The effect of water supply on volatile oil content may very well differ for the hydrophyton *Mentha* species as compared with the xerophyton *Lavandula* species. Similarly, the data are ambiguous with respect to the response and tolerance to water stress.

Difficulty arises with studies connected with water supply in the field, as a richness in precipitation almost always goes along with a reduction in the number of sunny hours. According to the work of Rowson (121) with *Datura* and other Solanaceae species and the work of Steinegger and Gessler (136) with *Datura,* the alkaloid content in these plants is reduced in areas with high precipitation. Again, the lack of light may be responsible for reduced alkaloid synthesis. Any generalization of species is probably unjustified since a high precipitation-low alkaloid relationship does not hold for *Solanum laciniatum,* a plant that has been investigated to the utmost detail in this respect.

Observations of *Solanum dulcamara* (16, 97) indicate that water supply modifies the accumulation of glyco-alkaloids parallel with modification in primary production. On the basis of data from 3 vegetation periods, the alkaloid content was significantly related to the sum of precipitation for the 2 weeks prior to measurement, and the closeness of relationship between alkaloid content and precipitation was indicated by the correlation coefficient of 0.95.

A universal concept has not been formed in connection with alkaloid synthesis and water supply in *Papaver somniferum.* An evaluation of data in the literature is encumbered as, in most cases, no distinction was made between alkaloid production and alkaloid accumulation (alkaloid level) in plants. While Yadev *et al.* (162) and Hotyn and Novikova (71) have reported that a favorable water supply increases opium and morphine yield, a summarizing study by Dános (41) indicates that rainy weather following flowering and pollination reduces alkaloid content.

Investigations performed under controlled conditions (20) provide some explanation of the uncertainty formed with respect to alkaloid level. Cultivation of a spring cultivar ('Kompolti M'), an intermediate maturing cultivar ('Reading'), and an autumn-sown cultivar ('Ankara') under cold and warm growth conditions in a culture media at 40-, 70-, and 90-percent saturation demonstrated that any modifying effects of water on alkaloid level were of secondary importance. The amount of alkaloids (appearance of codeine) was primarily dependent upon temperature (Figure 20). The quantitative

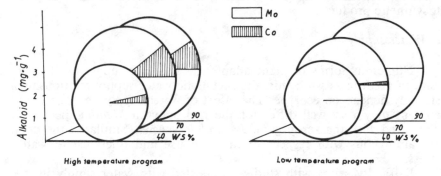

Figure 20. The Accumulation of Morphinanes in Poppy Capsules as Affected by Temperature and Water Stress. The appearance of codeine (Co) with morphine (Mo) was dependent upon temperature. Total morphinan content was decreased under a water stress (WS = percent water saturation of soil). Data of Bernáth and Tétényi (20).

values for alkaloids cannot be considered as characteristic since the relative alkaloid level measured at 40-percent saturation is probably related to damage to overall plant processes resulting in reduced primary production.

In the case of *Digitalis lanata* of the glycoside plants, our observations are identical to those of Balbaa *et al.* (5). Irrigation increases the plant biomass and, through it, the glycoside yield. A more complex conception on the effects of water has developed in the case of terpenoid species. In the very water-demanding *Mentha piperita,* the volatile oil level was higher by 0.3 to 0.5 percent at flowering in irrigated plants as compared with nonirrigated plants. On the basis of the data of Schröder (130) and Kerekes and Hornok (75), it appears that the increase in volatile oil content following irrigation is characteristic for the species. There is an intensive reduction in oil content after flowering.

The role of the plant developmental stage in relation to water supply and secondary product formation can be determined by examining 3 years of data on *Mentha piperita* collected by Penka (113). The observed changes are similar to those reported earlier for *Mentha piperita* (76). In the case of *Matricaria chamomilla*, which is adapted for drier growing conditions, irrigations do not influence the volatile oil content (74); in fact, the plant appears expressly developed for dry conditions (113). The species-dependent relationship was also demonstrated through the investigations of Penka (113). Several volatile oil-yielding species can be arranged into groups based on the effect of water supply on volatile oil synthesis:

- The percentage of volatile oil may increase with irrigation [*Carum carvi* (fruit, shoot), *Foeniculum vulgare* (fruit), *Archangelica officinalis* (root)].
- The volatile oil content does not change with irrigation [*Pimpinella saxifraga* (surface shoot), *Melissa officinalis* (surface shoot)].
- The volatile oil content may be reduced with irrigation [*Petroselinum hortense* (root, above-ground parts), *Lavandula spica* (flowering shoot)].

The above classification can be accepted, but only in a general informative nature since, under field conditions, the natural supply of precipitation influences the effect of irrigation. Gershenzon *et al.* (54) reported that increasing water stress will initiate a reduction of double bond C_4-C_8 and that the transformation of pulegone and piperitenone in the direction of isomenthone and piperitone, respectively, is accelerated. In contradiction of others (53), they conclude that an increase in volatile oils cannot be associated with regulation of transpiration.

d. Role of soil and nutrient supply

Through chemical, physical, and biological means, soil has a complex effect on the growth, development, dry-matter production, and special product production of the plant. As far as the chemical factors are concerned, data on soil pH and primary production are readily available. Species tolerant of soil acidity are known (*Arnica* and *Polypodium*), and species that appear to require alkaline conditions for optimum production are also known (*Primula, Adonis,* and *Hyssopus*) (158). However, little evidence relating soil pH to the accumulation of special products has been reported. McNair (101) reported a positive relationship between alkaline soil and the formation of alkaloids, and a positive effect of the alkaline soil on volatile oil content of *Valeriana officinalis* has been emphasized by Berbec (11) and in *Matricaria chamomilla* by El-Badry and Hilal (45).

A relationship between the nutrient elements and metabolic processes leading to the formation of special products in the plant is certainly important, but details have not been elaborated (158). In spite of this, numerous data are available indicating that the supply of nutrients does have an influence on the formation and accumulation of special products. As demonstrated by Vágújfalvi (154) in experiments with *Datura innoxia,* application of soil nutrients during growth will change both plant production and alkaloid levels. However, optimum plant production and alkaloid levels are not in congruence. The greatest plant growth was obtained with maximal nitrogen supply and the highest alkaloid level developed at the medium nutrient level. Similar responses have been noted for production of alkaloids in *Nicotiana tabacum, Ricinus communis, Vinca perenne,* and *Catharanthus roseus* (109). No optimum soil nutrient effect has been noted for alkaloid production in *Solanum laciniatum* and *Solanum dulcamara* (16).

Results of experiments with alkaloid production in poppies were recently summarized by Dános (41) and Morász (104). Maximal capsule production and highest alkaloid level developed at a 2:2:1 ratio of nitrogen, phosphorous, and potassium, respectively (107). A surplus of phosphorous compared with nitrogen apparently reduces the internal nitrogen concentration and, simultaneously, the alkaloid content. Costes *et al.* (35) have studied the effect of nitrogen forms NO_3^- and NH_4^+; phosphate; and the cations Mg^{2+}, Ca^{2+}, Na^+ in sand culture. Nitrogen had the greatest physiological effect on plants and modified the formation of alkaloids with the anion NO_3^- proving to be the most efficient form of nitrogen. An accumulation of calcium ions also increased the formation and plant content of alkaloids. Other reports (57, 104, 131) indicate that the supply of boron can stimulate or inhibit the development and accumulation of alkaloids in poppy.

The interaction of nutrient supply and light can be examined from studies on alkaloid development in poppy (20). Experiments with the cultivar 'Kek Duna' under controlled conditions indicated that the nutrient supply level scarcely influenced the accumulation of alkaloids under short-day, low light level (8 klx) conditions or under short-day, high light level (32 klx) conditions (Figure 21). However, at a light level of 16 klx, there was a significant nutrient response and the quantity of both co-alkaloids was maximal under a relatively high level of nitrogen. Apparently, the extremely low light level and the high light level limited or encouraged, respectively, the development of alkaloids to such a great extent that any response from soil nutrients could not be observed.

High light levels and raised nutrient levels appear to induce equivalent biosynthetic changes. This supports the assumption of Nowacki *et al.* (109) that some amino acids have a "feedback" effect, inhibiting protein synthesis. When an increase in nitrogen level or an acceleration of precursor flow from high light levels enables the

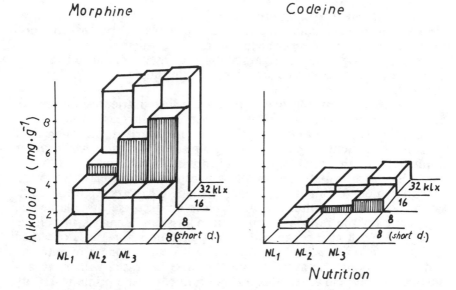

Figure 21. The Effect of Light and Soil Nutrition on Morphine and Codeine Accumulation in Poppy Capsules. An effect of soil nutrition (NL = relative nutrition level) could only be observed at the 16 klx illumination level. Data of Bernáth and Tétényi (20).

increased formation of amino acids, a metabolic shift takes place to reestablish equilibrium in the plant, with the amino acids being transformed and stored in nontoxic forms. Thus, the biosynthetic pathways to secondary products from phenylalanine and tyrosine are stimulated.

For the terpenoid plant species, a relatively complex relationship between soil nutrients and volatile oil synthesis has developed. On the basis of field experiments, Hornok (67) reported maximal volatile oil content (3.33 percent) at an average (60 kg N/ha + 40 kg P_2O_5 /ha + 40 kg K_2O/ha) nutrient level following the fertilization of *Anethum graveolens*. Adding several soil nutrients to *Foeniculum vulgare* (40 kg N/ha + 80 kg P_2O_5/ha + 40 kg K_2O/ha on a sandy soil) and to *Lavandula angustifolia* (60 kg N/ha + 60 kg P_2O_5/ha + 170 kg K_2O/ha) reduces volatile oil content (51). Investigations with *Mentha arvensis* indicate an increase in crop yield of about 100 percent (at an unchanged volatile oil level) from an increased supply of nitrogen and phosphorus (4).

A complete understanding of fertilizer responses, however, can only be expected from controlled experiments. From this perspective, Vágújfalvi (151) has investigated the effect of nutrient supply on the production of pot-growing *Matricaria chamomilla*. Increasing nitrogen and phosphorous supplies reduced the amazulene content of the flower. The reduction in product may be connected to the relative moderate nutrient demand of the species, as a positive effect is observed with even small increases in nutrients. In pot-growing and field-growing *Mentha piperita* (a more nutrient-demanding crop), increases in nitrogen levels significantly increased volatile oil content from the 0.6 to 1.0 percent in plants lacking nitrogen to 2.5 percent in plants with added nitrogen (154).

The effect of nitrogen can be seen, using nutrient solutions, to demonstrate how increasing the nitrogen level increases the volatile oil content (67, 75). Wahab (157) has investigated the change of volatile oil content of potted and field-planted *Ocimum basilicum* as influenced by the interaction of nitrogen, phosphorous, and potassium. Increases in both nitrogen and phosphorous increased the volatile oil content (from 0.3 percent to about 0.6 percent) while additional potassium resulted in an increase or decrease of volatile oil, depending on the ratio of nitrogen to potassium. Changes in volatile oil content with changes in soil fertility are similar to those observed in *Valeriana officinalis* (15). Depending on the amounts of nitrogen and phosphorous, the average root thickness increased with increased nutrient supply. However, this did not influence the optimum fertility value (medium nutrient level) for volatile oil content.

A generalization of universal validity with respect to fertility and production of terpenoids can hardly be imagined. Experiments conducted under very controlled conditions have yet to establish any relationship between the effective nutrient demand of the species and the development of volatile oil.

e. Effect of biotic factors

The relationship between the biotic (plant and animal) factors and the formation level of special products has not been widely investigated. Any relationship is rare and is verified with difficulty. While the roles of intraspecific (density of stand) and interspecific competition (weeds) are well-known with respect to primary production, an effect on the level of special products is not certain. However, in some instances, a biotic effect on secondary production has been supported. Pathogenic fungi are known to affect the level of special products. For example, *Septoria* infections reduce the glycoside content of *Digitalis lanata*. *Phytophtora infestans* can cause a loss of 16 to 20 percent in the steroid glyco-alkaloid content of *Solanum laciniatum* (95). Under field, greenhouse, and plant tissue culture conditions, *Dendryphion penicillatum* and *Alternaria alternata* have been demonstrated to decompose about 10 percent of the alkaloids accumulated in a poppy head within 24 hours (82).

III. REGULATION OF "SPECIAL PRODUCTION" IN THE ECOSYSTEM

The objective of physio-ecological and production-ecological investigations is to understand the regularities of the ecosystem and, in this way, establish definitive backgrounds of knowledge. All of the evaluation points, which are considered fundamental for regulating special plant production, are presented schematically in Figure 22. Being acquainted with them does not mean that production can be

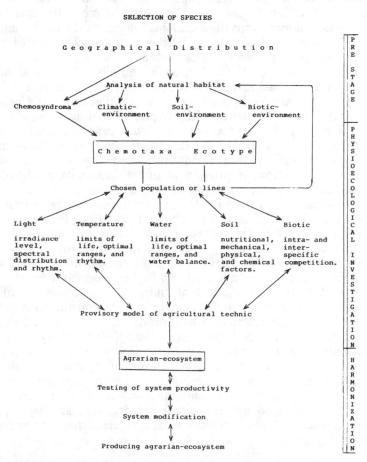

Figure 22. Ecological Experimental Research Steps for Establishing Productivity of Secondary Substances.

regulated, but at least the environmental influences can be recognized.

A. Natural or Quasinatural "Medicinal Plant" Ecosystems

In a natural system producing special compounds, the starting point for successful human influence is to acquire knowledge on the phytocenosis comprising the species. But, for the most part, investigations on a rational system estimate the static state even if all vegetative growth for the life cycle is summed. Essential proof for judging the stage and developmental direction of the ecosystems and the phytocenosis is generally not offered, and the time dimension of phytocenosis-producing special compounds remains essentially unknown. Consideration of the time dimension is made imperative by the day-to-day human activities that lead to a reduction in natural localities of "medicinal plants" and from this, a declaration of more and more species that need to be protected.

Enlargement of special production in the natural or quasinatural ecosystem may be achieved by increasing the dominance of the producing species and/or by improving the individual plant's production capacity. A method successfully applied in Hungary was that of oversowing the natural phytocenosis of *Matricaria chamomilla* using high-quality seeds to increase the dominance and, at the same time, intensifying the individual production capacity of each plant. Through plant selection, improvement of products with high volatile oil content and favorable composition was achieved (140) and, in the course of small plot experiments, the tolerance of the species to environmental factors could be determined (74, 138). By oversowing, a dominant population with favorable active compounds and of a higher production capacity was introduced into the natural phytocenosis. Thus, the relative biological equilibrium decomposed by collection could be reestablished at a higher production level.

In the West-Bengalian areas of India, the development of the quasinatural ecosystem of the *Cinchona* can be considered a classic example of successful adaptation of a production species (3, 29). The acclimatization of species began more than 100 years ago, starting with analyses of original native localities. Under the new conditions, *Cinchona* developed a self-regulating, dominant system of high production with a minimum of human influence. Intraspecific and interspecific competitions for optimal content of secondary compounds were developed by controlling growing area and by relating chemotypes and ecotypes (species) within an ecosystem for exposure and altitude.

B. Introduction of a New Ecosystem

The establishment of new (agro) ecosystems can be equally motivated by biological and economical considerations. From a biological point of view, establishment of such an ecosystem becomes necessary when the natural presence of a species (such as *Adonis vernalis*) has become rare and the natural ecosystem, as a source of special production, has ceased to exist. The ensurance of stable values of chemical components may be a determining factor in introducing artificial production systems. Such was the case with *Vinca minor, Catharanthus roseus,* and *Dioscorea deltoidea.*

Defining the geographical distribution presents a basis for the estimation of the chemism (the ecological demand of the species selected) and the natural growing conditions. The importance of work on temperature requirements and various adaptation capacities of species-producing special compounds is indicated by data of Duke and Hurst (43). As with temperature, other environmental variables such as water supply, soil and nutrient supply, and altitude may be equally determinant factors and thus, the analyses of these factors may offer essential information for developing growing conditions of an (agro) ecosystem.

An already elaborated peculiarity of the work involved in acquiring knowledge on special plant production as compared with agrarian models is the need for optimization of the quantity and quality of special products and not of production in general (88). The formation of the dynamic production model (114), comprising the complex action mechanisms, however, should be formed from the simple elements.

To establish and fit a new production system into an agricultural environment is not a simple task even if a suitable level of physio-ecological knowledge has been obtained. Some limiting factors to emphasize in the establishment of a new system are these:

- Once the plant is introduced (many times originating from extremely different climatic conditions), an alteration (generally negative, but sometimes positive) between biological demand and the prevailing growing conditions may develop. A positive effect of environmental change, for example, is demonstrated by *Solanum laciniatum* and *Catharanthus roseus.* These 2 species show a phanerophyton form under the native condition but can be cultivated as a terophyton one-year life form in Hungary.
- Regulation of environmental factors experimentally determined to promote growth and production cannot be modified (or can only be slightly modified) in the field. With respect to light and temperature, acclimatization remains the primary means for establishment of plants in a new habitat. Selection of the most suitable soil type, the addition of a water supply, and providing adequate soil fertility are more easily optimized. Intraspecific competition and interspecific competition can also be easily optimized through planting patterns and weed control, respectively.
- Introduction of a new system requires accommodation to the agrotechnical (technological) procedures already available and

practiced. Systems for producing special plant compounds must fit into ongoing agriculture where such factors as the sequence of crops, the optimal size of production unit, and relationships to other farm operations must be considered. The practical importance of rotation of crops, consideration of carry-over herbicidal action from previous crops, and understanding of the role of insects and diseases are well recognized.

C. Optimization of Producing (Agricultural) Ecosystem

The optimization or alteration of an already producing system can be justified by several factors. The application of a new chemotaxon, ecotype, or selected species may require the development of new techniques. A change in agricultural background, the development of intensive growing conditions, or the introduction of more up-to-date technological methods may enable profitable crop production where none was available previously. The maximal utilization of the agro-ecological potential of a locality, which is scarcely avoidable today, can only be realized by a reorganization based on ecological principles of special production.

The starting point and the objective of regulation is the producing (agricultural) ecosystem. The relatively shorter recognition process based only on feedback from previous systems should be opposed. Optimization of a producing system can best be accomplished by understanding the relationship between plants and environmental limitations.

IV. REFERENCES

1. Akahori, A., M. Togami, and T. Iwao. 1970. Studies on the steroidal components of domestic plants. 59. Effect of light on steroidal sapogenins of *Dioscorea tokoro* Makino. Chem. Pharm. Bull. 18:436–439.

2. Antoun, M.D. and M.F. Roberts. 1975. Some enzymes of general metabolism in the latex of *Papaver somniferum*. Phytochemistry 14:909–914.

3. Aslam, S.M.A., C. Doraswamy, C. Venkitaseshan, G.N. Govindan. 1977. *In* C.K. Atal and B.M. Kapur, eds. *Cultivation and Utilization of Medicinal and Aromatic Plants*. Regional Res. Lab. Jammu-Tawi. pp. 54–60.

4. Bains, D.S., J.S. Sarma, S.S. Saini. 1977. *In* C.K. Atal and B.M. Kapur, eds. *Cultivation and Utilization of Medicinal and Aromatic Plants*. Regional Res. Lab. Jamu-Tawi. pp. 191–203.

5. Balbaa, S.I., S.H. Hilal, and M.Y. Haggag. 1971. The effect of irrigation and nitrogenious fertilizers on the growth and glycosidal content of *Digitalis lanata*. Planta Med. 20:54–59.

6. Balbaa, S.I., S.H. Hilal, and M.Y. Haggag. 1971. A study of the effect of some factors on the growth and glycosidal content of *Digitalis lanata* Ehrh. grown in Egypt. Q. J. Crude Drug Res. 11:1689–1696.

7. Bazzaz, F.A., D. Dusek, D.S. Seigler, and A.W. Haney. 1975. Photosynthesis and cannabionoid content of temperate and tropical populations of *Cannabis sativa*. Biochem. Syst. Ecol. 3:15–18.

8. Behnke, H.D. 1976. Ultrastructure of sieve-element plastids in Caryophyllales (Centrospermae) evidence for the delimination and classifications of the order. Plant Syst. Evol. 126:31–54.

9. Bell, E.A. and B.V. Charlwood. 1980. *Secondary Plant Products*. Springer-Verlag, New York. 674 p.

10. Bellomaria, B., K.K. Hruska, and G. Valentini. 1981. Composizione degli olii essenziali di *Thimus longicaulis* C. Presl. in varie localita dell'Italia centrale. G. Bot. Ital. 115:17–27.

11. Berbec, S. 1965. Wplyw roznych dawk wapina na worst, plonowanie oraz jakosc surowka kizlka lekarskiego (*Valeriana officinalis* L.) Ann. Univ. Mariae Curie-Sklodowska. Sect. E. Agric., Lublin. 20:233–248.

12. Bernáth, J. 1971. Az orvosi csucsor (*Solanum laciniatum* Ait.) bogyókötődését és a generativ szervek elrugását kiváltó meteorológiai tényezők. Herba Hung. 10(1):21–32.

13. Bernáth, J. and D. Földesi. 1974. Összefüggés az orvosi csucsor (*Solanum laciniatum* Ait.) levelének szolaszodin tartalma, valamint a léghőmérsékleti viszonyok valtozasa között. Herba Hung. 13(3):37–43.

14. Bernáth, J., D. Földesi, and Zs. Lassányi. 1973. A tápanyagellátottság es a talajtipus hatása a macskagyökérre (*Valeriana officinalis* L. ssp. *collina* Wallr.) I. Herba Hung. 12(2–3):45–63.

15. Bernáth, J., D. Földesi, Zs. Lassányi, and I. Zámbó. 1975. A tápanyagellátottság és a talajtipus hatása a macskagyökérre (*Valeriana officinalis* L. ssp. *collina* Wallr.) II. Herba Hung. 14(2–3):37–46.

16. Bernáth, J. and P. Tétényi. 1978. Ecological factors — adaptability relationship of steroid alkaloid production based on investigation of examen two species, *Solanum laciniatum* Ait. and *Solanum dulcamara*. L. Acta Bot. Acad. Sci. Hung. 24(1–2):41–55.

17. Bernáth, J. and P. Tétényi. 1979. The effect of environmental factors on growth, development, and alkaloid production of poppy (*Papaver somniferum* L.) I. Responses to day-length and light intensity. Biochem. Physiol. Pflanz. 174:468–478.

18. Bernáth, J. and P. Tétényi. 1980. Alteration in compositional character of poppy chemotaxa affected by different light and temperature conditions. Acta Hortic. 96:91–99.

19. Bernáth, J. and P. Tétényi. 1981. The effect of environmental factors on growth, development, and alkaloid production of poppy (*Papaver somniferum* L.) II. Interaction of light and temperature. Biochem. Physiol. Pflanz. 176:599–605.

20. Bernáth, J. and P. Tétényi. 1982. Environmental control on formation of poppy alkaloids. National Congress on Medicinal Plants, Sofia. Oct. 15–16.

21. Bernáth, J., P. Tétényi, I. Horváth, and I. Zámbó. 1976. A fény intenzitásának és szinképösszetételének hatása a szteroid alkaloidok képződésére. Herba Hung. 15(1):43–53.

22. Bernáth, J., P. Tétényi, I. Horváth, and I. Zámbó. 1978. A különböző származásí és kemizmusu *Solanum dulcamara* L. klónok szteroidaglikon-

tartalmának a fény szinképösszetételből függo változása. Herba Hung. 17(1):57–64.

23. Bernáth, J., P. Tétényi, Zs. Lassányi, and E. Dobos. 1985. Effect of light and temperature on morphology and productivity in *Digitalis lanata* Ehrh. Acta Bot. Hung. In press.

24. Bernáth, J., T. Tischner, and A. Ábrányi. 1982. *Nóvénykörnyezet es szabályozása*. Akadémiai Kiadó, Budapest. 241 p.

25. Blunden, G. and K. Jewers. 1976. The steroidal sapogenin content of *Agave sisalana* from different geographical locations. Herba Hung. 15:35–41.

26. Brink, N.P. 1961. *Kultura pashlena pticeva*. Med. Promst. SSSR. 17 p.

27. Brukin, A.I. 1971. Soderhanie morfina v korobockah maka zavishimosti ot srokov uborki. Byull. Gl. Bot. Sada. 78:27–29.

28. Burbott, A.J. and W.D. Loomis. 1967. Effects of light and temperature on the monoterpenes of peppermint. Plant Physiol. 42:20–28.

29. Chatterjee, S.K. and I.K. Lama 1977. Cultivation of cinchona in West Bengal. *In* C.K. Atal and B.M. Kapur, eds. *Cultivation and Utilization of Medicinal and Aromatic Plants*. Regional Res. Lab. Jammu-Tawi. pp. 61–67.

30. Choudhary, D.K. and B.L. Kaul. 1982. The alkaloids of *Papaver somniferum* L. and their biosyntheses. Indian Drugs 19:229–232.

31. Cosson, L. 1969. Influence de l'eclairement sur les variations ontongeniques des tenezres en scopolamine et en hyoscyamine des feuilles de *Datura metel*. Phytochemistry 8:2227–2233.

32. Cosson, L., A. Escudero-Morales, and N. Cougoul. 1978. La regulation ecophysiologique du metabolisme des alcaloides tropaniques. Hyoscyamine et scopolamine. Plant Med. Phytother. 12:319–326.

33. Cosson, L., P. Chouard, and R. Paris. 1966. Influence de l'eclairement sur les variations ontongeniques alcaloides de *Datura tatula*. Lloydia 29(1):19–25.

34. Cosson, L. and J.C. Vaillant. 1976. Les alcaloides tropaniques des feuilles du *Duboisia* myoporoides neocaledonien. Phytochemistry 15:818–820.

35. Costes, C., Y. Milhet, C. Candillon, and G. Magnier. 1976. Mineral nutrition and morphine production in *Papaver somniferum*. Physiol. Plant. 36:201–207.

36. Crawford, D.J. and T.J. Mabry. 1978. Flavonoid chemistry of *Chenopodium fremontii*. Infraspecific level. Biochem. Syst. Ecol. 6:189–192.

37. Croteau, R., A.J. Burbott, and W.D. Loomis. 1972. Apparent energy deficiency in mono- and sequi-terpene biosynthesis in peppermint. Phytochemistry 11:2937–2948.

38. Culberson, C.F. and W.L. Culberson. 1976. Chemosyndromic variation in lichens. Syst. Bot. 1:331–338.

39. Culberson, C.F., W.L. Culberson, and A. Johnson. 1983. Genetic and environmental effect on growth and production of secondary compounds in *Cladonia cristatella*. Biochem. Syst. Ecol. 11:77–84.

40. Dalev, D., L. Iliev, and R. Ilieva. 1960. Poppy cultivation in Bulgaria and the production of opium. Bull. Narc. 12:25–36.

41. Dános, B. 1968. A *Papaver somniferum* L. teljesitményalakulására vonatkozó vizsgálatok, különös tekintettel az alkaloidprodukcióra. Kandidátusi értekezés, Budapest.

42. Davis, P.H. and V.H. Heywood. 1963. *Principles of Angiosperm Taxonomy*. Oliver Boyd, Edinburgh.

43. Duke, J.A. and S.J. Hurst. 1975. Ecological aplitudes of herbs, spices, and medicinal plants. Lloydia 38:404–410.

44. Eisenhuth, F. 1955. Untersuchungen über die Modifikation der Leistung un der Qualität bei *Valeriana officinale* durch Anbautechnik und Standort. Pharmazie 501–506.

45. El-Badry, D. and M.H. Hilal. 1975. A preliminary study of the effect of pH of irrigation water on the production of chamomile flower-heads. Annals of Agricultural Science of Moshtohor 3:183.

46. Ellenberg, H. 1973. *Ökosystemforschung.* Springer-Verlag, Berlin. 280 p.

47. Evans, F.J. and P.S. Cowley. 1972. Variation in cardenolides and sapogenins in *Digitalis purpurea* during germination. Phytochemistry 11:2729–2733.

48. Fairbairn, J.W. and S. El-Masry. 1968. The alkaloids of *Papaver somniferum* L. VI. Bound morphine and seed development. Phytochemistry 7:181–187.

49. Firmage, D.H. 1981. Environmental influences on the monoterpene variation in *Hedeoma drummondii.* Biochem. Syst. Ecol. 9:53–58.

50. Flück, H. 1955. The influence of climate on the active principles in medicinal plants. J. Pharm. Pharmacol. 7:361–383.

51. Földesi, D. 1978. Édeskömény. *In* L. Hornok, ed. *Gyógynövények Termesztése és Feldolgozása.* Mezőgazdasági Kiadó, Budapest. pp. 147–151.

52. Franz, Ch., A.C. Izmir, and J. Holzl. 1983. Influence of the growing site on the quality of *Mentha piperita* L. oil. 4th Symposium of ISHS. May 26–29. Angers.

53. Fries, N., K. Flodin, J. Bjurman, and J. Parby. 1974. Influence of volatile aldehydes and terpenoids on the transpiration of wheat. Naturwissenschaften 61:452.

54. Gershenzon, J., D.E. Lincoln, and J.H. Langenheim. 1978. The effect of moisture stress on monoterpenoid yield and composition in *Satureja douglasii.* Biochem. Syst. Ecol. 6:33–43.

55. Gibbs, R.D. 1974. *Chemotaxonomy of Flowering Plants.* McGill-Queer University Press, Montreal.

56. Golcz, L. 1965. Dawkowanie nawozow mineralnych pod Psianke Wrebna. *Solanum laciniatum* Ait. Herba Pol. 11:208–217.

57. Gorgiev, M. and V. Hot. 1982. Uticaj povecanja koncentracije bora u zemljistu na prinos i zastuplejnost, morfina i proteina u maku (*Papaver somniferum* L.) Arh. Poljopr. Nauke. 43:95–106.

58. Gozin, A.A. and V.S. Jasnecov. 1982. Vlianie uslovij sredi na soderjanie biologicheski aktivnih veshestv v nekotorih lekarstvennih restenijah. Rastit. Resur. 18:363–367.

59. Grahle, A. and C. Höltzel. 1963. Effect of light on essential oil of the leaves of *Mentha piperita* L. Naturwissenschaften 50:552.

60. Harborne, J.B. 1976. Functions of flavanoids in plants. *In* T.W. Goodwin, ed. *Chemistry and Biochemistry of Plant Pigments.* Academic Press, London. pp. 736–779.

61. Harborne, J.B. 1977. *Introduction to Ecological Biochemistry.* Academic Press, London. 241 p.

62. Harborne, J.B. 1980. Plant phenolics. *In* E.A. Bell and B.V. Charlwood, eds. *Secondary Plant Products.* Springer-Verlag, Berlin. pp. 329–402.

63. Hawkes, J.G. 1968. Chemotaxonomy and Serotaxonomy. Academic Press, London.

64. Hegenauer, R. 1962-1973. Chemotaxonomie der Pflanzen. Birkauser Verlag, Basel. Vol. I–VI.

65. Hertel, H. 1978. Systematik der Flechten. Bericht uber die Jahre 1976 und 1977 mit einigen Nachtragen Prog. Bot. 40. Springer-Verlag, Berlin. 358 p.

66. Heywood, V.H., J.B. Harborne, and B.L. Turner. 1978. The Biology and Chemistry of the Compositae. Academic Press, London.

67. Hornok, L. 1978. Gyógynövények termesztése és feldolgozása. Mezőgazdasági Kiadó, Budapest. 356 p.

68. Horváth, I., J. Bernáth, and P. Tétényi. 1977. Effect of spectral composition of light on dry matter production in Solanum dulcamara L. ecotypes of different origin. Acta Acad. Sci. Hung. 26:345–354.

69. Hotyn, A.A. 1968. Efirmomaslithnie shirje i technologia efirnih masel. Kolos, Moskva. pp. 35–44.

70. Hotyn, A.A., J.A. Gubanov, P.T. Kondratenko, and V.V. Seberstov. 1967. Lekastvennie rastenia. SzSzSzR Kolos, Moskva. 172 p.

71. Hotyn, A.A. and P.J. Novikova. 1968. Lekarstvennie rasthenie. VILR. Trudii, Moskva. 13:30–40.

72. Jankulov, I. 1972. Izmenenie v sodersanieto i sootnosetieto na tropanovite alkaloidi pri rastenijatretironi s UV svetlina. Rast. Nauki. Sofia. 9(8):15–21.

73. Karnick, C.R. 1972. The effect of photoperiod on steroidal sapogenins and other constituents in Dioscorea deltoidea Wall. Ann. Bot. 36:605–610.

74. Kerekes, J. 1962. A viz hatása a kamilla (Matricaria chamomilla L.) virághozamára és hatóanyagára. Herba Hung. 1:57–64.

75. Kerekes, J. and L. Hornok. 1972. Adatok a borsosmenta (Mentha piperita L.) öntözéséhez és tápanyagellátásához. Herba Hung. 11:39–44.

76. Klimesova, E. and J. Klimesova. 1960. Vliv zavlah na rust a obsah silic u maty peprne (Mentha piperita) Hudson behem ontogeneze. Cesk. Farm. 9:49–55.

77. Kondratenko, P.T., N.P. Brink, G.P. Stolopnikov, and S.M. Kuthonbaiev. 1968. Vozdelivanie paslena doltshatovo v orosaemmih zemliah Kazahstana. Kajnar. Alma-Ata. 95 p.

78. Kreeb, K. 1974. Okophysiologie der Pflanzen. Veb Gustav Fisher Verlag, Jena. 211 p.

79. Kuznyecova, G.K. and V.S. Hazanov. 1973. O spektralnoj effektivnosti fothosintheza nekatorih alkaloidnosnih rastenij pri adoptacii k svetu rasnovo khatsestva. Fiziol. Rast. 3:554–557.

80. Lange, O.L., P.S. Nobel, C.B. Osmond, and H. Ziegler. 1983. Physiological Plant Ecology IV. Springer-Verlag, Berlin. 644 p.

81. Larcher, W. 1975. Physiological Plant Ecology. Springer-Verlag, Berlin. 252 p.

82. Laughlin, J.C. and D. Munro. 1982. The effect of fungal colonisation on the morphine production of poppy. Papaver somniferum L. capsules. J. Agric. Sci. 98:679–686.

83. Lavigne, C., L. Cosson, R. Jacques, and E. Miginiac. 1979. Influence de la duree quotidienne d'eclairement et de la temperature sur la croissance,

la floraison et la composition chimique de l'essence chez le *Jasminum grandiflorum* L. Physiol. Veg. 17:363–373.

84. Lee, Chang Ki and Hyung, Kooh Kim. 1970. Investigation into the geographical differences in alkaloid content of Korean opium. Bull. Narc. 22(2):41–46.

85. Levy, M. and K. Fuji. 1978. Geographic variation of flavonoids in *Phlox carolina*. Biochem. Syst. Ecol. 6:117–125.

86. Lincoln, D.E. and J.H. Langenheim. 1978. Effect of light and temperature on monoterpenoid yield and composition in *Satureja douglasii*. Biochem. Syst. Ecol. 6:21–32.

87. Ljakin, A.S.V. 1977. Vlianie oshadkov na rost, rasvitie i urasai maka. Sbor. Vopr. Agronomii, Frunse. 157 p.

88. Loomis, R.S. 1983. Productivity of agricultural systems. *In* O.L. Lange, P.S. Nobel, C.B. Osmond, and H. Ziegler, eds. *Physiological Plant Ecology* IV. Springer-Verlag, Berlin. pp. 151–172.

89. Loomis, W.D. 1967. Biosynthesis and metabolism of monoterpenes. *In* J.B. Pridham, ed. *Terpenoids in Plants*. Academic Press, London. pp. 59–82.

90. Luckner, M. and B. Diettrich. 1982. Cardenolide formation in tissue cultures of *Digitalis lanata*. National Congress on Medicinal Plants. Sofia. October 14–16.

91. Mabry, T.J. 1980. Betalains. *In* E.A. Bell and B.V. Charlwood, eds. *Secondary Plant Products*. Springer-Verlag, Berlin. pp. 513–533.

92. Máthé, I. 1959. Über die Standortverhältnisse von *Acorus calamus* L. und Vorkommen in Ungarn. Acta Bot. Acad. Sci. Hung. 5:79–86.

93. Máthé, I. 1960. A kamilla (*Matricaria chamomilla* L.) magyarországi termőhelyei. MTA Bio. Csop. Közl. 4:235–254.

94. Máthé, I., Jr. 1974. Hazánkban honos vagy meghonositható *Solanum* fajok es változatok alkaloid produkciójának vizsgálata tekintettel az ökológiai viszonyokra. Kandidátusi értekezés, Budapest.

95. Máthé, I. and D. Földesi. 1965. Az orvosi csucsor (*Solanum laciniatum* Ait.) Magy. Kulturflorája 24. Akadémiai Kiadó, Budapest. 80 p.

96. Máthé, I. and I. Máthé, Jr. 1973. Data to the European area of the chemical taxa of *Solanum dulcamara* L. Acta Bot. Acad. Sci. Hung. 19(1-4):441–451.

97. Máthé, I., Jr. and I. Máthé. 1973. Néhány talajtápelem hatása a *Solanum dulcamara* üvegházi Körülmények között. Herba Hung. 12:29–39.

98. Máthé, I., Jr. and I. Máthé. 1976. Steroids of *Solanum dulcamara* L. and their variability. Congress on Solanaceae. July 15–19. Birmingham.

99. Máthé, I. and I. Précsényi. 1966. Changing of vincamine agent in *Vinca minor* L. according to region and the year of growth. Acta Agron. (Budapest) 15:273–283.

100. Máthé, I., D. Vágujflavi, and M. Kovács. 1969. Néhány ökológiai tényező és az alkaloidtartalom változása *Vinca minor* állományban. Bot. Kozlem 56:93–97.

101. McNair, J.B. 1942. Soil acidity in relation to alkaloid and cyanogenetic glucoside production. Lloydia 25:208.

102. Mears, J.A. 1980. Flavonoid diversity and geographic endemism in *Parthenium*. Biochem. Syst. Ecol. 8:361–370.

103. Milletti, G. and G. Frenguelli. 1975. Nutrizione minerale e tenore in digossina sulla *Digitalis lanata* Ehrh. Fitoterapia 46:247–253.

104. Morász, S. 1979. *A Mák Termesztése.* Mezőgazdasági Kiadó, Budapest. 80 p.

105. Mothes, K. and H.R. Schütte. 1969. *Biosynthese der Alkaloide.* VEB Deutscher Verlag der Wissenschaften, Berlin. 730 p.

106. Muravjeva, V.J., P.T. Kondratenko, and N.P. Brink. 1969. Dinamika shoderjania solasodina v paslene dolchatovo. Rastit. Resur. 5:187–190.

107. Naumova, G.E. and V. Seberstov. 1972. O vlianii fosfora na urhosai mashithnovo maka i shoderjanie alkaloidov. Agrochimiya (Moscow) 5:36–39.

108. Nicholls, K.W. and B.A. Bohm. 1982. Quantitative flavonoid variation in *Lupinus sericeus.* Biochem. Syst. Ecol. 10:225–231.

109. Nowacki, E., M. Jurzysta, P. Gorski, D. Nowacka, and G.R. Waller. 1976. Effect of nitrogen nutrition on alkaloid metabolism in plants. Biochem. Physiol. Pflanz. 169:231–240.

110. Nowinski, M. 1956. Wplyw czynnikow ekologicznych na zawartosc zwiazkow czynnych w roslinach leczniczuch. Biul. Nauk. Poznan. 2:94–116.

111. Pavlov, P. and S. Ilieva. 1972. Certain biochemical changes in the initial developmental phases of *Salvia sclarea* plants grown in different light. Rastenievud. Nauki. 9:13–19.

112. Pelletier, S.W. 1970. *Chemistry of Alkaloids.* Van Nostrand Reinhold Company, New York. 795 p.

113. Penka, M. 1963. Kvantita a knalita sklizne zavlazovanych rostlin. Folia. 4. University J.E. Purkyne, Brno.

114. Penning De Vries, F.W.T. 1983. Modeling of growth and production. *In* O.L. Lange, P.S. Nobel, C.B. Osmond, and H. Ziegler, eds. *Physiological Plant Ecology* IV. Springer-Verlag, Berlin. pp. 117–150.

115. Phillipson, J.D., S.S. Handa, and S.W. El-Dabbas. 1976. N-oxides of morphine, codeine, and thebaine and their occurrence in *Papaver* species. Phytochemistry 15:1297–1301.

116. Remmert, H. 1980. *Ökologie.* Springer-Verlag, Berlin. 304 p.

117. Rhoades, D.G., D.E. Lincoln, and J.H. Langenheim. 1976. Preliminary studies of monoterpenoid variability in *Satureja douglasii.* Biochem. Syst. Ecol. 4:5–12.

118. Roberts, M.F. and M.D. Antoun. 1978. The relationship between L-DOPA decarboxylase in the latex of *Papaver somniferum* and alkaloid formation. Phytochemistry 17:1083–1087.

119. Robinson, T. 1968. *The Biochemistry of Alkaloids.* Springer-Verlag, Berlin. 149 p.

120. Rovesti, P. 1975. Incidenze ecologiche sulla composizione degli oli essenziali. Nota XII. Gli oli essenziali di *Ocimum suave* Wild. dell Africa orientale. Riv. Ital. Essenze, Profumi, Piante I. Offic, Aromi, Saponi, Cosmet, Aerosol. 57:321–323.

121. Rowson, J.M. 1954. Alkaloid biogenesis in plants with special reference to *Datura* and allied genera in the Solanaceae. J. Pharm. Belg. 36:195.

122. Runeckles, V.C. and E.E. Conn. 1974. *Metabolism and Regulation of Secondary Plant Products.* Academic Press, New York. 249 p.

123. Saleh, M. 1970. The effect of the air temperature and the thermoperiod on the quantity and the quality of *Matricaria chamomilla* L. Mededelingen Landbauhochenschele Wegeningen 15:17.

124. Saleh, M. 1973. Effect of light upon the quantity and quality of *Matricaria chamomilla* oil. III. Preliminary study under controlled conditions. Planta Med. 24:337–340.

125. Sander. H. 1963. Chemische Differenzierung innerhalb der Art *Solanum dulcamara* L. Planta Med. 11:303–316.

126. Sárkány, S.-né. 1962. A hatóanyagtartalom változása különböző eredetü *Vinca minor* L. állományok földfeletti hajtásaiban a tenyészidő folyamán. Herba Hung. 1:156–167.

127. Sárkány, S., A.-né. Michels, K. Nyomákay, and G.-né Verzár-Petri. 1967. A mák magjának, különböző korí fiatal növényeinek szöveti felépitése, finomszerkezeti vonatkozásai és az alkaloidképződés kérdése. Herba Hung. 6:239–251.

128. Sárkány, S., G.-né. Verzár, A.-né. Michels, and S.-né. Sárkány. 1966. Az alkaloidképződés tanulmányozása a szövetstrukturával és a szervdifferenciáltsággal összefüggésben a *Papaver somniferum* L.-ban. Herba Hung. 5(2–3):40–50.

129. Schneider, M. and K. Kuzminska. 1975. Wstepne badania nad wplywem wilgotnosci gleby na plony maku lekarskiego (*Papaver somniferum* L.) Rocz. Akad. Roln. Poznaniv. 82:151–155.

130. Schröder, H. 1963. Untersuchungen über den Einfluss unterschiedlicher Wasserversorgung aut Erträge, Gehalte an ätherischem Öl, Transpirationsquotinten, Blattgrössen und relative Öldrüsendichten bei einigen Arten aus der Familie der Labiaten. Pharmazie 18:47–58.

131. Seberstov, V.V. and L.I. Arsjuhina. 1966. Vlianie mikroelementov na urahsaj i sodherjanie dejstvujushih veshestv u korobockah maslichnovo maka. Lekarstvennie rhastenia. VILR. Trudi, Moskva. 13:30.

132. Semple, J.C. and J.E. Averett. 1975. Flavonoid variation in *Xanthisma texanum*: Infrapopulation and interpopulation variation. Biochem. Syst. Ecol. 3:11–14.

133. Singh, P. 1977. Cultivation of Digitalis ssp. *In* C.K. Atal and B.M. Kapur, eds. *Cultivation and Utilization of Medicinal and Aromatic Plants.* Regional Res. Lab. Jammu-Tawi. pp. 81–85.

134. Skursky, L. and G.R. Waller. 1972. Biochemical and physiological relation ricinineal N-dimethyl ricinine in *Ricinus communis*. Biochem. Physiol. Alkaloide, 4th. Int. Symp.

135. Smith, P.M. 1976. *The Chemotaxonomy of Plants.* Edward Arnold Limited, London. 313 p.

136. Steinegger, E. and G.F. Gessler. 1956. Beeinflussung von Wachstum und Wirkstoffgehalt bei *Datura* durch artfremde Stoffe. Sci. Pharm. 24:5–11.

137. Sváb, J.-né. 1978. Macskagyökér. *In* L. Hornok, ed. *Gyógynövények termesztése és feldolgozása.* Mezőgazdasági Kiadó, Budapest. pp. 152–156.

138. Sváb, J.-né., C. El-Din Awaad, and T. Fahmy. 1967. The influence of highly different ecological effects on the volatile oil content and composition in the chamomille. Herba Hung. 6:177–199.

139. Swain, T. 1966. *Comparative Phytochemistry.* Academic Press, London. 543 p.

140. Tétényi, P. 1963. *Infraspecifikus kémiai taxonok és a gyógynövénynemesités.* Doktori értekezés, Budapest. 536 p.

141. Tétényi, P. 1970. *Infraspecific chemical taxa of medicinal plants.* Akadémiai Kiadó, Budapest. 225 p.

142. Tétényi, P. 1978. Illóolajos növényfajok kémiai differenciálódása. Herba Hung. 17(1):11–27.

143. Tétényi, P., E. Tyihák, I. Máthé, I., and J. Sváb. 1962. Untersuchungen über die Azulenverbindungen der Achillea-Arten. Pharmazie 17:463–466.

144. Tétényi, P. and D. Vágújfalvi. 1965. Veranderungen des Alkalodgehalts von Papaver somniferum L. Pharmazie 20:731–734.

145. Tookey, H.L., G.F. Spencer, M.D. Grove, and W.F. Kwolek. 1976. Codeine and morphine in Papaver somniferum grown in controlled environment. Planta Med. 30:340–348.

146. Tóth, Gy. 1969. A Solanum laciniatum szelekciós nemesitéséről. Herba Hung. 8(1–2):113–120.

147. Tucakov, J. and N. Kristic. 1965. Prilog farmakognozijskom procavanju Solanum laciniatum Ait. gajenog u SR Sribiji. Acta. Pharm. Jugoslacica. 15:97–105.

148. Turkhede, B.B., D.E. Rajat, and R.K.U. Singh. 1981. Consumptive water use by opium poppy. Indian J. Agric. Sci. 51:102–107.

149. Tso, T.C. 1972. Physiology and Biochemistry of Tobacco Plants. Dowden, Hutchinson, and Ross, Stroudsberg, PA. 393 p.

150. UN Narcotics Laboratory. 1975. Relationship between Environment and Phenantrene Alkaloid Content. Research proposal, Geneva. 7 p.

151. Vágújfalvi, D. 1962. Az ásványi táplálkozás hatása a kamilla. Matricaria chamomilla L. növekedésére és prokamazulén-tartalmára. Herba Hung. 1:65–72.

152. Vágújfalvi, D. 1964. Az alkaloidok anyagcseréje Atropa belladonna magvak csirázásakor. Herba Hung. 3:165–178.

153. Vágújfalvi, D. 1967. A gyógynövények fontosabb hatóanyagai és képződésük a növényekben. Külső tényezők és kezelések módositó hatása. Herba Hung. 6(3):175–196.

154. Vágújfalvi, D. 1967. Gyógynövények ásványi táplálkozásának vizsgálata. In J. Sarkadi, ed. Trágyázási kisérletek 1955–1964. Akadémiai Kiadó, Budapest. 479 p.

155. Vágújfalvi, D. 1968. Alkaloidos növények élettani vizsgálata. Kandidátusi értekezés, Budapest. 268 p.

156. Vo Hong Nga, J. Bernáth and P. Tétényi. 1976. Az ökológiai tényezők hatása a Solanum dulcamara populációra. Herba Hung. 15(2):31–44.

157. Wahab, A.S.A. 1982. Effect of N,P,K—Supply on Growth, Yield and on the Active Principles of Some Medicinal Plants. Kandidátusi értekezés, Budapest.

158. Waller, G.R. and E.K. Nowacki. 1978. Alkaloid Biology and Metabolism in Plants. Plenum Press, New York. 294 p.

159. Walter, H. 1979. Vegetation of the Earth. Springer-Verlag, New York. 274 p.

160. Weeks, W.W. 1970. Physiology of alkaloids in germinating seed of Nicotiana tabacum. Ph.D. thesis. University of Kentucky, Lexington, KY.

161. Willuhn, G. 1966. Untersuchungen zur Chemischen Differenzierung bei Solanum dulcamara L. Planta Med. 14:408–420.

162. Yadav, R.L., R. Mohan, and D.V. Singh. 1982. Opium and seed yield of Papaver somniferum L. irrigated at different available soil moisture levels. Indian Drugs 19:260–263.

The Chemistry, Pharmacology, and Commercial Formulations of Chamomile

Connie Mann and E. John Staba
**Department of Medicinal Chemistry and
Pharmacognosy, College of Pharmacy, University of
Minnesota, Minneapolis, MN 55455**

CONTENTS

I. INTRODUCTION

The chamomiles, important medicinal plants cultivated principally in Europe, are of 2 distinct plant types: Roman chamomile, *Chamaemelum nobile* (L.) All., (formerly *Anthemis nobilis* L.) and German chamomile, *Matricaria recutita* L. More than 4,000 tons of the chamomiles are produced annually (220), with German chamomile accounting for most of the tonnage. Both dried flowers and the essential oils extracted from the chamomiles are of economic importance. Because of the chamomiles' widespread use and economic significance, much research in the botanical, horticultural, and pharmacological areas has been conducted. The objective of this review is to summarize and highlight the chemical and pharmacological knowledge gained in recent years and to bridge this information with medicinal uses and product formulations of the chamomiles.

II. BOTANY AND TAXONOMY OF CHAMOMILE

Prior to any serious consideration of the chemical composition of chamomile, the botanical and taxonomical identity of chamomile needs to be understood. The chemical composition of the plants is strongly dependent upon the genotype, and Roman and German chamomiles have often been confused in the literature with each other and with other plants of the same genus (Table 1).

Roman chamomile has been incorrectly reported to contain a hollow recepticum (166) and to have a disagreeable, fetid odor (209). *Anthemis cotula*, rather than German chamomile, has been reported to be Wild Chamomile (48). Nomenclature confusion especially occurs if one relies upon the older literature that incorrectly reports *Anacyclus pyrethrum* (Pellitory Root) as *Anthemis pyrethrum* (211), German chamomile as *Pyrethrum chamomilla* and *Matricaria chamomilla* (89), and Stinking Mayweed as *Pyrethrum parthenium* (23). Related to German chamomile botanically, but not resembling the plant at all, is *Oremis multicaulis*, from which an oil extracted from the flowering tops is used in perfumery and is referred to as Moroccan chamomile oil (8).

Chamomile products in the market are sometimes adulterated with *Anthemis*, *Chrysanthemum*, and other similar plants (Table 1). Differences in flower morphology between the 2 species are illustrated in Figure 1. Further discussion on the biological and botanical characteristics of the chamomiles has been reported (6, 9, 24, 35, 60, 67, 80, 111, 119, 130, 133, 148, 180, 198, 203, 214).

TABLE 1. Botanical Identity of the Chamomiles and Plant Sources That Have Been Used as Adulterants.

A. *Chamomiles*		
Family: Asteraceae (Compositae)	*Synonyms*	*Ref.*
Chamaemelum nobile (L.) A11. *(Anthemis nobilis* L.)	Roman Chamomile English Chamomile Garden Chamomile Lawn Chamomile Sweet Chamomile Manzanilla (Little apple) Whig Plant Scotch Chamomile ("single" flowers) May-then True Chamomile	198, 201
Matricaria recutita L. *(Tripleurosperumum recutita)* *(Chamomilla recutita* (L.) Rauschert) *(Matricaria chamomilla* L. (1753), pro parte)	German Chamomile Hungarian Chamomile Wild Chamomile	99, 150
B. *Plant Sources Used As Adulterants*		
Anthemis arvensis	Corn Chamomile	
Anthemis cotula	Stinking Chamomile Stinking Mayweed Dog Fenel Wild Chamomile	
Anthemis montana		79
Anthemis tinctoria	Yellow Chamomile Ox-Eye Chamomile Golden Marguerite	
Chamomilla suaveolens (Pursh) Rydb. *(Matricaria matricarioides* (Less.) Porter, pro parte)	Pineapple Weed Rayless Mayweed	198
Chrysanthemum leucanthemum		
Matricaria perforata Merat *(Matricaria inodora* L.) *(Tripleurospermum inodorum* (L.) Koch)	Scentless Mayweed Scentless Chamomile Wild Chamomile Corn Feverfew	150, 198

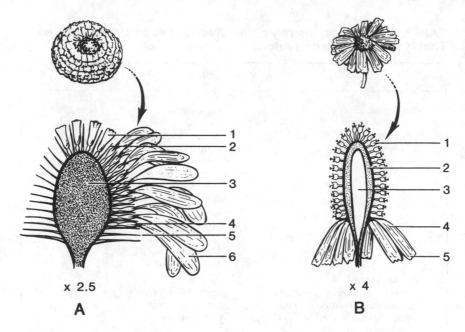

Figure 1. The Flowers of Roman and German Chamomile.

A. Roman Chamomile	B. German Chamomile
1. Tubular disc floret	1. Tubular disc floret
2. Paleae	2. Receptacle
3. Receptacle	3. Air space
4. Stigma	4. Ligulate ray floret
5. Involveral bracts	5. Floret ribs
6. Ligulate ray floret	

III. PLANT COMPOSITION

German and Roman chamomile, used for centuries as medicinal plants (primarily due to the azulene content of the extracted essential oils), are quite dissimilar in their essential oil and chemical composition. While there are, for example, several flavonoids and other compounds common to both chamomiles, each plant type should be considered separately. Moreover, in addition to the genetic influence (87, 107, 140, 191, 192) on oil composition, many other factors outside the scope of this review, such as plant age (41, 124, 163, 204), plant part (28), environmental variables (2, 36, 58, 82, 109, 125, 171, 186, 207), management practices (1, 43, 62, 105, 108, 156, 158, 175, 205, 217, 218, 219), and postharvest handling (25, 60, 112), are also known to affect essential oil and chemical composition of the chamomiles.

A. Essential Oils

1. Roman Chamomile Oil

A steam-distilled essential oil is extracted from the flower heads of Roman chamomile with oil yields of approximately 1.75 percent of plant fresh weight (165). Double-headed flowers usually yield above 0.7 percent volume of distilled oil per unit weight of fresh flowers (15). Roman chamomile oil is almost insoluble in glycerin, almost completely soluble in mineral oil and most fixed oils, and soluble with haziness in propylene glycol (165, 173). One milliliter of oil will dissolve in 2 milliliters of 80 percent alcohol, although sometimes with precipitation (173). Solubility in 70-percent alcohol is 1 part oil in 6 parts alcohol (165). Selected physiochemical properties of oil of Roman chamomile are presented in Table 2. More detailed reports on the nature of the essential oil of Roman chamomile have been published (22, 75, 132).

The essential oil of Roman chamomile has been recognized as safe (GRAS) by the U.S. Food and Drug Administration (70, 199), the Council of Europe (145), and the Flavoring Extract Manufacturers' Association (145).

2. German Chamomile Oil

Oil of German chamomile is collected from flower heads, either by steam distillation or by solvent extraction, for yields of 0.24 to 1.9 percent of fresh plant tissue (121). The oil consists of several high-temperature boiling components, and distillation requires high-pressure steam for 7 to 13 hours to remove the oil from the plant material. Redistillation of the steam distillation waters is necessary for efficient oil extraction from the chamomile plant as some constituents of the oil are soluble in large quantities of warm water, and the high specific gravity (0.91 to 0.95) of the oil leads to a milky emulsion of the essential oil flowing off in the original distillation water. Losses in oil can also occur due to the tendency of German chamomile oil to crystallize and form deposits on the walls or condenser tubes during extraction (60).

The distillation process affects the quantities and composition of the oil. Distillation, using the 4-hour European Pharmacopeia method, typically yields 0.33 milliliters of oil per 100 grams of tissue, while distillation, using the 2-hour German Pharmacopeia method (DAB7), typically yields 0.29 milliliters of oil per 100 grams of tissue (128, 129). The length of the steam distillation extraction period does influence the yields of essential oil. Higher percentages of chamazulene and farnesene are produced by distilling for 4 instead of 2 hours, and distilling smaller quantities of plant material at one time yields greater quantities of oil (82). A formula for estimating the essential oil content of tissue dried at 105 °C and extracted by the DAB7 method has been developed (123).

Azulenes give the deep, ink blue color characteristic of German chamomile oil. Little, if any, relationship exists between the azulene content and total oil distilled from the tissue (130). Azulenes form under acidic conditions and during distillation.

The distilled oil is soluble in propylene glycol but insoluble in glycerin and mineral oil (200). The oil does not usually dissolve clearly in 95-percent alcohol (200). Some selected physiochemical properties are presented in Table 2. The refractive index and optical rotation of German chamomile oil appear to be undetermined due to

TABLE 2.   Selected Physiochemical Properties of Roman and German Chamomile Oil.[a]

	Roman	German
Specific gravity	.089 to 0.91	0.91 to 0.95
Ester value	250 to 310	< 40
Refractive index @ 20 °C	1.44 to 1.45	--
Acid value	<15	5 to 50
Optical rotation @ 20 °C	-1 to +4	--

[a]Data modified from Furia and Bellanca (47) and Schaefer and Stein (173).

the intense blue color (59). Typical measured concentrations of ingredients in German chamomile essential oil are presented in Table 3.

The solvent-extracted oil is prepared by maceration and percolation and repercolation of flower heads with extracting solvents such as ethanol and water, glycerin and propylene glycol, and sunflower oil. The more polar the extracting solvent, the higher the flavonoid glycoside content of the oil. Using a less polar-extracting solvent increases the concentration of terpene compounds and flavonoid aglycones in the oil (142). Hydroalcoholic extracts of tissue are made, using 25- to 75-percent alcohol solutions. One extract is prepared by macerating flowers in propylene glycol (200 g flowers/kg solvent); another extract is prepared by digestion of flowers in sunflower oil (200 g of flowers/kg of oil) at room temperature (7). Patents have been awarded for procedures involved in extracting stabilized oils (45).

The extracted oil, highly viscous and often grainy, generally has a very deep blue color due to the high chamazulene content. The extracted oil is darker, more viscous, and more opaque than distilled

TABLE 3. Chemical Constituent Content of German Chamomile Oil.[a]

Component	Concentration (g/100 ml oil)
α – Bisabolol	6
α – Bisabololoxide A	7.8
α – Bisabololoxide B	35
Chamazulene	6.1
Spathulenol	1.2
cis-En-yn-dicycloether	6.4
Farnesene	12

[a]Data of Becker *et al*. (11).

oil and has an older, heavier, and more tenacious odor than distilled oil (8). Extracted oil contains a higher percentage of spiroethers than distilled oil. Hernarian, a coumarin derivative, appears in the extracted oil but not the distilled oil (28). Solids sometimes separate from the oil at low temperatures, and the color of the oil will change from blue to brown with time (8). Alcohol and water extractions that use alkaline substances to increase the stability of the oil produce a yellow- or green-colored extract as the azulenes are not formed under alkaline conditions (130, 131). The azulene in the oil adds a very stable rubbery note to the odor. Extracted oil has an enhanced fixative effect (8).

Many times, high-boiling solvents used in the extracting procedure remain as impurities in the oil and create undesirable odors. Total solvent used in the extraction process is often 1,000 times the amount of expected extract; thus, even a small percentage of extracting solvent left in the oil can represent a high percentage of the constituents in the extracted oil (8). An absolute oil is made from the German chamomile essential oil by extracting the essential oil with alcohol to produce a resin and subsequently extracting the resin for the absolute (131).

The essential oil of German chamomile has been recognized as safe (GRAS) by the U.S. Food and Drug Administration (70, 199), the Council of Europe (145), and the Flavoring Extract Manufacturers' Association (145).

B. Extraction, Isolation, and Identification of Chemical Constituents

Many laboratory procedures, recently reviewed by Schilcher (176), have been used to extract, isolate, and identify the chemical constituents of chamomile essential oils. The thin-layer, gas chromatographic, and high-performance liquid chromatographic procedures used for the analysis of German chamomile oil, flavonoids, and contaminants such as pesticide, heavy metal, and ethylene oxide residues within the oil have been detailed (27, 113, 161, 177, 191). Additional reports (26, 83, 104, 115, 142, 143) have summarized extracting and analyzing methods for German chamomile oil, coumarins, flavonoids, tannins, polyacetylenes, esters, alcohols, and triterpenoids. Comprehensive extraction, gas chromatographic, and mass spectra studies for Roman chamomile flowers collected at various stages of development have also been detailed (74, 139, 140).

Classical thin-layer procedures are often used for the separation and analysis of German chamomile flowers (113, 157) and tea (16) and Roman chamomile flavonoids (182) and related compounds (15). Both classical and pressurized thin-layer systems have been used for the analysis of German chamomile oil with the totally closed, pressured ultramicro chamber (PUM) and high-performance plates recommended for most efficient separations (135, 136).

In addition, a number of gas chromatographic systems have been developed for the analysis of German chamomile oil (113, 142, 143, 185), Roman chamomile oil (139, 140), and the head space above extracted oil (21). Droplet counter-current chromatography (DCCC) has been used for separating the nonpolar compounds (11); normal phase high-performance liquid chromatography (HPLC) has been used for the differentiating of spiroethers (152) and the coumarins, umbelliferone, and herniarin (153); and reversed-phase HPLC has been used for detailing flavones and glycosides (154) present in German chamomile. Spectral UV, IR, MS, and NMR data for identification of the essential oils (75, 200), bisaboloids (37, 38, 78), chamazulenes (96), flavonoids (116, 151), and hydrocarbons (185) of chamomiles have been reported. Although methods of analysis for determination of essential oil vary between the European and German pharmacopoeias, the content of essential oil is similar if extracted by either method (127, 129).

The need for specific chamomile product formulations sometimes requires special handling and extraction procedures to be used during processing. For example, the temperature at which the flowers are dried and the temperature and pH of the extraction process significantly affect the chamazulene content of the essential oil (112). The highest essential oil and prochamazulene content is obtained after drying plant material in the shade at 22 to 25°C. Slight losses (up to 7 percent) of prochamazulene, but with no reduction in plant essential oil content, occur with drying in a stationary bulk dryer with active ventilation at 40 to 45°C. A stationary steam dryer induces significant loss of prochamazulene and essential oil. In another study, the greatest loss of active compounds in the essential oil generally resulted from storage of plant material at -6 to 25°C and 55 to 95 percent humidity (206). Lyophilized plants frequently yield more oil than air-dried plants (28).

Super-critical gas extraction (12) increases the overall "sensory" properties of chamomile tea concentrates (212). Dioxolane derivatives have been used to prepare more stable chamomile extracts (91) and beta-cyclodextrins are known to stabilize the oil (190). A comparison of paper, polyester-polyethylene, polypropylene-paper, and polyethylene-paper laminates indicates polypropylene-paper is the best wrapping material for use in plant storage (206).

C. Chemical Constituents

Many chemical constituents have been identified in the chamomiles (Table 4). Of these compounds, certain ones appear more important (on the basis of quantity and/or pharmacological activity) to the character of the plants and can be designated as major constituents (Figure 2). The discussion in this report is limited to these compounds. Details on the chemistry of the major constituents of the chamomiles are presented in Table 5. Other characteristics of the major chamomile constituents are summarized in Table 6.

The major constituents of Roman chamomile oil are terpene hydrocarbons, oxygenated terpenes, and esters of angelic and tiglic acid. Roman chamomile oil has one of the highest content of esters of any known essential oil, with angelic and tiglic acid esters comprising about 85 percent of the oil (121). Of the terpenoids, 1,8-cineole and transpirocarvone are reported to be in greatest quantity in the oil (140). Chamazulene is formed from a natural precursor during distillation and the quantity of chamomile in the oil depends upon the origin and age of the flowers (206). The chamazulene content will decrease with time during storage (206).

German chamomile chemotypes are reported to contain oils with and without chamazulene (European origin), with α-bisabolol (Portuguese and Spanish origin), with α-bisabolonoxide A and α-bisabololoxide A (European, Bulgarian, and Turkish origin), and with α-bisaboloxide B (Argentine origin) (87). Further genetic differentiation has been illustrated by qualitative and quantitative analyses of oil from 11 different German chamomile chemotypes, where considerable variation in flavonoid concentration and only small differences in coumarin and phenolic acid content were detected among the chemotypes (Table 7) (157). Depending upon the chemotype, plants appear to be dominant in either bisabolol or bisabolonoxide A

TABLE 4.   Chemical Constituents of Roman and German Chamomile.[a]

Terpenoids	Roman References	German References
Anthemol	48, 139, 208	-
Azulene	48, 140	13, 48, 160
Bisabolene	139	197
β-Bisabolene	106	-
α-Bisabolol	-	38, 82, 121
α-Bisabololoxide A	-	11, 38, 174
α-Bisabololoxide B	-	11, 38, 174
α-Bisabololoxide C	-	174
α-Bisaboloneoxide A	-	11, 38, 92
Borneol	140	28, 149
B-Bourbonene	106	-
α-Cadinene	106, 139	-
Calamene	-	138
Camphene	21, 140	-
3-Carene	-	138
B-Caryophyllene	118, 140	160
cis-Caryophyllene	-	160
Caryophyllenepoxide	-	160
Chamazulene	139, 142, 165	11, 17, 47
Chamomillol	-	160
1,8-Cineole	118, 140	-
α-Copaene	118, 140	-

[a]This list of constituents in the chamomiles includes most identified compounds. However, the list should not be considered definitive as chemical makeup will differ among chemotypes and among plants grown in different environments. For ease of reference, the compounds' common names have generally been presented.

TABLE 4 (cont.)

Terpenoids	Roman References	German References
B-Copaene	118, 140	-
α-Cubebene	106	138
B-Cubebene	106	-
p-Cymene	118, 140	-
3-Dehydronobilin	85	-
α-p-Dimethylstyrene	118	-
3-Epinobilin	85	-
1,10-Epoxynobilin	85	-
Eucannabinolide	85	-
Farnesene	139	120
trans-α-Farnesene	-	160
trans-β-Farnesene	-	11, 160
Farnesol	25	28, 125
Germacrene-D	106	-
Guaiazulene (1,4-dimethyl-7- isopropylazulene)	-	28, 149
Humulene	106	-
Hydroxyisonobilin	172	-
Limonene	21	-
Linear sesquiterpene lactone	-	215
Matricarin	-	19, 103, 210
Matricin	-	39, 103, 121
α-Muurolene	-	138

TABLE 4 (cont.)

Terpenoids	Roman References	German References
β-Myrcene	118, 140	-
Myrtenal	118, 140	-
Myrtenol	140	-
Nerolidol	121	-
Nobilin	85	-
α-Pinene	21, 118, 140	-
β-Pinene	21, 118, 140	-
Pinocamphone	118, 140	-
α-*trans*-Pinocarveol	118, 140	-
α-*trans*-Pinocarvone	140	-
Sabinene	118, 140	-
β-Selinene	106	-
Spathulenol	-	11, 44
α-Terpinene	118, 140	-
Thujone	-	28
Xanthoxylin	-	138

Flavonoids	Roman References	German References
Apigenin	121, 220	33, 116, 157
Apigenin-7-(6″-o-acetyle) glucoside	-	116
Apigenin-7-apiosylgluoside (apiin)	121, 182	116, 121

TABLE 4 (cont.)

Flavonoids	Roman References	German References
Apigenin-7-glucoside (2″, 3″)-diacetate	182, 220	116, 121, 157
Apigenin-7-glucoside (apigetrin)	-	155
Apigenin-7-glucoside (3″,4″)-diacetate	-	155
Axillarin	-	33
Chrysoeriol	-	32, 33, 157
Chrysoeriol-7-glucoside	-	116
Chrysoplenol	-	32, 33
Chrysosplentin	-	33
6,7-Dimethoxyquercetin	-	32
6,3-Dimethoxyquercetin	-	32
Eupaletin	-	32, 33
Eupatoletin	-	33
6-Hydroxy-luteolin-7-glucoside	-	116
Isorhamnetin		33, 116
Isorhamnetin-7-glucoside	-	116
Jaceidin	-	32, 33
Kaempferol	-	33
''Lipophiles Flavon''	-	116
Luteolin	182	116, 121, 157
Luteolin-4′-glucoside	-	116

TABLE 4 (cont.)

Flavonoids	Roman References	German References
Luteolin-7-glucoside	121, 182, 220	116, 157
Luteolin-7-rhamnoglucoside	-	116
6-Methoxy-kaempferol	-	32,33
Patuletin	-	33, 116, 157
Patuletin-7-glucoside	-	116
Quercetagetin-3,5,6,7,3',4' hexamethylether	-	157
Quercetagetin-3,6,7,3',4' pentamethylether	-	157
Quercetagetin-3,6,7,3' tetramethylether	-	157
Quercetin	-	116, 157
Quercetin-3-galactoside (hyperin, hyperosid)	-	116,
Quercetin-7-glucoside (quercimeritrin)	-	116, 157
Quercetin-3-rutinoside (rutin)	182	116, 121
Quercetrin	121	-
Spinacetin	-	33

Other Organics	Roman References	German References
Amino acids	-	121, 123
Anthemic acid	48, 67, 210	-
Ascorbic acid	-	123
Bornyl acetate	-	28, 149

TABLE 4 (cont.)

Other Organics	Roman References	German References
(-)-Butane-1,3-diyl-1-([Z]-2′-methyl- 2′-butenoate)-3-isobutyrate	194	-
n-Butanol	139	-
Butyl angelate	21, 118, 140	-
Capric acid	-	123
Caprylic acid	-	123
Carrotanacetone homologues	195	-
Catechin tannin	-	142
Chamomilla ester I	-	160
Chamomilla ester II	-	160
Chlorogenic acid	-	123
Choline	121	58, 121
Crimson red aldehyde	-	138
β -Damascenone	195	142
Dehydromatricana ester	220	-
cis-en-yn-Dicycloether	-	11, 152, 160
trans-en-yn-Dicycloether	-	82, 152, 160
2,4-Dihydroxybenzoic acid (syringic acid)	-	157
2,5-Dihydroxybenzoic acid (gentisic acid)	-	157
2,3-D-Dihydroxycinnamic acid (anthenoblic acid)	79, 220	-
3,4-Dihydroxycinnamic acid (caffeic acid)	73, 79, 142	157

TABLE 4 (cont.)

Other Organics	Roman References	German References
ε-1-(2,6-Dimethylphenyl) -2-buten-1-one	195	-
Epicatechol	71	-
Ethyl benzoate	-	142
Ethyl decanoate	-	142
Ethyl palmitate	-	142
Ethyl phenylacetate	-	142
Ferulic acid	73, 142	-
Fructose	-	123
Furfural	-	60
5-(3-Furyl)-2-methyl-1 -penten-3-ol (lepalol)	195	-
5-(3-Furyl)-2-methyl-1 -penten-3-one (lepalone)	195	-
Galactose	-	123
Gallic acid tannin	-	142
Geraniol	-	123
Glucose	-	123
Herniarin	-	47, 153, 159
Hexylacetate	118, 140	-
Hexylbutyrate	21	-
Hydrocarbons	-	185
4-Hydroxy-3-methoxy- benzoic acid (vanillic acid)	-	157

TABLE 4 (cont.)

Other Organics	Roman References	German References
3-Hydroxy-4-methoxycinnamic acid (isoferulic acid)	-	157
3-(2-Hydroxyphenyl)-2-propenoic acid (o-cumaric acid)	-	157
3-(4-Hydroxphenyl)-2-propenoic acid (p-cumaric acid)	-	157
3-Hydroxy-2-methylidene-butyric acid angelate	106	-
Isoamyl angelate (isopentyl)	21, 140	-
Isoamyl butyrate (isopentyl)	21	-
Isoamyl-2-methylbutyrate	21	-
Isoamyl propionate	139, 140	-
Isobutanol	102	-
Isobutyl angelate	21, 140	-
Isobutyl butyrate	140	-
Isobutyl isobutyrate	21	-
Isobutyl isovalenianate	140	-
Isobutyl-2-methylbutyrate	21	-
4-Isopropenyl benzaldehyde	195	-
4-Iospropenyl toluene	140	-
5-Isopropenyl-2-(2-methylpropyl)-2-cyclohexen-1-one	196	-
5-Isopropyl-2-propyl-2-cyclohexen-1-one	196	-

TABLE 4 (cont.)

Other Organics	Roman References	German References
Linoleic acid	-	123
Malic acid	-	123
Methacrylic acid and esters	60, 139, 140	-
4-Methoxybenzoic acid (anisic acid)	-	157
3-Methylamyl angelate	140	-
3-Methyl-1-butanol (isopentyl or isoamyl alcohol)	139	-
3-Methylbutyl angelate	118	-
2-Methylbutyl butyrate	118	-
α-Methylbutyl isobutyrate	140	-
2-Methylbutyl-2-methylbutyrate	21	-
2-Methylbutyl-2-methyl propionate	118	-
3-Methylidene-4-oxpentyl angelate	106	-
2-Methylidenepropane-1,3-diyl -1-[z]-2'- methyl-2'-butenoate) 3-isobutyrate	194	-
d-3-Methyl-pentanol	102, 139	-
3-Methylpentyl angelate	118	-
2-Methylpropane-1,3-diyl-1 [Z]-2' -methyl-2'-butenoate] 3- isobutyrate	194	-
2-Methyl-2-propyl angelate	21, 118	-
2-Methylpropyl butyrate	118	-
2-Methylpropyl 2-methyl butyrate	118	-

TABLE 4 (cont.)

Other Organics	Roman References	German References
2-Methylpropyl 3-methyl butyrate	118	-
Niacin	-	123
Oleic acid	-	123
Palmitic acid	-	123
Pectic acid	-	213
Phenolic acid	20	159
Perillyl alcohol	-	123
Polyacetylene	13, 80	142
Polysaccharides	-	51, 52, 53, 54, 110
Propyl angelate	21, 140	-
Rhamnose	-	123
Salicylic acid	-	123
Scopoletin-7-glucoside	121, 220	-
Scopoletol	73, 220	-
Sinapic acid	-	157
Tannin	48, 210	57, 216
Taraxasterol	220	-
Thiamine	-	123
Tiglic acid and esters	140, 210	-
Triacontane	102	123
Umbelliferone	-	102, 121, 153
Xylose	-	123

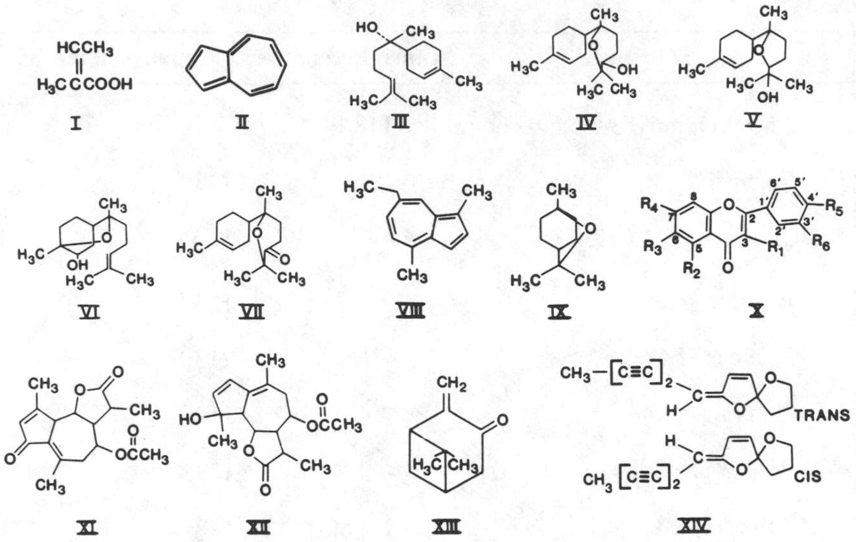

Figure 2. The Chemical Structure of Major Compounds in Chamomiles.

I. Angelic acid

II. Azulene

III. (–)-α-Bisabolol

IV. (–)-α-Bisabololoxide A

V. (–)-α-Bisabololoxide B

VI. (–)-α-Bisabololoxide C

VII. (–)-α-Bisabolonoxide A

VIII. Chamazulene

IX. 1,8-Cineole

X. Flavonoids

XI. Matricarin

XII. Matricin

XIII. Pinocarvone

XIV. Spiroethers

production (44). However, the actual quantity of bisabolol in oil probably depends upon the plant's growth environment (42). The quantity of prochamazulene/chamazulene in German chamomile oil appears genetically controlled (87).

German chamomile oil also contains en-yn-dicycloether, several terpenoids, azulenes, and a large number of different flavonoid compounds (20, 32, 33, 111, 121, 197). As in Roman chamomile, the azulenes in the oil are formed from natural plant precursors during distillation (130).

D. Biosynthesis of the Essential Oil

Attempts have been made to trace the synthesis of chemical constituents in the essential, oils of the chamomiles by using radioactively labeled starting components. Injecting 1-^{14}C acetate into the receptacle of German chamomile flowers leads to approximately a 2-percent incorporation of radioactive carbon into the tissue (84). The

TABLE 5. The Major Chamomile Chemical Constituents and Their Selected Properties.

	Common Name	Chemical Name	Chemical Formula	CA Number[a]	Physical Constants[b]
I.	Angelic acid	(Z)-2-methyl-2-butenoic acid (210)	$C_5H_8O_2$	565-63-9	Bp_{12} 86°C Bp_{760} 185°C $UV_{max}(H_2O)$ 217 nm
II.	Azulene	Bicyclo [5.3.0] deca-1,3,5,7,9-pentaene cyclopenta-cycloheptene (210)	$C_{10}H_8$	275-51-4	Mp 98.5-99°C
III.	(−)- α -Bisabolol	(−)-(1′S, 2S)-6-methyl-2-(4-methyl-3-cyclohexen-1-yl)-5-hepten-2-ol (40)	$C_{15}H_{26}O$	515-69-5	Bp_{13} 154–156°C ND_{20} 1.4939
IV.	(−)- α -Bisabolol-oxide A	(−)-(1′S, 3S, 6S)-tetrahydro-2,2,6-trimethyl-6-(4-methyl-3-cyclo-hexen-1-yl)-2H-pyran-3-ol (40)	$C_{15}H_{26}O_2$	22567-36-8	Bp_{10} 156–158°C
V.	(−)- α -Bisabolol-oxide B	(−)-1″S,2′S,5′)-1-methyl-1-[tetrahydro-5-methyl-5-(4-methyl-3-cyclo-hexen-1-yl) furan-2-yl] ethanol (40)	$C_{15}H_{26}O_2$	26184-88-3	Mp 99°C ND_{20} 1.5010
VI.	(−)- α -Bisabolol-oxide C	1,3-dimethyl-3-(4-methyl-3-pentyl)-2-oxabicyclo [2.2.2] octan-6-ol	$C_{15}H_{26}O_2$	59861-08-4	Mp 99–100°C
VII.	(+)- α -Bisabololn-oxide A	(+)-1′S,6S)-tetra-hydro-2,2,6-tri-methyl-6-(4-methyl- 3-cyclohexen-1-yl)-2H-pyran-3-one (40)	$C_{15}H_{24}O_2$	58985-73-2	
VIII.	Chamazulene	1,4-dimethyl-7-ethylazulene (210)	$C_{14}H_{16}$	529-05-5	Bp_{12} 161°C UV_{max} 370 nm
IX.	1,8-Cineole (eucalyptol, cajeputol)	1,8-epoxy-p-methane	$C_{10}H_{18}O$	470-82-6	Bp 175–177°C Mp 1.5°C ND_{20} 1.455–1.460
X.	Flavonoid (parent structure)		$C_{15}H_{10}O_2$[c]		
XI.	Matricarin (proazulene)	4-(acetyloxy)-3,3a, 4,5,9a,9b-hexahydro-3,6,9-trimethyl-azuleno [4,5-b]furan-2, 7-dione	$C_{17}H_{20}O_5$	5989-45-5	Mp 190–191°C UV_{max} 225 nm

[a]CAS Number=*Chemical Abstracts Registry Service Handbook* number.
[b]Bpn=boiling point at pressure of n millimeters of mercury; °C = degrees centigrade. Mp=melting point; nm=naometers; ND_{20}=refractive index; $UV_{max}(H_2O)$=light absorption peak; [α] = optical rotation.
[c]Rn with side chains as hydrogen atoms; chemical name, chemical formula, CAS number, and physical constants vary depending upon side chains of the parent compound.

TABLE 5 (cont.)

XII. Matricin (prochamazulene)	(−)-(3S,3aR,4S, 9R,9aS,9bS)-4-acetoxo-2,3,3a, 4,5,9,9a,9b-octahydro-9-hydroxy-3,6,9-trimethylazuleno [4,b-b]furan-2-one	$C_{17}H_{22}O_5$	29041-35-8	Mp 159°C [α] +30 in chloroform
XIII. Pinocarvone (*trans*-pinocarvone)	2(10)-pinen-3-one	$C_{10}H_{14}O$	19890-00-7	Bp4 67–69°C
XIV. Spiroethers (*cis*- and *trans*-en-yn-dicyclo-ether)	2-(2,4-hexadiyn-ylidene)-1,6-diox-aspiro[4,4]non-3-ene	$C_{13}H_{12}O_2$	16863-61-9	*trans* Mp 48.5–49.5°C *cis* [α] 20.5°C–104.4° as oil in ether

highest concentration of ^{14}C in tissue, following injection with the labeled acetate, occurred after some days and was located in en-yn-dicycloether and an unknown polar compound. Large differences in the incorporation of acetate, mevalonic acid, and leucine into the bisaboloids of 3 German chamomile chemotypes have been reported a few hours after application of the starting ^{14}C-labeled components (81). Angelic, isobutyric, and methacrylic esters of Roman chamomile appear to be derived from amino acids by oxidative degradation (196). Biogenetically, α-bisabolol first forms α-bisaboloxide A and then α-bisabolonoxide A. α-Bisaboloxide B can also be formed from α-bisabolol (114, 174).

The site of synthesis for various components of chamomile essential oils has not been extensively studied. Schilcher (174) suggests that a sesquiterpene glycoside associated with the biomembranes in the cytoplasm or in the excretory glandular trichomes is involved in the biosynthesis of German chamomile oil. A positive prochamazulene (matricin) content has been established histochemically in the glandular hairs of both the yellow tubular (202) and the ligulate (117, 184) flowers of German chamomile. One study reports that the tubular flowers contribute 68 to 70 percent of the weight of the flower and contain more oil (1.14 percent) than ligulate flowers with the receptacles (0.76 percent) (28). The flower receptacles of German chamomile are reported to contain 2 to 3 times more oil than either the tubular or ligulate flowers (130). The receptacles contain the highest tissue concentration of farnesene, borneol, en-yn-dicycloether, and α-bisaboloxide A, particularly if collected in the morning (28). A diurnal rhythm in concentration of α-bisabolol and certain other sesquiterpenes, but not oil content, has been observed in German chamomile flowers using periodogram and cosinor analyses (164). Increases in plant content of en-yn-dicycloether, bisabolol, and chamazulene occur in the mornings and evenings (28). Increases of farnesene and bisabolol oxides are observed in the mornings but not

TABLE 6. Characteristics of the Major Chamomile Chemical Constituents.

Compound	Characteristics
I. Angelic acid	Isomerized to tiglic acid by boiling. Esters of angelic and tiglic acid comprise about 85 percent of the essential oil from Roman chamomile (121). Has a spicy odor and is soluble in hot water, alcohol, and ether. Classified as a sedative (210). Also present in plants such as *Angelicae archangelica* L. of the Apiaceae family (59).
II. Azulene	Blue-colored component of chamomile essential oil. The color is related to the 5 conjugated double bonds and can range in different azulenes from blue to violet or green. Derived from matricarin during steam distillation. An antiinflammatory agent (59) also present in essential oils of other plants such as camphor, wormwood, and eucalyptus.
III. (−)- α-Bisabolol IV. (−)- α-Bisabololoxides A V. (−)- α-Bisabololoxides B VI. (−)- α-Bisabololoxides C VII. (−)- α-Bisabolonoxide A	Both geometric and steroisometric isomers are possible. The isopropylid type structure in chamomile is (−)-α-bisabolol and comprises up to 50 percent of the essential oil in some species of German chamomile (37). (−)-α-Bisabolol is oxygenated to 4 different compounds, of which 3 have been reported to have the "S" configuration (38). The bisabolols possess a number of biologically active properties (86, 93, 97).
VIII. Chamazulene	First isolated in 1926 and synthesized in 1960 (210). Derived from matracin with catalyzing action of steam and/or pH during distillation. Initially credited with all medicinal properties of German chamomile. Also present in such plants as wormwood and yarrow (210).
IX. 1,8-Cineole	An oil with the odor of camphor. One of the more abundant terpenoid compounds of Roman chamomile (140). Used in pharmaceutical preparations as a mild anesthetic and antiseptic (59). Occurs in as many as 260 essential oils (59).
X. Flavonoids	Visible compounds (mostly yellow) that absorb light in range of 250 to 380 nm. Present as free flavonoids or glycones with 36 recognized in German chamomile and 7 recognized in Roman chamomile (20, 32, 33, 72, 76, 113, 116, 121). Many soluble in water, creating a yellow-colored tea. Some flavonoids may have medicinal properties (64). Occur widely in many plant species.
XI. Maricarin XII. Matricin	Both considered to be precursors of azulenic compounds: matricarin toazulene and matricin to chamazulene (39, 77, 101, 130, 142, 220). The quantity of matricin in flower is used as a standard for chamazulene content (123).
XIII. Pinocarvone (*trans*-pinocarvone)	The major component of Roman chamomile. Also reported in Spanish *Eucalyptus globulus* oil (140).

TABLE 6 (cont.)

XIV. Spiroethers	Both *cis-* and *trans*-en-yn-dicycloether occur in oil of German chamomile. Other spiroethers have also been reported in German chamomile (26). The *cis* form, more pharmacologically potent than *trans* form, has antispasmodic and antiinflammatory activity (14, 152).

evenings. A change in chemical constituency during the day leaves only traces of farnesene in tissue by evening. No diurnal rhythm in content of farnesol has been measured. These changes in composition were reported to be not significant in terms of harvesting (164). Fluctuations in concentrations of compounds have also been observed in Roman chamomile (167).

IV. MEDICINAL APPLICATIONS

A. Medicinal Preparations and Uses

In many countries throughout the world, Roman and German chamomile products are widely used as remedies for minor digestive disorders, as skin washes and fomentations, and as mild sedatives.

TABLE 7. Range in Chemical Constituents of the Essential Oil among German Chamomile Chemotypes.[a]

Constituent	Flower Content (mg/100 g of tissue)
Essential oil	590 to 992
α-Bisabolol	traces to 5.1
α-Bisabololoxide A	13.1 to 74.4
α-Bisabololoxide B	1.3 to 8.6
α-Bisabolonoxide A	5.0 to 66.8
Chamazulene	traces to 9.8
En-yn-dicycloether	7.5 to 12.0
Farnesene	3.0 to 12.2

[a]From data of Reichling *et al.* (157).

Preparations of warm and cold infusions of German and Roman chamomile serve as medicinal agents and as health-related beverages, representing the largest use of chamomile flowers on the market. Both chamomiles have been employed as anti-inflammatory, antibacterial, antispasmodic, and sedative agents. Hydrophobic and hydrophilic components of German chamomile have smooth muscle relaxant effects (3, 98). Extracts have been reported to have deodorant and astringent properties, to promote granulation and epithelization, to alleviate pain and irritation, to gently cleanse wounds and ulcers, to increase sloughing of necrotic tissue, and to aid prophylaxis and therapy of irradiated skin injuries (86). Commercial products have been formulated from chamomile for cystitis (23), dental afflictions (147), shaving emulsions (162), veterinary uses (10), and cosmetic applications (101).

Infusions, made by steeping fresh or dried flowers in water (15 g/240 ml) are used both internally and externally (123). Large doses of a warm infusion have been used as an emetic, while cold infusions have been used as a digestive aid and for colic, fevers, and flatulence (146, 211). Infusions are applied externally as a fomentation or as a wash on wounds and sores. Infusions are also used in hair formulations. Decoctions, prepared by boiling flowers in water, are used as antispasmodic agents (90).

Several chamomile flower preparations are commercially available for use in health products. Milled whole flowers with short sections (approximately 2.5 centimeters) of stem attached are used for tea production. Disc flowers, called "pollen," are additives in many commercial products (126). Seeds of chamomile are added to teas to increase density (126). A rubbing oil made from fresh or dried flowers steeped in olive oil for 24 hours has been used for painful joints and swellings (87).

Although tinctures made from chamomile flowers are also commercially available, these products are commonly prepared in the home. The Roman or German chamomile flowers are extracted with 30- to 50- or 70-percent alcohol, respectively, at a ratio of 20-percent weight of flowers per volume of alcohol (47). Since alcohol is used in preparing the tincture, the constituents in the tincture are similar to the chemical constituents in the essential oils extracted with alcohol.

Many of the commercial German chamomile products are made from fluid extracts standardized to a minimum value of chamazulene and α-bisabolol (123). For example, a common standardized German chamomile product on the market is Kamillosan®(Table 8). On the West German market, at least 18 different medicinal preparations can currently be identified as containing German chamomile. These preparations are recommended for a variety of external and internal uses. However, extracted chamomile products should not be used in the eyes because of the residual alcohol content.

TABLE 8. A Standardized Preparation of German Chamomile Extract.[a]

Kamillosan®, a product of Chemiewerke Homburg Pharmaceutical, Division of Degussa, Frankfurt, West Germany.

Formulation	Constituents
Liquid	100 milliliters of alcoholic extract standardized to contain 150 milligrams of essential oil from flowers; minimum content of 3 milligrams of chamazulene and 50 milligrams of α-bisabolol.
Ointment	400 milligrams of dry extract and 20 milligrams of essential oil mixed in 100 grams of a fatty ointment base; minimum content of 0.4 milligrams of chamazulene and 7 milligrams of α-bisabolol.

[a]Both formulations of Kamillosan® are used on inflammations of the gums and oral cavity, rectum and urogenital region, and other mucous membranes (86). The formulations are also used for skin baths and enemas and as aids in curing bronchitis, stomach ulcers, digestive disorders, wounds, and dermatitis (168).

B. Pharmacology

The pharmacology and toxicology of a plant and plant products are directly related to the active constituents. Unless a chamomile preparation is described in terms of the individual constituents, predictable and reproducible pharmacological effects may not occur. Countries such as Germany, where medicinal uses of chamomile are extensive, have developed standards for the essential oil content of the flower and for the chamazulene and α-bisabolol content of various products (123).

The azulenes of both species of chamomile have been documented to be antiallergenic and anti-inflammatory (34), although the mechanism of action is unclear. Stern and Milin (183) have suggested the azulenes prevent discharge of histamine from tissues by activating the pituitary-adrenal system, causing the release of cortisone. Cortisone prevents the action of fibrolysin that normally initiates proteolysis and histamine release, giving antiallergenicity activity. Meer and Meer (130) have suggested that azulenes cause histamine release through mechanical and chemical means, activating cellular resistance and speeding the process of healing. The prevention of allergic seizures by the azulenes suggests that the inhibition of histamine release is the true mechanism of action. Azulenes have been shown to prevent allergic seizures in guinea pigs as long as 60 minutes after administration (183).

The anti-inflammatory effects of extracts from the chamomiles have been demonstrated in several tests. Oral intake of prochamazulene (matricin) has proved to be an effective therapeutic agent in the carrageenin inflammation test on a rat paw (179). The activity of the azulenes chamazulene and guaiazulene in a carrageenin inflammation test are about equal to each other but less therapeutically active than prochamazulene 2 to 3 hours after application (94). Anti-inflammatory activity for other constituents in German chamomile has also been reported (Table 9)(179).

TABLE 9. Anti-inflammatory Activity of German Chamomile Extracts.

Compound	Anti-inflammatory Test	
	CE[a]	CPG[b]
	$(ED_{50}$ in mg/kg oral$)^c$	
Essential Oil	--	35
Azulene	850	30
Guaiazulene	1100	32
Bisabolol	2200	34
Phenylbutazone	16	33
Indomethacin	4.5	4.5

[a]Carrageenin edema of a rat paw.
[b]Cotton pellet granuloma in rats.
[c]Effective dose for use of 50 percent of animals; data of Shipochliev *et al.* (179).

Azulene compounds are known to stimulate liver regeneration. Subcutaneous treatment of partially hepatectomized rats with azulene compounds, including guaiazulene, will initiate formation of new tissue (49). Oil from German chamomile plants has a similar action in rats, but oil from Roman chamomile plants contains a lower concentration of azulenes than German chamomile oil and will not stimulate liver regeneration after subcutaneous application (49). Similarly, guaine, a hydroderivative of the sesquiterpene alcohol guaiol, is not an effective subcutaneous treatment for partially hepatectomized rats. However, both guaine and oil from Roman chamomile plants are effective therapeutic agents if given orally. Apparently, the gastrointestinal tract of the rat may initiate sufficient aromatization of the sesquiterpenes to increase their effectiveness.

One of the principal components of German chamomile, α-bisabolol, is reported to have anti-inflammatory, antibacterial, antimycotic, and ulcer-protective properties with low toxicity (92). The anti-inflammatory activity of α-bisabolol is greater than that of bisabololoxide A, bisabololoxide B, bisabolonoxide A, (±)-α-bisabolol, or (+)-α-bisabolol (97). Anti-inflammatory activity of α-bisabolol has been demonstrated in yeast fever of the rat, ultraviolet erythema of the guinea pig, and adjuvant arthritis of the rat (97, 98).

Ulcer development induced by indomethacin, stress, and ethanol in animal tests is inhibited by α-bisabolol (189). Healing times for ulcers induced by chemical stress or heat coagulation are reduced by α-bisabolol (189). The commercial chamomile extract Kamillosan®inhibits ethanol-induced ulceration (189). *In vitro* studies with bisabolol have demonstrated a dose-dependent antipeptic activity (not related to pH) that will decrease the proteolytic activity of pepsin by 50 percent when α-bisabolol is administered in a ratio of 1 to 0.5 (95). α-Bisabolol and α-bisabol oxides are also generally considered to be smooth muscle relaxants (3, 95). However, α-bisabolol loses effectiveness after contact with the substrate (95).

Spiroether occurs in the *cis-* and *trans-* configuration in German chamomile, and the *cis-* form of this compound has been demonstrated to inhibit the development of dextran-induced edema and decrease plasmakininogen in rats (14). However, *cis*-en-yn-dicycloether does not inhibit local edema caused by the injection of serotonin, histamine, or bradykinin (14). The smooth muscle relaxing effects of *cis*-en-yn-dicycloether are not linearly dose-dependent (3), but this compound is more active than papaverine on the isolated intestine of guinea pigs and rabbits (152). En-yn-dicycloether does not decrease anaphylactic shock in guinea pigs (152). A local inflammatory reaction is produced by injection of en-yn-dicycloether into the blood stream (14).

The sesquiterpenoids nobilin, 1,10-epoxynobilin, and 3-dehydro-nobilin (compounds that occur in Roman chamomile) have demonstrated antitumor activity against human tumor cells with *in vitro* studies (65, 121). Hydroxy-isonobilin is reported to have an effective dose (ED_{50}) cytotoxicity level against HeLa of 0.56 μ/ml and against KB of 1.23 μg/ml. This activity at a low concentration (less than the arbitrary acceptable test level of 4 μg/ml) qualifies hydroxy-isonobilin for further testing (56).

The flavonoids and coumarins from German chamomile must also be considered as having active medicinal properties (123). Apparently, flavonoids with free hydroxy groups at the 3', 4'-position exert beneficial effects on capillaries (64). The metals that prevent oxidation of ascorbate are chelated. Methyl transferase is inhibited, prolonging epinephrine effects, and the pituitary-adrenal axis is stimulated. Flavonoid glycosides and the flavones apigenin, luteolin, patuletin, quercetin, and apigenin monoglucosides are smooth muscle

TABLE 10. Smooth Muscle Relaxant Effect of the Various Chamomile Compounds.

Compound	Activity[a]
Apigenin	2.34 to 4.62
Apigenin-7(6″-0′acetyl) glucoside	0.29 to 0.55
Apigenin-7-glucoside	0.38 to 0.55
Apiin	0.60 to 0.11
Guercetin	0.46 to 1.09
Patuletin	0.56 to 0.81
Luteolin	0.30 to 0.64
α-Bisaboloi	0.71 to 1.17
Bisabololoxide A	0.39 to 0.55
Bisabololoxide B	0.44 to 0.56
German chamomile oil	0.03 to 0.05

[a]As compared to papaverine with *in vitro* studies. Papaverine activity = 1. Data of Isaac (193).

relaxants (Table 10) (3, 86). The coumarins, herniarin, and umbelliferone are also reported to have minor smooth muscle relaxant activity (130). In addition, many flavonoids have antiviral activity (64), and coumarins have demonstrated antibacterial activity (130).

C. Pharmacodynamics

Anti-inflammatory effects of German chamomile extracts predominate externally, and smooth muscle relaxing effects predominate internally. In initiating smooth muscle relaxation, active components of German chamomile were reported to reside mainly in the water-soluble components of decoctions (90). Treatment of tissue with extracts of German chamomile increases the requirement for acetylcholine and histamine to induce muscle contractions and decrease maximal muscle contractility (40). However, the effects of chamomile on smooth muscle are less than the usual therapeutic doses of atropine. Extracts of German chamomile are reported to enhance uterine tonus (178).

Anti-inflammatory, antipeptic, and smooth muscle relaxant effects of German chamomile extracts on the stomach and duodenum of humans have been demonstrated through gastric biopsies and cytological studies (86). Extracts can be used to help healing after operations on the large intestine and urogenital system (86). Excessive use of extracts as chamomile teas, however, may result in stomach muscle flaccidity (134) and emesis (146, 211).

Extracts of German chamomile apparently do have some sedative effects. Orally administered infusions of German chamomile during cardiac catheterization induced a deep sleep in 10 of 12 patients tested even though some pain is involved in the catheterization procedure and no medication had been given to the patients before treatment (55). Except for a small increase in mean brachial artery pressure, the infusion had no observable cardiac effects. This sedative action of German chamomile has been attributed to the presence of the amino acid tryptophan in the infusion, although support for this hypothesis has not been documented (69).

External applications of German chamomile extracts are reported to change the metabolism of cells in guinea pig skin by increasing creatine phosphate and ATP and decreasing glucose-6-phosphate content (86). This change in energy-dependent processes could aid cellular regeneration and inhibit inflammation. A growth inhibitory effect of German chamomile extracts has also been noted on streptococcal toxins, gram (+) micro-organisms, and fungi (5, 29, 86, 187, 188).

Extracts of German chamomile may be helpful to patients with mucosal and cutaneous infections (141). In a clinical study, individuals with habitual cephthal, pemphigus vulgaris, lichen rubber mucosa, exfoliatio areata lingual, or glossodynia (mucosal affections) were treated with mouthwashes of diluted chamomile extracts. The treated patients indicated that, except in the case of glossodynia, chamomile mouthwashes used 5 to 6 times daily (alternated with water or saline for comparison) provided a cooling and astringent effect.

For evaluation of chamomile therapy against cutaneous infections, patients with acute skin alterations on lower legs from dermatitis statica were treated with Kamillosan®. Dressings containing Kamillosan®, in addition to the standard basic treatment of calcium, corticosteroids, and antihistamines, were applied to the infected legs during the first few days. Anti-inflammatory, deodorant, cooling, and slight anesthetic effects were noted by patients from the treatment with chamomile-containing Kamillosan®.

V. TOXICOLOGY

The acute toxicity of Roman and German chamomile oil appears to be relatively low. No phototoxicity has been reported for either chamomile, although acetylenic compounds in many Asteraceae can cause photodermatitis (144). With rabbits, both the oral LD_{50} (dose lethal to 50 percent of the animals) and the dermal LD_{50} of either oil exceeded 5 g/kg of body weight (145). Applied to the backs of hairless mice, the undiluted oils produced no noticeable toxic effects. When applied to normal or abraded rabbit skin for 24 hours, the undiluted oils of both species of chamomile produced some limited irritation. A 48-hour closed-patch test with humans using 4 percent chamomile oils in petrolatum produced no observable irritation (145).

The *Registry of Toxic Effects of Chemical Substances* (122) reports that the LD_{50} of oral $(-)$-α-bisabolol for rats is 14.85 g/kg of body weight and 11.35 g/kg of body weight for mice. No teratogenic effects have been observed at any of the bisabolol dosage levels tested (61). The LD_{50} for orally administered chamazulene in rats is 10 g/kg of body weight, while the LD_{50} for intermuscularly-administered chamazulene in mice is 3 g/kg of body weight (122).

Long-term oral administration of German chamomile extracts to rats produced no teratogenicity or signs of changes in prenatal development (86). Cutaneous application of German chamomile onto rabbits daily for 3 weeks produced no observable toxicity. Inhalations of German chamomile extracts by guinea pigs daily for 3 weeks also produced no signs of toxicity. Long-term oral administration of German chamomile extracts to rats and dogs produced no observable toxicity. Operant rat behavior was not depressed with Roman chamomile essential oil except at the highest dose tested (500 mg/kg of body weight) (46).

VI. ALLERGENICITY

Allergic reactions are often a potential problem with plants due to the variety of compounds within a plant. Anaphylaxis and contact dermatitis have been reportedly induced by the chamomiles (18, 119).

The acute allergenicity to chamomile plants and plant products is generally thought to be quite low (68). However, the development of allergic reactions can be serious, and persons with known sensitivity to other members of the Asteraceae family (such as ragweed, asters, and chrysanthemums) may best be advised to avoid contact with German chamomile, Roman chamomile, or chamomile products. In an allergic study of individuals with known or suspected allergies to Asteraceae, 2 of 25 patients were allergic to the chamomiles, and cross-reactivity was observed between other Asteraceae plants and the chamomiles (66).

A number of compounds (3-carene, α-pinene, limonene, and myrcene) known to cause contact dermatitis are in Roman chamomile oil (31). Sesquiterpene lactones are suggested as sensitizing agents (66), and a number of sesquiterpene lactones are known allergens (31). The prerequisite for allergic activity of sesquiterpene lactones is an exocyclic α-methylene group (144). Deacetyl-matricarin has produced positive test reactions in a sesquiterpene lactone-sensitive patient (137). Nobilin, a sesquiterpene lactone occurring in Roman chamomile, is also potentially allergenic (137).

In a patch test for Roman chamomile oil and extract, 4 of 490 individuals had a positive response (137). Incidents of dermatitis and one case of anaphylaxis have been reported following contact with Roman chamomile (137). An incidence of anaphylaxis from ingestion of chamomile tea has also been reported (18).

A possible serious source of allergic reactions is the contamination of chamomile flowers or chamomile products with other related, but more allergenic, plants. Related species of plants are sometimes unknowingly sold as chamomile or used as adulterants (Table 1). *Anthemis cotula*, known as mayweed or dog fennel, is sold in the American Southwest as chamomile (88). This plant has been used in the past for control of hysteria (209) and is reported to have some medicinal properties in common with the chamomiles (89). However, *Anthemis cotula* is a well-recognized skin irritant (4, 169, 197), and a patch test has produced vesicular erythematous skin lesions within 24 hours on nearly all children and adults tested (169). The proper identification and purity of the chamomiles and chamomile products should always be established in order to minimize the number of allergic reactions.

VII. COMMERCIAL FORMULATIONS

In addition to medicinal applications, extracts of the chamomiles are used as a scent or scent enhancer in several cosmetic products (7), a nonirritating hair dye (170), and occasionally, as a flavoring agent in alcoholic beverages (7). The essential oil of Roman chamomile is added as a trace ingredient to perfumes to give a fresh, warm note and depth. Both steam-distilled and solvent-extracted German chamomile oil are used in quality perfumes to create a rich undertone (8). The essential oil of German chamomile is also added to soaps, lotions, and creams (Table 11) (47, 145).

Several compounds in Roman and German chamomile are responsible for the scent. Farnesol, present in the essential oil of both chamomiles, is used in fragrances to create harmony and to enhance floral odors (193). The farnesol is normally in the *trans- trans-* form and produces an odor similar to linden blooms and angelica seeds.

TABLE 11. Commercial Products Containing Chamomile Oils.[a]

Product	Content of Roman or German Chamomile Oil in Product (% oil)	
	Usual	Maximum
Creams	0.0020	0.020
Detergents	0.0005	0.006
Perfume	0.0400	0.400
Soap	0.0050	0.060
	Roman	German
	(UL/liter)	
Alcoholic beverages	20.0	1.0
Baked goods	4.3	6.5
Candies	4.3	3.8
Ice creams	3.3	6.1
Nonalcoholic beverages	2.3	2.6

[a]Data of Furia and Bellanca (47) and Opdyke (145).

Concentrated farnesol has a weak odor whereas low concentrations have a sweet, tenacious, floral odor (193).

Borneol, present in both Roman and German chamomiles, and bornyl acetate, present in German chamomile, have a piney, camphoraceous odor and are used to perfume soaps and detergents (50). α-Bisabolol in German chamomile has a pleasant odor and is used in perfumes as a fixative (193). Nerolidol, reported to be in Roman chamomile, has a sweet, tenacious odor suggestive of roses and apples and is used to harmonize compositions with floral components. Pure nerolidol has a weak but persistent odor (193).

Newly isolated ketones such as (E)-1-(2,6-dimethylphenyl)-2-buten-1-one, 4-isopropenylbenzaldehyde, 5-(3-furyl)-2-methyl-1-penten-3-ol, and 5-(3-furyl)-2-methyl-1-penten-3-one are reported to add to the odor of Roman chamomile oil (195). Of these compounds, 4-isopropenylbenzaldehyde has the strongest odor, one resembling a cuminaldehyde-type odor.

The low toxicity and yellow-coloring agents (apigenin, apigenin glucoside, and other flavonoids) in both Roman and German chamomile flowers have promoted their use in vegetable hair dyes (170). The flowers are used in hair rinses, packs, and shampoos to add yellow color to hair. A hair rinse, produced from a strong infusion of flowers made with boiling water, is generally poured over the hair several times after shampooing. Packs of chamomile flowers, preferably Roman, are made with 2 parts powdered flowers mixed with 1 part kaolin or Fuller's earth from which a thin paste (made in boiling water) is applied to the hair.

The resultant hair color following use of chamomile-based hair dyes depends upon the original hair color and the length of application time, although repeated applications of chamomile to any hair color are reported to produce a brilliant yellow (170). For a less glaring yellow color, chamomile is mixed with henna, *Lawsonia inermis* L. Some examples of commercial hair formulations are presented in Table 12.

TABLE 12. Use of Chamomiles in Hair Formulations.[a]

Product	Ingredients	Composition (%)		
Rinse	Roman chamomile flowers, powdered	40		
	Oil of chamomile	0.2		
	Alcohol (20%) to make . . .	100		
	Dilute 10 ml of product to 1 liter with water.			
Powdered shampoo	German chamomile flowers, powdered	10		
	Mild organic acid	5		
	Sodium lauryl sulfate	85		
	Oil of chamomile for perfume	Trace		
Liquid shampoo	Chamomile infusion	10		
	Sodium lauryl sulfate	30 to 40		
	Water	50 to 60		
Dye Mixture (Chamomile: Henna)	3:1	1:1	1:3	
Original Hair Color	Expected Hair Color			
Blond	Golden blonde	Red gold	Golden red	
Light brown	Light auburn	Auburn	Auburn	
Dark brown	Chestnut	Red brown	Dark auburn	

[a]Data from Sagarin (170).

Acknowledgements

The authors wish to thank Ms. Randi Tesdahl, Mr. Dave Casper, Ms. Shari Fodness, and Mr. John H. Staba for their invaluable assistance in compiling and editing the original manuscript and references.

VIII. REFERENCES

1. Abou-Zeid, E.N. and S.S. El-Sherbeeny. 1974. Preliminary study on the effect of gibberellic acid on quality and quantity of the volatile oil of *Matricaria chamomilla*. Egypt. J. Physiol. Sci. 1:63–70.

2. Abou-Zied, E.N. and A.M. Rizk. 1973. Phytochemical investigation of *Anthemis nobilis* L. growing in Egypt. Qual. Plant. et Mater. Veg. 22:141–144.

3. Achterrath-Tuckermann, U., R. Kunde, E. Flaskamp, O. Isaac, and K. Thiemer. 1980. Pharmacological investigations with compounds of chamomile. V. Investigations on the spasmolytic effect of compounds of chamomile and Kamillosan®on the isolated guinea pig ileum. Planta Med. 39:38–50.

4. Addo, H.A., B.E. Johnson, and W. Frain-Bell. 1980. A study of the relationship between contact allergic sensitivity and persistent light reaction. J. Dermatol. 103:20–21.

5. Aggag, M.E. and R.T. Yousef. 1972. Antimicrobial activity of chamomile oil. Planta Med. 22:140–144.

6. Amat, A.G. 1982. Interes farmacobotanico de las "Manzanillas": Principios activos, sustituyentes y estado taxonomico. Acta Farm. Bonaerense 1:49–52.

7. Andre, M.M. 1984. Letter to E. John Staba, College of Pharmacy, University of Minnesota, June 5.

8. Arctander, S. 1960. *Perfume and Flavor Materials of Natural Origin.* P.O. Box 114, Elizabeth, NJ. 736 p.

9. Bailey, L.H. and E.Z. Bailey. 1976. *Hortus Third.* Macmillan, New York. 1290 p.

10. Bartos, J. 1972. Dietan (linseed, chamomile, oak bark) in the prevention and treatment of gastro-enteritis in new-born calves. Veterinaria (Prague) 14:39–42.

11. Becker, H., J. Reichling, and W-C Hsieh. 1982. Water-free solvent system for droplet counter-current chromatography and its suitability for the separation of non-polar substances. J. Chromatogr. 237:307–310.

12. Behr, N., O. Von Ettingshausen, H. Van der Mei, and R. Wuest. 1982. Components of chamomile by extraction with carbon dioxide. Patent EP 58365 Al. August 25.

13. Bohlmann, F. and W. Skuballa. 1970. Polyacetylenic compounds. 175. Synthesis and biogenesis of Anthemis-thioethers. Chem. Ber. 103:1886–1893.

14. Breinlich, J. and K. Scharnagel. 1968. Pharmakologische Eigenschaften des EN-IN-Dicycloaethers aus *Matricaria chamomilla.* Arzneim.-Forsch. 18:429–431.

15. *British pharmacopoeia.* 1980. Vol. 1. Her Majesty's Stationery Office, London. 940 p.

16. Bsonek, K. 1979. Mikro-DC, eine rationelle Variante der Duennschicht-Chromatographie fur das Apothekenlabor. Pharm. Ztg. 124:755–758.

17. Buckingham, J. and S.M. Donaghy. 1982. *Dictionary of Organic Compounds.* Mack Printing Co., Easton, PA. 5769 p.

18. Casterline, C.L. 1980. Allergy to chamomile tea. J. Am. Med. Assoc. 244:330.

19. Cekan, Z., V. Prochazka, V. Herout, and F. Sorm. 1959. [On terpenes. CI. Isolation and constitution of matricarin, another guaianolide from camomile (*Matricaria chamomilla*).] Collect. Czech. Chem. Commun. 24:1554–1557. Taken from Chem. Abstr. 53:20121f.

20. Chaumont, J.P. 1969. Polyphenols (flavonoids, phenolic acids, coumarins) of the capitula of the Roman camomile (*Anthemis nobilis*). Plant. Med. Phytother. 3:167–174.

21. Chialva, F., G. Gabri, P.A.P. Liddle, and F. Ulian. 1982. Qualitative evaluation of aromatic herbs by direct headspace GC analysis. Applications of the method and comparison with the traditional analysis of essential oil. J. High Resolut. Chromatogr. Chromatogr. Commun. 5:182–188.

22. Chretien-Bessiere, Y., L. Peyron, L. Benezet, and J. Garnero. 1970. A contribution to the knowledge of the constitution of the essential oil of Roman camomile (*Anthemis nobilis* L.). Soc. Chim. Fr. Bull. 1:381–382.

23. Christopher, J.R. 1976. *School of Natural Healing.* BiWorld Publishers, Inc., Provo, UT. 653 p.

24. Culpepers, N. *Complete Herbal.* W. Foulsham & Co., Ltd., London. (reprint) 430 p.

25. Czabajski, T. and S. Doerffer. 1978. Attempts to mechanize the harvest of the flowers of common chamomille (*Matricaria chamomilla*) by using an adapted combine. Wiad. Zielarskie 20:3–4.

26. Debska, W. and T. Bartkowiakowa. 1978. Determination of bisabolol, 'spiroether'[5-(hexa-2, 4-diynylene)-2,2',3',4',5,5'-hexahydro-2,2'-spirobifuran] and chamazulene in *Matricaria chamomilla* flower heads. Acta Pol. Pharm. 35:699–700.

27. Debska, W. and S. Domeracki. 1973. Determination of residual pesticides and their degradation products in vegetable drugs and crude drugs. I. Content of organochlorine pesticides in *Matricaria chamomilla* flower heads. Herba Pol. 19:15–22.

28. DePasquale, A. and R. Silvestri. 1976. Content of active substances in the various parts of "*Matricaria chamomilla* L." Essenze Deriv. Agrum. 45:292–298.

29. Detter, A. 1981. Germination inhibitors as drugs? Investigation of the growth inhibiting effects of a chamomile and yarrow extract. Pharm. Ztg. 126:1140–1142.

30. El-Kholy, S.A. and M.M. Saleh. 1980. Effect of thiamine and ascorbic acid on the yield, essential oil, and chamazulene formation in *Matricaria chamomilla* L. Ain Shams Univ. Fac. of Agric. Res. Bull. 1409:19.

31. Evans, F.J. and R.J. Schmidt. 1980. Plants and plant products that induce contact dermatitis. Planta Med. 38:289–316.

32. Exner, J., J. Reichling and H. Becker. 1980. Flavonoide in *Matricaria chamomilla*. Planta Med. 39:219.

33. Exner, J., J. Reichling, T-C-H. Cole, and H. Becker. 1981. Methylated flavonoid-aglycones from "Matricariae Flos." Planta Med. 41:198–200.

34. Farnsworth, N.R. and B.M. Morgan. Herb drinks: Chamomile tea. J. Am. Med. Assoc. 221:410.

35. Felklova, M. and M. Jasicova. 1978. Active compounds of *Matricaria chamomilla*. Cesk. Farm. 27:359–366.

36. Felklova, M., M. Jasicova, L. Trnkova and P. Ciutti. 1981. Effect of mineral nutrients upon the yield and quality of chamomile flowers (*Matricaria chamomilla* L.). Acta Fac. Pharm. Univ. Comenianae 36:69–102.

37. Flaskcamp, E., G. Nonnenmacher, and O. Isaac. 1981. On the diastereoisomerism of natural and synthetic -bisabolols. Z. Naturforsch. 86b:114–118.

38. Flaskcamp, E., G. Nonnenmacher, G. Zimmermann, and O. Isaac. 1981. On the stereochemistry of the bisaboloids from *Matricaria chamomilla* L. Z. Naturforsch. 86b:1023–1030.

39. Flaskcamp, E., G. Zimmermann, G. Nonnenmacher, and O. Isaac. 1982. Studies on the characterization of the chamazulene precursor matricin from *Matricaria chamomilla*. Z. Naturforsch. 37b:508–511.

40. Forster, H.B., H. Niklas, and S. Lutz. 1980. Antispasmodic effects of some medicinal plants. Planta Med. 40:309–319.

41. Franz, Ch. 1980. Content and composition of the essential oil in flower heads of *Matricaria chamomilla* L. during its ontogenetical development. Acta Hortic. 96:317–321.

42. Franz, Ch., D. Fritz, and F.-J. Schroder. 1975. Influence of ecological factors on the essential oils and flavones of two camomile cultivars. 2. Effect of light and temperature. Planta Med. 27:46–52.

43. Franz, Ch., J. Hoelzl, and C. Kirsch. 1983. Influence of nitrogen, phosphorus and potassium fertilization on camomile [*Chamomilla recutita* (L.) Rauschert, syn. *Matricaria chamomilla* L.]. II. Effect on the essential oil. Gartenbauwissenschaft 48:17–22.

44. Franz, Ch. and I. Wickel. 1979. The composition of essential oil in crossing- and selfing-progenies of *Matricaria chamomilla* L. Planta Med. 36:281–282.

45. Frey, M., L. Cotenescu, I. Stancescu, V. Dobrescu, and E. Nichiforescu. 1980. Stabilized extract of *Matricaria chamomillae* flowers. Rom. Patent 68709, June 30.

46. Fundaro, A. and M.C. Cassone. 1980. Effect of the essential oils of chamomile, cinnamon, absinthium, mace, and origanum on operant behavior in rats. Boll. Soc. Ital. Biol. Sper. 56:2375–2380.

47. Furia, T.E. and N. Bellanca, eds. 1975. *Fenaroli's Handbook of Flavor Ingredients*, 2d ed. Vol. 1. CRC Press, Inc., Cleveland, OH. 771 p.

48. Gathercoal, E.N. and E.H. Wirth. 1947. *Pharmacognosy*, 2d ed. Lea & Febiger, Philadelphia, PA. 756 p.

49. Gershbein, L.L. 1977. Regeneration of rat liver in the presence of essential oils and their components. Food Cosmet. Toxicol. 15:173–181.

50. *Givaudan Index, The* 1949. 1st ed. Givaudan-Delawanna, Inc., New York. 378 p.

51. Gorin, A.G. and A.I. Yakovlev. 1974. Polysaccharides of *Matricaria chamomilla*. I. Monosaccharide composition of a polysaccharide complex. Khim. Prir. Soedin. 10:137–141.

52. Gorin, A.G. and A.I. Yakovlev. 1974. Polysaccharides of *Matricaria chamomilla*. I. Monosaccharide composition of the polysaccharide complex. Chem. Nat. Compds. Engl. Transl. 10:151–154.

53. Gorin, A.G. and A.I. Yakovlev. 1975. Chemical study of acid sugars of the polysaccharide of *Matricaria chamomilla*. Nauch. Tr. Ryazan. Med. Inst. 50:5–9.

54. Gorin, A.G. and A.I. Yakovlev. 1975. Products of the enzymic hydrolysis of *Matricaria chamomilla* polysaccharides. Sb. Nauchn. Tr. - Ryazan. Med. Inst. 50:9–12.

55. Gould, L., C.V. Ramana Reddy, and R.F. Gomprecht. 1973. Cardiac effects of chamomile tea. J. Clin. Pharmacol. 13:475–479.

56. Grabarczyk, H, B. Drozdz, B. Hladon, and J. Wojciechowska. 1977. Sesquiterpene lactones Part XV. New cytostatic active sesquiterpene lactone from herb of *Anthemis nobilis* L. Pol. J. Pharmacol. Pharm. 29:419–423.

57. Greenish, H.G. 1933. *A Textbook of Pharmacognosy*, 6th ed. J. & A. Churchill, London. 564 p.

58. Grejtovsky, A. 1976. Study of the effect of activity of B-fructofuranoxidase in soil upon choline and ethereal oil contents in camomile. Farm. Obz. 45:399–404.

59. Guenther, E. 1949. *The Essential Oils*, Vol. 2. D. Van Nostrand Co., New York. 852 p.

60. Guenther, E. 1952. *The Essential Oils*, Vol. 5. D. Van Nostrand Co., New York. pp. 433–445.

61. Habersang, S., F. Leuschner, O. Isaac, and K. Thiemer. 1979. Pharmacological studies with compounds of chamomile. IV. Studies on toxicity of (–)α-bisabolol. Planta Med. 37:115–123.

62. Haikal, M. And M. Badr. 1982. Effect of some GA_3 and CCC treatments on the growth and oil quantity and quality of chamomile. Egypt. J. Hortic. 9:117–123.

63. Halasova, J. and D. Busova. 1974. Ecological factors and their influence on the essential oil content of chamomile in eastern Slovakia. Nase Liecive Rastliny 11:99–103.

64. Harborne, J.B., T.J. Mabry, and H. Mabry., eds. 1975. The Flavonoids. Part 2. Academic Press, New York.

65. Hartwell, J.L. 1968. Plants used against cancer. A survey. J. Nat. Prod. 31:71–170.

66. Hausen, B.M. 1979. The sensitizing capacity of *Compositae* plants. III. Test results and cross-reactions in *Compositae*- sensitive patients. Dermatologica 159:1–11.

67. Hebert, B.E., K.W. Ellery, and F. Hemming. 1948. *Textbook of Practical Pharmacognosy*. Bailliere, Tindall and Cox, London. 372 p.

68. Hegyi, E. 1979. Development tendencies of contact allergy. Allerg. Immunol. 25:104–115.

69. Heinerman, J. 1979. The Science of Herbal Medicine. Bi-World Publishers, Orem, UT. 318 p.

70. Herb ratings by the FDA. 1978. Health Foods Business, June. pp. 53–61.

71. Herisset, A., J.P. Chaumont, and R. Paris. 1970. Roman camomile (*Anthemis nobilis*) polyphenols. Plant. Med. Phytother. 4:189–200.

72. Herisset, A., J.P. Chaumont, and R. Paris. 1973. Flavonoids of Roman chamomille (*Anthemis nobilis* L.), a single flower variety. Plant Med. Phytother. 7:234–240.

73. Herisset, A., J.P. Chaumont, and R. Paris. 1974. Acid phenols and coumarins of the Roman camomile (*Anthemus nobilis* L.), simple variety. Plant Med. Phytother. 8:306–313.

74. Herisset, A., J. Jolivet, and J.P. Chaumont. 1975. Attempts at industrial extraction of essential oil of Roman camomile from the total of aerial parts of the plant (*Anthemis nobilis*). Plant Med. Phytother. 9:140–147.

75. Herisset, A., J. Jolivet, and P. Rey. 1972. Differentiation of some essential oils of similar composition. VI. Essential oil from common chamomile (*Anthemis nobilis*) and wild chamomile (*Matricaria chamomilla*). Plant Med. Phytother. 6:194–203.

76. Herisset, A., R.R. Paris, and J.P. Chaumont. 1971. Flavonoids in Roman camomille (*Anthemis nobilis* L.). Plant Med. Phytother. 5:234–239.

77. Herout, V. and F. Sorm. 1957. Terpenes. LXXX. Structure of matricine, a guaianolide from camomile (*Matricaria chamomilla*). Chem. Listy 51:756–763.

78. Herrmann, R. 1982. New method for detection and determination (–)-alpha-bisabolol in chamomile extracts. Dtsch. Apoth. Ztg. 122:1797–1800.

79. Heywood, V.H. and S.R. Chant. 1982. *Popular Encyclopedia of Plants*. Cambridge University Press, Cambridge. 368 p.

80. Heywood, V.H., J.B. Harborne, and B.L. Turner. 1977. *The Biology and Chemistry of the Compositae*, Vol. I, II. Academic Press, New York. 1189 p.

81. Hoelzl, J. 1979. Investigations on the biosynthesis of sesquiterpenes and spiroethers of *Matricaria chamomilla* L. Planta Med. Abstr. A:226.

82. Hoelzl, J. and G. Demuth. 1975. Influence of ecological factors on the composition of the essential oil and the flavones in *Matricaria chamomilla* of different origin. Planta Med. 27:46–52.

83. Hoelzl, J. and G. Demuth. 1975. Influence of ecological factors on the formation of essential oils and flavones of camomiles anthemis of various origin. I. Critical comparison of quantitative determination methods. Planta Med. 27:37–45.

84. Hoelzl, J., C. Franz, D. Fritz, and A. Voemel. 1975. Biosynthesis of the essential oil by *Matricaria chamomilla*. 1. ^{14}C-labelling of the substances of the essential oil. Z. Naturforsch. 30c:853–854.

85. Holub, M. and Z. Samek. 1977. Isolation and structure of 3-epinobilin, 1,10-epoxynobilin and 3-dehydronobilin - other sesquiterpenic lactones from the flowers of *Anthemis nobilis* L. Revision of the structure of nobilin and eucannabinolide. Collection Czech. Chem. Commun. 42:1053–1064.

86. Homburg Pharma Germany, Division of Degussa. *Kamillosan Scientific Information*. Frankfurt (Main), W. Germany. 12 p.

87. Honcariv, R. and M. Repcak. 1979. Chemotypes of *Matricaria chamomilla* L. Herba Pol. 25:261–267.

88. Huxtable, R.J. 1980. Herbal teas and toxins: Novel aspects of pyrrolizidine poisoning in the United States. Perspect. Biol. Med. 24:1–15.

89. Hylton, W.H., ed. 1974. *The Rodale Herb Book*. Rodale Press Book Division, Emmaus, PA. 653 p.

90. Ingianna, J. and E. Gambassi. 1982. Mecanismo de la accion antiespasmodica intestinal de las flores de *Matricaria chamomilla* L. Rev. Biol. Trop. 30:85–90.

91. Isaac, O. 1975. Stable pharmaceutical extract containing 2,2-dimethyl-4-hydroxymethyl-1,3-dioxolane. Ger. Offen. 2,340,914 (Cl. A61K) 27 Feb.

92. Isaac, O. 1979. Pharmacological investigations with compounds of chamomile I. On the pharmacology of (-)-α-bisabolol and bisabolol oxides (Review). Planta Med. 35:118–124.

93. Isaac, O. 1980. Chamomile therapy-experimentation and verification. Dtsch. Apoth. -Ztg. 120:567–570.

94. Isaac, O. and G. Kristen. 1980. Alte und neue Wege der Kamillentherapie. Med. Welt 31:1145–1149.

95. Isaac, O. and K. Thiemer. 1975. Biochemical studies on camomile components. III. *In vitro* studies about the antipeptic activity of (-)-bisabolol. Arzneim.-Forsch. 25:1352–1354.

96. Jakovlev, V., O. Isaac, and E. Flaskamp. 1983. VI. Investigations on the antiphlogistic effects of chamazulene and matricine. Planta Med. 49:67–73.

97. Jakovlev, V., O. Isaac, K. Thiemer, and R. Kunde. 1979. Pharmacological investigations with compounds of chamomile II. New investigations on the antiphlogistic effects of (-)-α-bisabolol and bisabolol oxides. Planta Med. 35:125–140.

98. Jakovlev, V. and A. von Schlichtegroll. 1969. Zur entzuendungshemmenden Wirkung von (-)-α-Bisabolol, einem wesentlichen Bestandteil des Kamillenoels. Arzneim.-Forsch. 19:615–616.

99. Jeffrey, C. 1979. Note on the lectotypification of the names *Cacalia* L., *Matricaria* L. and *Gnaphalium* L. Taxon (28) 349–351.

100. Jellinek, J.S. 1970. *Formulation and function of cosmetics.* Transl. G.L. Fenton. John Wiley and Sons, Inc. New York. 586 p.

101. Kalemba, D., T. Boruch, and J. Gora. 1982. Extracts of plants and their cosmetic application. Part III. Extracts from inflorescence of *Matricaria chamomilla* L. Pollena: Tluszcze, Srodki Piorace Kosmet. 26:108–113.

102. Karrer, W. 1958. *Konstitution und Vorkommen der Organischen Pflanzenstoffe (exclusive Alkaloide. Birkhaeuser Verlag, Basel. 1207 p.*

103. Karrer, W., E. Cherbuliez, and C.H. Eugster. 1977. *Konstitution und Vorkommen der Organischen Pflanzenstoffe (exclusive Alkaloide. Birkhauser Verlag, Basel. 1038 p.*

104. Kirs, L. 1980. Effect of surfactants on the extraction of flowers of *Matricaria chamomilla* L. and *Matricaria matricarioides*. Tartu Riikliku Ulik. Toim. 523:33–40.

105. Kisgeci, J., D. Adamovic, S. Stanacev, and V. Lukic. 1982. Effect of the sowing method and seed rate on the yield and quality of a Yugoslav chamomile population. Bilt. Hmelj. Sirak. 14:45–50.

106. Klimes, I., D. Lamparsky, and E. Scholz. 1981. Occurrence of new bifunctional esters in Roman camomile oil (*Anthemis nobilis* L.) Helv. Chim. Acta 64:2338–2349.

107. Kocurik, S. 1979. Content variability of the ethereal oil and chamazulene in wild chamomile (*Matricaria chamomilla* L.) (East Slovakian region). Pol'nohospodarstvo 25:67–75.

108. Kocurik, S. and V. Dovjak. 1977. Cultivation of true chamomile below the Tatra mountains. Nase Liecive Rastliny 14:3–6.

109. Kocurik, S. and V. Dovjak. 1979. Effect of molybdenum and boron on dry matter production and drug yield in chamomile (*Matricaria chamomilla*). Nase Liecive Rastliny 16:69–74.

110. Kocurik, S. and L. Gianits. 1979. Saccharides of the flowers of camomile (*Matricaria chamomilla* L.). II. Water-soluble polysaccharide. Farm. Obz. 48:111–118.

111. Konovalova, O.A. and K.S. Rybalko. 1982. Biologically active substances of German camomile. Rastit. Resur. 18:116–127.

112. Konovalova, O.A., K.S. Rybalko, and G.I. Klimakhin. 1981. Effect of drying conditions on the essential oil and prochamazulene content of *Matricaria chamomilla*. Khim.-Farm. Zh. 15:71–72.

113. Kubeczka, K.H., ed. 1982. *Aetherische Ole*. Georg Thieme Verlag, Stuttgart. pp. 104–115.

114. Kubeczka, K.H., ed. 1982. *Aetherische Ole*. Georg Thieme Verlag, Stuttgart. pp. 214–224.

115. Kunde, R. and O. Isaac. 1979. Identification of racemic α-bisabolol in specialities made from chamomile extracts. Planta Med. 35:71–75.

116. Kunde, R. and O. Isaac. 1979. On the flavones of chamomile (*Matricaria chamomilla* L.) and a new acetylated apigenin-7-glucoside. Planta Med. 37:124–130.

117. Lassanyi, Zs., G. Stieber, and E. Tyihak. 1978. Investigations into the volatile oil secretory system of chamomillae anthodium (Flos) I. The histochemical analysis of glandular hairs. Herba Hung. 17:31–42.

118. Lawrence, B.M. 1981. Progress in essential oils. Perfume. Flavor. 6:59–63 April/May.

119. Lawrence, B.M. 1984. Progress in essential oils. Perfume. Flavor. 9:35–45.

120. Lemberkovics, E. 1979. Farnesene isomers in chamomile oil. Sci. Pharm. 47:330–332.

121. Leung, A.Y. 1980. *Encyclopedia of Common Natural Ingredients: Used in Food, Drugs, and Cosmetics*. John Wiley & Sons, New York. 296 p.

122. Lewis, R.J., Sr. and R.L. Tatken, eds. 1980. *Registry of Toxic Effects of Chemical Substances*, Vol. I. National Instit. Occupational Safety and Health, Cincinnati, OH. 828 p.

123. List, P.H. and L. Hoerhammer. 1976. *Hagers Handbuch der Pharmazeutischen Praxis*. Vol. 5. Springer-Verlag, Berlin. pp. 710–719.

124. Marczel, G. and V.G. Petri. 1979. Essential oil production and composition during the ontogeny in *Matricaria chamomilla* L. Herba Hung. 18:325–329.

125. Mathe, I. 1972. Chemical composition changes of the *Matricaria chamomilla* grown in Hungary. Mezhdunar. Kongr. Efirnym Maslam 4:106–108.

126. McCaleb, R.G. 1984. [Letter to E. John Staba, College of Pharmacy, University of Minnesota.] May 3.

127. Mechler, E. 1979. The yield of essential oils according to the two different methods of European pharmacopoeia and German pharmacopoeia, 7th edition. Planta Med. 36:278–279.

128. Mechler, E. and K.A. Kovar. 1977. Vergleichende Bestimmungen des aetherischen Oels in Drogen nach dem Europaeischen und dem Deutschen Arzneibuch. Dtsch. Apoth.-Ztg. 117:1019–1029.

129. Mechler, E. and E. Ruckdeschel. 1980. The yield of essential oils according to the two different methods of European pharmacopoeia and German pharmacopoeia, 7th edition. Acta Hortic. 96:125–132.

130. Meer, G., Jr. and W.A. Meer. 1960. Chamomile flowers. Am. Perfum. November.

131. Meer, W.A. 1984. [Letter to E. John Staba, College of Pharmacy, University of Minnesota.], May 15.

132. Merkes, K. 1981. Drugs with essential oil: *Anthemis nobilis* L. Roman chamomile. PTA Repetitorium 29–32.

133. Messerschmidt, W. Discrepancies in the declaration of chamomile Spitzner. Krankenhaus-Apotheke 30:95–96.

134. Michael, P. 1980. *All Good Things Around Us.* Holt, Rinehart and Winston, New York. 240 p.

135. Mincsovics, E., E. Tyihak, J. Nagy, and H. Kalasz. 1979. Thin-layer chromatographic investigation of components in essential oil of *Matricaria chamomilla* L. by means of classical and pressurized chamber systems. Planta Med. 36:296.

136. Mincsovics, E., E. Tyihak, J. Nagy, and H. Kalasz. 1980. Thin-layer chromatographic investigation of components in essential oil of *Matricaria chamomilla* L. by means of classical and pressurized chamber systems. Acta Hortic. 96:181–188.

137. Mitchell, J. and A. Rook. 1979. *Botanical Dermatology.* Greengrass. Vancouver. 787 p.

138. Motl, O. and M. Repcak. 1979. New components from camomile essential oil. Planta Med. 36:272–273.

139. Nano, G.M., T. Sacco, and C. Frattini. 1973. General study of Anthemis. Essenze Deriv. Agrum. 43:107–114.

140. Nano, G.M., T. Sacco and C. Frattini. 1976. Botanical and chemical studies on *Anthemis nobilis* L. and some of its cultivars. Essenze Deriv. Agrum. 46:171–175.

141. Nasemann, T. 1975. Kamillosan therapy in dermatology. Z. Allgemeinmed. 25:1105–1106.

142. Negoescu, E., M. Botea, L. Mutihac, C. Faraianu, M. Culea, and N. Palibroda. 1982. Qualitative study on compositions of extracts obtained from Romanian chamomile flowers. Rev. Chim. (Bucharest) 33:162–166.

143. Negoescu, E., L. Mutihac, M. Botea, C. Faraianu, N. Palibroda, and M. Culea. 1981. A study on the chemical composition of a volatile oil obtained from wild chamomile (*Matricaria chamomillae*). Rev. Chim. (Bucharest) 32:902–908.

144. Neil Towers, G.H. 1979. *Toxic Plants.* Proc. 18th Annual Meeting Soc. Eco. Bot., The University of Miami, Coral Gables, FL. Kinghorn, A.D., Ed. Columbia University Press, New York. 195 p.

145. Opdyke, D.L.J. 1974. Monographs on fragrance raw materials. Chamomile oil German and Roman. Food Cosmet. Toxicol. 12:851–853.

146. Osol, A. and G.E. Farrar, Jr. 1950. *The Dispensatory of the United States of America.* J.B. Lippincott Co., Philadelphia. 2057 p.

147. Pambuccian, G. and A. Condurache. 1981. Use of some medicinal plants in the post extractional treatment of the alveolan wound--histological aspects Rev. Chir. Oncol. Radiol. Orl. Oftalmol. Stomatol. Stomatol. 28:61–68.

148. Quincy, J. 1742. *English Dispensatory.* Thomas Longman, London. 700 p.

149. Rahjes, J. 1980. Drugs with essential oil. VII. *Matricaria chamomilla* L. - camomile. PTA-Repetitorium 1:1–3.

150. Rauschert, S. 1974. Nomenklatorische Probleme in der Gattung *Matricaria* L. Folia Geobot. Phytotaxon. 9:249–260.

151. Redaelli, C., L. Formentini, and E. Santaniello. 1980. Apigenin 7-glucoside and its 2″- and 6″-acetates from ligulate flowers of *Matricaria chamomilla*. Phytochemistry 19:985–986.

152. Redaelli, C., L. Formentini, and E. Santaniello. 1981. High-performance liquid chromatography of *cis*- and *trans*-en-in-dicyclo ethers (spiro ethers) in *Matricaria chamomilla* L. flowers and in chamomile extracts. J. Chromatogr. 209:110–112.

153. Redaelli, C., L. Formentini, and E. Santaniello. 1981. HPLC determination of coumarins in *Matricaria chamomilla*. Planta Med. 43:412–413.

154. Redaelli, C., L. Formentini, and E. Santaniello. 1981. Reversed-phase high-performance liquid chromatography analysis of apigenin and its glucosides in flowers of *Matricaria chamomilla* and chamomile extracts. Planta Med. 42:288–292.

155. Redaelli, C., L. Formentini, and E. Santaniello. 1982. Apigenin 7-glucoside diacetates in ligulate flowers of *Matricaria chamomilla*. Phytochemistry 21:1828–1830.

156. Reichling, J. and H. Becker. 1980. Use of herbicide in growing chamomile *Matricaria chamomilla* 4. Herba Hung. 19:73–86.

157. Reichling, J., H. Becker, J. Exner, and P.-D. Draeger. 1979. Vergleichende Untersuchung verschiedener Handelsmuster von Matricariae Flos: Aetherisches Oel, Flavonoide, Cumarine, Phenolcarbonsaeuren und Pflanzenschutzmittelrueckstande. Pharm. Ztg. 124:1998–2005.

158. Reichling, J., H. Becker, and A. Voemel. 1977. Herbicides in cultivation of *Matricaria chamomilla* L. I. Communication: Influence of herbicides on the composition of the essential oil. Planta Med. 32:235–243.

159. Reichling, J., R. Beiderbeck, and H. Becker. 1979. Comparative studies on secondary products from tumors, flowers, herb, and roots of *Matricaria chamomilla* L. Planta Med. 36:322–332.

160. Reichling, J., W. Bisson, H. Becker, and G. Schilling. 1983. Composition and accumulation of essential oil in *Matricariae* radix (2. Communication). Z. Naturforsch. 38c:159–164.

161. Reifenstein, H. and F. Pank. 1975. Triazine residues in medicinal herbs. Pharmazie 39:391–393.

162. Reinke, S. 1979. Nonfoaming Facial and Shaving Emulsion. German Offen. Patent: DE 3027079-AL.

163. Repcak, M., J. Halasova, R. Honcariv, and D. Podhradsky. 1980. The content and composition of the essential oil in the course of anthodium development in wild camomile (*Matricaria chamomilla* L.). Biol. Plant. 22:183–191.

164. Repcak, M., B. Smajda, P. Cernaj, R. Honcariv, and D. Podhradsky. 1980. Diurnal rhythms of certain sesquiterpenes in wild camomile (*Matricaria chamomilla* L.). Biol. Plant. 22:420–427.

165. Reynolds, J.E.F., ed. 1982. *Martindale: The Extra Pharmacopoeia*. The Pharmaceutical Press, London. 2025 p.

166. Riotte, L. 1974. Chamomile can do it. Org. Gard. Farming 21:86–87.

167. Rombaux, J. and R. Larvelle. 1960. Les variations diurnes de la teneur en essence des capitules de camomille. J. Pharm. Belg. 15: 269–274.

168. *Rote Liste.* 1982. Editio Canto, Aulendorf.

169. Rowe, A.H. 1934. Camomile (*Anthemis cotula*) as a skin irritant. J. Allergy 5:383–388.

170. Sagarin, E., ed. 1957. *Cosmetics Science and Technology.* Interscience Publishers, Inc., New York. pp. 492–493.

171. Saleh, M. 1973. Effects of light upon quantity and quality of *Matricaria chamomilla* oil. III. Preliminary study of light intensity effects under controlled conditions. Planta Med. 24:337–340.

172. Samek, Z., M. Holub, H. Grabarczyk, B. Drozdz, and V. Herout. 1977. The structure of *Hydroxyisonobilin*--A cytostatically active sesquiterpenic lactone from the leaves of *Anthemis nobilis* L. Collect. Czech. Chem. Commun. 42:1065–1068.

173. Schaefer, J. and M. Stein. 1972. Reasons for differences in essential oil quality of the chamomile. Mezhdunar. Kongr. Efirnym Maslam, (Mater.), 4th 2:247–253.

174. Schilcher, H. 1977. Biosynthesis of (–)α-bisabolols and bisaboloxide. Planta Med. 31:315–321.

175. Schilcher, H. 1978. Influence of herbicides and some heavy metals on growth of *Matricaria chamomilla* L. and the biosynthesis of the essential oils. Acta Hortic. 73:339–341.

176. Schilcher, H. 1982. Analysis methods of the ingredients of *Matricaria chamomilla* L. Aetherische Oele: Ergeb Int. Arbeitstag. Ed. Karl-Heinz Kubeczka. Thieme, Stuttgart, W. Germany. 104–115.

177. Schilcher, H. 1982. Residues and impurities in medicinal plants and drug preparations. Planta Med. 44:65–77.

178. Shipochliev, T. 1981. Extracts from a group of medicinal plants enchancing uterine tonus. Vet.-Med. Nauki 18:94–98.

179. Shipochliev, T., A. Dimitrov, and E. Aleksandrova. 1981. Anti-inflammatory action of a group of plant extracts. Vet.-Med. Nauki 18:87–94.

180. Simon, J.E., A.E. Chadwick, and L.E. Craker. 1984. *Herbs: An Indexed Bibiliography 1971–1980.* Archon Books, The Shoe String Press, Inc., Hamden, CT. 770 p.

181. Spengler, H. and G. Weisflog. 1947. Extractum Chamomillae fluidum. Pharm. Acta Helv. 22:190–203.

182. Stahl, E. and S. Juell. 1982. Thin layer chromatography for identification of pharmacopeial drugs. Standardization by thin layer chromatography of flavonoid-containing drugs. Dtsch. Apoth.-Ztg. 122:1951–1957.

183. Stern, P. and R. Milin. 1956. Die antiallergische und antiphlogistische Wirkung der Azulene. Arzneim.-Forsch. 6:445–450.

184. Stieber, G., Z. Lassanyi and E. Tyihak. 1979. Investigations of the volatile oil secreting system of the Chamomillae anthodium (Flos). II. Changes in the prochamazulene content of glandular hair in the camomile (*Matricaria chamomilla*) flower during ontogeny. Herba Hung. 18:27–39.

185. Stransky, K., M. Streibl, K. Ubik, J. Kohoutova, and L. Novotny. 1981. The hydrocarbon composition of camomile (*Matricaria chamomilla* L.). Fette, Seifen, Anstrichm. 83:347–354.

186. Svab, J., G. Marczal, V.G. Petri, and E. Rajki. 1980. Cold-treatment effect on the flower and volatile oil building of chamomile (*Matricaria chamomilla* L.). Herba Hung. 18:235–244.

187. Szalontai, M., P.G. Verzar, and E. Florian. 1976. Data on the antifungal effect of the biologically active components of *Matricaria chamomilla* L. Acta Pharm. Hung. 46:232–247.

188. Szalontai, M., P.G. Verzar, and E. Florian. 1977. Study of the antimycotic effects of biologically active components of *Matricaria chamomilla* L. Parfuem. + Kosmet. 58:121–127.

189. Szelenyi, I., O. Isaac, and K. Thiemer. 1979. Pharmacological experiments with compounds of chamomile. III. Experimental studies on the ulcer protective effect of chamomile. Planta Med. 35:218–227.

190. Szente, L., M. Gal-Fuzy, and J. Szejtli. 1982. Stabilization of chamomile oil with beta-cyclodextrin. Proc. Int. Symp. Cyclodextrins 1st 1:431–442.

191. Tanker, M., N. Tanker, and E. Atasu. 1981. Research on Turkish *Matricaria* species II: Chromatographic comparison of *M. chamomilla* var. recutita L., var. pappulosa margot and reuter and *M. macrotis* Rech. Fil. Doga. 5:169–172.

192. Tanker, M., N. Tanker, and E. Sayron. 1977. Research on the Turkish *Matricaria* species. I. Comparison between natural and cultivated samples. Doga. 1:25–29.

193. Theimer, E.T., ed. 1982. *Fragrance Chemistry*. Academic Press, New York. pp. 225–228.

194. Thomas, A.F. 1981. The occurrence of some novel diesters in Roman camomile oil (*Anthemis nobilis*). Helv. Chim. Acta 64: 2397–2400.

195. Thomas, A.F. and J-C. Egger. 1981. Novel ketones from Roman camomile oil. Helv. Chim. Acta 64:2393–2396.

196. Thomas, A.F., M. Schouwey, and J-C. Egger. 1981. 136. Homologues of p-menthane derivatives in Roman camomile. Helv. Chim. Acta 64:1487–1495.

197. Thune, P.O. and Y.J. Solberg. 1980. Photosensitivity and allergy to aromatic lichen acids, *Compositae* oleoresins and other plant substances. Contact Dermatitis 6:81–87.

198. Tutin, T.G., V.H. Heywood, N.A. Burges, D.M. Moore, D.H. Valentine, S.M. Walters, and D.A. Webb. 1976. *Flora Europaea*, Vol. 4. Cambridge University Press, Cambridge. 505 p.

199. U.S. Code of Federal Regulations. 1982. Title 21: 172.510, 182.10; April.

200. U.S. *Food Chemicals Codex*. 1981. 3d ed. National Academy Press, Washington, DC. 735 p.

201. vanKetel, W.G. 1982. *Anthemis nobilis* is now designated *Chamaemelum nobile*. Contact Dermatitis 8:143.

202. Vaverkova, S. 1982. Histochemical determination of prochamazulene in distinct developmental stages of the anthodium *Matricaria chamomilla* L. II. Farm. Obz. 51:255–259.

203. Vaverkova, S. and A. Herichova. 1979. Effect of 3-cyclohexyl-2, 6-dioxy-4-methylpyrimidine on cell division of *Matricaria chamomilla* L. Nucleus, (Calcutta). 22:174–176.

204. Vaverkova, S. and A. Herichova. 1980. Histochemical proof of prochamazulene at different stages of development of the flower crown of *Matricaria camomilla* L. Biologia (Bratislava) 35:753–757.

205. Vrzalova, J. and L. Nespor. 1971. Variations in the yield and quality of camomile (*Matricaria chamomilla* L.) due to application of various amounts of calcium nitrate and some growth stimulants. Brno Acta Univ. Agr. Fac. Agron. 19:257–266.

206. Walenciak, M. and A. Korzeniowski. 1983. [Effect of storage conditions on the content of substances in *Matricaria chamomilla.*] Zesz. Nauk.-Akad. Ekon. Poznaniu, Ser. 1, 88:98–99, 1981. Taken from Chem. Abstr. 98:166747, 1983.

207. Wali, A.K.A.S. 1980. Yield and volatile oil content of chamomile *Matricaria chamomilla* as affected by water supply. Herba Hung. 19:65–72.

208. Wallis, T.E. 1955. *Textbook of Pharmacognosy*. 3d ed. Little, Brown and Co., Boston. 578 p.

209. Weiner, M. 1980. *Weiner's Herbal*. Stein and Day, New York. 224 p.

210. Windholz, M., ed. 1983. *The Merck Index*. 10th ed. Merck & Co., Inc., Rahway, NJ. 1463 p.

211. Wood, G.B. and F. Bache. 1845. *The Dispensatory of the United States*. 6th ed. Grigg and Elliot, Philadelphia. 1368 p.

212. Wuest, R., H. Pfeiffer, and H. Van der Mei. 1982. Plant Extracts with Sensory Properties. Patent EP 62893 AL October 20.

213. Yakovlev, A.I. and A.G. Gorin. 1977. Structure of pectic acid of *Matricaria chamomilla*. Khim. Prir. Soedin. 2:186–189.

214. Yamazaki, F. and I. Nishioka. 1980. Discrimination of several floral crude drugs morphology of pollen grains. Shoyakugaku Zasshi 34:259–265.

215. Yamazaki, H., M. Miyakado, and T.J. Mabry. 1982. Isolation of a linear sesquiterpene lactone from *Matricaria chamomilla*. J. Nat. Prod. 45:508.

216. Youngken, H.W. 1948. *Textbook of Pharmacognosy*. 6th ed. The Blakiston Co., Philadelphia. 1063 p.

217. Zalecki, R. 1971. Cultivation and fertilizing of the tetraploid *Matricaria chamomilla* L. I. Planting date. Herba Pol. 17:367–375.

218. Zalecki, R. 1972. Cultivation and fertilizing of the tetraploidal form of *Matricaria chamomilla* L. III. Mineral fertilizing. Herba Pol. 18:184–196.

219. Zalecki, R. 1978. Factors affecting the (essential) oil and azulene content in common chamomile (*Matricaria chamomilla*). Wiad. zielarskie 20:2–4.

220. Zwaving, J.H. 1982. Wild and roman chamomile, differences and similarities of the active constituents. Pharm. Weekbl. 117:157–165.

Medicinal Plants of Israel: An Ethnobotanical Survey

D. Palevitch
Department of Medicinal and Spice Crops, Agricultural Research Organization, The Volcani Center, Bet Dagan, Israel

Z. Yaniv
Department of Medicinal and Spice Crops, Agricultural Research Organization, The Volcani Center, Bet Dagan, Israel

A. Dafni
Institute of Evolution, Haifa University, Haifa, Israel

J. Friedman
Department of Botany, The G.S. Wise Faculty of Life Sciences, Tel-Aviv University, Ramat Aviv, Israel

CONTENTS

I. INTRODUCTION

An extensive ethnobotanical survey was conducted in Israel on plants known in folk medicine for their therapeutical properties. This information was gathered and recorded in order to preserve knowledge about the traditional herbal medicines; with the greater use of modern medicine and the diminishing practice of folk medicine, such knowledge is threatened with extinction.

The reported medicinal uses of 68 species are based on interviews with 100 informants representing different ethnic groups and different geographical regions. The collected data are arranged in this review according to the medicinal properties of the species.

Although a considerable amount of information regarding medicinal plants has been published, no ethnobotanical survey with thorough geographical coverage has been conducted in Israel. Field surveys in the Middle East (with almost no comparative literary evidence) have been reported by Bailey and Danin (7), Guest (31), Hareuveni (33), Hooper (34), Levy (38), Osborn (43), and Queden (45). A literary work on the Middle East with no field survey has been completed by Abou-Chaar and Ades (1), Al-Rawi, Chakravarty (4), and Alami *et al.* (5), Chopra *et al.* (12), and Fahmy (22). Field surveys in North Africa, accompanied by detailed comparative bibliographies, were reported by Boulos (8). Similar work on the species growing in Israel was done by Dafni (16), Dafni *et al.* (18), and Yaniv *et al.* (55). Some survey material related to medicinal uses of plants in northern Israel has also been published (18, 44, 55).

Some investigations have detailed phytochemical-pharmaceutical information of particular species or genera, such as *Achillea santolina* (52), *Capparis* (3), *Nerium oleander* (20), *Pancratium* (2), *Ruscus aculeatus* (21), and *Thymelaea hirsuta* (26). Other studies are referenced by Dafni *et al.* (18).

Historical aspects of herbal medicine in the Mediterranean region have been discussed in studies by Gunther (32), ancient Greece; Grieve (29), European herbal medicine; Ruweiha (47), Lebanon; Tackholm and Drary (51), ancient Egypt; Levey and Khaledy (37), early Arabic medicine; Budge (9), ancient Syria; and Crowfoot and Baldensperger (14), Arabic herbalism in Palestine.

The survey discussed in this report, completed during the time period 1981–83, was conducted throughout Israel, including the northern part with the cooler Mediterranean climate and the southern part with arid Saharo-Arabian conditions. Information regarding folk medicinal practices was collected for about 150 plants with the main species, based on quotations, presented in this report. Identity of the plants was confirmed by comparing plant material with live specimens and photographs of known plants. The claim of a medicinal property was recorded only if mentioned by at least 3 separate informants. All of the interviewed informants had been active as herbal healers throughout the years and most of them were still active at the present time. Any individual's involvement in practical herbal healing was greater in more remote isolated settlements as compared with localities that were closer to modern medical services. Seventy-five percent of the healers were above the age of 60; 80 percent of them were males.

Ethnic analyses indicated the existence of a large variety of groups in the northern part of Israel, such as Bedouins (23 informants), Druze (20 informants), Moslem Arabs (15 informants), and Christian Arabs (6 informants); in the southern part of Israel, almost all the informants were Bedouins. The relatively high number of Druze and Bedouin healers was expected as these individuals live in remote villages and nomadic settlements less influenced by modern medical practices.

Information regarding the practice of folk medicine among Jewish groups was not covered in this review as Jewish settlements in Israel are relatively new and the European influence in the selection and practice of herbal medicine is very strong. Some of the available information on Jewish use of herbal medicines is reported by Friedman (25) and Riami (47).

II. MEDICAL USES OF NATIVE PLANTS

The collected field data on 68 species are summarized in the following tables. Plants are listed in alphabetical order according to family and then according to species within the family. All information is organized according to reported medical properties of the plants. Plant parts utilized, method of preparation, and product administration are described and referenced to other reports of medicinal use.

A. Native Plants Used to Treat Animal Bites

Family and Botanical Name	Therapeutical Indications	Plant Part	Preparation and Use	Ref. No.
APIACEAE (UMBELLIFERAE)				
Eryngium creticum	Scorpion bites	Leaves	Eaten	
Lam.	Snake bites	Root	Ground, soaked in water, and spread on bite	33
APOCYNACEAE				
Nerium oleander L.	Dog bites	Flowers	A few eaten daily for 40 days	
ASTERACEAE (COMPOSITAE)				
Matricaria aurea (Loeffl.) Sch. Bip	Snake bites	Leaves	Tisane prepared and consumed	29
RUTACEAE				
Ruta chalepensis K.	Snake bites	Leaves	Tisane prepared and consumed	32
	Head lice	Leaves	Decoction prepared and used as hair rinse	
THYMELAEACEAE				
Thymelaea hirsuta (L.) Endl.	Snake bites	Branches	Burned and ash applied to bite	

B. Native Plants Used to Treat Diabetes

Family and Botanical Name	Plant Part	Preparation and Use	Ref. No.
APIACEAE			
Ammi visnaga (L.) Lam.	Flowers and seeds	Decoction prepared and consumed daily	
Eryngium creticum Lam.	Leaves	Decoction prepared and consumed as needed	
ASTERACEAE			
Achillea fragrantissima (Forssk) Sch. Bip	Herb[a]	Tisane prepared and consumed	52
Inula viscosa (L.) Ait	Leaves	Tisane prepared and consumed daily	
Matricaria aurea (Loeffl.) Sch. Bip	Leaves	Tisane prepared and consumed daily	
CAESALPINACEAE			
Ceratonia siliqua L.	Seeds	Tisane prepared and consumed for 40 days	
CAPPARACEAE			
Capparis spinosa L.	Fruit	Boiled and decoction prepared and consumed	
Cleome droserifolia	Leaves	Mix 1 teaspoon in glass of water, boil, and drink each morning	7
CARYOPHYLLACEAE			
Paronychia argentea Lam.	Leaves	Tisane prepared and consumed daily for 40 days	38

[a]All above-ground parts of plant.

B. Native Plants Used to Treat Diabetes (cont.)

Family and Botanical Name	Plant Part	Preparation and Use	Ref. No.
CHENOPODIACEAE			
Atriplex halimus L.	Leaves	Tisane prepared and consumed daily	24 40
CUCURBITACEAE			
Citrullus colocynthis (L.)	Dried fruit	Ground and 1/2 teaspoon of powder consumed daily	
	Pulp	Cooled until soft and spread over legs	8
LAMIACEAE (LABIATAE)			
Teucrium polium L.	Leaves	Tisane prepared and consumed daily	
MIMOSACEAE			
Prosopis farcta (Banks et Sol.) Macbride	Root	Root peeled, boiled in water, and decoction consumed	
PAPILIONACEAE			
Trigonella foenumgraecum	Seeds	Ground seeds consumed or tisane prepared and consumed	12 35
ROSACEAE			
Sarcopoterium spinosum L. (sp.)	Roots	Roots boiled and decoction consumed as needed	11 49 50

C. Native Plants Used to Treat the Digestive System

Family and Botanical Name	Therapeutical Indications	Plant Part	Preparation and Use	Ref. No.
ANACARDIACEAE				
Pistacia lentiscus	Abdominal pains	Young branches	Decoction prepared and consumed	
	Abdominal pains	Resin	Tisane prepared and consumed or drops of resin chewed	46
	Diarrhea	Young branches and fruits	Infusion prepared[a]	29
Rhus coriaria L.	Abdominal pains	Fruits	Soaked in water; water consumed	10
	Diarrhea	Fruits	Infusion prepared[a]	
	Liver diseases	Fruits	Eaten or juice drunk	
APIACEAE				
Ammi visnaga (L.) Lam.	Diarrhea and intestinal parasites	Seeds	Decoction prepared[a]	
Eryngium creticum Lam.	Ulcers and intestinal parasites	Seeds	Mixed with honey to form candy and consumed every morning for 40 days	33

[a]Procedure for use of preparation is unknown.

C. Native Plants Used to Treat the Digestive System (cont.)

Family and Botanical Name	Therapeutical Indications	Plant Part	Preparation and Use	Ref. No.
Foeniculum vulgare Mill.	Abdominal pains in babies (colic)	Seeds	Decoction prepared[a]	25
Pituranthos tortuosus (Def.) Benth x Aschers	Abdominal pains and intestinal parasites	Leaves	Tisane prepared and consumed	38
APOCYNACEAE				
Nerium oleander L.	Jaundice	Leaves and flowers	Boiled in water; water used to wash body	
ASTERACEAE				
Artemisia herba-alba Asso.	Abdominal pains and intestinal parasites	Leaves	Infusion prepared and consumed every morning on empty stomach	5 25 32
Inula viscosa (L.) Ait.	Hemorrhoids	Flowers	Dried in the sun, cut, mixed with olive oil, and spread around anus	
	Diarrhea	Leaves	Juice squeezed and consumed as drops	29
Matricaria aurea (Loeffl.) Sch. Bip.	Abdominal pains	Flowers	Infusion prepared and consumed as needed	19

C. Native Plants Used to Treat the Digestive System (cont.)

Family and Botanical Name	Therapeutical Indications	Plant Part	Preparation and Use	Ref. No.
Varthemia iphionoides Boiss et Bl.	Abdominal pains and intestinal gas	Leaves	Infusion prepared[a]	
	Indigestion and food poisoning	Leaves	Cut, soaked, and eaten	38
BORAGINACEAE				
Anchusa strigosa	Abdominal pains	Roots	Cut, boiled, and decoction prepared and consumed as needed	
CAESALPINACEAE				
Ceratonia siliqua L.	Abdominal pains and diarrhea	Fruits	Decoction prepared and consumed as needed	38
CHENOPODIACEAE				
Atriplex halimus L.	Constipation and intestinal gas	Roots	Cut, decoction prepared, and one glass a day consumed for 2 weeks	8
CRUCIFERAE				
Moricandia nitens Viv Dur & Barr	Abdominal pains and diarrhea in children	Leaves	Infusion prepared[a]	

C. Native Plants Used to Treat the Digestive System (cont.)

Family and Botanical Name	Therapeutical Indications	Plant Part	Preparation and Use	Ref. No.
CUCURBITACEAE				
Citrulus colocynthis (L.) Schrad	Constipation	Fruit	Dried and ground; 1/2 teaspoon a day eaten	25 46
	Hemorrhoids	Seeds	Crushed in oil and applied to area	4 53
Ecbalium elaterium (L.) A. Rich.	Jaundice	Fruit	Drops of juice applied to nostrils; fruit smelled; or fruit boiled and water drunk	1
	Constipation	Fruit	Parts eaten	28
	Hemorrhoids	Fruit	A bandage is soaked in juice and applied to anus	12 29
EUPHORBIACEAE				
Euphorbia hierosolymitana Boiss. ex Boiss.	Abdominal pains and constipation	Latex	Drops of latex swallowed	35
FAGACEAE				
Quercus calliprinos Webb	Ulcers	Galls	Decoction prepared[a]	

C. Native Plants Used to Treat the Digestive System (cont.)

Family and Botanical Name	Therapeutical Indications	Plant Part	Preparation and Use	Ref. No.
	Abdominal pains	Flowers	Dried and infusion prepared[a]	
	Diarrhea	Fruit	Fruit eaten	
Quercus ithaburensis Decne	Abdominal pains, diarrhea, and ulcers	Green-galls	Cooked in water and 1/2 glass of water consumed each day	46
LAMIACEAE				
Corydothymus capitatus (L.)	Abdominal pains	Leaves	Infusion prepared[a]	
Majorana syriaca (L.) Rafin	Intestinal problems	Leaves	Infusion prepared and 2–3 teaspoons are consumed with honey	
	Intestinal parasites	Leaves	Extracted in olive oil for 2 weeks and oil with sugar consumed as drops	38
Micromeria fruticosa (L.) Druce	Abdominal pains and diarrhea	Leaves	Infusion prepared[a]	
Micromeria myrtifolia Boiss. et Hohen	Abdominal pains	Leaves	Infusion prepared with *Pistacia lentiscus*[a]	
Salvia fruticosa Mill	Abdominal pains and ulcer pains	Leaves	Tisane prepared and consumed	25

C. Native Plants Used to Treat the Digestive System (cont.)

Family and Botanical Name	Therapeutical Indications	Plant Part	Preparation and Use	Ref. No.
	Dysentery	Leaves	Steam bath	
Satureja thymbra L.	Constipation and abdominal pains	Leaves	Concentrated infusion prepared[a]	
Teucrium polium L.	Abdominal pains in babies and loss of appetite	Leaves	Tisane prepared and consumed	
LAURACEAE				
Laurus nobilis L.	Diarrhea and vomiting in babies	Leaves and fruit	Decoction prepared and consumed as drops	25
LILIACEA				
Asphodelus microcarpus Salzm et Viv.	Jaundice	Rhizomes	Boiled with *Trigonella* leaves, filtered, and water consumed	
	Intestinal gas	Rhizomes	Soaked in water, filtered, and water consumed	
Urginea maritima (L.) Bak	Hemorrhoids	Bulb	Crushed with soap powder and applied to anus	
	Constipation	Bulb	Dried scales eaten	36

C. Native Plants Used to Treat the Digestive System (cont.)

Family and Botanical Name	Therapeutical Indications	Plant Part	Preparation and Use	Ref. No.
MIMOSACEAE				
Prosopis farcta (Banks et Sol) Macbride	Dysentery and hemorrhoids	Fruits	Decoction prepared or crushed with oil and applied to area	4 34
OROBANCHACEAE				
Cistahche tubulosa (Schenk) Wright	Jaundice	Entire plant	Decoction prepared[a]	
PAPILIONACEAE				
Alhagi maurorum Medik	Diarrhea with blood	Roots	Decoction prepared, evaporated to concentrated extract, and consumed as needed	34
	Constipation and abdominal pains	Seeds	Decoction prepared[a]	25
Glycyrrhiza glabra L.	Ulcers	Root	Decoction prepared[a]	10
Retama raetam (Forssk.) Webb	Abdominal pains	Leaves	Tisane prepared and consumed	38
Trigonella foenumgraecum L.	Abdominal pains and food poisoning	Seeds	Decoction prepared and consumed as a tea	35

C. Native Plants Used to Treat the Digestive System (cont.)

Family and Botanical Name	Therapeutical Indications	Plant Part	Preparation and Use	Ref. No.
PRIMULACEA				
Cyclamen persicum Mill.	Diarrhea and abdominal pains	Leaves	Eaten	29
RHAMNACEAE				
Rhamnus alaternus L.	Jaundice	Young branches	Boiled in water until yellow and water consumed every morning or steam bath	
Ziziphus spinachristi (L.) Desf.	Abdominal pains	Seeds	Ground and decoction prepared[a]	4, 8
	Constipation	Leaves	Decoction prepared[a]	
	Intestinal parasites	Fruits	Decoction prepared[a]	
ROSACEAE				
Sarcopoterium spinosum (L.) (Sp.)	Abdominal pains and indigestion	Root	Boiled in water and consumed as needed	
RUTACEAE				
Haplophyllum tuberculatum (Forssk.) Ad Juss.	Abdominal pains	Leaves	Tisane prepared and consumed	8
Ruta chalepensis L.	Abdominal pains	Leaves	Tisane prepared and consumed	12

C. Native Plants Used to Treat the Digestive System (cont.)

Family and Botanical Name	Therapeutical Indications	Plant Part	Preparation and Use	Ref. No.
SCROPHULARIACEAE				
Verbascum cremobium Murb.	Dysentery and hemorrhoids	Leaves	Tisane prepared and consumed	
SOLANACEAE				
Lycium europeum L.	Abdominal pains in children	Leaves	Crushed and a sweetened tisane prepared and consumed	
TAMARICACEAE				
Tamarix aphylla (L.) Karst	Abdominal pains	Leaves	Decoction prepared[a]	25

D. Native Plants Used to Treat Problems Associated with Ears

Family and Botanical Name	Therapeutical Indications	Plant Part	Preparation and Use	Ref. No.
CAPPARACEAE				
Capparis spinosa L.	Hearing problems	Root	Crushed in warm oil and drops of oil placed in ear	32

D. Native Plants Used to Treat Problems Associated with Ears (cont.)

Family and Botanical Name	Therapeutical Indications	Plant Part	Preparation and Use	Ref. No.
LILIACEAE				
Urginea maritima (L.) Bak	Deafness	Bulb	Fried in oil and drops of oil placed in ear	32
MYRTACEAE				
Myrtus communis L.	Earaches	Leaves	Oil extracted and drops of oil placed in ear	
RUTACEAE				
Ruta chalepensis L.	Earaches	Leaves	Boiled and ear treated with steam bath	25

E. Native Plants Used to Treat Eye Ailments

Family and Botanical Name	Therapeutical Indications	Plant Part	Preparation and Use	Ref. No.
Eryngium creticum Lam.	Cataracts	Seeds	Ground, mixed with sugar, and powder spread over the cataract	
Foeniculum vulgare Mill.	Failing eyesight	Seeds	Decoction is prepared and consumed as needed	8

[a]All above-ground parts of plant.

E. Native Plants Used to Treat Eye Ailments (cont.)

Family and Botanical Name	Therapeutical Indications	Plant Part	Preparation and Use	Ref. No.
ASTERACEAE				
Inula viscosa (L.) Ait.	Eye infections	Herb[a] ground	Immersed in boiling water and eye held above steam	
Matricaria aurea (Loeffl.) Sch. Bip.	Eye infections	Flowers	Infusion prepared and drunk	38
Varthemia iphionoides Boiss. et Bl.	Eye ailments	Leaves	Immersed in cold water and applied as wet dressing or wet leaves applied to eye	
CARYOPHYLLACEAE				
Paronychia argentea Lam.	Blindness	Dried flowers	Ground with sugar and powder spread above eyes	
CUCURBITACEAE				
Ecbalium elaterium (L.) A. Rich	Eye infections	Fruits	Boiled, water filtered, and water used as eye drops	
FAGACEAE				
Quercus ithaburensis Decne.	Eye infections	Galls	Burned, ground, and powder applied to affected area	

E. Native Plants Used to Treat Eye Ailments (cont.)

Family and Botanical Name	Therapeutical Indications	Plant Part	Preparation and Use	Ref. No.
LAMIACEAE				
Marrubium vulgare L.	Eye infections	Leaves	Juice squeezed from leaves and used as eye drops	
Micromeria fruticosa (L.) Druce	Contaminated eye	Leaves	Boiled in water and water used to wash eyes	
MALVACEAE				
Malva nicaensis All.	Eye infections	Leaves	Boiled in water and water used as eye drops	46
MIMOSACEAE				
Prosopis farcta (Banks et Sol.) Macbride	Eye infections	Branches	Crushed, mixed with sour milk, and spread over eyes	
PAPAVERACEAE				
Glaucium corniculatum (L.) Rudolph	Eye infections	Petals	Petals squeezed and juice used as eye drops	38
	Eye infections	Entire plant	Plant boiled in water and decoction used as eye drops before retiring or plant ground and squeezed with juice used as eye drops	

E. Native Plants Used to Treat Eye Ailments (cont.)

Family and Botanical Name	Therapeutical Indications	Plant Part	Preparation and Use	Ref. No.
PRIMULACEAE				
Cyclamen persicum Mill.	Eye infections	Bulb	Crushed and strained with juice used as eye drops	
RHAMNACEAE				
Ziziphus spinachristi (L.) Desf.	Eye infections	Seeds	Powdered dry seeds mixed with olive oil and spread over eyes	
	Eye infections	Roots	Baked in open fire, crushed, mixed with *Verbascum* and *Pistacia* leaves, and applied to the eye	
RUTACEAE				
Haplophyllum tuberculatum (Forssk) Ad. Juss.	Eye infections	Leaves	Squeezed and juice diluted with water, for use as eye drops	
Ruta chalepensis L.	Strained eyes	Leaves	Cold compress prepared from decoction	
SCROPHULARIACEAE				
Verbascum eremobium Murb.	Cataracts	Leaves and flowers	Squeezed and juice used as eye drops or flowers dried, crushed, mixed with sugar, and spread over eyes	8

E. Native Plants Used to Treat Eye Ailments (cont.)

Family and Botanical Name	Therapeutical Indications	Plant Part	Preparation and Use	Ref. No.
SOLANACEAE				
Lycium europaeum L.	Eye infections and cataracts	Leaves	Squeezed and juice applied as eye drops or diluted with water and consumed with coffee 3 times daily	
Hyoscyamus aureus L.	Eye infections	Leaves	Decoction prepared and used as eye drops	8
Solanum nigrum L.	Eyesight	Leaves	Steam bath	8
TAMARICACEAE				
Tamarix aphylla L. Karst.	Eye infections	Bark	Ground, burned over fire, and mixed with sugar to form powder for application to eye; or broiled and mixed with salt for application to eye	

F. Native Plants Used to Treat Headaches and Fever

Family and Botanical Name	Therapeutical Indications	Plant Part	Preparation and Use	Ref. No.
ANACARDIACEAE				
Pistacia lentiscus L.	Fever	Young leaves	Decoction prepared and consumed 3 times daily	
APIACEAE				
Foeniculum vulgare Mill.	Headaches and weakness	Seeds	Decoction prepared[a]	
Pituranthos tortuosus (Desf.) Benth & Aschers & Schweinf.	High fever in children	Leaves and branches	Cooked in water with *Varthemia* leaves; patient washed with water	
ASTERACEAE				
Achillea fragrantissima (Frossk.) Sch. Bip.	Fever and general weakness	Herb[b]	Soaked in water and water used to wash patient	
Chrysanthemum coronarium L.	Fever and headaches	Yellow flowers	Cooked in water and water consumed	
Inula viscosa (L.) Ait.	Fever	Leaves	Steam bath	
	Headaches	Leaves	Crushed and mixed with water; bandage soaked in water and applied to head	

[a]Procedure for use of preparation is unknown.

[b]All above-ground parts of plant.

F. Native Plants Used to Treat Headaches and Fever (cont.)

Family and Botanical Name	Therapeutical Indications	Plant Part	Preparation and Use	Ref. No.
	General weakness	Leaves	Steam bath	
Matricaria aurea (Loeffl.) Sch. Bip.	Fever, headaches, and general weakness	Flowers	Tisane prepared and consumed	14 34
Phagnalon rupestre (L.) DC.	Headaches	Herbs[b]	Tisane prepared and used as gargle	
Varthemia iphionoides Boiss. et Bl.	Headaches	Leaves	Tisane prepared and consumed	
CHENOPODIACEAE				
Anabasis articulata	Headaches	Leaves	Cooked and head rinsed with water or cooked to a sticky mix with soap and egg and the mix spread onto head	
CRUCIFERAE				
Moricandia nitens (Viv) Dur & Barr	Fever, especially in babies	Leaves	Crushed, cooked in water, and water drunk	
LAMIACEAE				
Micromeria myrtifolia	Headaches	Leaves	Tisane prepared and consumed	
Salvia fruticosa (L.)	Headaches	Leaves	Tisane prepared and consumed	

F. Native Plants Used to Treat Headaches and Fever (cont.)

Family and Botanical Name	Therapeutical Indications	Plant Part	Preparation and Use	Ref. No.
MYRTACEAE				
Myrtus communis L.	Headaches	Leaves	Dried, ground, soaked in wine vinegar until red, and applied externally on head	54
PAPILIONACEAE				
Glycyrrhiza glabra L.	Fever	Root	Boiled in water for 4–5 hours, cooled, and drunk	29
RUTACEAE				
Haplophyllum tuberculatum (Forrsk.) Ad. Juss	Fever and headaches	Herb[b]	Cut, made into a sticky mix, and spread on head or cooked in water and body washed in water	
Ruta chalepensis L.	Fever and headaches	Leaves	Tisane prepared and consumed or cooked in water, oil added and massaged onto forehead	25 28 32

G. Native Plants Used to Treat Heart Disorders and Circulation

Family and Botanical Name	Therapeutical Indications	Plant Part	Preparation and Use	Ref. No.
ANACARDIACEAE				
Rhus coriaria L.	Swollen legs and poor circulation	Fruits	Crushed, diluted with water, and spread over swollen legs	
APIACEAE				
Foeniculum vulgare Mill	Heart disease	Seeds	Decoction prepared and consumed as needed	
APOCYNACEAE				
Nerium oleander L.	Weak heart	Leaves	Decoction prepared and consumed as needed	19 25
	Internal bleeding	Leaves	Decoction prepared and 3 drops in a glass of milk consumed 3 times a day	5
ASTERACEAE				
Achillea fragrantissima (Forrsk.) Sch. Bip.	Heart pains	Green herb[a]	Boiled and tea consumed as needed	
Artemisia herb-alba Asso.	Heart pains	Leaves	Infusion prepared and consumed in the morning on an empty stomach	

[a] All above-ground parts of plant.

[b] Procedure for use of preparation is unknown.

G. Native Plants Used to Treat Heart Disorders and Circulation (cont.)

Family and Botanical Name	Therapeutical Indications	Plant Part	Preparation and Use	Ref. No.
Matricaria aurea (Loeffl.) Sch. Bip.	Weak heart	Flowers	Infusion prepared and consumed as needed	
Varthemia iphionoides Boiss. et Bl.	Heart disorders	Leaves	Infusion prepared and one cup consumed every morning	46
CARYOPHYLLACEA				
Paronychia argentea Lam.	Heart pains	Leaves	Boiled in water (300 grams per liter) for 2 days until water is red; 2–4 cups of water drunk each day	
CHENOPODIACEAE				
Atriplex halimus L.	Heart disorder	Leaves	Decoction prepared and consumed as needed or steam bath for legs	
FAGACEAE				
Quercus calliprinos Webb	Heart pains	Cones	Cooked in water and water drunk as needed	
Quercus ithaburensis Deche	High blood pressure	Cones	Cooked in water and water drunk as needed	

G. Native Plants Used to Treat Heart Disorders and Circulation (cont.)

Family and Botanical Name	Therapeutical Indications	Plant Part	Preparation and Use	Ref. No.
LAMIACEAE				
Corydothymus capitatus (L.) Reich	Heart disorders	Leaves	Infusion prepared and consumed as needed	
	Dropsy	Leaves	Decoction prepared and consumed for 40 days	
Majorana syriaca (L.) Rafin	Weak heart	Leaves	Crushed with honey and eaten	42
Marrubium vulgare L.	Heart pains	Leaves	Infusion prepared and consumed	
Micromeria fruticosa (L.) Druce	Heart disorders and high blood pressure	Leaves	Infusion prepared and consumed	
Micromeria myrtifolia Boiss. et Hohen	Heart pains	Leaves	Infusion prepared and consumed	
Satureja thymbra L.	Heart pains	Leaves	Infusion prepared[b]	
	Swollen legs and poor circulation	Leaves	Compresses made and applied to legs	

G. Native Plants Used to Treat Heart Disorders and Circulation (cont.)

Family and Botanical Name	Therapeutical Indications	Plant Part	Preparation and Use	Ref. No.
LILIACEAE				
Asphodelus microcarpus Salzm. et Viv.	Dropsy	Thick roots	Crushed roots boiled in water or steam bath	29
ROSACEAE				
Sarcopoterium spinosum L. (Sp.)	Poor blood circulation	Seeds	Decoction prepared and consumed as needed	
RUTACEAE				
Ruta chalepensis L.	Poor blood circulation	Herb[a]	Infusion prepared and consumed as needed	23
URTICACEAE				
Urtica pilulifera L.	Hemorrhaging	Leaves	Juice extracted from leaves and applied to affected area	4

H. Native Plants Used to Treat Kidney Diseases

Family and Botanical Name	Therapeutical Indications	Plant Part	Preparation and Use	Ref. No.
ANACARDIACEAE				
Pistacia lentiscus L.	Kidney stones	Young branches	Boiled in water and water consumed until patient better	25
APIACEAE				
Eryngium creticum Lam.	Kidney stones	Roots	Decoction prepared and consumed	
	Gall bladder problems	Leaves	Decoction prepared and consumed cold every morning	54
Ammi visnaga (L.) Lam.	Kidney stones	Flowers	Decoction prepared and consumed in increasing doses	12
ASTERACEAE				
Achillea fragrantissima (Forssk.) Sch. Bip.	Kidney stones	Green herb[a]	Cooked and consumed	
	Edema	Herb[a]	Decoction prepared and consumed as needed	
Varthemia iphionoides Boiss. et Bl.	Edema	Leaves	Infusion prepared and consumed as needed	

[a]All above-ground parts of plant.

[b]Procedure for use of preparation is unknown.

H. Native Plants Used to Treat Kidney Diseases (cont.)

Family and Botanical Name	Therapeutical Indications	Plant Part	Preparation and Use	Ref. No.
CARYOPHYLLACEAE				
Paronychia argentea Lam.	Kidney stones and edema	Green leaves	Boiled in water until liquid red (2 days) and then 2–4 glasses a day are consumed	1
CHENOPODIACEAE				
Anabasis articulata (Forssk.) Moq.	Edema	Herb[a]	Cooked with sugar and consumed for 7 days	
LAMIACEAE				
Satureja thymbra L.	Edema	Leaves	Infusion prepared and consumed as needed	25
Teucrium polium L.	Kidney and genital infections	Leaves	Infusion prepared and consumed as needed	
LILIACEAE				
Ruscus aculeatus L.	Kidney stones and edema	Root	Ground, decoction prepared, and consumed as needed	1 29
Urginea maritima L. Bak.	Edema	Bulb	Scales dried and eaten	4

H. Native Plants Used to Treat Kidney Diseases (cont.)

Family and Botanical Name	Therapeutical Indications	Plant Part	Preparation and Use	Ref. No.
MIMOSACEAE				
Prosopis farcta (Banks et Sol.) Macbride	Kidney stones	Root	Decoction prepared and consumed	
OROBANCHACEAE				
Cistanche tubulosa (Schenk) Wright	Kidney stones and edema	Herb[a]	Decoction prepared and consumed as needed	
PAPILIONACEAE				
Alhagi maurorum Medik	Kidney stones	Rhizomes	Boiled until water yellow (overnight) and consumed 2 to 3 times a day	22
Glycyrrhiza glabra L.	Kidney stones and edema	Roots	Decoction prepared and consumed as needed	29 32 37
POLYGONACEAE				
Polygonum equisitiforme Sm.	Edema	Herb[a]	Decoction prepared for 10 minutes and then consumed in the morning for 3–4 days	41
	Kidney diseases	Herb[a]	Decoction prepared[b]	

H. Native Plants Used to Treat Kidney Diseases (cont.)

Family and Botanical Name	Therapeutical Indications	Plant Part	Preparation and Use	Ref. No.
PRIMULACEAE				
Cyclamen persicum Mill.	Edema	Bulb	Crushed and decoction prepared	12
ROSACEAE				
Sarcopoterium spinosum L. (Sp.)	Edema	Fruits	Cooked in water and patient bathed in water	
RUTACEAE				
Ruta chalepensis L.	Kidney stones	Leaves	Oil extracted and drops of oil added to tea and drunk	
URTICACEAE				
Urtica pilulifera L.	Edema	Leaves	Decoction prepared and consumed	15

I. Native Plants Used to Treat the Nervous System

Family and Botanical Name	Therapeutical Indications	Plant Part	Preparation and Use	Ref. No.
ANACARDIACEAE				
Pistacia lentiscus L.	Muscle paralysis	Leaves	Steam bath with leaves of *Inula* and *Eucalyptus*	
	Muscle paralysis	Fruits	Decoction prepared and consumed	
APOCYNACEAE				
Nerium oleander L.	Bone fractures	Leaves	Steam bath	
ASTERACEAE				
Artemisia herba-alba Asso.	Neuralgia	Leaves	Extracted (5 leaves in 1 1/2 cups of water), sweetened, and consumed as needed	
Chrysanthemum coronarium	Muscle aches	Leaves	Steam bath for legs	
Inula viscosa (L.) Ait.	Muscle spasms	Leaves	Steam bath	
	Bone fractures	Leaves	Steam bath to soften area and bandage	
	General tonic	Leaves	Steam bath	
	Local paralysis	Leaves	Extracted oil massaged into area	

[a]Procedure for use of preparation is unknown.

I. Native Plants Used to Treat the Nervous System (cont.)

Family and Botanical Name	Therapeutical Indications	Plant Part	Preparation and Use	Ref. No.
	Nervousness	Roots	Decoction prepared and spread on body	
Matricaria aurea (Loeffl.) Sch. Bip.	General pain and muscle pains	Flowers	Crushed in olive oil, spread on affected area, and exposed to sun	
	General tonic	Flowers	Tea prepared with leaves of *Ruta* and consumed as needed	
BORAGINACEAE				
Ancusa strigosa Banks et Sol.	Weariness and exhaustion	Leaves	Decoction prepared[a]	
	Temporary paralysis	Roots and bark	Decoction prepared and spread externally on affected area	
CAPPARACEAE				
Capparis spinosa L.	General pain	Roots	Powdered roots applied to area for 15 minutes	5
	Neuralgia	Roots	Decoction prepared and consumed	

I. Native Plants Used to Treat the Nervous System (cont.)

Family and Botanical Name	Therapeutical Indications	Plant Part	Preparation and Use	Ref. No.
CUCURBITACEAE				
Citrullus colocynthis (L.) Schrad.	Paralysis and muscle spasms	Fruits	Steam bath	
Ecballium elaterium (L.) A. Rich	Insanity	Seeds	Crushed in water and drunk	
	Neuralgia	Fruits	Crushed in olive oil and spread on area	
EUPHORBIACEAE				
Euphorbia hierosolymitana Boiss. ex Boiss.	Depression and fears	Seeds	Boiled in water and drunk	
FAGACEAE				
Quercus ithaburensis Decne	Weariness and exhaustion	Fruits	Cooked and eaten	
LAMIACEAE				
Cordydothymus capitatus (L.) Reich.	Paralysis and blindness	Leaves	Steam bath daily for a month, including head	
Majorana syriaca Boiss. et Hohen	Dizziness	Green leaves	Chewed	

I. Native Plants Used to Treat the Nervous System (cont.)

Family and Botanical Name	Therapeutical Indications	Plant Part	Preparation and Use	Ref. No.
Micromeria fruticosa (L.) Druce	Weariness and exhaustion	Leaves	Tisane prepared and consumed	
Micromeria myrtifolia Boiss. et Hohen	Stress	Leaves	Tisane prepared and consumed	
Satureja thymbra L.	Swollen legs	Leaves	Cooked in water and legs soaked in water	
	Stress	Leaves	Tisane prepared and consumed	
	Paralysis	Leaves	Steam bath	
	Weariness, exhaustion, and dizziness	Leaves	Tisane prepared and consumed or ground and mixed in honey for eating (1 teaspoon each day)	
LILIACEAE				
Urginea maritima (L.) Bak	Neuralgia in legs and spine	Bulb	Applied to area and exposed to the sun	
	Bone fractures	Bulb	Crushed into a sticky mix and applied to fracture for a month	

I. Native Plants Used to Treat the Nervous System (cont.)

Family and Botanical Name	Therapeutical Indications	Plant Part	Preparation and Use	Ref. No.
MIMOSACEAE				
Prosopis farcta (Banks et Sol.)	Knee pains	Root	Ground, boiled, made into bandages for affected area	
PAPILIONACEAE				
Retama raetam (Forssk.) Webb.	Backaches	Leaves and branches	Steam bath to affected area or cut up leaves applied directly to affected area or crushed, made into glue with dough, and applied to affected area	7
	Arm and leg paralysis	Upper branches	Steam bath	
PRIMULACEA				
Cyclamen persicum Mill.	Bone fracture	Bulb	Cut thinly, bandages soaked and tied to affected area for 3 weeks	
	Nerve infections	Bulb	Cut, soaked in alcohol for 2 months, with the extract applied externally to affected area	

I. Native Plants Used to Treat the Nervous System (cont.)

Family and Botanical Name	Therapeutical Indications	Plant Part	Preparation and Use	Ref. No.
RUTACEAE				
Ruta chalepensis L.	Local paralysis	Roots	Bandage made with crushed root	
	Local paralysis	Leaves	Crushed with olive oil and massaged onto area	12 25 46
	Nervous tension	Leaves	Eaten with *Allium cepa*	
	General pain	Leaves	Steam bath prepared	
	Insanity	Leaves	Dried, mixed with milk, and applied to head	
SCROPHULARIACEAE				
Verbascum cremobium Murb.	Pains in legs and shaking hands	Leaves	Boiled in water and used in bandage	
SOLANACEAE				
Solanum nigrum L.	Neuralgia	Leaves	Decoction prepared and used as massage	33
	Backaches	Fruit	Steam bath for 40 days with salt	
	Breast pains	Leaves	Crushed and applied to area	

I. Native Plants Used to Treat the Nervous System (cont.)

Family and Botanical Name	Therapeutical Indications	Plant Part	Preparation and Use	Ref. No.
	Swollen legs	Leaves	Crushed, cooked with fat, and spread on affected area	
URTICACEAE				
Urtica pilulifera L.	Weariness and exhaustion	Leaves	Collected in April, boiled in water, and water drunk	4
	Pains in legs and muscle spasms	Leaves	Boiled in water and water consumed	
ZYGOPHYLLACEAE				
Balanites aegyptica (L.) Del.	Neuralgia	Seeds	Oil extracted and applied to area	
	Local paralysis	Root	Boiled in water and extract spread on affected area	
	Dizziness	Seeds	Baked and inhaled or decoction prepared and consumed	
Peganum harmala L.	Nervousness, weariness, and exhaustion	Seeds	Steam bath prepared	8 19

J. Native Plants Used to Treat the Reproductive System

Family and Botanical Name	Therapeutical Indications	Plant Part	Preparation and Use	Ref. No.
APIACEAE				
Eryngium creticum Lam.	Low libido	Root	Decoction prepared and consumed	48
APOCYNACEAE				
Nerium oleander L.	Delayed menstruation	Leaves	Steam bath or crushed and mixed with honey and 2 teaspoons of mix consumed each day	
ASTERACEAE				
Achillea fragrantissima (Forssk.) Sch. Bip.	Delayed menstruation	Green herb	Boiled in water and drunk	
Artemisia herba-alba Asso.	Male impotence	Leaves	Infusion prepared and consumed	
Inula viscosa L.	Female infertility	Entire plant	Steam bath applied to genital area or leaves crushed and applied to anus	
CAPPARACEAE				
Capparis spinosa L.	Male and female infertility	Root and flower	Decoction prepared and consumed or crushed and applied to male organ	7

ªAll above-ground parts of plant.

J. Native Plants Used to Treat the Reproductive System (cont.)

Family and Botanical Name	Therapeutical Indications	Plant Part	Preparation and Use	Ref. No.
EUPHORBIACEAE				
Euphorbia hierosolymitana Boiss. ex-Boiss.	Excessive libido	Latex	Drops of white latex added to a drink	
LAMIACEAE				
Teucrium polium L.	Delayed menstruation	Leaves	Cooked and eaten	15
	Nausea during pregnancy	Leaves	Dried, ground, fried, and eaten	
PAPILIONACEAE				
Retama raetam (Forssk.) Webb.	Female infertility	Branches	Steam bath for barren woman	
PRIMULACEAE				
Cyclamen persicum Mill.	Female infertility and low libido	Bulb	Bulb crushed and extracted juice drunk	29
RANUNCULACEAE				
Clematis cirrhosa L.	Male impotence	Juice of plant	Applied to genital area or drunk every morning with honey for 7 days	

J. Native Plants Used to Treat the Reproductive System (cont.)

Family and Botanical Name	Therapeutical Indications	Plant Part	Preparation and Use	Ref. No.
RUTACEAE				
Haplophyllum tuberculatum (Forssk.) Ad. Juss	Female sterility	Herb[a]	Steam bath	8
SOLANACEAE				
Solanum nigrum L.	Potential miscarriage	Fruits	Decoction prepared and consumed	
URTICACEAE				
Urtica pilulifera L.	Male impotence	Seeds	Eaten	29

K. Native Plants Used to Treat the Respiratory System

Family and Botanical Name	Therapeutical Indications	Plant Part	Preparation and Use	Ref. No.
ANACARDIACEAE				
Pistacia lentiscus L.	Sore throat	Leaves	Decoction prepared	
	Mucus in the respiratory tract	Leaves	Ground and powder inhaled	

[a]Procedure for use of preparation is unknown.

[b]All above-ground parts of plant.

K. Native Plants Used to Treat the Respiratory System (cont.)

Family and Botanical Name	Therapeutical Indications	Plant Part	Preparation and Use	Ref. No.
ASTERACEAE				
Artemisia herba-alba Asso.	Colds and coughs	Leaves	Infusion prepared[a] or leaves cooked in milk	8 38
Inula viscosa (L.) Ait.	Mucus in the respiratory tract	Leaves	Steam bath	29
Matricaria aurea (Loeffl.) Sch. Bip.	Coughs and colds	Flowers	Infusion prepared and consumed as needed	25 45
CAESALPINACEAE				
Ceratonia siliqua L.	Coughs	Fruits	Decoction prepared[a]	
CAPPARACEAE				
Capparis spinosa L.	Coughs	Ripe fruits	Decoction prepared and consumed for 3 days	12 25
CHENOPODIACEAE				
Atriplex halimus L.	Chest pains	Leaves	Decoction prepared and spread over body	37
	Coughs	Leaves	Decoction prepared and drunk	

K. Native Plants Used to Treat the Respiratory System (cont.)

Family and Botanical Name	Therapeutical Indications	Plant Part	Preparation and Use	Ref. No.
FAGACEAE				
Quercus calliprinos Webb	Coughs	Fruits	Decoction prepared, sweetened, and consumed	
Quercus ithaburensis Decne	Asthma	Galls	Ground, immersed in water, and drunk	
LAMIACEAE				
Majorana syriaca (L.) Rafin.	Coughs	Leaves	Crushed in honey and eaten	7
Micromeria fruticosa (L.) Druce	Colds, coughs, and runny noses	Leaves	Infusion prepared[a]	
Micromeria myrtifolia Boiss. et Hohen	Lung diseases	Leaves	Decoction prepared and evaporated until one half remains[a]	
Salvia fruticosa L. Mill	Colds and coughs	Leaves	Infusion prepared[a]	54
Satureja thymbra L.	Mucus in respiratory tract	Leaves	Infusion prepared[a]	
LAURACEAE				
Laurus nobilis L.	Colds	Leaves	Steam bath, alone or with leaves of *Salvia fruticosa, Ruta chalepensis* , and *Satureja thymbra*	15

K. Native Plants Used to Treat the Respiratory System (cont.)

Family and Botanical Name	Therapeutical Indications	Plant Part	Preparation and Use	Ref. No.
MIMOSACEAE				
Prosopis farcta (Banks et Sol.)	Asthma	Root	Crushed in water and a small glass of the water drunk before meals	
	Coughs and mucus in respiratory tract	Fruit	Crushed with sugar, cooked, and consumed as needed	
PAPILIONACEAE				
Glycyrrhiza glabra L.	Lung diseases	Root	Peeled, left in water for 12 hours, and extract consumed with sugar	15 27 29
RUTACEAE				
Ruta chalepensis L.	Coughs	Leaves	Steam bath with water spread on body or ground and powder mixed with *Matricaria* in bandage around chest	
	Asthma	Leaves	Infusion prepared, mixed with leaves of *Laurus nobilis,* and consumed or leaves boiled in oil and oil spread on body	

K. Native Plants Used to Treat the Respiratory System (cont.)

Family and Botanical Name	Therapeutical Indications	Plant Part	Preparation and Use	Ref. No.
SOLANACEAE				
Hyoscyamus aureaus L.	Mucus in respiratory tract	Leaves	Steam bath	19
Solanum nigrum L.	Sore throat	Leaves	Dried and ground with flour, or made into spread with fat, and applied to affected area	
TAMARICACEAE				
Tamarix aphylla (L.) Karst.	Colds	Root and bark	Steam bath	
THYMELAEACEAE				
Thymelaea hirsuta L. Ende.	Coughs and asthma	Roots	Cooked in water until extract concentrated; with steam inhaled	8 26
	Coughs and asthma	Seeds	Added to flour before baking	
ZYGOPHYLLACEAE				
Peganum harmala L.	Coughs and colds	Seeds	Decoction prepared and consumed daily	8
		Herb[b]	Boiled and steam inhaled	7

L. Native Plants Used to Treat Rheumatism

Family and Botanical Name	Therapeutical Indications	Plant Part	Preparation and Use	Ref. No.
ASTERACEAE				
Achillea fragrantissima Forssk.	Rheumatism	Green herb[a]	Steam bath	
Inula viscosa L.	Rheumatism	Herb[a]	Steam bath	14 54
Varthemia iphionoides Boiss. et Bl.	Rheumatism	Leaves	Steam bath	
CAPPARACEAE				
Capparis spinosa L.	Rheumatism	Root and fruit	Ground and powder applied to affected area for a short time or steam bath	5 12 28 34
CHENOPODIACEAE				
Atriplex halimus L.	Rheumatism	Leaves	Steam bath with patient left to sweat	
CRUCIFERAE				
Moricandia nitens (viv) Dur & Barr	Backaches	Roots	Cooked into glue and spread on back	
FAGACEAE				
Quercus calliprinos Webb	Rheumatism	Acorns	Oil extracted from acorns, applied to joints, or ground and powder spread on joints	

[a] All above-ground parts of plant.

L. Native Plants Used to Treat Rheumatism (cont.)

Family and Botanical Name	Therapeutical Indications	Plant Part	Preparation and Use	Ref. No.
LAMIACEAE				
Corydothymus capitatus (L.) Reicib	Rheumatism	Leaves	Cooked in olive oil and spread on joints	
Salvia triloba (L.) Mill.	Rheumatism	Leaves	Steam bath	
Satureja thymbra L.	Rheumatism	Leaves	Steam bath	
LAURACEAE				
Laurus nobilis L.	Rheumatism	Fruits	Oil extracted and massaged onto area	15 29
PAPILIONACEAE				
Alhagi maurorum Medik	Rheumatism	Roots	Steam bath from crushed roots	19
Retama raetan (Forssk.) Webb	Backaches	Leaves	Steam bath to affected area or crushed leaves applied to affected area or glue made with cut upper branches and dough applied to affected area	
RHAMNACEAE				
Ziziphus spinachristi (L.)	Rheumatism	Root and branches	Steam bath or glue made from roots and dough applied to back	

L. Native Plants Used to Treat Rheumatism (cont.)

Family and Botanical Name	Therapeutical Indications	Plant Part	Preparation and Use	Ref. No.
RUTACEAE				
Haplophyllum tuberculatum (Forssk.) Ad. Juss.	Backaches	Leaves	Steam bath or poultice made with green leaves applied to affected area	8
Ruta chalepensis L.	Rheumatism	Leaves	Crushed with olive oil and massaged on painful joints or steam bath	12 46
SOLANACEAE				
Hyoscyamus aureus L.	Rheumatism	Leaves	Steam bath	
Solanum nigrum L.	Backaches	Fruits	Steam bath with salt treatment for 40 days	
TAMARICACEAE				
Tamarix aphylla (L.) Karst.	Rheumatism	Roots and bark	Steam bath	38
URTICACEAE				
Urtica pilulifera L.	Arthritis	Leaves	Body massaged with leaves	15
ZYGOPHYLLACEAE				
Balanites aegyptica (L.) Del.	Arthritis	Seeds	Oil extracted and spread over body	14

L. Native Plants Used to Treat Rheumatism (cont.)

Family and Botanical Name	Therapeutical Indications	Plant Part	Preparation and Use	Ref. No.
		Roots	Crushed, decoction prepared and spread on painful joints	
Peganum harmala L.	Rheumatism	Seeds	Steam bath or oil extracted and spread over affected area	7 8

M. Native Plants Used to Treat Skin Ailments

Family and Botanical Name	Therapeutical Indications	Plant Part	Preparation and Use	Ref. No.
ANACARDIACEAE				
Pistacia lentiscus L.	Eczema	Resin	Mixed with olive oil and honey in equal amounts, boiled and spread over hands	54
APIACEAE				
Eryngium creticum Lam.	Open wounds and cuts	Leaves and roots	Cut and applied to wounds	
APOCYNACEAE				
Nerium oleander L.	Eczema and skin irritations	Leaves and flowers	Boiled in water until concentrated and water spread on skin or juice squeezed from leaves onto skin or leaves boiled, mixed with soap, salt, and kerosene and applied to skin; skin will peel	
ASPLENIACEAE				
Ceterach officinarum DC.	Cuts and wounds	Herb[a]	Dried, ground, and powder added to cuts and wounds	14

[a]All above-ground parts of plant.

M. Native Plants Used to Treat Skin Ailments (cont.)

Family and Botanical Name	Therapeutical Indications	Plant Part	Preparation and Use	Ref. No.
ASTERACEAE				
Chrysanthemum coronarium L.	Burns	Petals	Cut and applied to affected area	
Inula viscosa (L.) Ait.	Open wounds	Leaves	Applied fresh to wound or dried and powder spread on wound or juice squeezed onto wound	33
Matricaria aurea (Loeffl.) Sch. Bip.	Open wounds	Flowers	Dried, powdered, and applied to affected area	32
	Open wounds	Leaves	Cut and applied to affected area	
Phagnalon rupestre (L.) DC.	Burns	Stem	Wood dried, ignited, and used to cauterize the ache	7
	Leprosy	Herb[a]	Decoction prepared and consumed	
Varthemia iphionoides Boiss. et Bl.	Wounds	Leaves	Applied to wound in either fresh or crushed form	25

M. Native Plants Used to Treat Skin Ailments (cont.)

Family and Botanical Name	Therapeutical Indications	Plant Part	Preparation and Use	Ref. No.
BORAGINACEAE				
Achusa strigosa Banks et Sol.	Open wounds	Leaves	Crushed and applied to wounds or boiled in olive oil and spread on wounds	
CAESALPINACEAE				
Ceratonia siliqua L.	Wounds on tongue	Fruits	Honey from plant material spread on tongue	
CAPPARACEAE				
Capparis spinosa L.	Open wounds	Leaves	Epidermis peeled and used as wound covering	
CHENOPODIACEAE				
Anabasis articulata (Forssk.). Moq.	Scabies	Stems	Cut, cooked, and glue made with dough spread on skin	
CRUCIFERAE				
Moricandia nitens Boiss. et Bl.	Wounds	Leaves	Applied to wound in either fresh or crushed form	25
CUCUBITACEAE				
Ecbalium elaterium (L.) A. Rich	Skin diseases	Fruit	Juice mixed with infusion of *Nerium oleander* and spread on skin	46

M. Native Plants Used to Treat Skin Ailments (cont.)

Family and Botanical Name	Therapeutical Indications	Plant Part	Preparation and Use	Ref. No.
EUPHORBIACEAE				
Euphorbia hierosolymitana Boiss.	Wounds and warts	Latex	Spread on skin	8
Mercurialis annua L.	Open wounds	Herb[a]	Fresh or dried material powdered and applied to wounds	
FAGACEAE				
Quercus ithaburensis	Wounds	Galls	Ground into powder and applied to wound	29
LAMIACEAE				
Marrubium vulgare L.	Open and infected wounds	Leaves	Cooked in olive oil and applied to wounds or boiled in water and spread on wound or decoction prepared and mixed with soap and spread on wounds	46
Micromeria fruticosa (L.) Druce	Wounds	Leaves	Decoction prepared and used to make compresses	

M. Native Plants Used to Treat Skin Ailments (cont.)

Family and Botanical Name	Therapeutical Indications	Plant Part	Preparation and Use	Ref. No.
Satureja thymbra L.	Open wounds	Leaves	Oil extracted and applied to affected area or bandage wet with decoction applied to affected area	
Teucrium polium L.	Open wounds	Leaves	Crushed and spread over wounds	15
LAURACEAE				
Laurus nobilis L.	Crusted scabs	Fruit	Oil extracted and spread over skin	10 29
LILIACEAE				
Asphodelus microcarpus Salzm. et Viv.	Dry skin on feet, eczema and warts	Rhizomes	Juice extracted and spread over dry skin	17 33
Urginea maritima (L.) Bak.	Head wounds	Bulb	Crushed with olive oil and applied to affected area	29
MALVACEAE				
Malva nicaenis All.	Wounds	Leaves	Crushed and applied to affected area	46
	Swellings	Fruits	Cooked with egg yolk and white flour; applied to affected area	

M. Native Plants Used to Treat Skin Ailments (cont.)

Family and Botanical Name	Therapeutical Indications	Plant Part	Preparation and Use	Ref. No.
MYRTACEAE				
Myrtus communis L.	Skin irritation in newborns	Leaves	Dried leaves powdered and used as a talcum or immersed in olive oil and used as lotion	10 32 34
PAPILIONACEAE				
Glycyrrhiza glabra L.	Open wounds and peeled skin	Seeds	Crushed and spread on affected area	10
	Open wounds and peeled skin	Leaves	Applied fresh to peeled areas	
Retama raetam (Forssk.) Webb	Infected wounds	Leaves	Dried, boiled in water, and water used to wash affected area or crushed and applied to affected area	7 35
Trigonella foenumgraceum L.	Open wounds	Leaves	Cooked in oil and spread on affected area	19 25
PRIMULACEAE				
Cyclamen persicum Mill.	Open wounds, abscesses, eczema, and skin burns	Bulb	Juice applied to affected area or applied as bandage or mixed with oil and applied to burns	32 39

M. Native Plants Used to Treat Skin Ailments (cont.)

Family and Botanical Name	Therapeutical Indications	Plant Part	Preparation and Use	Ref. No.
RHAMNACEAE				
Ziziphus spinachristi L.	Open wounds	Fruit	Infusion prepared and spread over skin	12
	Baldness	Branches	Cut and juice used as hair wash	8
ROSACEAE				
Sarcopoterium spinosum L.(Sp.)	External inflammations	Root	Boiled in water and rubbed onto affected area	
RUTACEAE				
Ruta chalepensis L.	Infected wounds	Leaves	Infusion prepared and used to wash affected area	
SOLANACEAE				
Lycium europeum L.	Skin irritation	Herb[a]	Decoction prepared and used as wash on affected area	
Hyoscyamus aureus L.	Open wounds	Leaves	Crushed with olive oil and spread over affected area	

M. Native Plants Used to Treat Skin Ailments (cont.)

Family and Botanical Name	Therapeutical Indications	Plant Part	Preparation and Use	Ref. No.
Solanum nigrum L.	Open wounds	Leaves	Crushed and applied to wounds or burned to ash and spread over wounds or cooked and used on wounds or squeezed for juice and juice used on wounds or crushed with animal fat and used on wounds	
	Open wounds	Fruit	Boiled in animal fat and spread over affected area	8
	Skin irritations	Fruits	Crushed and spread over affected area	
TAMARICACEAE				
Tamarix aphylla L.	Open wounds and eczema	Root and bark	Ground and powder spread on wound	12 15
THYMELAEACEAE				
Thymelaea hirsuta (L.) Endl.	Open and infected wounds, skin irritations	Bark and branches	Burned to ashes and ashes applied to affected area	26

M. Native Plants Used to Treat Skin Ailments (cont.)

Family and Botanical Name	Therapeutical Indications	Plant Part	Preparation and Use	Ref. No.
URTICACEAE				
Parietaria judaica L.	Open wounds	Leaves	Applied fresh to affected area	1
Urtica pilulifera L.	Open wounds	Seeds	Dried, powdered, and spread on affected area	
	Infected wounds	Leaves	Used as cover for affected area	
	Infected wounds	Fruits	Ground in water and spread over affected area	
	Pain around wounds	Leaves	Rubbed in skin around affected area	15
ZYGOPHYLLACEAE				
Peganum harmala L.	Open and infected wounds (adults and babies)	Seeds	Roasted, ground, boiled in oil, and spread over wounds	8

N. Native Plants Used to Treat Toothaches

Family and Botanical Name	Therapeutical Indications	Plant Part	Preparation and Use	Ref. No.
ANACARDIACEAE				
Rhus coriaria L.	Tooth and gum aches	Fruits	Infusion prepared and used as mouthwash	32
APIACEAE				
Eryngium creticum Lam.	Gum tonic	Leaves	Eaten	
ASTERACEAE				
Inula viscosa (L.)	Toothache	Flowers	Boiled in water until yellow and water gargled	29
Matricaria aurea (Loeffl.)	Tooth and gum aches	Flowers	Infusion prepared	8
Phagnalon rupestre (L.) DC.	Toothache	Herb[a]	Infusion prepared and gargled	
LAMIACEAE				
Majorana syriaca (L.) Rafin	Toothache	Leaves	Crushed and juice applied to area or decoction prepared and gargled	14
	Gum infestations	Leaves	Crushed with salt and rubbed on gums	42
	Unclean teeth	Leaves	Chewed daily	

[a]All above-ground parts of plant.

N. Native Plants Used to Treat Toothaches (cont.)

Family and Botanical Name	Therapeutical Indications	Plant Part	Preparation and Use	Ref. No.
Satureja thymbra L.	Tooth decay	Leaves	Oil extracted and placed on teeth	
MIMOSACEAE				
Prosopis farcta (Banks et Sol.) Macbride	Toothache	Fruit	Crushed and applied to teeth	
PRIMULACEAE				
Cyclamen persicum Mill.	Toothache	Bulb	Juice squeezed onto teeth	
RHAMNACEAE				
Ziziphus spinachristi (L.) Desf.	Tooth decay and toothache	Fruit	Eaten	
	Gum problems	Roots	Ground and powder rubbed onto teeth	4
ROSACEAE				
Sarcopoterium spinosum L. (Sp.)	Toothache	Roots	Decoction prepared and gargled	
SOLANACEAE				
Hyoscyamus aureus L.	Tooth decay and toothache	Seeds and leaves	Crushed and placed on teeth or fried with fat and smoke inhaled	

N. Native Plants Used to Treat Toothaches (cont.)

Family and Botanical Name	Therapeutical Indications	Plant Part	Preparation and Use	Ref. No.
Lycium europeum L.	Toothache and gum problems	Leaves	Decoction prepared and gargled	
	Toothache and gum problems	Bark	Burned and ashes applied to teeth	7
TAMARICACEAE				
Tamarix aphylla L. Karst.	Toothache	Seeds, leaves, and stems	Cooked and steam inhaled	32
ZYGOPHYLLACEAE				
Peganum harmala L.	Toothache	Seeds	Crushed and placed on teeth or cooked and steam inhaled	8

III. DISCUSSION

The existing traditions of herbal medicine among the ethnic groups, primarily in the rural areas of Israel, have been collected, summarized, and described in this chapter. Most of the recorded herbal medicinal treatments were for external ailments including wounds, bites, bone fractures, toothaches, and eye troubles. External treatments were recommended for these external ailments.

The herbal medicines recommended by healers for internal use consisted mainly of remedies for disturbances of the digestive system. Oral consumption of these remedies was advised by the healers. Narcotic and poisonous plants, utilized in the past, such as *Hyoscyamus* spp., *Mandragora officinalis* and *Datura* spp., are not now being used, due to their toxicity. The inhabitants of desert areas use narcotic plants like *Peganum harmala, Hyoscyamus aureus* and *Euphorbia hierosolymitana*, but special care is used in preparation and administration.

Surprisingly, some plants common to herbal practice in early Arabic medicine and in Europe were not being used in the surveyed area. Since these observations are based on information collected in the field, we are unable to explain, at this time, the reasons some plants are no longer in use. Examples of such plants are *Melissa officinalis, Mentha* spp., *Anagallis arvensis*, and *Adianthum capillus-veneris*.

Most of the surveyed medicinal uses involved using only one plant species. Mixtures were used rarely and mainly in steam bath applications. In the past, however, mixtures containing up to 40 different plants were commonly used (33, 38).

No gradual or stepwise treatment was recorded except for one interesting example: the treatment of gastric ulcers with acorns of *Quercus calliprinos* involved acorns that are rich in tanins, astrigent, and able to absorb irritating liquids around the ulcer; cumin that prevented vomiting; and *Matricaria* flowers that are analgesic and able to heal the wound. Some traces of the Doctrine of Signatures were still being practiced. For example, the yellow decoction obtained from *Cictanche tubulosa, Rhamnus elaternus*, and *Ecaballium elaterium* were used for treatment of jaundice.

The use of plants as herbal medicines appeared related to cultural background of the people. In the northern part of Israel, where several ethnic groups coexist, the same plants had many different therapeutic applications. Even in the same northern village, different side-by-side cultural traditions utilized plants differently with little or no cultural exchange of herbal medicines. However, the homogeneous population in the south, consisting usually of Bedouins, has fewer medicinal uses but a greater number of identical uses for the same plant among the several informant healers. For example, in the north, *Inula viscosa* has 19 uses, *Solanum nigrum* has 11 uses, and *Salvia fruticosa* has 7 uses; not one of the plants used in the south had more than 6 uses. Our findings support those described for the Bedouins of Sinai and the Negev by Bailey and Danin (7), reflecting similar herbal medicine practices within a wide geographical area of the arid zone.

Preparation of the different herbal remedies was simple and included tisane, docoction, extract of crushed leaves, cooked plant parts, and steam bath. Only in a few cases was the oil extracted from leaves for medicinal use.

A comparative study of early Arabic medicine (36) revealed that herbal remedies have decreased in importance (37), probably due to the spread of modern medicine to even the most remote villages. An exception in our study was an informant from the Shomron (Samaria) area who, in addition to his knowledge of the local plants, owned and used a number of old and new books and practiced herbal medicine according to the traditional medicine of earlier times. Herbal healing with plants in Israel, as practiced by different ethnic groups, appears to be a result of influences from neighboring cultures and the development of a local folklore.

Acknowledgements

We wish to thank Nisim Krispill, Yosef Ziv, Salman Abu-Rocon, Uri Eliav, and the late Uri Zeira, who helped us in the various stages of this project.

Special thanks are due to Yoel Amiran of the National Council for Research and Development for his assistance in obtaining the financial support for this project and for his continuous encouragement. Above all, our appreciation extends to all of the informants who readily reported their views and experiences during the interviews.

This work was supported by a grant from the National Council for Research and Development. Contribution from the Agricultural Research Organization, The Volcani Center, Bet-Dagan, Israel, No. 1155-E series.

IV. REFERENCES

1. Abou-Charr, C.I. and J. Ades. 1961. Medicinal plants of Lebanon. Pakistan J. Sci. Indust. Res. 4:153–157.

2. Ahmed, Z.F., A.M. Rizk, and F.M. Hammouda. 1964. Phytochemical studies on Egyptian *Pancracium* species. Lloydia 27:115–134.

3. Ahmed, Z.F., A.M. Rizk, and F.M. Hammouda. 1972. Glucosinolates of Egyptian *Capparis* species. Phytochemistry 11:250–256.

4. Al-Rawi, A. and H.L. Chakravarty. 1964. *Medicinal Plants of Iraq.* Tech. Bull. Min. Agric. Baghdad, No. 146. 109 p.

5. Alami, R., A. Macksad, and A.R. El-Gindy. 1975. *Medicinal Plants in Kuwait.* Ministry of Health, Kuwait.

6. Avitzur, S. 1972. *Everyday Life in Israel in the 19th Century.* Am. Hasefer Publishers, Israel (in Hebrew). 258 p.

7. Bailey, C. and A. Danin. 1981. Bedouin plant utilization in Sinai and the Negev. Econ. Bot. 35:145–162.

8. Boulos, L. 1983. *Medicinal Plants of North Africa.* Reference Publications Inc., Algonac, MI. 286 p.

9. Budge, E.A.W. 1913. *The Syrian Book of Medicines.* Oxford University Press, London. 609 p.

10. Campbell, Thompson A. 1949. *A Dictionary of Assyrian Botany.* The British Academy, London, 312 p.

11. Carraz, G., A. Boucherle, and A. Dardas. 1968. Activité hypoglycémiante des triterpènes pentacycliques dans le diabète hypersulénique. C.R. Hebd. Seances Acad. Sci. Serie D. 266D:293–294.

12. Chopra, R.W., S.L. Nayar, and I.C. Chopra. 1956. *Glossary of Indian Medicinal Plants.* Council of Scientific and Industrial Research, New Delhi. 330 p.

13. Conway, D. 1973. *The Magic of Herbs.* Jonathan Cape, London, 158 p.

14. Crowfoot, G.M. and L. Baldensperger. 1932. *From Cedar to Hyssop.* The Sheldon Press, London, 196 p.

15. Culpeper, N. 1643. *Complete Herbal.* London. 430 p.

16. Dafni, A. 1980. *Plant Folklore in Israel.* Gestlit, Haifa (in Hebrew). 92 p.

17. Dafni, A. and A. Dafni. 1975. On some economical and medicinal plants in the Bedouins. Tewa wa'Aretz 17:233–240 (in Hebrew).

18. Dafni, A., Z. Yaniv, and D. Palevitch. 1984. Ethnobotanical survey of medicinal plants in northern Israel. J. Ethnopharmacol. 10:295–310.

19. Dastur, J.F. 1970. *Medicinal Plants of India and Pakistan.* D.C. Taraporevala Sons and Co. Private Ltd., Bombay. 212 p.

20. Elkiey, M.A., A.M. Elmoghazy, S.A. Salem, and M.S. Karawya. 1970. Macro and micromorphology of *Nerium oleander* L. grown in Egypt. U.A.R. J. Pharm. Sci. 11:123–136.

21. El-Sholy, M., J.E. Knap, D.J. Statkin, and P.L. Schiff. 1975. Constituents of *Ruscus aculeatus.* Lloydia 38:106–108.

22. Fahmy, I.R. 1956. The medicinal plants of the Middle East. Lebanese Pharm. J. 4:12–56.

23. Flück, H. 1976. *Medicinal Plants.* Transl. J.M. Rowson. W. Foulsham and Co., Ltd. Berks, England. 188 p.

24. Frenkel, G., P.F. Kraicer, and J. Shani. 1972. Diabetes in the sand-rat: Diabetegenesis, responses to mannoheplulose and *Atriplex* ash. Diabetologia 8:313–318.

25. Friedman, A. 1966. Folk medicine of the Eastern Jews in the Galilee. M.Sc. thesis. School of Pharmacy, The Hebrew University of Jerusalem, Israel (in Hebrew). 162 p.

26. Garbo, S.A., S.M. Khafagy, and T.M. Sarg. 1970. Phytochemical investigations of *Thymelea hirsuta.* U.A.R. J. Pharm. Sci. 11:101–106.

27. Gibson, M.R. 1978. Glycyrrhiza in old and new perspectives. Lloydia 41:348–354.

28. Githens, I.S. 1948. *Drug Plants of Africa.* University of Pennsylvania Press, The University Museum, Philadelphia. 125 p.

29. Grieve, M. 1974. *A Modern Herbal.* Hafner Press, New York. 888 p.

30. Grundon, M.F. 1979. A new quinoline alkaloid from *Ruta graveolens.* Phytochemistry 18:1768–69.

31. Guest, E. 1933. Notes on plants and plant products with their colloquial names in Iraq. Bull. Iraq Dep. Agric. Baghdad. No. 27. 111 p.

32. Gunther, R. 1934. *Greek Herbal of Dioscoides, Illustrated by a Byzantine A.D. 512. In English by I. Goodyear, A.D. 1655.* Hafner Publishing, London. 701 p.

33. Hareuveni, A. 1930. Medicinal and magic plants of the Arabs in Israel. Harefuah 4:113–127 (in Hebrew).

34. Hooper, D. 1937. *Useful Plants and Drugs of Iran and Iraq.* Publ. No. 387. Field Museum of Natural History, Chicago. 241 p.

35. Leung, A.Y. 1980. *Encyclopedia of Common Natural Ingredients used in Food, Drugs and Cosmetics*. Wiley Interscience Pub., New York. 409 p.

36. Levey, M. 1966. *The Medical Formulary or Aqrabadhin of Al-Kindi*. The University of Wisconsin Press, Madison, WI. 410 p.

37. Levey, M. and Al Khaledy, N. 1967. *The Medical Formulatory of Al-Samarquandi*. University of Pennsylvania Press, Philadelphia. 102 p.

38. Levy, S. 1978. *Medicine, Hygiene and Health of the Bedouins of South Sinai*. Society for the Protection of Nature in Israel, Tel Aviv (in Hebrew). 92 p.

39. Lust, B. 1977. *About Herbs*. Thorsons Publishers Ltd., England. 660 p.

40. Mertz, W., E.E. Roginski, W.A. Gordon, W.W. Harrison, J. Shani, and F.G. Sulman. 1973. *In vitro* potentiation of insulin by ash from saltbush (*Atriplex halimus*). Arch. Int. Pharmacodyn. Ther. 206:121–128.

41. Miller, R. and D.J. Greenblatt. 1976. *Handbook of Drug Therapy*. Clarkson N. Potter Inc. Publishers, New York. 1126 p.

42. Ochana, R. 1956. *Mareh Hailadim*. Ochana Publishers, Tiberias, Israel (in Hebrew). 122 p.

43. Osborn, D.T. 1968. Notes on medicinal and other uses of plants in Egypt. Econ. Bot. 22:165–177.

44. Palevitch, D., A. Dafni, and Z. Yaniv. 1982. *Survey of Israeli Flora as a Source of Drugs*. Nat. Council Resource Development N.C.R.D. (Isr.) 2–82 Jerusalem, Israel (in Hebrew).

45. Queden, S. 1974. Heimishce arneipflanzen der Arabischen. Planta Med. 26:65–75.

46. Riani, Y. 1963. Medicinal Drugs of the Yemenite Jews. M.Sc. thesis. School of Pharmacy, The Hebrew University of Jerusalem, Israel (in Hebrew). 102 p.

47. Ruweiha, A. 1978. *Herbal Medicine*. Beirut (in Arabic). 559 p.

48. Satyavati, G.V., K.K. Raina, and M. Sharma. 1976. *Medicinal Plants of India*, Vol. I, A–G. Council of Medicinal Research, New Delhi, India, 487 p.

49. Shani (Mishikinsky), J., B. Joseph, and F.G. Sulman. 1970. Fluctuations in the hypoglycaemic effect of *Poterium spinosum* L. (Rosacae). Arch. Int. Pharmacodyn. Ther. 185:344–349.

50. Steinmetz, G.F. 1965 *Poterium spinosi cortex radicis*--A new agent against diabetes. Acta Phytother. 12:2–6.

51. Tackholm, V. and M. Drar. 1954. *Flora of Egypt*, Vol. III. Bull. Fac. Sci. Cairo Univ., Cairo. 30 p.

52. Twaij, H.A. 1983. Some pharmacological studies of *Achillea santolina* L. and *Achillea micrantha* M.B. Fitoterapia 1:25–32.

53. Tyler, V.E., L.R. Brady, and J.E. Robbers. 1976. *Pharmacognosy*, 7th ed. Lea and Febiger, Philadelphia. 537 p.

54. Tzizik, B. 1952. *Otzar Hatzmachim*. Tzizik Publishers, Herzliya, Israel (in Hebrew). 509 p.

55. Yaniv, Z., A. Dafni, and D. Palevitch. 1982. Labiatae as medicinal plants in Israel. *In* N. Margaris, A. Koedam, and D. Vokoc, eds. *Aromatic Plants*. Martinue Nijhof Publishers, The Hague. pp. 265–268.

56. Zaitscheck, D. and S. Levontin. 1972. Further information about essential oils of Labiatae in Israel containing phenols. Harokeach Haivri 14:284–298 (in Hebrew).

Index

Compiled by Fred Ramey